For Murray

We are our
Stories

Nov 2011

Feminism and Voluntary Action

Also by Linda Mahood

SOCIAL CONTROL IN CANADA: ISSUES IN THE SOCIAL CONSTRUCTION OF DEVIANCE (*edited with Bernard Schissel*)

POLICING GENDER, CLASS AND FAMILY: BRITAIN, 1850–1932

THE MAGDALENES: PROSTITUTION IN THE NINETEENTH CENTURY

Feminism and Voluntary Action

Eglantyne Jebb and Save the Children, 1876–1928

Linda Mahood
Associate Professor of History, University of Guelph, Ontario, Canada

© Linda Mahood 2009

All rights reserved. No reproduction, copy or transmission of this
publication may be made without written permission.

No portion of this publication may be reproduced, copied or transmitted
save with written permission or in accordance with the provisions of the
Copyright, Designs and Patents Act 1988, or under the terms of any licence
permitting limited copying issued by the Copyright Licensing Agency,
Saffron House, 6–10 Kirby Street, London EC1N 8TS.

Any person who does any unauthorized act in relation to this publication
may be liable to criminal prosecution and civil claims for damages.

The author has asserted her right to be identified as the author
of this work in accordance with the Copyright, Designs and Patents Act
1988.

First published 2009 by
PALGRAVE MACMILLAN

Palgrave Macmillan in the UK is an imprint of Macmillan Publishers Limited,
registered in England, company number 785998, of Houndmills, Basingstoke,
Hampshire RG21 6XS.

Palgrave Macmillan in the US is a division of St Martin's Press LLC,
175 Fifth Avenue, New York, NY 10010.

Palgrave Macmillan is the global academic imprint of the above companies
and has companies and representatives throughout the world.

Palgrave® and Macmillan® are registered trademarks in the United States,
the United Kingdom, Europe and other countries

ISBN-13: 978-0-230-52560-3   hardback

This book is printed on paper suitable for recycling and made from fully
managed and sustained forest sources. Logging, pulping and manufacturing
processes are expected to conform to the environmental regulations of the
country of origin.

A catalogue record for this book is available from the British Library.

A catalogue record for this book is available from the Library of Congress.

10   9   8   7   6   5   4   3   2   1
18   17   16   15   14   13   12   11   10   09

Printed and bound in Great Britain by
CPI Antony Rowe, Chippenham and Eastbourne

For two Rebel Daughters:
My mother Pat Kingery and my daughter Lucy Satzewich

Contents

List of Illustrations

Acknowledgements

In the preparation of this manuscript I have had the privilege of meeting many fascinating and dedicated people and the advantage of researching and writing in many invigorating places in Europe and North America. This book would never have been written without the encouragement from members of Eglantyne Jebb's family. Lionel and Corinna Jebb allowed me to use family papers and showed great patience and hospitality whenever I flew across the Atlantic by permitting me to work in the beautiful rooms on the estate where Eglantyne grew up. Ben Buxton generously copied Buxton family papers and arranged for me to interview his father, the late David Buxton who shared with me memories of his aunt Eglantyne and his parents, Charles and Dorothy Buxton. Sadly, I never met the person who remembered Eglantyne the best, her niece, the late Eglantyne Roden Buxton. Her devotion to her aunt and fervent insistence that this story is told correctly has steered my research.

The Social Science and Humanities Research Council of Canada and the University of Guelph have generously funded this research. I cannot thank warmly enough two former *Save the Children* archivists of the 1990s, Rodney Breen and Susan Snedden. They provided me with piles of photocopies, a private screening of George Mews' films, insight into the modern *Save the Children* and access to the kettle. Archivists and librarians of the following collections must also be mentioned: Friend's House (London), National Council of Women (Metropolitan Archive, London), Women's International League for Peace and Freedom (London School of Economics, London), Keynes family papers (British Library, London), Scottish Women's Hospitals (Mitchell Library, Glasgow), Cambridge Ladies Discussion Society and Cambridge Charity Organization Society (Municipal Archive, Cambridge), Save the Children International Union (*Archives d'Etat*, Geneva), Lady Caroline Jebb papers (Sophia Smith Collection, Smith College, Massachusetts), Charles Kay Ogden papers (McMaster University, Ontario). Research papers have been presented at academic conferences in Liverpool, Birmingham, Glamorgan, Amherst, Marquette, Saskatoon and the International Institute of Sociology in Krakow. Papers have also been presented in community halls where many self-identified *Save the Children* volunteers have shared the ethos of volunteering. Material in this books appears in abridged forms in, *Women's History Review*, 17:1 (February 2008), pp. 1–20, *Voluntary Action*, 5 (2002), pp. 71–88, *History of Education*, 35:3 (May 2006), pp. 349–371 and *Journal of Historical Sociology,* 22:1 (March 2009), pp. 55–83. Thanks must be given for permission to use photographs and quotes from Jebb and Buxton family papers and Lady Caroline Lane Reynolds Jebb Papers, Sophia Smith Collection, Smith College. Every attempt has been made to contact other copyright holders and I apologize if copyright material has inadvertently been used.

Many associates, colleagues and friends have helped me in different ways. Professors Barbara Littlewood, Kevin James and James Snell read and commented on early drafts of the manuscript. Jacqueline Murray's assistance with Chapter 7 was invaluable. Vic Satzewich read and discussed many drafts of this manuscript and collaborated on the Russian famine. For contributions of various other kinds, I am grateful to Professors Dominique Marshall, David Smith, Pat Starkey, June Purvis, Terry Crowley, Donna Andrew, Bill Cormack, Sofie Lachapelle and Catherine Carstairs. Alix Sutton-Lalani and Freya Goddard provided copyediting assistance. Longtime Guelph SCF volunteer, Pat McCraw has helped my students and me. Katrina Vukovic and Bonnie Sawyer were excellent research assistants. Graduate students, Paulette Gehl and Meghan Cameron worked on the Canadian Save the Children Fund. Lucy Satzewich assisted with the transcription of the 'Boots Scribbling Diary' and helped me to unravel its complexities. Dorothy Emslie, MD, FCFP has shared her medical expertise concerning Eglantyne's medical history and with Briar Long, MD, FRCP(C) interpreted the 'Conversations with a Departed Friend'. No doubt mistakes due to jet lag, deteriorating documents and misjudgements have crept in. I hope that they are few and I take full responsibility for them. For over a decade of terms and vacations, tryouts and triumphs, Anne Kennedy, Janet Diebel, Dorothy Emslie, Sue Perry and for much longer my sisters, Beth Berquist and Lori Bossen have constituted a sphere of friendship and a supportive source of love and laughter. My final thanks go to Jack: this book would not exist without your ardent insistence that I neglect you, your *Huskie* sweats and all that juice service. You will join me in dedicating it to Lucy who inspires us all. Now Vic: *and then there were two…*

List of Abbreviations

AOS	Agricultural Organization Society
COS	Charity Organizations Society
CLDS	Cambridge Ladies Discussion Society
FFC	Fight the Famine Council
HAIA	Home Arts and Industries Association
ICRC	International Committee of the Red Cross
ICW	International Council of Women
LMH	Lady Margaret Hall, Oxford University
LN	League of Nations
MRF	Macedonian Relief Fund
NCW	National Council of Women
NCWGB	National Council of Women of Great Britain
SCF	Save the Children Fund
SCIU	Save the Children International Union
SWH	Scottish Women's Hospitals
WILPF	Women's International League for Peace and Freedom

Prologue: No Silk-Blouse Social Worker

Perhaps it is a consciousness of the co-operation of Fate, which gives one an instinct about one's destiny. More probably, not at all...[1]

'I've never cared for my work here,' confessed a distraught young settlement worker. 'I can't get on with uneducated people and the slum surroundings revolt me...[M]y work takes more courage than I've got and it seems quite useless.' It was not the long hours that bothered her. It was the clientele, their bullying and begging, their insolence and dishonesty. It is 'crushing me like a heavyweight', she said. It was a low moment when the 21-year-old social worker finally mouthed the words: 'I do not love the poor'.[2] Today when social workers speak such words, their feelings are recognized as professional burn out, the solutions to which range from stress management to a change of career. In 1912, the way out was less clear to Eglantyne Jebb, who reflected in her unpublished novel, 'The Ring Fence', upon 'the horror and squalor' and the 'sacrifices' of a 'silk blouse' social worker.[3] From the point of view of one of her working-class protagonists, 'the poor were like "toys" for the rich...Their ideas, their battles, their catastrophes, their passionate longing for freedom' are all 'the playthings of a superior class'. The poor 'craved to possess their souls', and the rich responded with bribes and 'an occasional institute'.[4] An upper-class character agreed 'Charity' was a 'ridiculous' word but a 'decent misnomer' to cover 'a multitude of sins'.[5] Everyone in Jebb's imaginary community affirmed 'philanthropists were humbugs'.[6]

Whether or not Eglantyne really doubted the power of collective voluntary action, she was one of half a million British women at the turn of the century who felt the pull of what was variously called philanthropy, voluntary social work, public work and in the most extreme cases, 'slumming', which involved putting on a disguise and living

1

amongst the poor in what Seth Koven calls a cross-class masquerade.[7] Eglantyne spent most of her life as a voluntary social worker in organizations devoted to charity work and campaigns for social action. A few months after completing the never-to-be-published semi-autobiographical 'The Ring Fence', she began raising funds for the Macedonian Relief Fund (MRF) and went to the Balkans to inspect refugee hospitals. She also became the editor of *The Plough*, a newsletter devoted to co-operative farming and alternative agriculture under the auspices of the Agricultural Organization Society (AOS). In 1918, while serving as the honorary secretary of an anti-blockade lobby group called the Fight the Famine Council (FFC), she founded the Save the Children Fund (SCF) with her sister Dorothy Frances Buxton. The main purpose of the Jebb sisters' new charity was to raise money for the child victims of the First World War. When Eglantyne was arrested in May 1919 in Trafalgar Square for distributing uncensored SCF leaflets, she told a reporter for the *Daily Mirror* that if the publicity surrounding her arrest provided food for one starving child, then the five-pound fine was the 'equivalent to victory'.[8] Over most of the next decade until her death in 1928, Eglantyne served as honorary secretary of the SCF and vice-president of the Save the Children International Union (SCIU). In 1922, she led a group of feminists, pacifists and intellectuals to collaborate on the Declaration of the Rights of the Child, which was ratified by the League of Nations (LN) in 1924. For a woman who declared that voluntary action was humbug, these are incongruous activities.

In *Schools of Citizenship*, Frank Prochaska agrees with Ralf Dahrendorf's assertion that charities are 'untidy organizations'. Whether they have a political agenda that is only implied or are a direct attack on the government of the day, charities 'raise the thorny issue of how a society should be administered'.[9] Schools of thought ranging from Marxism to social control see society in terms of class conflict and power relations. For Prochaska, studies of charity written by scholars from these perspectives have, in a way, 'demonised philanthropy as a form of "bourgeois hegemony"', elite self-interest and social engineering because it seems out of step with progressive politics and social transformation.[10] Studies of children's charities do likewise. In 1969, Anthony Platt defined 'child-savers' as a group of well-heeled humanitarians who regarded child welfare as a matter of conscience and morality.[11] According to Jacques Donzelot, philanthropists and child-savers encircle, invade and suffocate the family.[12] In Britain by the end of the nineteenth century, the child-saving movement amounted to the surveillance of working-class children by doctors, teachers, social workers and the police.[13] From these perspectives the term 'do-gooder', like moral entrepreneur, is pejorative.[14] Of course, there is nothing new in making fun of the philanthropist. Since the 1880s *Punch* satirists had been lampooning philanthropists, especially the 'Lady Bountiful',[15] for her egotistical self-indulgence. At the grass-roots, even contemporary social workers ridiculed the cold hand of charity. In 1902, Eglantyne mocked the diamonds on the 'very white' fingers of the honorary secretary of the Cambridge Charity Organization Society.[16] Ten years later in 'The Ring Fence' she created a satirical dinner-party conversation where the guests all agreed that although pauperism was a pressing social question, the more pressing social problem was the well-to-do women who got carried away with their social work. 'Once women of a household take to that', says Lord Copefied, 'domestic peace is at an end. Late for meals, out in the evening, too tired to do anything, short skirts…irritability and nervous breakdown. I don't blame them indeed when they get cross, for what woman can keep her temper when her hair is out of curl?'[17] Though it is hard to disagree with some of the broader conclusions about charities drawn by critics, their observations do little to help us to understand what the opportunity to do volunteer work represented in women's lives in the late nineteenth and early twentieth centuries.

When I first came across Eglantyne Jebb's humanitarian work in the 1990s while working on late-Victorian philanthropy and the child-saving movement, I discovered that the available snippets of information about her were drawn from a rather narrow range of sources. Eglantyne never wrote her own life story; however, she saved many letters and diaries and various childhood memories which appear in her later private writing and fiction. After her death in 1928, her sister Dorothy Buxton prepared two short monographs, *Save the Child!* and *The White Flame*, with Edward Fuller of the SCF executive committee. Carolyn Steedman would say that these books are not 'innocent secondary source[s]',[18] for they were intended to raise funds and the profile of the SCF in the 1930s when it was in serious financial trouble. Buxton and Fuller construct an image of Eglantyne as the 'sister of all the world' and a martyr for child welfare.[19] These sentiments reappeared in Fuller's *The Right of the Children* (1951), which commemorated the SCF's 30th anniversary, Kathleen Freedman's *If Any Man Build* (1965) and Richard Symond's *Far Above Rubies: The Women Uncommemorated by the Church of England* (1993).[20] These authors paint a hagiographical portrait of Jebb as a saintly woman whose destiny was humanitarian work and an untimely death. This view effaces her early work as a grammar school teacher and her social and investigative work for the Charity Organization Society (COS), her political work, personal goals and ambition and the labour of countless other SCF volunteers and committee members.

In the early 1960s Eglantyne's niece Eglantyne Buxton observed that 'philanthropy is colossally out of fashion now',[21] however the political climate of the decade confirmed her conviction that Jebb had been an important social pioneer, and the death of her mother, Dorothy, in 1963 freed her to take control of her aunt's image. Eglantyne Buxton regarded the early histories of the SCF, which her mother had helped create, as 'vague hero-worshipping' and a misrepresentation of Jebb's original internationalist philosophy and commitment to social responsibility. In defiance of the spirit of the times she decided to rescue her aunt, whose work she greatly admired, from the SCF's representation of her as a 'plaster saint'.[22] Buxton prepared some notes for a biography,[23] and Buxton's cousin Eglantyne Mary Jebb recommended Francesca Wilson to write it. Like Buxton, Eglantyne Mary and her late sister Geraldine Jebb shared an enduring fascination with Eglantyne Jebb, to whose inspiration they attributed their distinguished professional careers as leading British educationalists.[24] In the early 1960s Eglantyne Mary Jebb had recently retired from her position as principal of the Froebel Institute and vice-chairman of the SCF, where she had been a council member since 1943. Wilson was an old friend of Geraldine Jebb. They first met around 1909, when they were Newnham students at Cambridge. Although Wilson and Eglantyne Jebb never met, the SCF sponsored some of Wilson's relief work between 1920 and 1940, as she described in many of her books: *In the Margins of Chaos* (1944), *Aftermath* (1947), *They Came as Strangers* (1949). After the Second World War, Wilson worked with the survivors of Dachau concentration camp on behalf of the United Nations.[25]

Wilson, E. M. Jebb and Buxton immersed themselves in the project. While Wilson interviewed Jebb's few surviving friends, the younger Eglantynes sorted and re-sorted family papers. Wilson declared she did not want to restate much of the information that had already been published which she dismissed as 'boring mysticism', and every one agreed. Wilson's goal was to 'reconstruct' Jebb's life 'historically and sociologically',[26] an approach which was a bold departure from the 'saint of children' image brokered by the SCF. The final biography entitled, *Rebel Daughter of a Country House* appeared on the eve of Wilson's 80th birthday; it was dedicated to all three Eglantynes and the memory of Geraldine. The *Times* ignored it; however, other newspapers did review it and their critics suggested that it fell short of the writer's vision. The *Church Times* dismissed it as a 'ladylike biography'. The reviewer suggested that 'a critical analytical objectivity might have thrown Eglantyne into relief as one of the most interesting social pioneers.'[27] The *Sunday Times* suggested that 'perhaps the earnestness of the book is the only really effective way to convey the almost mystical elations and black despairs of a woman scarred with the classic marks of saintliness'.[28] The *Daily Telegraph* noted that 'Eglantyne Jebb was an interesting complex character who deserved to be rescued from obscurity, though the witty, radiant creature we are assured she was is overshadowed...by the earnest do-gooder'.[29] Wilson's severest critic, however, was Buxton, who called *Rebel Daughter* 'very feeble and superficial' because of its 'lack of historical perspective and paltry emphasis on relief work'.[30] It is difficult for a modern reader to disagree with the tone of the reviews. Buxton was right – *Rebel Daughter* was not well grounded in the history of the time, and the earlier hagiographical account of the selfless, mystical idealist inevitably crept back in. This is not surprising, after all, this was how everyone remembered her, and the only sources of information available to Wilson were family papers and the fond recollections of devoted relatives and friends. But *Rebel Daughter* must have ruffled some feathers within the SCF, for it made 'no attempt to advertise it in their Jubilee year'![31]

Given the way that Eglantyne Jebb's life story has been framed in SCF biographical accounts and in *Rebel Daughter*, it is not surprising that she has failed to attract the attention of many modern academic researchers. The hagiographical representation of her achievements explains her poor showing in the canon of women's studies literature and history. Many feminist scholars have been more interested in suffrage pioneers, trade unionists, radical politics and ordinary women than in conservative 'women worthies'.[32] Consequently, as Ellen Ross has recently observed, old-fashioned charity work and the 'seemingly tame institutions' like settlement houses and children's charities are not well known. Neither do we know much about how unpaid work in these organizations 'prepare a generation of women for leadership'.[33]

Eglantyne Jebb was an Oxford-educated member of the Shropshire elite and there were certainly elements of the Lady Bountiful in her child-saving worldview, which cannot be excused from the women-centred perspective of modern feminism. In the same vein, after the Second World War the tweedy SCF, with its tradition of royal patronage and high-street shops, top-down non-participatory relief projects and child 'adoption' schemes is an example of European economic and cultural colonialism-cum-imperialism and out of step with the academic field of international development. Nevertheless, Soma Hewa and Darwin Stapleton argue that the modern *Save the Children* charity is recognized today as a 'brand name' among international non-governmental organizations with a stature similar to Oxfam, Amnesty International, Friends of the Earth and Greenpeace.[34] *Save the Children* publications and website state that it still supports Jebb's original principles and Declaration of the Rights of the Child, which was adopted by the United Nations.

Scholars have emphasized the importance of gender in the history of philanthropy and the role women played in the development of local and national social-welfare institutions. By the mid-nineteenth century, modern industrial nations realized that they could no longer leave the well being of the individual to the *laissez-faire* market mechanisms, which had presumably been responsible for Britain's earlier economic success. Rapid population growth and burgeoning urbanization were seen to have created human problems, which could not easily be solved, by traditional rural paternalism or the English Poor Law. Daily, thousands of charities and church societies fed, clothed and visited the poor. According to Lynn Hollen Lees, the foot soldiers in this work were middle- and upper-class women whose efforts produced a great deal of information about the causes and consequences of poverty, drunkenness, immorality and disease.[35] In Prochaska's estimation there was 'enough poverty and distress in English society to satisfy every woman's charitable inclination', whatever her age or marital status.[36] Brian Harrison proposes that many 'respectable housewives and spinsters' took great pleasure in slumming. 'Indeed, reclaiming the intemperate was probably effective a remedy for boredom and invalidism as alcohol itself'.[37]

There is no single reason why so many women participated in volunteer work. Harrison detected 'recurring biographical patterns' which suggests 'altruism is certainly not the whole story'.[38] The decision to volunteer for a cause was individual and the experience highly personal, but certain generalizations can be made. What women actually did in the field of reformist or benevolent charity work depended upon a range of circumstances, including their social class, family position, education, religiosity and personal inclination. For a large number of women charity work was an expression of a profound religious conviction, which Julia Parker says can be explained only in 'mystical terms' as a calling. For such women, charity work was a spiritual right or rite.[39] At the same time, argues Maria Luddy, charity work could be a source of pleasure, adventure or rebellion, because it enabled the worker to escape from the monotony and constraints of domestic life and to display her talent, experience and intelligence. Charity work was an opportunity to travel at home or abroad and to find one's voice and express political opinions by speaking out against injustice and hypocrisy.[40] After the First World War expanded the opportunities available to women, many women chose to continue in philanthropy. As honorary secretary of the Save the Children Fund, Eglantyne gave newly enfranchised women a chance to see first-hand the consequences of war, and many volunteers continued to educate themselves about child famine in the course of doing international relief work.[41] It needs to be stressed, however, that not all women who did paid or unpaid social work found it rewarding. For some it was a loathsome burden and a thankless duty. Charity workers were well aware that the work could be physically, mentally and morally exhausting. Ross and Koven point out that by the late-Victorian period speculating about the 'queer' sexualities of spinster-bluestockings, social-worker-types and busy-bodies had become a part of popular culture.[42] These negative stereotypes were a drawback; however, they did not stop thousands of women from volunteering in soup kitchens, organizing milk and boot campaigns, running youth clubs at a settlement house, hostessing snowball teas for waifs' homes or wearing an 'SCF' armband and taking up a money box for starving children.

Liz Stanley says that 'in a sense it is *only* biography which can make available to us the detailed processes of historical change.'[43] Stanley does not mean a 'conventional linear "jigsaw" model of biography', which puts the subject under a microscope, 'honing in on each small detail of a person's life' so that the masterly biographer can make authoritative claims to the 'truth' about what her subject was 'really' like.[44] No, Stanley rejects the microscope approach to biography in favour of a kaleidoscope so 'each time you look you see something different.[45] For Stanley, the 'feminist biographer' captures the full complexity and mosaic patterning of her subject's life and the lives of contemporaries so she can say my subject 'was like that *and* like that'.[46] The question arises, what sort of biography is mine? According to Jill Lepore, new subgenera of biography, called microhistory, or 'histories of self' emerged in the 1990s. Such studies explore 'rather ordinary people in whose lives many significant social forces and events converge'.[47] Microhistorians differ from biographers because they tend to identify with the topic rather than the subject. My goal is to blend the techniques of feminist biography and microhistory, and like *Rebel Daughter*, reconstruct Jebb's life historically and sociologically. As such this study is not an organizational history of the Save the Children Fund, nor is its goal to rescue another woman whose history has been hidden or lost, though this may be one of the results. As a microhistory this book uses Jebb's life as a lens through which to see the part that voluntary social work played in Jebb's life and the lives of middle and upper-class women born in the final decades of Queen Victoria's reign.

In the six decades covered by this study, the position of women in British society changed dramatically. As a member of the late Victorian Shropshire elite, Jebb's life cuts across a number of important class, gender and cultural conjunctions. To understand change in women's history requires recognition of the intersection of history and biography. This involves the examination of the interplay between, on the one hand, the individual, society and the subjective 'self', and on the other hand, existing ideas surrounding class, gender, marriage, family responsibilities and interpersonal networks along the lines suggested by the sociologist C. W. Mills in the late-1950s in *The Sociological Imagination*.[48] In the 1970s, feminists rephrased Mills's idea as 'the personal is political' and women's history grew up around the 'integration between the public and the private', which remains 'a major goal of a generation of feminist scholars.'[49] This approach enables us to see how a study of a women's voluntary social work networks can go beyond what Ross described as 'sentimental images of female selflessness, satirical lady bountiful stereotypes, or social-control simplifications' and how voluntary social action produced a generation of feminists leaders.[50]

Beryl Haslam refers to women born in the late 1870s and 1880s as the cohort who bridged the gap between the Victorian feminist pioneers and the generation who came of age in the early 1920s.[51] It is only when we look closely at individual women's 'careers' that we fully appreciate the historical and biographical intersection of contemporary ideas surrounding professional responsibilities, marriage and family duties, women's networks and the struggles this generation faced. As we shall see, they were the earliest beneficiaries of expanded opportunities for women in higher education; however, the pace of their educational advancements had outstripped political and social changes. Many women of this generation found their ambitions stifled by the restrictions imposed upon their sex by law, social convention, credentialism and, for those who did not marry, cultural ideas regarding the dependent role of what was called the 'daughter-at-home'. It is true that 'many doors were closed, [but] they discovered a crack in the doors of philanthropic societies'.[52] Martha Vicinus argues that voluntary social work offered much compensation to unmarried women, including the chance to have a career, display their talent and gain access to a network of like-minded friends outside one's family.[53] Many of the century's 'new women' with education, leisure and financial means devoted their lives to philanthropic causes and social campaigns.

Steedman argues that biographies are written in response to the political and social climate in which biographers find themselves.[54] On 8 June 2004, long time Guelph, Ontario *Save the Children, Canada* volunteer, Pat McCraw, arranged for me to attend a reception held in honour of *Save the Children* president, Her Royal Highness The Princess Royal, who was in Toronto to present an award to a United Nations special envoy for HIV/AIDS in Africa. While executing my clumsy curtsy, I quickly explained this project to her. She told me that she believed it was time for us to examine the woman behind the many myths that have grown up around Eglantyne Jebb. All writers of biography have difficulty constructing a 'real' person from archival documents. Some scholars claim that it is an impossible task because biography is merely fiction and bears no relationship to the actual life as it was lived by the subject. June Purvis argues that such a '…postmodern critique itself is a product of a particular historical response in time and does not invalidate the necessity for biography….[A] study of any particular life can help illuminate choices, situations and events, as well as aid our understanding of the person being studied'.[55] The clash over *Rebel Daughter* in the 1960s illustrates what modern feminist biographers like Ros Pesman call the unstable intersections and boundaries between biography and autobiography. Her questions about 'how women tell stories about their own lives and those of others' are similar to Liz Stanley's epistemological problem of 'knowing other lives'.[56]

Researching and writing about 'people, living or dead, is tricky work', according to Lepore, 'it is necessary to balance intimacy with distance, while at the same time being inquisitive to the point of invasiveness'.[57] Biographers and microhistorians inevitably develop relationships with their subjects and how they see them determines what they look for in the archive. As such all biographical explanations will be selective, the question is how does one sift through and interpret the private and public written word, visual images and interviews with surviving family objectively without imputing modern meanings, motives and messages? What can modern readers learn from historical life writing about women of the past? How does the writer account for her 'self' or subjectivity in the writing process?[58] My interpretation of Jebb's life differs from Wilson's *Rebel Daughter* and SCF hagiography due to important difference in the sources available to us. I have been able to draw upon the vast field of feminist history and the autobiographies and biographies of Jebb's contemporaries. These sources have enabled me to view Jebb's life kaleidoscopically, from different angles and perspectives, and to see her life in the context of the life stories of women around her and ultimately to assess which experiences were unique to Eglantyne and which were shared by other women of her class and generation. To that end, by isolating historical and personal moments in Jebb's life, I have enabled readers to see women's history in action.

There is no single archival collection of Eglantyne Jebb's papers. As a professional sociologist and historian whose previous work has focused on the history of childhood, family and voluntary and state agencies, I have been particularly interested in extant primary sources that elucidate private life and public policy. In this biography I have focused a great deal on the unpublished letters, diaries and personal writings of the entire Jebb family. The majority of Eglantyne's personal letters and her mother's and sisters' diaries are currently in the possession of her family. I have supplemented these where possible with the letters and diaries of members of Jebb's circle; notably, Lady Caroline Jebb's diary and letters to family in America, John Maynard's letters to Duncan Grant and Dorothy Buxton's letters to C. K. Ogden of *Cambridge Magazine*. Hundreds of miscellaneous personal letters to Jebb from SCF volunteers were found in the files of the Save the Children Fund in London. Moreover, there are dozens of 'confidential' letters from Jebb to Suzanne Ferrière and other colleagues in the Save Children International Union archive in Geneva where Eglantyne was living when she died.

The two main collections of letters are Dorothy Gardiner's (née Kempe) correspondence with Eglantyne from the time they met at Lady Margaret Hall (LMH) in 1895 to around 1914. When Eglantyne died Gardiner retyped Eglantyne's side of the correspondence before giving it to Dorothy Buxton in 1929. The second series of letters is Jebb's correspondence with Margaret Hill (née Keynes). In 1928 Dorothy Buxton approached Hill for Eglantyne's letters. Hill gave her hundreds written between 1911 and 1914 and her assurance that the most intimate letters had been burned.[59] In 1956 Dorothy copied these letters into an old *Boots Scribbling Diary* from 1947. She admitted 'taking out the endearments' and made other alterations because of ambiguities about the nature of the relationship between Margaret and Eglantyne. After *Rebel Daughter* was published in 1967, David Buxton destroyed more of Eglantyne's letters. Those that have survived are as intriguing as the burned letters must have been. For Catherine Clay calls letters a 'textual medium that comes closest to "conversation"'. The presence of the other is 'woven into the writer's own self-imaging...It is in the endless possibilities of this space that the pleasures of these texts, and of the friendships they construct, take shape'.[60] As valuable as letters are to historians, Margaretta Jolly says 'the physical death of a letter can only be symbolic'.[61] She looks upon 'the burned letter' as an 'archival motif of revenge, cleansing and commemoration.'[62] Jolly would say that when Dorothy copied her dead sister's letters into the *Boots Scribbling Diary*, she 'unburned' them; as did Wilson when she deliberately left her research notes for *Rebel Daughter* tucked in among Jebb's personal papers.

The second type of historical sources used in this study are the more formal subcommittee minute books, inter-office correspondence and annual reports of organizations with which Eglantyne and members of her family worked. These include the Home Arts and Industrial Association (HAIA), the Cambridge Ladies Discussion Society (CLDS), the Cambridge Charity Organizations Society, *Cambridge Magazine*, the Society of Friends, the International Council of Women and National Council of Women (Great Britain) (NCWGB), the Women's International League for Peace and Freedom (WILPF), the Save the Children Fund and the Save Children International Union in Geneva. These sources provide behind-the-scenes details and episodic 'snapshots' of Eglantyne's involvement with a large number of feminist, pacifist or reformist organizations. Here, my methodology has been to create a chronological narrative that covers Jebb's whole life through a close textual analysis of the documents. I have tried to shed light on Jebb's personality without losing sight of the larger historical context. My decision to provide lengthy quotes from her letters, fiction and non-fiction prose and essays is not to 'cut and paste' around tricky issues but to give the reader a chance to hear Eglantyne's own words. Eglantyne was most comfortable communicating with people through her pen. My intention is to elucidate her subjective 'experience' of being a woman, a daughter, a sister, a friend and a public figure and show how she understood her successes as well as her failures.

This book follows a chronological narrative approach. Little in Eglantyne Jebb's life story is truly intelligible unless we begin at the beginning in her childhood home on a 100-acre estate in Shropshire. The subject of Chapter 1 is the lives of Eglantyne's parents, Arthur Trevor and Eglantyne Louisa Jebb. In this chapter we examine the role that philanthropic worked played for the social elite and see the making of a late-Victorian marriage, a family and a nascent charity: The Home Arts and Industries Association, which Mrs Jebb founded in 1882. The subject of Chapter 2 is Eglantyne and her sisters. By focusing on the socialization of late-Victorian girls, this chapters show that like other home-schooled girls who grew up surrounded by servants and female relatives and friends in large country houses, the Jebb sisters participated in charity work and home visiting. Chapter 3 examines the historically unique experience of attending Lady Margaret Hall at Oxford University in the late 1890s, where Eglantyne encountered the first of many women who influenced the direction of her life and her decision to enter Stockwell Teacher Training College, which is the focus of Chapter 4. Chapter 5 examines Eglantyne's brief career as a schoolmistress living among the poor in Marlborough, where she developed a dislike for hands-on social work. Chapter 6 focuses on Eglantyne's life in Cambridge, where she moved with her mother in 1900. Her work with the Charity Organization Society developed her expertise as a social investigator and a committeewoman and she later became a mentor to a new generation of social workers. Chapter 7 examines Eglantyne's intimate friendship with Margaret Keynes and the time she spent travelling as her mother's companion from 1909 to 1913. Chapter 8 shows that when Eglantyne returned to England she was increasingly drawn to direct action organizations and to people who were combining their personal, spiritual and political ideologies with social action. From 1913 to 1919 Eglantyne worked for a number of direct actions organizations. This earlier work prepared her to take over the leadership of the Save the Children Fund. Chapter 9 examines how Eglantyne set up the national and international infrastructure of the SCF and her battles with the press and public opinion. Chapter 10 reveals the development of her commitment to internationalism and belief that an alliance between the Save the Children International Union and League of Nations would redefine the boundaries of voluntary and state action and put children's rights on the international agenda. The legacy of Eglantyne Jebb and other early *Save the Children* women is examined in the epilogue.

1

The Lady Bountiful and the Country Squire: Lessons in Life, Love and Woodcarving

On Christmas Eve in 1882, Eglantyne Jebb's mother wrote in her diary, '[Y]ou are almost done 1882, the most wonderful year of my life. A lifetime of experience crowded into the last 6 months'.[1] She was referring to the woodcarving lessons she had organized for the needy village children around Ellesmere. At the time, she did not know that her Home Arts and Industries Association (HAIA) would soon be one of the most influential arts and education charities in England. Like other members of the rural elite, Mr and Mrs Jebb realized that although the accumulation of wealth was important, participation in philanthropy and charitable activities was also a passport to enhanced social status and social integration, but there was more to what Mrs Jebb called her 'fearless' new career than simply complying with the rules, conventions and duties of the family's social position. Her charitable impulses sprang from a deepening social consciousness. In 1882 she wrote, '[W]e have long talked of Women's Rights and Women's work...our first right and our best work is to aid the men of our generation in bringing up a happier and more prosperous race—and this indeed is nothing but what our country has a "Right" to claim from us'.[2]

In *Philanthropy and Police*, Donna Andrew observes that 'important elements of continuity' connect charity work over the centuries. It was always 'an important agent in...social change...a central area for special experimentation and a central avenue for individual and social action.'[3] Major historical studies of nineteenth-century charity and philanthropy in Britain have documented transformations in the administration of charitable aid. In *Citizen, State and Social Welfare in Britain*, Geoffrey Finlayson divides the history of charity into separate political, economic and ideological phases. Beginning with voluntary alms-giving salvation-based charity of the late eighteenth century,

1.1   The Jebb Family, source: Jebb Family

moving to poor-law reform and the rational scientific Charity Organ-ization Society model of the end of the nineteenth century, and conclud-ing with the gradual emergence of the early welfare state in the early twentieth century, Finlayson asserts that whatever the context, men and women of the elite classes regarded charity and philanthropy as serious business.[4] The Jebb family had been members of the Shropshire squiro-cracy since the 1830s. Eglantyne's father was a member of the Board of Guardians and Provident Society and her mother had founded a charity to teach village children marketable handicrafts. According to Eglantyne, 'the men served on the larger public bodies and the women visited the cottages with soup and advice'.[5] This chapter shows how Eglantyne's parent's personal inclinations, social class consciousness and material interests conformed to late-nineteenth century trends in voluntary action. Drawing on family letters and diaries, we can also see how women's phil-anthropy represented more than a genteel pastime for ladies of leisure; it could also be a source of adventure and rebellion. The lives of Eglantyne's parents can serve as a lens through which to see the making of a late-Victorian marriage, a family and a nascent charity.

Eglantyne's mother was Eglantyne Louisa Jebb of Killiney, Ireland; she was known in her family as 'Tye'. Her future sister-in-law said that she 'was a great beauty in her day' and refused many 'suitors' of 'fortune and family'.[6] Tye once announced that she would only marry in order to change her dreadful last name, but fate had other plans for her.[7] In 1871, a distant English cousin, Arthur Trevor Jebb, the son of a prosperous Shropshire landowner, won her hand. Although the exact relationship between the Irish and English Jebb families was never officially traced, Tye's and Arthur's fathers met at boarding school in Oswestry, where many rich Irish Protestants sent their sons to be educated, and they became life-long friends. Their children met for the first time when Arthur was 20 and Tye was 15 and a visitor at her future in-laws' estate.[8] Surviving letters and diaries reveal nothing about their courtship or marriage settlement; however, an American sister-in-law, who knew a great deal about such things, said Arthur was 'pretty rich' and 'heir to three thousand pounds a year and a country house'. Tye had made 'a good match'.[9]

The marriage ceremony of Arthur and Tye took place on 12 April 1871 at Monkstow Church in Dublin, with the Reverend John Jebb, Canon of Hereford officiating.[10] The 25-year-old bride then moved from her seaside childhood home in County Dublin to Ellesmere, and her new home on the Jebbs' 100-acre estate, called the Lyth, which included vast grazing lands and a spacious two-storey house with large windows that opened all the way to the ground.[11] Her new household also included Arthur's 30-year-old unmarried sister, Louisa Jebb, and their widowed father. Tye conformed very well to the ideal image of the Victorian angel of the house. She acknowledged the primacy and authority of her husband, whom she called 'Dear Lord' or 'Dearest Husband'. In her diary she wrote, 'My darling husband, how I worship him. I wonder if anyone has a lovelier soul'.[12] Dreamy and artistic by nature, she was more interested in reading, painting and making calls than in managing a large strange household of 12 servants, and she never questioned why Arthur's sister continued as mistress of the house.[13] This was a division of labour that suited everyone because Arthur was away a great deal and Tye was soon pregnant with her first child, and five more followed in close succession. Emily was born in February 1872, Louisa in August 1873, Richard in September 1874, Eglantyne in August 1876, Gamul in April 1880 and Dorothy in March 1881. Arthur was pleased and wrote, 'little Tye seems not a bit the worse—quite the reverse—only her eyes a little more liquid than usual…Nothing delights her more than being a mother'.[14]

Whereas late-Victorian women are seen mainly in relation to their families, as daughters, sisters and mothers, Leonore Davidoff has observed that historians portray men as one-dimensional 'autonomous' social actors 'unencumbered by intimate relationships and domesticity'.[15] This makes it difficult to see them within the boundaries of family life. Arthur Jebb's letters to his wife in the 1870s and 1880s reveal that providing for his family was central to his masculine identity and complicated because the boundaries of class and authority were in flux in the late-Victorian period. At the time of his marriage, he was 31 and had enjoyed a suitably long bachelorhood; however, he did not know how long it would be until he would inherit the family estate and like many young gentlemen with a growing family to support, Arthur struggled to balance his demanding roles as a husband, father and breadwinner.

Arthur was educated at Harrow and went on to Balliol College, Oxford, where he earned a third-class Bachelor of Arts degree in 1864. He trained as a barrister though he does not appear to have practised law. He must have felt curtailed by an allowance that was not large enough to support a growing family because in 1872 he was forced to try his hand at breadwinning. Jillian Sutherland claims that after 1870s the Church and the Bar were no longer 'the most usual career for young men just down from the Universities with no great distinction (first class degrees were the exception rather than the rule) or clear direction in life'.[16] Instead, many such young gentlemen found careers as school inspectors in the rapidly expanding bureaucracy of the Education Department, which had been created by the recent education acts. Like Arthur, most prospective inspectors were men in their early 30s. Barely a tenth had any teaching experience, although some had a clear sense of mission and social conscience, the majority, 'in so far as they can be discovered to have done anything at all', were also, like Arthur, 'briefless barristers, or at least had eaten the requisite number of Bar dinners'.[17] Accordingly, it was not unreasonable for Arthur to anticipate a successful career with the Education Department.

Arthur's initial appointment in 1873 as Inspector of Returns in the London Office was only temporary. He was excited by the challenge, but also bothered because he was forced to run his household from his lodgings at the New University Club in St James Street. He missed his young family and complained about the 'boorish manners' and 'prodigious appetites' of the 'Parsonic element' who 'roared dogmatically'. The cleric's 'conversation' dominated the dining room[18] and made him feel out of place. He was also understandably worried about Tye, for pregnancy and childbirth were dangerous for women of all classes in the late nineteenth century. He wrote her encouraging letters, which he addressed to 'Pussy' and 'Dear Wife'. Hints of their physical intimacy are inferred by references to his cold feet. Tye tried to reassure him by sending cheerful little watercolours and drawings. Gratefully he responded, 'a picture done so pretty—can come through the post and shows husband how very well she really is'.[19] Arthur was anxious for news of his babies, 'little Emily and Wesa': 'Do not suppose that Doddie does not care to hear about his children. He loves them'.[20] He took an active interest in their health, filled out and returned their immunization forms himself, and reminded Tye that 'children must be vaccinated within three months after birth'.[21] When it was his son Richard's turn, he said the boy 'should commence the course of suffering to which human flesh is heir'.[22] When Emily was slow learning to talk, he wrote jokingly to his anxious wife, 'I suppose she does not talk in order to reflect the more'.[23]

Although Arthur tried to be an affectionate husband and attentive father, worries about finances and his future with the Education Department began to dominate his letters. He cleared '25 shillings *per diem*—but not reckoning Sundays and holidays'[24] and was feeling sorry for himself when he wrote, 'it will be so much more pleasant for Pussie if she has not to pawn her trinkets. I should not like to think of the little things creeping forth mysteriously from her jewel box'.[25] In a thwarted effort to economize, he experimented with second-class travel, but 'the smells…were horrible' and the 'carriage was so dirty' that his 'newest and freshest colour bags were almost spoiled'.[26] Not wishing to look like a second-class traveller, he ordered 'two brand new pair of boots' to be delivered to the Lyth. When he informed Tye of his purchase he asked guiltily, 'is not Pussie glad that husband has had the courage to order new boos [boots]?'[27] Two months later though, he realized that he could not go home for Emily's birthday. 'It is entirely a question of money…I do not wish to appear mean but appear mean I must. It is only by the most rigid economy that I can put by 6 pence for those that come after me…If I have made every effort in my power, if no self-denial in my part has been wanting, little Emily ought to judge me gently'.[28]

In the late nineteenth century, families of the upper-middle class and gentry whose sons and sons-in-law needed paid employment peddled their influence within the ranks of the civil service, but Tye's family influences were clerical. If Arthur had chosen the church like her brother, Heneage, his future might have been secure. When Heneage abandoned his legal studies for the church, his parents were confident that they had sufficient influence to get him a living, but it would take 'some crumpled rose leaves'.[29] Arthur quickly realized that his prospects were reduced because of 'a person named Gladstone' and other 'internal corruption', which foisted 'outsiders' upon 'the Office'. He calculated that he was 'about 30th in line' for six inspectorships.[30] He drew the conclusion that 'no labour—no good service, faithfully rendered' was going to get him any form of permanent employment. 'Work confessedly does not count—nor character—nor education.'[31] By contrast, 20 years later the Jebbs acquired influence in the Education Department through the friendship of Tye's brother Sir Richard Jebb with Sir John Gorst, the Minister of Education. When Arthur's daughter Eglantyne left Stockwell Teacher Training College in 1898, she was immediately offered an inspectorship. Realizing that the appointment was based on her privileged class position, and not her talent or expertise, she turned it down. Arthur's lack of success may have been due to his lack of family influence or connections within the Liberal Party, however, his high-mindedness may have offended his superiors.

In 1874, Arthur returned to the Lyth, where he helped his father manage the estate until he inherited it in 1878. He was then free to devote himself entirely to his new position as landowner. Work and home life were inseparable at the Lyth, and the Jebb marriage seemed to conform to the companionate ideal.[32] Arthur and Tye shared a love of nature and a passion for poetry, books and their children. Arthur confided the burdens of running the estate to Tye and made sure that she understood the economic basis of land ownership, agriculture markets, hiring fairs and labour shortages. He wrote, 'that infernal American Trust Fund is again going down'.[33] After speaking against the Tenant's Rights Bill at a meeting of the Shropshire Chamber of Agriculture, he told Tye that he hoped his remarks would not appear in the press.[34] He explained to her exactly how Sir Edmond Beckley managed to generate revenue by leasing parcels of his estate[35] and that it took 15 people two hours to spread the hay to dry, unfortunately the endeavour was ruined by 'the worst thunderstorm...you could sail toy boats on the croquet ground'.[36] Rain struck again in 1882 and '£100 worth of hay was lost'.[37] Arthur, who kept a close eye on the domestic servants and household economy, reported to Tye that 'in 90 days Elaine sent out 70 handkerchiefs to the wash and Harriet 72 aprons'. Consequently, 'Elaine ought to go back to Switzerland, and Harriet ought not to be made parlour maid or have an advance of wages.'[38] In 1883, desperate to find a dairymaid at the hiring fair, he 'interviewed one dairymaid—the only one apparently in Oswestry—and she gravely demanded of me 40 per annum...We get a [bargain] by way of a nursemaid...at 8 pounds a year'.[39] Later that month he composed a verse for Tye about labour shortages: 'The big tree is in full leaf/the birds are in full song/the cows are not in full milk/nor are the labourers in full employment/some of us find doing nothing not unpleasant.'[40]

Arthur's letters to Tye illustrate his high regard for her intelligence and his expectation that she could and should understand the economic basis of their livelihood. As with other members of their class, their attitude toward their servants was 'central to the ruling-class consciousness'.[41] Like other Victorian paterfamilias Arthur adhered to a paternalist philosophy, which appeared overly generous to his American sister-in-law: '[Arthur] keeps a perfect army of poor people going, old servants pensioned, labourers taken on when the place does not need them, to give them work'.[42] Finlayson argues that '"private" paternalism could easily shade into "public" philanthropy',[43] and here the Jebb family's actions indicate that they realized that charitable activities could improve their standing in Ellesmere society.[44]

Arthur was a Liberal Unionist with a staunch conservative streak and an ardent opponent of Gladstonian Liberalism. He was very civic-minded and involved in a number of charitable causes. Like most conservative Victorians, he believed that voluntary charity was the best way of helping the poor. His solution to social welfare problems embodied the views expressed by Samuel Smiles in *Self-Help* (1859). Smiles emphasized the spirit of individual hard work, discipline and deferred gratification. In principle, the idea was that whatever is done for individual men or entire classes of people would remove the stimulus for and necessity of doing it for themselves. Where 'men were subjected to over-guidance and over-government', the inevitable tendency was to 'render them comparatively helpless'.[45] Arthur endorsed Smiles' doctrine of self-help wholeheartedly.

Since the late eighteenth century, friendly and benevolent societies like the Shropshire Provident Society had offered the working class a means of insuring themselves against the 'vicissitudes' of life, particularly illness, old age and death.[46] Arthur participated in the Shropshire Provident Society and believed it was his duty to promote self-help and fight pauperism; personally, he favoured the workhouse. On 7 April 1888, in protest against the 'debauching system' of outdoor relief, he dashed off angry letters to the *Times,* asking, '[W]hy should [their families]…make any effort to relieve them so long as public money is to be made for the purpose? As regards the undeserving poor, why should not idleness and improvidence be permitted to bring with them their natural punishment?'[47] According to his daughter Emily's short memoir, Arthur 'made a principle of placing himself at the disposal of all, and of never hiding behind an intermediary in the disagreeable concerns of life'.[48]

Arthur and his sister Louisa contributed a substantial amount of money to the Provident Society and the creation of the local hospital.[49] Their generosity improved their social position. Arthur proudly took his place among the local elite, upper ranks of the middle class, businessmen and landowners on the Uban District Council, the Board of Guardians and the Shropshire Provident Society, which distributed local relief to the sick, injured and indigent, weeded out the undeserving poor from the deserving and rewarded self-reliant provident behaviour.

Arthur Jebb's letters in the 1870s and 1880s have shown how a young husband and father balanced his private life with his public roles of landowner and breadwinner in the competitive arena of civil service, but what about Tye? Eglantyne Jebb and her mother both hold places in the history of women and philanthropy as founders of important charities for children. As we shall see, they shared a profound commitment to promoting social justice and improving the lives of the poor, but their approaches to voluntary action embodied different philanthropic traditions for women. Many late-Victorian women trod softly around the political side of their work, whereas their daughters embraced charity and politics as means of social criticism and social reform. Nevertheless, for conservative late-Victorian women, charity work still provided a way of expressing profound religious convictions, talent and intelligence. It was also a means of escaping the constraints of domestic life, speaking out against injustice and finding one's voice. Tye's diaries and letters to her husband challenge the one-dimensional portrait of the Victorian angel of the house, whose only role in life was to create a comfortable home and promote her husband's and children's status in society.[50] This stereotype, which casts women solely in relational roles, as daughters, wives and mothers, conceals the fact that in the late nineteenth century many middle- and upper-class married women were struggling to escape the confines of prescribed class and gender roles and to have public lives of their own.

Tye had a pampered upbringing. Though she did not have servants in livery or a title like her richer relatives, she had her own maid who went with her to the Lyth to dress her and do her hair.[51] According to Caroline Slemmer, who married Tye's brother Richard in 1874, by sheer effort her mother-in-law had kept up an illusion that the family was wealthier than they actually were. In truth, they had no 'fortune' to look forward to. Tye was fortunate to have 'married a rich man'[52] and her brother Richard was a brilliant and resourceful scholar, but Heneage and Bob were as 'helpless as young princes'.[53] Caroline said Bob 'takes a fancy to one penniless girl after another, but never by any chance do his affections fall on one he could possibly marry'.[54] Indisputably, Tye's marriage was the most significant attachment of her life. There is no evidence that she had ever wanted anything radical like a career and no evidence that Arthur wanted her to be more than an efficient wife and mother, so perhaps he could not be blamed for being less than enthusiastic when her interests in the affairs of the world outside of her family began to grow.

Like many upper-middle-class women, Tye had had an uneven and incomplete education; she was not a scholar like her famous brother Richard, though she had been permitted to take art classes at the Royal Dublin Society School of Art and won a prize at the second-grade examination of 1870.[55] Any hopes she may have had of pursuing art as a serious vocation were likely dashed by the lack of professional opportunities for women. Nonetheless, Tye was intelligent and deeply religious and determined to improve herself through her deep love of art, literature and poetry. In her diary she wrote frequently and eloquently about the things that mattered to her. Reflecting upon her years of married life, in 1882, she wrote, 'When I think how little worth the having I was 12 years ago, I like to think this—that I am perhaps [now] worth the having'.[56] The reason for Tye's awakening confidence was not her secure domestic life or her six children who ranged in age from ten to one, but what she called her 'fearless' new career.

There are competing accounts of how Tye's new career began, but the version she preferred to tell and hear told was that 'one day she found a boy in tears. He was picking up stones from one of their fields' which had been 'his duty in the past and apparently would be for the years ahead'. Tye, unable to bear the thought of such a wasted young life,[57] created a charity she called the Home Arts and Industries Association. The purpose of her charity was to provide the financial and human resources necessary to teach the children of local farm labourers how to make handcrafts to sell so they might have extra money that would protect their families from the perils of poverty and the dangers of the workhouse.[58] A more historically grounded version of events suggests that like other enlightened gentlewomen in the 1880s, Tye was very familiar with the work of William Morris and the aesthetic theories of John Ruskin. She had recently read *The Minor Arts: Porcelain Painting, Wood-carving, Stencilling, Modelling, Mosaic Work* by an American barrister named Charles Godfrey Leland who was travelling around England giving lectures to ladies and gentlemen on how to advance 'culture among the poor' by setting up arts and handicraft classes for local children and young adults.[59] The idea had not originated with Leland either, for according to Anne Anderson, an organization called the Cottage Arts Association had been giving Saturday classes in handcrafts since 1867 to working-class boys who were likely to take up the trades.[60]

Whichever version of the story one accepts, Tye did start a charity in 1882, and with the help of some local lady volunteers began giving woodcarving lessons in the servants' hall to cottagers' children around the Lyth. To improve her teaching methods, Tye read up on Friedrich Froebel's theories of early childhood development and his system of training hand and eye and used them to show the children how to 'duplicate' simple rustic designs in wood, brass and clay. There was more to her woodcarving classes than making saleable handcrafts, however. Tye saw the children's creative labour, including china work, inlaying, spinning and weaving as a solution to the long-term economic and social problems because factory work deskilled workers. 'The apprenticeship system had broken down', she wrote, 'and the school system was inadequate to take its place'. Regrettably, she remarked, children were no longer 'lovingly, little by little', taught the family trade by their parents.

> Nature's methods are superseded in our England…The father works at one place, the mother often at another, the child is at school, and very little wholesome home teaching survives. The skilled work of the Englishman is no longer, necessarily, the best of its kind, and this is having its effect upon the country'.[61]

With missionary zeal, Tye devoted herself to spreading the gospel of arts, crafts and culture throughout Shropshire.

For a late-Victorian landowning family like the Jebbs, there was nothing unusual in charitable activities. Rural 'landowning paternalists' were the founders of friendly societies, savings banks and schools, and their sisters, wives and daughters founded ladies' visiting committees and oversaw the day-to-day running of such institutions, 'especially those in the interests of women and children'.[62] The Quaker reformer Hannah Moore said that 'charity is the calling of a lady; the care of the poor is her profession…female philanthropy [would] bind rich and poor together in an invisible chain of sympathy…mitigating distress and softening class hostility.'[63] Although philanthropy was seen as a natural part of the educated classes' wider social and religious duty, Jacques Donzelot has argued that it had a political dimension as well. In his view, philanthropy was not simply an apolitical pastime for Victorian gentlefolk, but a deliberate act of authority by the rich towards poor.[64]

Many late-Victorian philanthropic activities, especially those concerning rural children, reflected a wider goal of creating future citizens
and disciplined agricultural workers. For women, the rhetoric of social
motherhood gave them permission to meddle in the family life of the
poor.[65] Tye's HAIA was no exception. Anderson argues that by main-
taining a 'disinterested amateur status', lady volunteer art teachers
could maintain that their work was not for personal gain, but for
the common good; to civilize the lower classes and thus produce good
citizens.[66] Tye would have agreed, she wrote, 'our work seeks to bind
together the social life of the country…it is not only the pupils who are
educated, but the taste of the neighbourhood is raised'.[67] Success
would be achieved when the 'dignity of the "work of the hands" was
restored to the labouring classes'.[68] There were limitations to the work,
however, and nobody was thinking of removing the barriers of class
relations. Unlike Leland, who saw handicrafts as training for future
artisans, Tye wanted to teach a hobby, which could fill up the leisure
time of people of good character. She did not 'fancy for a moment'
that peasant children would be made into artisans or 'aspire to excel in
Fine Art'. She asserted that

> there was a vast difference between living, breathing marble, and a
> simple chiselled pattern; between a highly-finished grand likeness of
> the mind and body of a man, and an outline on a brass tray, or
> china plate – all the difference indeed, between the Art of Greece
> and that of Japan…Home Arts, as the name implies, means rather
> simple, useful, early forms of Art, such as the young and ignorant
> can aspire to practice with interest, and to good purpose, after very
> few lessons.[69]

Julia Parker argues that the place of charity work in women's lives was
a function of their social class and family position, aptitude and talent,
and personal inclination.[70] Tye discovered that she could give 'capital'
carving lessons but teaching volunteer lady art teachers or children
were not her 'forte'.[71] Before long she became bored and decided that
her next step should be to pick up her pen. Despite the fact that she
had never written anything for publication before, with the blessing of
Canon Harold, 'who called at lunch', she decided to write an article
called 'A New Ladies' League' about how ladies' handicraft classes
could help poor children. It was a suitable topic for a lady's pen, and
Canon Harold 'highly approved' of the 'name'.[72] Tye put her heart and
soul into the article, which, however, by the time it appeared a month

later in the *Temperance Visitor,* had a significantly more radical title: 'The Rights of Women'. But its only debt to Mary Wollstonecraft was the name. Tye began her long article with a heavy dose of the Book of Genesis and moved from a detailed account of how the infant Moses was saved by a Pharaoh's daughter to Napoleon Bonaparte's call to the mothers of France to rebuild the nation. She finally concluded with Sir Edwin Chadwick's challenge (following Froebel) to the ladies of England to grace the crèches of the population's poorest. Thus, in her article, Tye provided theological, historical and moral justification for women's role as the natural 'helpmeets' of men. She envisioned a 'network of women's work brightened by women's love which shall embrace in its fold every child...We have long talked of women's rights and women's work—surely this is our first right and our best work, to bear our part in bringing up a happier race'.[73]

Over the next two years Tye worked harder, wrote more and advanced in her 'new fearless career' from lady volunteer art teacher to prominent local philanthropist. With her children in tow, she spent entire days collecting five-guinea subscriptions; handing out samples of woodcarving; and discussing art classes, Celtic designs, Froebel, Ruskin, Buddhism, the 'sacred body of the east', her own aesthetic theories and the effect of temperance on poverty with any reform-minded member of the local elite who cared to listen. Her diary was quickly filled with appointments, teas and correspondence with important philanthropists, clergy and the managers of the local Boys' Industrial Home and the Cripples Home.[74] She even received a letter from Robert Browning, 'who seemed amused' by the project.[75] On the day of her daughter Eglantyne's sixth birthday, Tye was truly excited to learn that her article for the *Temperance Visitor* would be reprinted as a leaflet. She began to draft a book about 'how to hold classes in woodcarving' and wrote to Captain William Booth, promising to donate 'any possible profits accruing from it' to the Salvation Army.[76] Tye thought she must use her writing as another way of helping the poorest of the poor. No one including her coachman could escape the crusade. One day after lunch, poor Evans was subjected to a discussion about the 'desirability of men of his class having a "second string to their bow" in the way of work'.[77]

Although charity work was a moral and spiritual mission for pious gentlewomen, it was also recognized as a form of serious work for society women, whose private and public lives were circumscribed by its strict 'rules, conventions and rituals'.[78] As the wife of a landowner, Tye understood that it was her responsibility to move her family onward and upward by making connections within society; charity work was one of the ways that wives and daughters of the elite classes did this. Tye was promoting herself, her daughters, the Jebb family name and the Home Arts and Industries Association. Her reaction on the day that Lady Brownlow called upon her illustrates the rules of late-Victorian social etiquette and the part they played in charity work.

Lord and Lady Brownlow were the cream of Ellesmere society. Their Bridgewater estate consisted (by the end of the First World War) of '60,000 acres scattered across England'.[79] The Jebbs did not move in their social circle and Tye could never have approached Lady Brownlow without an introduction. However on the 20th of September 1882, Tye was having an At-Home and was astonished when Lady Brownlow arrived. Tye recorded the details of this decisive personal and social victory in her diary. She wrote:

> In the afternoon as I had finished tea in walked Etty and to my surprise Lady Brownlow. A beautiful sweet lady, sweet and graciously mannered in dark blue serge–ruff and cardinal coloured satin lining. She would know all about the carving and half doubting whether I did well, I went on to speak of my Irish classes and then she asked me if I knew Lady Spencer. I said 'no' and she said 'she is a great friend of mine, would you like me to send her some of your papers?' To which I gladly assented.[80]

Tye recognized the Victorian expression 'do you know?'[81] It designated rigid social boundaries and meant that an invitation to higher society might be forthcoming. The following Sunday after church, with Louisa, Emily, Eglantyne and Richard by her side, Tye cautiously approached Lady Brownlow at the church gate. To her relief, Lady Brownlow asked for her papers and invited her to call later at Ellesmere House. The rule was that once invited to a person's home, no further sign of social acceptability was considered necessary.[82] After 'more talk'; Lady Brownlow agreed to be 'my "leader" in the Ladies Association'.[83] The first hurdle was jumped. Tye had secured a titled patron for her HAIA, which was the ultimate goal of any new Victorian charity.[84] With this the wheels quickly began to turn.

By 1883, the position of the Home Arts and Industries Association as an important new charity was assured and Tye gained access to an exciting new social circle. The first annual meeting was held in 1884. Lord Brownlow became the founding president and the 'head and shoulders' of the Working Council and Walter Besant, the novelist and social reformer, took on the role of Honorary Treasurer. By 1885 the association comprised between 70 and 80 branches in different town and villages, with offices and studios in London offering classes fo training paid teachers in design and drawing. The prospectus liste 48 vice-presidents; many of who were distinguished titled patron of the Royal Academy of Art. Over the next ten years the HAIA becam renowned for its extravagant annual exhibitions, which were attende by celebrities and members of the royal family.[85]

Although most well-to-do Victorian women did charity work, fev actually took their good works into the realm of politics and becam 'reformers'. Yet the ground between charitable reform and politica action was shaky in the late nineteenth century. In the early 1880s when Tye often travelled to Dublin to take care of her ailing parents she was struck by the devastating poverty of the Irish villages sh passed and particularly, the misery of the Irish children, which sh described in her diary:

> ...the way [from] Killiney to King William's town...seems straight a an arrow...steep and rough and unspeakably dreary; bare, blue bo without limit, rough people in small force working languidly a their scanting or peats, or do no work at all looking hungry in thei rags; helpless, air as of creatures sunk beyond hope, look[ed] int one of their huts under pretence of asking for a draught of water dark, narrow, two women nursing, other young woman on foot as i for work; but it is narrow, dark, as if the people and their lives wer covered under a tub or 'tied in a sack' all things smeared over to with the languid green...these were the wretched population I saw in Ireland.[86]

One Sunday Tye reflected upon the words of a hymn she and her chil dren sang in church: 'There's a home for little children above the brigh blue sky...there's a rest for little children'.[87] Her mind wandered to th starvation in Ireland and the mothers and babies who were being turne away from the overcrowded shelters.[88] It occurred to her that Irish people 'being Celtic in race, and thus quick of sense and fancy and deft in hand would be 'specially qualified for such Art-Instruction'.[89] She immediately decided to concentrate her own HAIA work on saving the 'wretched population' in her native Ireland;[90] thereby applying her philanthropic work to a wider sociological and political problem. She had learned enough about agricultural production from her husband to think that th extra income earned from home crafts might provide a buffer against th cyclical agricultural slumps and over-dependence on backward method of tillage, grazing, growing and dairying. What was significant and unusual, however, was that Tye was a supporter of Irish Home Rule, which was not popular among the Anglo-Protestants and could have put her at odds with other members of the HAIA.[91] Tye was willing to take the risk. In her assessment it was time to go beyond charitable handouts and demand that the government provide grants for educational and practical training to 'deserving' Irish children who had a 'hereditary aptitude' for handiwork.[92] Tye quickly established some HAIA branches in Ireland, and before long, some controversial Irish nationalists and Young Irelanders like John Dillon and Charlotte O'Brien became aware of her activities. The Irish republican Michael Davitt began to write to her from Portland Gaol where he was imprisoned in 1882 and 1883.[93]

Charity work for late-Victorian women provided a way of expressing a profound religious conviction, using their talents and intelligence and finding an opportunity for a life outside the home. Through charity work many women 'found their voices' and a vocabulary that enabled them to speak against injustice'[94] which have been important themes in women's history.[95] In the early 1880s, Tye began to receive a great deal of attention from many important people who applauded her hard work and reforming zeal. It would appear, however, that she did not have the approval of the two most important men in her life, Arthur and her brother Richard; for once her charity work began to move from a genteel pastime toward the political arena, Arthur and Richard applied the brakes. At first, Arthur had supported her 'causes célèbres' and Tye appreciated it enormously. She wrote, 'O my darling—if ere anybody had the soul of a king it is you'.[96] Arthur also supported her writing at first, but as she began to talk more and more about Irish problems and Home Rule, he became anxious. Initially, Tye was deferential, handing Arthur the 'first proofs' of her article in *Nineteenth Century* for him to look at 'after breakfast'. They read them over together, and Arthur pointed out 'two or three little emendations of sentence—with his delicate and cultured taste for good English'. When he said he did 'not think it necessary to offer down my pleas for the labourers' she obediently toned them down.[97] Soon, though, Arthur began trying to moderate her reformist ideas, especially her application for government grants for education in Ireland:

> I wish I could be as sanguine as you in regard to your scheme. I never quite understood how cookery came to get a grant, I feel confident there can be no expansion of grants of this kind in the country. It is impossible not to see that anything is possible in regard to Ireland.

Money is thrown away there in sheer despair or rather desperation and no return is as much as looked for.[98]

Frank Prochaska has written that 'as a religion of social action, phil anthropy slowly challenged the complacency of women, gave them practical experience and responsibility, and perhaps most importantly it heightened their self-confidence and self-respect'.[99] Prochaska does not talk about the sacrifice and guilt that some women were made to feel in doing the work. As HAIA began to take Tye away from home more and more, Arthur objected to the amount of time she was spend ing away from her children. In letters he remarked that 'all the chil dren are near fairly well, and have completely forgotten Mamma'.[100] 'I would rather you taught a few little lads at the Lyth and did not under take classes in Ellesmere. In short I disapprove of the plan, and wish you had consulted me instead of Mrs Purvis'.[101] In May 1883, Tye received a particularly stern letter. Arthur had begun to refer to Charles Godfrey Leland as Uncle Charlie and mockingly blamed the shortage of competent farm labourers on Tye's handicraft movement:

> Dearest...we are going on here somehow, though Bet looks worn to a shadow and I am weak in the knee joints, and in the face ashy pale, [my sister] means to come here by and by when it suits her convenience and does not suit mine...a host of others assist me to tide over a difficulty which would have been provided for in old times by half our regular staff. Damned that education (wood carving included), which prevents mankind from having anything to say to drudgery or small pay.[102]

Arthur had no use for Gladstone and little sympathy with Home Rule and, influenced by the views of, Samuel Smiles, considered grants for Ireland to be a violation of the doctrine of self-help because they would never promote self-reliance.[103] Tye was hurt rather than amused by Arthur's mockery. In her diary she confided:

> My Dear Lord writes yesterday as usual you are wanted at home you must be more wanted where you are and with this reflection I must pacify my desire...I feel such a longing to acquire a greater mastery but the first obvious duties of life of home government—of—of family life. If only I may attain to this—it does not come naturally to me—and all of my life up to the last 5 years more of less inflicted me for doing it well...yet how distinctly that call comes! All I do

seems so little and then always feelings of weakness and yet and yet the work creeps on![104]

Tye's brother Richard also had strong ideas about the way that women should behave in public and private. In 1874 he had refused to buy his wife a sewing machine because he could not 'stand to hear the machine and dislikes any sewing that doesn't look refined'. She told her sister that once Dick had been 'dreadfully shocked' to find her 'sitting on the rug before the fire, eating a sweet biscuit for my luncheon and reading the newspaper. He said I seem to have a natural taste for squalid things...I try to shock what he calls his refinement as little as possible...A shy, self-conscious man cannot comprehend the ease and absence of terror another feels who is not self-conscious'.[105] Clearly, such 'a shy, self-conscious man' would also object to his sister discoursing in print or from the platform about the 'Irish problem'. Richard made his objections clear when they were visiting their mother in Ireland. Tye felt compelled to lie to him about her part in a lecture tour after he said, '"Well, mind you are not to make a speech—you mustn't make a speech"—Like a miserable wretch I assured him that Mrs L'Entrange "will do all the talking"'.[106] This was not the truth. In her diary, Tye admitted her lie: 'I shall—too speak...even if nothing further should be given to me to do',

> I have struck a spark now, which surely cannot die. My dream palace is nearer...than I thought. A holy temple (a temple of help) living stones...Oh Ireland, Ireland, crushed and broken...I will not let [them] take your little innocent children...Thank God who has given me words to say—and let him give me grace to speak it plain before I die.[107]

Though acknowledging that it took 'great strength of character' for women to 'make headway against the wishes of their husbands or parents', Prochaska concedes that it 'would be a distortion however, to suppose that female philanthropy succeeded without any support from men'.[108] The Victorian marital relationship, known as the 'marriage question', was the subject of intense discussion in the late nineteenth century. Between 1882 and 1886, the *Times* published hundreds of letters by feminists and non-feminists debating the implications of reshaping or revolutionizing the institution of matrimony. The Jebbs read the *Times* and were likely aware that numerous women and some men of their class found many features of the husband-wife relationship to be oppressive and were struggling to redefine it. When Tye wished to enter public life and her genteel woodcarving classes turned into a programme for radical social action, Arthur's angel of the house fell from grace. He could not see how an activist wife fitted into his domestic world, and he had no wish to be upstaged by her or to emulate the progressive marriages of contemporary social reformer like Josephine and Samuel Butler (married in 1852), Charles and Mary Booth (married in 1871), or Charity Organization Society founders, Henrietta and Samuel Barnett (married in 1872).[109] Arthur believed that he had the moral authority to guide his wife, children and servants towards a virtuous life. He believed that a 'woman's sphere was in the home' and there would be no 'career for them'. Even his 'shockingly' radical sister Louisa, who wrote pamphlets on Darwinism 'placed marvellous restraint on her strong convictions...out of loyalty to her brother'.[110]

The fact that Arthur was not interested in women's rights had implications for Tye's work. It has been said that in marriage, 'guilt, its uses, its effect, and the uses and effect of its intimate ally, principle' have been effective in controlling women's choices.[111] This can be applied to Tye's predicament. Early in her HAIA work she had posed the question: 'What shall I do, when I encounter...the antagonism, which seems so terribly prominent a feature in other people's experiences?' She was disappointed that by objecting to her career, Arthur and Richard became her antagonists, but she did not challenge their sovereign role.[112] Tye did not 'wish to be called a strong minded woman', however, she thanked 'God who has given me words to say'.[113] Sadly, this was the same woman who in her article, *The Rights of Woman* described the 'sense of the aimlessness, of uselessness, which urges so many women of leisure to go forth, "choosing rather to suffer" with the workers of the world' instead of enjoying

> the unsatisfying pleasures of an idle, fruitless life...the very consciousness of possessing this spare time begets a longing for a life which shall call forth in action capabilities and instincts which unused fill the soul with a sense of incompleteness and failure...Fruitless inaction *is* Death, helpful action *is* Life.[114]

In 1884, it was announced that Mrs Arthur Jebb had retired from public life; the official reason given was broken health. She reduced her work to a few local meetings a year and a couple of exhibitions in 1885 and 1886.[115] Her diary of the time suggests that there was nothing the matter with her health. She was 37 years old, and although nothing is known about her medical or reproductive history, she had always been energetic and in good health. She loved the outdoors, nature and walks in Shropshire and Wales with her family. Her diary makes no mention of miscarriages or of menstrual, prenatal or postnatal difficulties; nor does it suggest, apart from fatigue, that any of the six pregnancies gave her difficulty. Nevertheless, shortly after giving up her Home Arts work, she began to suffer from the mysterious maladies that afflicted many late-Victorian women. In September 1887 her sister-in-law was so alarmed by the transformation in Tye that she described Tye's symptoms in detail to a sister in America:

> She is frightfully thin and looks worn out, and I don't know how she can look so ill and have nothing the matter. I think she has a great fear present with her constantly. She says they may talk about overwork and the brain being tired and wanting rest, but she fears the indigestion and nausea have some other cause. She has a spot where she sometimes feels beating and uneasiness deep inside...Of course the Doctors have examined her very carefully...Her head is as strong and clear as ever, she can dictate letters by the hour, but she cannot read or write on account of the pain in her eyes...I think Arthur and the Doctors fear she may sink into a chronic nervous state, but that she is really seriously ill now, I feel not a doubt.[116]

In 1887 Tye's doctors found absolutely nothing wrong, but today acute loss of weight, severe dizziness, nausea, heart palpitations and depression are associated with a generalized anxiety disorder which used to be known as hypochondria. Parker writes that whatever the mixture of motives which led women into social service work, those who regarded it as an expression of God's work were able to 'defy opposition and to endure the disappointments and vicissitudes of their public lives'.[117] This being the case, those who believed, as Tye did, that she had failed to serve God in his chosen way suffered excessively. Tye felt guilty (in the Christian sense having sinned) for giving up her Home Arts work and abandoning the children of Ireland. She was unable to express her anger toward Arthur and her brother for their part in forcing her do so. She internalized her guilt and anger, which caused her depression. Tye suffered from this 'illness' for the rest of her life.

Eleanor Gordon and Gwyneth Nair observe that although late-Victorian 'married couples may have been counselled to love, honour and respect each other and husbands to temper their authority with affection, rarely do complex and intimate human relations neatly cor-respond with cultural prescriptions'.[118] This chapter has shown that after Arthur came into his inheritance, he was able to devote himself fully to being a husband, father and landowner. He was committed to modest philanthropy around Ellesmere and did not want to move in higher social circles. Though he was well educated and had modest literary aspirations, he could never bring himself to write anything other than letters to the newspapers and '*A Book of Psalms, Rendered into English Verse*', which Tye had published posthumously. Tye knew that Arthur was uncomfortable around her brother's sophisticated Cambridge University friends where he said he felt like 'the rusty old country squire among all the professors and learned people'.[119] He may have been disappointed by his own inability to make his mark on the world and perhaps grew jealous of his wife. In 1894, Arthur developed pneu-monia and died suddenly at the age of 55. Years after his death, Tye made apologies for him: 'On earth my Darling lived on a high plain, constantly misunderstood of men...My consolation is that at least I suffered him to go his own high way, and never...to worry him down to a lower level, as a would-be wiser woman would have done'.[120] In the 1930s Emily Jebb remembered him as a 'melancholy Lancelot'.[121]

Late-Victorian women trod softly around the political side of their work, but their daughters embraced charity and politics as methods of social criticism and social reform. Both generations discovered that voluntary work and social action could be a way of expressing pro-found personal convictions, talent and intelligence. This chapter has also shown that charity work could be a means of escaping the con-straints of domestic life, speaking out against injustice and find-ing one's voice. On Christmas Eve, Tye wrote, '[Y]ou are almost done 1882...If I should live, [how] shall I ever fit its moral into a story?'[122] Tye lived to be 80 years old. Early in 1920, she told her second daughter, Lil, that 'for many <u>many</u> years [her] earnest prayer' was that each one of her four daughters 'should have work to do that should be pleasing to God and that he would prosper you in doing of it'.[123] Perhaps Tye's moral for the year 1882 was that every woman, and particularly her daughters, should 'experience' the 'happiness, which arises from a sense of living to some purpose'.[124] Over the years, Tye became 'boundlessly ambitious'[125] for her daughters, who did not disappoint her. In the early 1920s the British government recognized Louisa (Lil) Jebb Wilkins for her work for the war effort, which led to the formation of the Women's Land Army. During the First World War,

Dorothy Jebb Buxton's name became synonymous with international peace work. Emily Jebb Ussher published a book protesting the attacks upon civilians by the Royal Irish Constabulary and the notorious *Black and Tans*, and Eglantyne Jebb founded the Save the Child International Union in Geneva. In 1921, Tye told her daughter Lil, 'What <u>wonderful</u> answers I have had'![126]

2
Raising Rebel Daughters: Lessons for Lives of Social Action

'Nothing particular "now-a-day" as people say.' (Eglantyne, aged 10)

'I have a fever for dolls', wrote nine-year old Eglantyne Jebb in 1886. In her diary she unleashed a flood of concerns about Alice, Emmie, a Scotch doll, her half-a-head doll and Old Lady Waxface, whom 'Father cannot bear'.[1] These were only a few of the handed-down and borrowed dolls whose misadventures Eglantyne described in detail in her diary. Like other late-Victorian girls, Emily, Louisa (Lil), Eglantyne and Dorothy Jebb were encouraged by their parents and governesses to record their activities and thoughts in diaries because it was believed that writing in a diary served an important pedagogical purpose. Not only was it a good method of introducing young girls educated at home to the mechanics of language; it was the foundation of more complicated feminine accomplishments like the writing of letters, poetry and short stories which would be enjoyed by people outside of the family circle. Anthony Fletcher says that late-Victorian girl's diaries are important 'reflective exercises in self-scrutiny'.[2] The historical significance of girls' diaries, letters and compositions, according to Carolyn Steedman, lies in what they reveal about what girls were taught, and by whom, and what they actually learned.[3] Eglantyne loved to write, and throughout her life the written word was her favourite method of communication about personal and political matters. This chapter shows that there is nothing in her girlhood diaries, letters and vignettes to suggest that she was more likely than any of her sisters to follow in her mother's footsteps and through philanthropy become the 'saviour' of unwanted, neglected and abandoned children. Yet the Jebb sisters' girlhood writing reveals a great deal about the complicated family dynamics and how their relationships with their father, mother, Aunt

2.1 Eglantyne Jebb, source: Jebb Family

Louisa and each other influenced the decisions Eglantyne made as she travelled from girlhood to young womanhood in the decades of the 1880s and 1890s.

Eglantyne was born in 1876. She was Arthur and Tye's fourth child. She had periwinkle eyes and red-gold hair and her mother's diary suggests that this sensitive and imaginative third daughter was regarded as the prettiest child. Tye was especially proud of Eglantyne's long wavy hair and wild-rose complexion. In the 1870s, the majestic old family name 'Eglantyne' was considered to be 'too pompous' for a child,[4] so Tye called Eglantyne 'Rufa' and the rest of the family called her 'Doey'. The other children had nicknames too. Louisa was always called 'Lil' or 'Lillie', Richard was 'Dick' or 'Bar', Emily and Gamul's names were shortened to 'Emmie' and 'Gam' and Dorothy was called 'Dora'. With two older sisters and an older brother, Eglantyne became a 'middle' child after Gamul and Dorothy were born in 1880 and 1881; however, she was determined not be classified as one of the younger siblings. At the age of nine, she wrote, 'I hope if anybody reads this journal, they shall not laugh at me for talking of Gamul and Dorothy as "the little ones".'[5]

As was normal for the late-Victorian English rural elite, the Jebb boys went away to school and their sisters remained at home. Thus the life that Eglantyne and her sisters recorded in their diaries, memoirs and semi-autobiographical stories resembled the lives of many other late-Victorian girls who grew up in large country houses surround by servants and busy civic-minded parents. Diaries are a taxing source for historians, Mary Abbott points out, 'articulate, confiding, readable diarists are rare'.[6] None of Lil's diaries have survived. Eglantyne was disappointed with herself because she was 'always beginning journals and leaving them off',[7] but she was a prolific writer just the same, and a great deal of her girlhood writing survives. Emily was the eldest and the pre-eminent family chronicler. When the Jebb sisters' diaries are read alongside other family papers, they reveal that each of girls had a highly distinctive personality and a sense of her own individual dignity and importance. What emerges most strongly in the domestic details of Dorothy, Eglantyne and Emily's diaries is how much their duties and responsibilities, grievances, disappointments and pleasures shaped each other's experiences. As for many girls of their class, the immediate family was at the centre of their worlds, to the extent that when Dorothy went away to boarding school in 1898, she told Dick, 'Girls are such unknown quantities to me, it will be amusing to see what they are like!'[8] Emily and Lil were the closest in age but had the least in common. When the boys were home from school, scientifically minded Lil spent most of her time with them or outdoors with Dorothy, who was deeply engrossed in her plant, animal and insect collections. In contrast, Emily and Eglantyne shared a passion for sketching and poetry. Emily wrote, 'after tea Doey and I read

Longfellow on the rocks by the river. Had late dinner and were ideal "young liddies"'.[9] Emily empathized with Eglantyne the day she fell off a plank into the lake right in front of the visiting Beasley brothers. 'Miss Doey, who was gone for a short visit to Blueland [daydreaming], suddenly was reminded where she was by a splash, and finding herself up to her waist in a muddy pool...[She] had to change everything she had on'![10]

Under the influence of philosophers like Rousseau and Locke and the romantic poetry of William Wordsworth, the Victorians constructed an idealized vision of childhood as a 'special time, the best of times, a time that was sanctified'.[11] This ideology was practical only in upper- and middle-class families, however. In Victorian domestic ideology, the home was the perfect primary agency of socialization for girls; functioning as a total institution where few other social groups could have much influence.[12] In the 1880s and 1890s a culture of the 'new girl' became apparent which stressed the importance of developing a young girl's spirit and body as well as her intelligence.[13] This emancipation, however, did not release them from strict Victorian ideas about the surveillance of girls and from rigid codes of moral and religious education. Young girls learned the class and gender roles they would one day play by observing the relationships amongst the most powerful adult role models in the household. In the case of the Jebb sisters, potential role models and teachers included their father, mother, Aunt Louisa Jebb, the governess and a dozen servants. Arthur Jebb died suddenly of pneumonia in 1894 when Emily was 22, Lil 21, Eglantyne 18 and Dorothy 13, but he had an important formative influence on their lives. Moreover, it was not unusual for families to call upon the unpaid child-rearing services of the female relatives who were part of the household. As the Jebb children grew older, a great deal of their education was given over to Arthur's unmarried sister Louisa, who was an influential member of the household.

Historians presume that when urbanization and industrialization forced men and fathers into the competitive world of work and industry, child rearing and nurturing were given over almost exclusively to the wives and mothers. The organization of family life on small rural estates, however, did not conform to the industrial pattern because work and family life were combined.[14] Consequently, after Arthur Jebb left London and the Education Department in 1873 and returned to the Lyth, he had more opportunity and freedom to participate in the nurturing of his young children than most historians of fatherhood would appreciate. Fatherhood was a source of delight for Arthur, who spent a great deal of time with his children and, unlike the fathers described by Fletcher, did not feel 'out of his depth in parenthood'.[15] Many of Arthur's letters to Tye, who was away a great deal in the early 1880s doing her Home Arts and Industries Association (HAIA) work, reveal that he felt quite at home in the nursery. In fact, he developed a knack for child psychology. With the application of 'reason', he coaxed Emily out of a 'terrible' tantrum over 'a blue ribbon'. Emily 'gave in like an angel...She runs after me all day saying..."Where you go, I will go."' This had impressed his Old Nanny Ruth.[16] By the time Dorothy was a toddler, he had her running around the nursery 'after the plate' of strawberries 'with her tongue out'.[17] As the children grew up, Arthur placed great value on his companionate relationships with them; there is no mention of harsh treatment by him in any surviving diaries or memoirs. He was much loved for the puns and poems he composed from their names,[18] and his hobbies and interests, like reading poetry, riding, fishing and hiking, became his daughters' and sons' hobbies and interests.

But there was more to late-Victorian fatherhood than amusing the children, for it carried with it heavy moral, social and political responsibilities. It was the pedagogical and moral obligation of the paterfamilias to guide the entire household towards a virtuous life. Men had to teach their children, servants and employees 'to love God and respect their betters'.[19] Thus, a father's teachings extended beyond immediate domestic realm into the world at large.[20] Arthur shared with other members of the late-Victorian British elite the belief that his own behaviour should stand as an example of what was expected of others.[21] Through word and deed he tried to teach his children their future moral and social responsibilities. This can be seen in the Jebb's daily routine, which included family prayers, the participation of the whole family in the civic activities of the Ellesmere Debating Society and also Arthur's adherence to the old Christmas tradition of dining in the servant's hall.

The strict daily routine of Jebb family life in the 1880s and 1890s was recorded in their diaries and short autobiographical essays. The day began at around 7:30, when everyone was expected to be downstairs for family prayers and breakfast, and it ended 'not a tick later than 10 o'clock', when the whole family was expected to be in bed. Victorian children raised in country houses learned that thrift was a virtue and waste a sin and that the austerities of life were for their own good. When Arthur wrote to Tye in 1882, 'We must live very economically this winter',[22] they all knew that he meant it. Tye's household records revealed that she calculated that it cost her '1s/1d a day per head (not counting game) to feed the family'.[23] Emily remembered the wintry 'cold lamp-lit house', the ice in the basins 'when we got up in the mornings' and the 'meagre' late dinners 'in evening dress' at which children over the age of 13 were expected to be present. She recalled that they 'always ate and prayed in the library, leaving a romantic tapestried dining room to occasions of high festival'.[24] Eglantyne's diary captured the design of the nursery, the network of servants and the 'rats' which were an extra attraction of the English country house: 'Our house has lot of those dear things, who gnaw on doors, eat our slippers, and make smells in the hall'.[25]

The Evangelical movement within the Church of England, as much as Non-conformists, Quakers, Unitarians, Congregationalists and Baptists, espoused an 'earnest and personal Christianity' through 'daily family life as well as public service'.[26] Victorian family culture also adopted from Christian teachings 'a highly moralized understanding of the family as a microcosm of God's Kingdom, and a concomitant reverence for and deference toward the head of the household'.[27] It would have seemed natural to Arthur to expect his wife and children to respect his authority as they respected God's authority. And family prayers and overall religious education were a medium through which he conveyed morality and the principles of social duty to his household.[28] With the exception of Aunt Louisa, who was an atheist, the Jebb's were all active members of the Church of England in the 1880s and 1890s. They took prayer, churchgoing and public service seriously. These activities expanded their role in the community and laid the foundation for the routines of country-house life.

In her short memoir, Emily says the day ended with family prayers.[29] Despite the strict religious education, none of her younger brothers and sisters appear to have been excessively introspective or to have developed a Victorian terror of sin. Eglantyne's diary shows that, like other late-Victorian children, she was interested in the rituals associated with death and in the concepts of heaven and hell.[30] The Jebb children were not discouraged from burying pets and other creatures in their own little corner of the family graveyard. They enjoyed performing mock funerals and administering sacraments. In fact, Eglantyne regarded a pet's funeral as a good occasion to compose an epitaph. Once they found a 'half dead' rabbit 'down by the moss', Eglantyne waited for him to die and then buried him, putting on his tombstone the following words:

> Under this stone a stranger lies
> No one laughs and no one cries
> Where he has gone and how he fares
> Nobody knows and nobody cares.[31]

Arthur recognized that it was his responsibility to teach his children the family's position in the British social system and their future civic duties. He was a barrister by training with a passion for the Ellesmere Debating Society. It is unclear whether the reason he expected his children to accompany him to the debating society meetings was that it was their duty or that he was proud of them and enjoyed taking them out. Either way, Emily and Eglantyne said they were expected to attend his debates, where they 'heard theories discussed from every possible angle'. Emily wrote, 'We were expected to sit mum so long as the debate was lively. But it if flagged, we had to help it out—but not for a moment were we allowed to suppose we really knew anything about anything'.[32] In her diary in 1893, Eglantyne described a meeting where Stanley Leighton 'preached' first, but 'made so many faces and gesticulations, and acted tragedy so badly, that [she] felt inclined to laugh'. Next up was an 'Irishman' who 'ranted and rolled his R's and thumped the table…Father gave a rather long and very interesting address, which was tremendously applauded'.[33] These theatrical community events were exciting occasions for Eglantyne. Though she did not understand what her father said, in her eyes he was the star of the event. It must be emphasized that although Arthur may have wanted his daughters to learn about the important social issues of the day, he was also an introverted man who may have felt more confident in a public forum when supported by four loyal and admiring daughters.

Arthur tried to set an example of paternalism and benevolence by adhering to the obligations of his class to servants. This can be seen in the half-century old Jebb family tradition of serving Christmas dinner to the servants. In his diary of 1890, Arthur wrote,

> Here we are having an old-fashioned Christmas with ice upon the water in our bedroom jugs, and snow upon the ground, and all my outdoor servants want to know what they are to do, well knowing that nothing can be done…The menu for the 6 maids within the 6 men without (and their families) totalled 45…plus such old friends as

Ruth…thrown in, was as follows…round of beef 54½ pounds, 2 fat geese, 5 plum puddings, and piles of mince pies. In the evening merry-making, songs and a fiddle. This they consumed (all of it no doubt) in two long rows each side of a long table in our servants' hall.[34]

The task for biographers who use children's diaries is to keep separate how the teaching was done from what was actually learned.[35] Emily's memoirs challenge the assumption that privileged children accepted class hierarchies as normal. Emily's description of being raised by Arthur reveals a generation gap. Arthur did not realize that 'the young democrats' among his children 'resented' his Christmas tradition and were embarrassed by it. Given the way they later chose to live their lives, Dorothy, Eglantyne and Lil likely suffered the most from their father's before-dinner speeches and were almost certainly mortified to be 'marshalled en masse in the already congested doorway whilst the coachman, like a seneschal of old, yelled "make way for the family, make way"'. Emily concluded, 'we might have been denizens of a castle and owners of a county 400 years or so ago'.[36]

Fathers are important role models in young girls' lives, whether they 'provide the first examples of paternalism—distance, indifference, or benevolence'.[37] When they grew up, Eglantyne and her sisters recognized the part their father played in teaching them the importance of community obligations and social service even though, as adults, they rejected his conservative politics, his opposition to women's right to higher education and careers, and his paternalist values. Emily, who was the most positive about Arthur, wrote, 'although he owned little more than a few Welsh farms, we grew up far more aware of what land-owning means than those people often are who own vast estates'.[38] In contrast, Lil devoted her professional life to promoting alternative methods of agriculture, such as smallholdings and co-operative farms. Dorothy married a member of the wealthy Buxton family, became a Quaker and a socialist and refused to keep servants, but Eglantyne was more quietly the harshest critic of all. In her semi-autobiographical novel called 'The Ring Fence', she made a scathing attack on the privileges, hypocrisies and prejudices of the rural landowning classes whose only sign of contrition was a futile philanthropy, which she calls an 'egoism' that 'eats into its heart like a canker'.[39] Whatever direction their individual careers took, however, the Jebb sisters' choices do demonstrate that they had internalized Arthur's most important dictum: 'Of those who lived in beautiful places much was required'.[40]

2.2   Jebb children with mother, source: Jebb Family

One cannot easily determine what Tye's daughters learned from her by looking only at their childhood diaries because she lived to the age of 80. In fact, Victorian gentlewomen did not arrange their lives entirely around their children, and so children's relationships with their child minders must also be considered. In the 1880s, Tye was so frequently away with her charity work, nursing her ailing parents or visiting friends that she left what her husband considered to be an excessive amount of her children's care to their nurses, governesses and his sister, Louisa. Once in 1882, after returning home from a long HAIA trip, Tye found that her 11-month-old daughter, Dorothy, acted afraid of her and she had great difficulty putting the anxious infant to sleep. Emily, Lil and Eglantyne must have observed their crying baby sister and their mother's annoyance, for later Tye 'told the little girls after they had gone to bed about Dorothy being shy with me' and made up some explanation or excuse about 'trusting' and never 'doubting...God's love and care'.[41] At the time Arthur was pressing her to give up her HAIA work and Tye wanted her older daughters to understand that charity work was a sacrifice she was making for God and that with His blessing all would be well.

Doing charity work with their mothers was a common experience for late-Victorian girls. Tye took her daughters with her on Home Arts fundraising expeditions and to woodcarving classes where they were able to observe women's philanthropic work and benevolent ladies of every description in action. Charity ladies felt 'free to visit any working class home at any time, to walk in and at once become involved in the life of the family asking questions, dispensing charity or giving orders'.[42] Anne Anderson says that for HAIA ladies, 'teaching art to the poor was deemed to be as socially responsible and beneficial as running a soup kitchen'. Anderson links the basic idea behind the HAIA to the '"Beauty and the Beast" syndrome'. It was a 'lady's mission' to refine 'the workingman'.[43] With their mother, Eglantyne and her sisters witnessed the abject and dehumanizing poverty of some of the cottage dwellers. These early experiences had a noticeable effect on Eglantyne. One day in 1882, when she was six years old, she burst into the nursery crying:

> Mother I've been reading a story about a wicked giant and a boy called Jack, and Jack went and got the castle where the giant lived from him—the castle belonged to Jack—and the giant had taken it way from his father—and had killed his mother and he nearly killed Jack too—For one day Jack was hiding and the giant came in and wanted his dinner and would have eaten Jack if he'd found him—and he said 'I smell the blood of an Englishman'—Surely it was an 'Irishman' in the old version?[44]

At a very young age, Eglantyne understood that her mother had to go away because she was helping poor Irish children. She was growing accustomed to the 'smell' of poverty and associated it with the people of Ireland.

Eglantyne knew she was supposed to pity poor children, but that did not prevent her from missing her mother terribly. One entry in Eglantyne's diary captures the mounting excitement of a highly anticipated homecoming: 'Mother should have come home today but Father had a letter putting it off till tomorrow'.[45] All day the restless 10-year old awaited her Mother's return: 'Lessons at 10 after that played with my dolls and wrote poetry till one...We had dinner. Wrote, lay in the hammock, did lessons, played with Marie till about 6 when (hip hip hurrah) MOTHER came home...(hip-hip-hurrah again)...All hip-hip-hurrah. Motherkins has been telling us about what she did at London (dreadfully jolly) and she has not finished yet'.[46] It was around this time that Eglantyne began her own imaginary rescue work. She collected all the broken dolls in the house and began pushing them around in an old perambulator. In her diary she described her Scotch doll, which was 'not pretty enough for Dorothy to play with', and old Lady Waxface whose 'fingers were ripped off' and her eyeball was 'falling into its head'. Eglantyne 'took its head...got some putty and encased the eyeball and stuck...it so could not fall back'.[47] When Lil teased her about being too poor to feed her doll-children, Eglantyne was furious and complained that Lily had 'invented poems' about her dolls: 'What she says is never true, one was how my big doll was very ugly and how I was too poor to let her have a pillow...and how I very meekly once tried to make her some clothes and bought two yards of silk and sopped it with milk...and how it all ended in me throwing it away. But that is not true. Not one bit of it'.[48]

Wherever Tye went in the early 1880s, she received a great deal of attention for her hard work. Eleven year-old-year Lil noticed the effect: 'It's all about Mrs Jebb,' she said one morning in 1882.[49] When Eglantyne and Dorothy attended the annual Arts and Crafts Exhibition in Birmingham in 1890, they wrote in their diaries that everyone asked after their mother.[50] It is obvious that they were proud of her and thought of her as an important local public figure. But Tye saw to it that her children knew more about the world than just the HAIA. When Eglantyne was nine, Tye told her all about the new science of phrenology, thereby giving her grave little daughter something more to worry about. Eglantyne wrote that her parents went to hear a 'thenologist (O don't know how to spell it)...mother came home and told me that heads which measured more than 22 inches round were full of brains, but were (sometimes) empty, those under 22 were on the way to idiotism and those under 18 were idiot'.[51] In 1886, Emily described a typical bedtime at Tydaw, the family's summer home in Wales: 'We had tea and went to bed with fidgeting Lill, where mother told us about Home Rule while the moon came out over the fir trees'.[52]

Tye's full-time philanthropic work ended by the mid-1880s, and afterwards she began to suffer from severe depression. From then on, Eglantyne and her sisters, like so many Victorian women, had the experience of nursing a sofa-ridden mother at some stage in their youth.[53] This was most distressing for Eglantyne and Dorothy, who were only ten and six when it began. In 1887, Tye's sister-in-law wrote that it would be 'the greatest misfortune that could happen to her family if she became a permanent invalid. She is the heart and centre. They have their father but they passionately worship their gentle refined intellectual mother'.[54] Tye may have been escaping the pressures of domesticity through social work and, later, unconsciously through illness, but she saw to it that her daughters understood her lessons about social justice. Her HAIA days were described in her daughter's adult writing as the greatest achievement of their mother's life. There is no question that the creativity Tye had shown in founding a movement influenced Eglantyne's later work even though she rejected the role of the Lady Bountiful in her own social and voluntary work. In 'The Ring Fence', Eglantyne describes in meticulous detail the damp interiors of rural cottages and she sympathized with the wretchedness of the village mothers while condemning the superior airs and graces of the landlord's wives. Later with the Save the Children Fund, she supported projects that promoted the liberation of oppressed regions and asserted that the SCF must never act as a philanthropist by coming from outside preaching about how people should look after their children.[55]

Fathers and mothers were not, however, the only adult influences on their sons' and daughters' lives. In many country houses before the First World War, even the most vigilant parents turned their infants and toddlers over to the care of servants and returned to their public duties, friends, careers and the social events that interested them. Parents could be quite ignorant of what went on in the nursery and the 'stamp' their servants put on their young children's characters.[56] Steedman has demonstrated that children's unpublished diaries 'offer rare insight into childcare and domestic education…into relationships with servants and other primary care givers…the growth of class consciousness and the idea of the social self'.[57] Like other children of their class, the Jebb children had nurses, maids and nannies. Some of their earliest memories were of the servants who ruled their domestic world, notably, a 'Scots nurse', a governess named Heddie Kastler, an elderly outdoor servant they called Neddy-boy and Crocus, a beloved maid.

For years the monarch of the nursery was a bad-tempered 'old Scotchwoman' who was prone to assaulting the nursemaids who 'displeased her'. Emily wrote, 'Crash went the unhappy girl to the bottom of three steps leading up to the nursery door – a process afterwards whitewashed to upper powers, as merely "putting her knee" to the wench'. Emily admitted that we were never 'kicked downstairs ourselves, not even beaten, we were frequently threatened with a stick which she used to rattle on the top of a cupboard, until Gamul climbed up and made off with it one day'.[58] In this environment, Eglantyne learned how to stand up for herself by defying the miserable nurse. After Tye became ill, Eglantyne took it upon herself to take care of the younger children. To amuse them, she began a family newsletter, called the *Briarland Recorder,* which she edited from 1889 to 1892. It contained many of her imaginative stories, poems and drawings.[59] She also filled in for her mother by reading to the younger children. In doing so she faced the ridicule of the 'bad tempered old Scotch nurse who yelled, "drop them lies"' whenever she discovered anyone enjoying the most 'innocent of fiction'. Eglantyne resorted to telling Gamul and Dorothy stories instead, but the old nurse came at them again, forbidding them from 'listening to them lies'.[60] Eglantyne continued making up stories for Dorothy and Gamul because she knew they enjoyed them. Along the way, she developed a love of writing, a passion for history books and a unique sense of humour and 'way of seeing things' that stayed with her for her entire life. Years later the idea of children helping children became a principle of the Declaration of the Rights of the Child.

In the late nineteenth century, gentility was not clearly definable, but 'it revealed itself in nuances that clearly distinguished members of the established and dominant classes'.[61] In Dorothy's assessment 'mother's idea of education' was still tinctured by 'pre-Victorian traditions as to what should be a young lady's accomplishments'.[62] Music and foreign languages counted as accomplishments, and many fashionable families hired foreign governesses. In the 1880s, the Jebbs engaged an austere Alsatian governess, named Heddie Kastler, who Dorothy said 'nearly equalled our six-foot father and towered above us small children, adding no doubt to the terror she inspired in me. She blighted every subject...thanks to her stupidity and bad temper'. In addition to French, Dorothy said, 'our first accomplishments had to include drawing and the piano'.[63] Dorothy hated the music lessons as much as she disliked the governess who taught them. She reported that she and Eglantyne 'shared to the full a curious hereditary inability of my father's family to reproduce or even recognize the simplest tune...[Our] total ineptitude...offered intolerable provocation'. During Eglantyne's lesson, which was first, Dorothy would sit outside waiting and watching 'for the opening of the schoolroom door, to reveal what degree of misery was pictured on E's face. If her eyes were <u>very</u> red I knew it boded a bad time also for me'.[64] Unlike Dorothy, Eglantyne formed a close attachment to Heddie Kastler. Dorothy said Eglantyne really seemed to 'love her, in spite of her appalling temper and degree of strictness, which was really cruel'. We do not know what Eglantyne really thought of the governess. She may have admired her, but she may also have been trying to make the best of a bad situation and protecting her little sister by befriending her enemy. Dorothy wrote, 'E called her "Reine" meaning monarch'.[65]

Eglantyne's closest attachment was to a nurse she called Crocus, who played the piano. She pretended that she and Crocus had been married 'in state in the sitting-room' and that Crocus was the mother of her ragged doll-children.[66] Four years later when Eglantyne attended Crocus's real wedding, she described it to Gamul, who was away at Marlborough College. She had taken part in an old folk custom of unmarried girls carrying 'a piece of wedding cake…upstairs to bed backwards' and put it under her pillow. She told Gamul that the 'dreams you dream would come true', but she was disappointed when she only dreamt that 'Lillie was singing!!! I think I'd prefer eating the [wedding cake] to sleeping on it'.[67] Crocus was replaced by a new Welsh maid named Celwin, 'who isn't half as easy to talk to…The first days we dressed in complete silence…But she has thawed a little now'.[68]

Eglantyne's other favourite servant was an elderly hired man the children called Neddy-boy, whom she included in her wildest outdoor games. Emily wrote that nobody in the family would ever forget the day that Eglantyne, holding her 'painted flags' and leading an imaginary army, was chased by her brother to the top of the 'earth heap near the potting shed' in a re-enactment of some tale of chivalry inspired by Sir Walter Scott. Eglantyne's 'wild rose complexion changed to poppy-hue…[as she] grimly gripped the elderly "boot-boy" by the legs, holding on for dear life, till the two of them slid down the sides of the earth heap together…Then she cried with blazing face, to a faithful old retainer, "Tear out his eyes, Neddy-boy, tear out his eyes!"'[69] Despite the close attachment that Eglantyne and her siblings developed with some servants, it is clear that they regarded the personal standards, morals and behaviour of these hired people to be different from their own codes, and their interactions with them were more casual than their interactions with their parents. Eglantyne did not realize how wide the gap was until she entered Stockwell Teacher Training College in 1899 and lived among working-class girls for a year. Far from enjoying a superior position as a gentleman's daughter, she was snubbed as an outsider by the other girls, who despite their lower-class background were the ones with the social power within the college. Eglantyne had not realized until then that loyalty and obedience and deference were not the same as genuine affection.

In some large Victorian families, relatives could be very influential role models. Since neither of Arthur's sisters had children of their own, Louisa Jebb and Emily Gilmore played a big part in Arthur's children's lives. In fact, Eglantyne and her sisters were saved from a conventional Victorian education, not only by their increasingly bed-ridden mother's high expectations for them, but also by the fact that as they grew up, more and more of their moral and academic education was left to Arthur's radical sister, Louisa, whom the children nicknamed 'Bun'. It was under her care that they received what, by the standards of the day, would have been considered a superior education. Their cropped-hair suffragist spinster aunt was the quintessential late-Victorian new woman, whom Emily described as 'masculine'. She and her brothers and sisters all regarded her as the 'heroine of our childhood…the inspirer of dreams, the instigator of many ideas'.[70]

To ensure that her daughters became accomplished young ladies, Tye supervised their drawing and painting lessons herself, while Aunt Louisa taught them 'carpentry, wood and metal turning, glass cutting and glazing…fretwork, the caning of chairs' so that they could help with Tye's Home Arts classes. Louisa Jebb also shared the family's enthusiasm for Home Arts and taught her nieces and nephews 'how to carve, to do basket and leather and metal repose work, to model in clay, to make mosaic tiles by chopping china cups to size with a formidable old fashioned dentists instrument, and then setting the chips in moulds'.[71] While other well-to-do girls were taught to love art for their own edification, in the Jebb family it had the added value of being a refinement they could disseminate to the poor.

Another important avenue of Victorian girls' education was 'self-education', particularly reading.[72] Louisa Jebb was a staunch believer in it. Emily recalled that 'with the instinct of a born educator Bun put within our reach the beginnings of knowledge as it was considered best begun in those enterprising eighties…I remember how we elder children all sat round her in a delighted circle, whilst with infinite zest she imparted English grammar, illustrated by the mistakes which Corbett's political opponents made in their Parliamentary speeches'![73] Louisa Jebb encouraged her nieces' independent reading and writing, though she and Emily Gilmore clashed over the reading habits of young ladies. One day after beginning to read Tennyson's *Promise of May* to the girls, Emily Gilmore 'left off in the middle' because she suddenly decided that it was 'most improper'.[74] As an extension of self-education, Louisa Jebb took them to castles, factories and Roman ruins, and in her workshop, she taught them how to 'make and use boomerangs, kites, popguns, bows and arrows, toboggans…stilts, fishing nets, and…over the bedroom fire to melt lead and cast bullets in an antediluvian instrument resembling a double spoon'. Emily recalled that of all her brothers and sisters, 'Eglantyne shared least in these occupations'; she preferred books, writing, story-telling and daydreaming.[75]

It was customary for late-Victorian girls to keep special travel diaries, which were believed to have educative value. The Jebb sisters kept many, which describe trips around England and Wales. When Dorothy went to Birmingham in 1894 she packed her diary, a copy of Green's geography and Dick's pocket atlas to mark the railway lines and stations stops. Emily's travel journals tell of crammed carriages, jockeying for seats, the ages, demeanour and characteristics of passengers, hotels and restaurants and the family's relaxed attitude toward travelling second-class. On a trip to Birmingham, rather than eat at a restaurant, Louisa Jebb took Emily, Lil and Eglantyne to dinner at the cooking school. Emily described many family trips to Tydaw and five family holidays, including a month in

2.3 Jebb children with Gilmores and Louisa Jebb, source: Jebb Family

Bala, Merionethshire in 1886, a trip to Overton Denbighshire in 1886 and three summer trips, in 1885, 1886 and 1887, to Marlborough and the 'whacking good Banbury cakes' her father bought them in Banbury.[76]

The organization of late-Victorian domestic life and the relationships between household members and the community constituted the first lessons that girls learned in the sexual division of labour. If her domestic relationships conform to the patterns she perceives in the world around her they will seem normal.[77] Here, the frequent visits to the Gilmores in Marlborough were not just something for the idle Jebb family to do, but an opportunity for the girls to cheer up their Aunt Emily, who was suffering from *maladies imaginaries* and confined to a bathchair, while their brothers Dick and Gamul returned to boarding school. Their uncle, James Gilmore, was a housemaster at the prestigious Marlborough College, where Dick and Gamul were pupils. On one trip to Marlborough the sisters were permitted to stay for a night in the boy's dormitories. From these visits to Marlborough College it would have been obvious to Emily, Lil, Eglantyne and Dorothy that an arm of outside experts were required to make boys like their brothers into properly educated English gentleman; on the other hand, their own educational needs could be met by the women who populated her immediate domestic world.

In the diaries of well-to-do girls educated at home, we read the minuscule, dull and mundane details of domestic routines. These are significant, however, because the words contain within them the seeds of a genteel female education.[78] In 1886, Eglantyne described a typical daily routine. While Dick and Gamul studied Latin and classics away at Marlborough College, she did her lessons with her sisters every morning until 10 and then practised the piano, picked gooseberries, helped her governess and Aunt Louisa make rhubarb pies and jam, and earned a few pennies pulling thistles and 6d for scraping paint off the foot baths. When visitors came to tea with her mother and aunt, Eglantyne joined them and later looked after her garden plot or attended the Shrewsbury Naturalist Society with her father. She always had lessons again from 5:00 until supper.[79] Although she was not expected to do routine domestic chores like cleaning or housework, young ladies were nonetheless expected to acquire the skills necessary to run a household and this required some detailed knowledge of what was involved in housekeeping. As an 'open book of socialisation'[80] Eglantyne's diary entries reveal how girls like herself learned to be young ladies.

In the late nineteenth century it was considered unladylike for unmarried daughters to work hence their dependence on male relatives was total. The 'money for each dress, each pair of shoes, had to be asked for and might be denied. In the same way money might be denied for subscriptions to a library or attendance at a course of lectures'.[81] It is unclear when the discussion of the higher education of the Jebb girls first began, but as we shall see in the next chapter, Arthur expected his sons to follow in his footsteps and read Greats at Oxford. No financial provisions had been made for his daughters. Despite their seemingly progressive early socialization and domestic education, Arthur's only expectation for them was that nothing should stand in the way of their marrying men of suitable social standing. The trouble began when Louisa Jebb announced that she had other ideas for her nieces' futures.[82] She wanted them to attend university and overrode her brother's opposition and paid their fees from her own private income. Eglantyne later described Oxford, where she spent three years, as her 'Jerusalem'.[83]

In their diaries, young girls' domestic experiences were recorded and objectified in their written words. Though it might be argued that girls wrote in diaries only because they were expected to, their diary entries reveal the way in which their experiences came to be categorized in relation to their particular social environment. Through the act of writing they created 'themselves'. The construction of this personal narrative helped them to reflect upon their own individual feelings and failings.[84] From Eglantyne's diary we learn that she enjoyed her lessons but was always glad for a 'half-holiday' or a sick day when lessons were cancelled. From February to April 1886 all of the children were inflicted with what ten-year-old Eglantyne called 'hoopung cough' and confined for weeks to the nursery. She enjoyed three things about the sickroom. First, their worried mother slept in the nursery. Second, Dick did not go back to school until May. Third, they skipped 'a good many lessons'. The bedridden and bored children amused themselves by playing popular Victorian children's games: draughts, Gobang and dominoes. Dick amused his sisters and brother by making a kite, creating a puzzle by pasting a picture on to wood, and putting on a magic lantern show. He and Lil mastered some conjurer's tricks. The most impressive consisted of cutting 'a piece of string into two pieces', knotting them together and blowing 'the knot off'.[85] That winter Eglantyne helped six-year-old Gamul start his first journal. 'I have to write on paper first everything he says for him to copy for he can't spell yet', she said. Gamul said that he wanted to write a journal so he would know when he 'was grown up what he did when he was little'.[86] From her superior position as elder sister, Eglantyne realized that he was only doing it to imitate Dick, who was also writing a journal. What she could not have known, however, was that her little brother would be the only one of her siblings never to grow up. He died of pneumonia, at the age of 16, while at school in Marlborough.

For their health and constitutions, late-Victorian young ladies were encouraged to enjoy outdoor pursuits, and their parents encouraged them all in gardening and horticulture as well as vigorous riding and hiking. There is no evidence that any restrictions were placed on the Jebb sisters' physical activity; they were allowed to be themselves and did not become the over-pampered, enfeebled miniature ladies portrayed in late-Victorian fiction. They climbed trees, tore their clothes, pounded down the road and over the fields on their ponies, played with their brothers, swam and fished with their father. They worked hard on their artwork and watercolours and academic lessons and were proud of themselves when they were successful. During the summers of 1885 and 1886, they spent their days pushing Aunt Nony in her bathchair up and down the roads, writing letters, catching butterflies, picnicking and sketching. When the Gilmores bought a tricycle they spent a great deal of time trying to learn to turn it. They extended their social circle by attending children's balls and parties and by playing with the children whose parents called to tea. When boys visited they played bowls or rounders or went to the gymnasium, where they 'swung and vaulted and had great fun'. At one tea with the Beasley boys, 'Gerald, Oliver, Alfred and Lewis, no girls;' they 'tried to see who could eat the most tea. Doey won, Gerald just behind. Played at bowls…Gerald donned a pair of boxing gloves'. If the guests were the Preston sisters, Eglantyne and her sisters sketched in their *Kate Greenway* books.[87]

Their games all seem to have been class- and gender-appropriate. Nevertheless, if they dirtied their clothes they were not punished.[88] Dorothy said that once when 'Doey and I went up the mountain…we went down the Wimberry slide…it was beautiful fun, but the wet soaked through onto Doey's dress and dirtied it'. All that Tye said when she saw 15-year-old Eglantyne's mud-soaked dress was that she would try to get some sacking 'which we can slide down the mountain in'.[89] One summer day when Emily was 13, after a 'whacking good tea under a tree on the edge of the wood' and a few games of prisoner's base and some ghost stories, Emily, Eglantyne, Lil and the three young

ladies who came with the Misses Prestons' drove home with their carriages dangerously close together and 'treated' the people on the streets
to a concert. 'Emmeline and Kathleen led off the orchestra...there was
nothing but "Pirate Kings, Men on a Dead Man's Chest", "John
Brown", and "Jolly Good Fellows", which we all joined in lustily'.
When the carriages drew up before the house, they all yelled at the top
of their voices

> Fifteen men on a dead man's chest
> Yo ho ho and a bottle of rum
> Drink and the devil had done for the rest
> Yo ho ho and a bottle of rum.

This sort of high-spirited behaviour by well-bred young ladies would
have been frowned upon in some families, but as soon as the Jebb
sisters arrived home they ran to tell Crocus and Emily Gilmore exactly
what they had done in order to shock them. They were not scolded,
shamed or punished.[90]

There is no direct reference to puberty in the girls' diaries; however,
many diary entries reveal a consciousness of growing up as indicated
by the restlessness and changes in mood that mark adolescence. When
Emily was 14 she began to complain of feeling 'tired and grumpy, idle,
stupid, and a good many other thing too'.[91] Eglantyne recorded changes
in Lil's health in her diary. She was probably worried because the invalidism of her mother and Emily Gilmore may have led her to associate
womanhood with illness. Eglantyne wrote, 'Lil's got a pain in her
head...they think it is...Newalgea, neralga, neralgeria, newalga, I'm not
myself if one of these aren't right'.[92] After Emily received news that a
beloved cousin was going to marry a clergyman named Mr Philpot, she
wrote that she felt 'very low and I don't know at what...I can't grasp
it. What an idiot I am...I ought to be very glad, but I don't feel as if
I could be when I don't know the man.' She later admitted that she
was 'jealous and selfish'. At church, 'the parson bobbed about...the
pulpit...talking about respect to parents, filial duty... He squinted...at
Lill, Dick and Doey...and perhaps their changed colour made him state
[it all] the harder'.[93] That spring Emily was sent to stay with the Gilmores
for a 'change of air', where she relaxed by reading about Burne Jones and
Hamilton's painting of Lady Hamilton. 'When I am in one of my moody
fits I like the *Wheel of Fortune* very much. I think Lady H **beautiful** as
Nature'.[94] When Eglantyne was 16 she announced that she did not want
to have dancing lessons with Dorothy again. 'Half the time is wasted

there, by the small children (none were at all as old as me last year) learning their steps'.[95] Clearly, she no longer thought of herself as a child.

According to Steedman, children reproduce feelings and emotional responses in their writing. The biographer's task is not to look to their writing for the roots of genius, the future adult poet or child protégé, but to use their texts 'to reconstruct the theories they evolved in order to become part of a particular society in a particular place and time'.[96] Emily said that Eglantyne read earlier and more than the other children, and Eglantyne's diary reveals that by the time she was ten she was creative, literate, tenderhearted and bright. According to Emily the 'mother best remembered by Eglantyne and Dorothy was often ailing'.[97] Caroline Jebb observed that the Jebb children 'worshipped their mother'.[98] Eglantyne's diary shows that she was worried a great deal about her dolls, Lil's headaches, Dorothy being afraid of the governess, but most of all her mother. She longed for her mother's approval, and by the age of 11 had appropriated her mother's role as caregiver to her two younger siblings, whom she called 'the little ones.' They withdrew together into Eglantyne's imaginary world. When she was 14, to cheer up her mother Eglantyne transcribed in a letter an entire play she had written, promising to 'act the same thing again when you are here'. She added, 'It made people laugh so'.

> ...It was neither a charade nor a play. It was called the 'Modern Queen Elizabeth'. I invented a little of it, a little I had read, and the others made suggestions. We rigged up a stage...made...a very high throne...on the top if it all, was Dorothy, with ruff and fan and crown, perched above us as Queen Elizabeth. You can imagine that she...orders us about, with her nose in the air...Gamul was courtier Great-talker...He had to come in first and say to Em: 'Well my sweet Sagacity, where is my Adorable Audacity' and then with another bow: 'Have you used Pears Soap this morning'...I had to kneel down to kiss Queen Elizabeth's toe, and tipple her over. Whereupon little Queen Elizabeth...stood on a tiptoe and slapped my face. I was greatly indignant and stalked away calling her 'a crooked old woman' and saying that I'd never come back. I had just before been making a speech about rage, 'discord and anger flying from Queen Elizabeth's face, like darkness from the sun'!!...Dorothy strutted up and down... [and]...made every one laugh.[99]

Historians of late-Victorian women and girls have shown that it was from within the confines of the largely female-dominated sphere of literary societies, at-home teas and charity bazaars that many remark-able women remerged as pioneers in the new female professions of education, medicine, social work and politics. Eglantyne and her sisters were among such women. How did their socialization and education produce a generation of remarkable young women with strong identities, high self-esteem, creativity, commitment to personal fulfilment and careers in social action? By studying documents by and about Victorian girls, Erna Hellerstein solves this seeming paradox. She suggests that the very intrusiveness of their own parents or professionals with pro-scriptive theories about how to mould a daughter's character instilled within the girls a 'belief in her own intrinsic significance'.[100] In many late-Victorian families, women and girls understood it was their 'duty' and 'right to take part in public affairs'.[101] This chapter has shown that in the pages of Eglantyne's diary, we can find her perched on the branch of a favourite tree, or watch her commanding an imaginary army, struggling to walk on her stilts, telling stories to her brothers and sisters or a pram filled with broken dolls, pulling thistle and writing a play. Although these diary entries are simply humdrum accounts of ordinary domestic life, they must, however, be read as evidence that Eglantyne Jebb was watching the world around her closely and regarding it with interest.

3
Educating Eglantyne: The Young Lady of Lady Margaret Hall

'When first I heard of your helping in our educational expenses, I began to take an interest in living, as opposed to dreaming', 18-year-old Eglantyne told her Aunt Louisa, adding, 'It must be a horrid thing to feel a dreadful door with "No Road" posted on it across your life'.[1] Eglantyne was at Lady Margaret Hall, Oxford from 1895 to 1897. She was aware that the opportunity to go to university was a great stepping-stone and she was determined to make her mark. This chapter shows that it was at Oxford that Eglantyne encountered the first of many women outside her family, who were to influence the direction of her life. She also discovered the range of careers, including scholar, nurse, teacher and social worker that were open to women of her class and generation.

Beginning in the 1860s, a small but growing number of British women had been fighting for the right to study academic subjects in the country's universities. Initially, those who succeeded were restricted, for the most part, to the supposedly 'feminine' subjects like biology, physiology and botany. They could not attend the same lectures as men and were not awarded degrees.[2] At Cambridge University, the first women students were admitted to Hitchin (later Girton) College in 1869. In the mid-1870s, Eglantyne's aunt, Louisa Jebb, had been one of these women. She took courses at Newnham College and was invited by Anne Jemina Clough to become Principal of Alexandra College in Dublin, an offer she declined because her atheism placed her at odds with the religious ethos of the college.[3] In 1878, Dr Edward Talbot of Keble College was determined to establish 'a small residential enterprise' for women at Oxford University, and the Association for the Education of Women was formed to raise funds for two women's colleges, Lady Margaret Hall (LMH) and Somerville, which opened in 1879.[4]

3.1   Eglantyne at Lady Margaret Hall, Oxford, source: Jebb Family

By the 1880s the question of the higher education of women had
slowly spread from the university community to the public at large, as
articles, essays and reflections about the lives of university-educated

women began to appear in the British press, women's journals and girls' magazines. Sally Mitchell points out that the press constructed both positive and negative images of the female students and 'girl graduates' for popular culture.[5] Negative images encompassed the fear that the stigma of 'intelligence' would ruin a woman's prospects for marriage and that the long hours of arduous study could damage her health.[6] Eleanor Lodge, a student and lecturer at LMH from 1890 to 1922, recalled that for girls, university 'was controversy mixed with excitement'.[7] At Lady Margaret Hall, Eglantyne noticed that people were still talking 'such a lot of rubbish about women'.[8] In 1900, another student, Agnes Mary Hamilton, said the women were regarded as 'a bit freakish' and she grew 'tired of being stared at'.[9]

Victoria Glendenning argues that while the supervised freedom of growing up in a beautiful Victorian country house might be ideal for a child, it was 'less sweet' for grown-up girls. 'If your father had enough money to keep you, marriage was the only possible reason for leaving home.'[10] In the Jebb family it had been assumed that after Marlborough College, Richard and Gamul would follow in their father's footsteps to Oxford. Emily, like many affluent English girls, went to Dresden in 1891 to study portrait painting.[11] But trouble began when Arthur clashed with his sister Louisa over Lil's future. Under Louisa's influence Lil had developed a strong aptitude for science, and her aunt thought the new agricultural course at Cambridge would be ideal for Lil, a suggestion at which Arthur Jebb balked. In the mid-Victorian period it was feared that men would not choose wives 'from the ranks of educated women' and so university would be of little 'use' to them.[12]

Late-nineteenth century medical opinion asserted that girls needed to develop healthy reproductive systems and those who expended 'their energy on intellectual achievements' risked 'breakdown, masculinity, sterility, or becoming mothers of sickly children'.[13] This point of view supported Arthur's suspicions. He was not as happy about the influence that Louisa Jebb had had on his daughters as Tye and the girls were. He may have regarded his suffragist sister who had attended Newnham College, then wrote pamphlets on Darwinian science and snickered at his objections as the embodiment of the masculine stereotype and proof of the 'dangers' of higher education for women. The Ellesmere locals surreptitiously referred to Louisa Jebb as 'man Jebb', whereas her nieces regarded her as 'the inspirer of dreams [and] the instigator of many ideas'.[14] Arthur told Tye that 'a ladies' college seems to me only a ladies' school with all its evils intensified, because the time of life is just the most impressionable and hazardous of any'.[15] He also claimed that he simply could not afford to send his daughters to university. In October 1891, he wrote to Tye, 'If a girl were marked with small-pox and had good abilities, if she were short-sighted as to make spectacles a perpetual necessity and had great common sense, if she were to be obliged hereafter to gain her livelihood as a teacher at some sad seminary, then there might be something to be said for Cambridge'.[16]

Many late-Victorian women who wished to enter institutions of higher learning encountered similar opposition, the usual argument being that money had been put aside only for their brothers' education. The suffrage activist, Helena Swanwick, who worked with Eglantyne and Dorothy in the Fight the Famine Council in 1919, said that her father was utterly indifferent to her education and that her mother supported higher education for women, but she drew the line when it came to her own daughter. When Swanwick won a scholarship to Girton College in 1882, her parents told her there was simply not enough money to supplement it. But her godmother, whom Swanwick forever afterwards thought of as a 'fairy godmother', heard about the problem and paid Swanwick's fees.[17] When Arthur announced that he could not spare 40 pounds per annum to send Lil to Newnham, Louisa Jebb interfered and paid the fees and Lil entered Newnham in 1892.[18] After Arthur's death in 1894, Tye supported higher education for women and encouraged Louisa Jebb to take a stronger role in decisions regarding the family. Louisa paid the fees so that Eglantyne could take a three-year history course at Lady Margaret Hall, and also so Dorothy could study economics and moral sciences at Newnham. Eglantyne, who wanted to become a writer, saw Oxford as a pathway toward that goal. She was very grateful to Louisa, to whom she wrote, 'I wish I were you...to send my family wherever so they wished on the road to learning.'[19]

Eglantyne went up to Oxford in what Vera Brittain described as the women's 'infiltration phase (1890–1900)'.[20] University authorities stood in *loco parentis* to the students and believed that women students needed special protection.[21] They were not allowed, for example, to belong to university societies or to attend tutorials with their male dons unchaperoned. Upon her arrival, Eglantyne was immediately presented with a long list of the rules that restricted her activities, including contact with her brother Richard, who was at New College. She told a cousin that after reading the rules, 'she sat down upon her trunk and considered whether she should leave immediately or stay up long enough to break all the rules and be sent down'.[22] Eglantyne even then found the prospect of rule breaking appealing, however, she was not yet ready to cause a scandal. Rather, she regarded the rules, which suited her temperament, as an exciting part of her new life at Lady Margaret Hall.

Eglantyne spent the first year in a small residence in Crick Road under the direction of Mary Talbot. It was a typical North Oxford villa, with a tiny back garden. In the basement was a small common room where the seven residents, called the 'Crickets', ate their meals. The day was divided between 'work' in their private bed-sitting rooms and lectures at Keble College. Otherwise, their walks, games and gatherings, such as the Saturday Evening Sociables, took place at Lady Margaret Hall itself.[23] Most of the students came from cultivated homes and 'a decent interval elapsed before formality gave place to the Christian or nicknames of familiar intercourse'.[24] Intimate friendships between the women students compensated for the lack of social intercourse with the men students and were the first friendships that many young women of this class had ever formed without their mothers' approval. Eglantyne's closest friend was a second-year student named Dorothy Kempe.[25] This formative and sustaining acquaintance lasted all their lives. Kempe recalled that she and Eglantyne 'paired off' whenever the opportunity arose. They were drawn to each other by their love of literature and poetry. Kempe remembered 'the thrill of interest with which, from a letter which I took to her, I discovered her Christian name! It seemed...entirely appropriate to her wild-rose charm and grace, and I longed girlishly for the moment when I might use it instead of the formal Miss Jebb'.[26]

Choosing one's own friends was only a taste of the freedom in store for this generation of female scholars. It was also the first time that many women of this class and generation had been released from the 'rigid genteel routine' of 'hostessing teas and preparing for ladies' bazaars', which in Glendinning's opinion, was 'not a rich enough prospect for an intelligent energetic young woman'.[27] Francesca Wilson, who was at Newnham with Eglantyne's cousin Geraldine Jebb in the early 1900s, said that only those who were there could appreciate how 'stimulating and exciting this little world was'. She described a heterogeneous group of young women from 'narrow' family backgrounds. Some she said were:

> exceptionally intelligent...all...eager for experience and knowledge, arrogant and immature, women...still in the making with wistfulness and despairs and dreams and hope. The talks we had, the explorations

of each other's minds were to many of us then far more stimulating and rewarding than our studies. We were proud of our friends, envious but not jealous of their beauty and their gifts.[28]

June Purvis points out that for this generation of woman students, college was the first time in their lives that they knew privacy or any measure of independence.[29] For example, a striking theme in early college autobiographies was the sheer bliss of possessing a room of one's own. Swanwick remembered her first days at Girton: 'To have a study of my own and to be told that, if I chose to put "Engaged" on my door, no one would so much as knock was in itself so great a privilege as to hinder me from sleep. I did not know till then how much I had suffered from the incessant interruptions of my home life.'[30] Eleanor Lodge, the ninth child in her family, found Lady Margaret Hall to be 'simply a revelation…of what life might be like. The very fact of having a room of one's own, a place one not only could work, but was expected to work, the possibility of independence…of getting up and going to bed according to one's own ideas and not those of others, made each day an adventure and a joy'.[31] Eglantyne, who had always shared a room with at least one sister, was struck by the contrast between the freedoms of Oxford and what suddenly appeared to be the restrictions of the Lyth, when she returned home for her first summer vacation. The incessant family interruptions and 'small talk' were irritating. She complained, 'I want to read'. She told Kempe that she was more interested in 'William III than in visitors' and she was tired of her mother's guests 'before they have come'. After she 'expressed [her] ill-concealed feelings on the subject' however, she knew that she must 'settle down to the placid smile of despairful resignation'.[32] Eglantyne's experience supports Purvis's suggestion that once these young women began to regard themselves as serious scholars, being constantly interrupted by the duties of daughter at home was 'especially unwelcome'.[33]

Eglantyne's initial plan was to do a two-year course of study in history, for which the first hurdle was to pass her 'prelims'. This was another historically unique experience for the early generations of women students. Unlike boys, who had suffered the academic humiliations of rigorous preparatory schools, girls like Eglantyne, who had been educated at home, had never directly experienced competition from their peers. It was obvious to Lodge that some of the students were wholly unprepared, having 'scarcely ever attended a lecture' before, and some had 'never written an essay'.[34] The pressure both alarmed and excited Eglantyne, who was determined to prove to her family, her tutors and herself, her intellectual capabilities and right to belong to the university community. She noticed that some students withstood the pressure better than others. From the fear of failure, to her devastation on behalf of Ethel Knox-Little, who failed her prelims,[35] to the graffiti on the desktops—in her finest college slang, Eglantyne described the 'vacant stares of desperation' upon rows of 'dismal faces' among the students.

> All agreed that the papers were easier than we had expected, yet after each one, a chorus of 'I'm ploughed!' went up from about thirty girls in the cloak room at the schools. Broken hearts seem to have been the corollary of examinations…We used to meet under-grads coming out after reading the results…some of them looked such absolute wrecks that it was quite an effort not to laugh. The desks in the exam rooms are covered with such remarks as: 'Good old smalls again!' and 'Dead ploughed' etc. To draw the man in front of you is a very favourite amusement when one's pen does not see its way to any more legal employment'.[36]

During her second term Eglantyne experienced a bereavement, which was common amongst Victorian families, the death of a sibling. On 11 March 1896, her 16-year-old brother Gamul, who was excelling in science at Marlborough College and hoping to study medicine, died. On 5 March Tye had received a letter from Gamul's housemaster telling her he had a chill, but before she could get there, Gamul had developed pneumonia and died. Eglantyne, Dick and Lil immediately returned to the Lyth to spend some time with their mother, aunt and Dorothy, who had been closest to Gamul. In the weeks that followed, Eglantyne kept up with her reading, in particular Sir Thomas More's *The History of Henry VII* and Richard Hooker's *Ecclesiastical Polity* from a 1625 edition they had at the Lyth. She also rode a great deal with Dick and her sisters.[37]

At the end of the term, Eglantyne stayed to help with the annual summer play which the Lady Margaret students performed for the working people in the neighbourhood of London Settlement House. She also attended Dick's New College commencement ball. Lady Margaret Hall adhered to the truism that 'the brother of one is not the brother of them all!'[38] Even young ladies who were their brother's escorts had to be chaperoned at mixed-sex college events. Eglantyne told Dorothy Kempe: 'Finally got an old lady to go…first to my brother's rooms and then on to the ball…We danced into the broad daylight—a college ball seems quite unlike any other, for it is so very juvenile…It really seemed all made up of other people's sisters and brothers, and a long line of obvious chaperones. There were no intermediates between the two'.[39] Clearly, Eglantyne did not think she needed to be protected from men, nor did she think that they needed to be protected from her.

Eglantyne and Dick travelled home together for the summer vacation. It had been a taxing year, and Eglantyne was happy to be back. She said she was never so glad to see the old familiar station or hear the coachman call her '"Miss Miglantyne", the nearest approach he can get to my name'.[40] Like a good undergraduate, she slept until noon the first day and spent the summer reading. As a scholar Eglantyne was developing a wide range of interests, which were well served by the books in the Jebb family library, where she found three volumes of Thomas Carlyle's *Fredrick the Great*, Archdeacon William Coxe's *History of the House of Austria* and Voltaire's *History of Peter the Great*. She also took a 'desperate fling' at financial history by starting a little notebook on taxation. After all of this effort had been expended; however, she acquired a copy of her tutor's 'list of books for the vac' and discovered to her 'horror' that nothing she had read was on it.[41] Thanks to the efforts of her governess, Heddie Kastler, Eglantyne's French was proficient, and she read a French history book that was 1,046 pages long. She told Dorothy Kempe, 'It is a monument of midnight oil after my own heart...one has to keep one's eyes wide open all the time to seize on the stray facts and fish them out of a sparkling sea of witty word painting; it is a great contrast to the historical works in my beloved native tongue'.[42] Eglantyne was deepening her knowledge of international history and had become interested in the philosophy of Voltaire and Rousseau. She had 'had no idea' that the eighteenth century 'had such a well-defined character of its own...the age of enlightened despots...with its everlasting negotiations, treaties, counter treaties, humbugging parchments and issues of alliances. The[y] kept fumbling in their dusty archives for "rights" on their neighbour's land [it] is positively amusing'.[43] The summer of 1896 concluded with a 'rather fun' reading party with Lil's and Richard's Cambridge and Oxford friends, constituting 'a very collegiate assembly' and 'shop' talk. Eglantyne also reported her 'first bicycle smash...damages not so bad...three spokes broken, mud guard twisted and tyre bruised'.[44]

Eglantyne returned to Oxford for her second year to discover that it was now Oxford that felt like home: '[B]elonging to it—to be linked on to the long chain of students—to feel one has that in common with all the children of Oxford, past, present and to come; and then the

training is so admirable: to have historians to coach one in history!...
[O]ne never gets enough of it'.[45] At Oxford, Eglantyne met people who
influenced her perception of herself. In her second year she was coached
by John A. R. Marriott and W. H. Hutton coached her in her third year.
Marriott had been permitted to tutor her without a chaperon because
another female student, Lilas Milroy, was with her, but she had to ask
Hutton to change the hour she had been assigned to meet him because
she was alone and 'someone must be <u>lecturing next door</u> at the same
time in order to <u>chaperon</u> me!' She thought it was ridiculous and it made
her feel awkward, because 'if it was sufficient for some one to be <u>next
door</u>, it would be sufficient if they came <u>next day</u>'.[46] Frankly, she was
more afraid for her intellectual safety than she was for her physical safety.
No chaperon could protect her from a tutor's attacks upon her ideas
and theories. Initially she was nervous and so 'shy...and so hopeless of
Mr. Hutton's acquiescence' that she sat 'silently miserable'. Then he
'stopped trotting out the old things' and asked her views. Eglantyne told
Dorothy Kempe:

> The unfortunate man did not know what he had let himself in for,
> my ideas suddenly fell out, helter skelter, very badly explained. I
> condemned the authorities, I said there were a great many things in
> Indian history, which I did <u>not</u> want to know, ('That's unfortunate,
> he remarked') others which I <u>did</u> want to know...Contenting
> himself with a few mild sarcasms...he fell in entirely with my views,
> and professed himself ready to do anything I wanted. I am therefore
> working to my heart's content. The joy of it, the joy of it.[47]

According to Purvis, many female students of the 1890s reported that
their tutors were not open to women students' opinions and tolerated
their presence 'more or less on sufferance'.[48] Hutton's 'mild sarcasms'
may have suggested that he was not particularly interested in Eglantyne's
'views' either. If he had regarded her as a serious scholar and on a par
with a male student, he would not likely have allowed her to restrict
her field of study to the areas of history that interested her. Some male
dons were candid about their dislike of tutoring the female students.
John Maynard Keynes said that 'the nervous irritation caused by two
hours contact with them is intense. I seem to hate every movement of
their minds. The minds of men, even when they are stupid and ugly,
never appears to me so repellent'.[49] One of the female students that
Keynes made an exception for was Dorothy Jebb, whom he had tutored
in 1902. He regarded her intelligence as 'exceptional'.[50]

At Lady Margaret Hall, Eglantyne learned to endure her tutor's criticisms and admitted that the examiner for the Margaret Evans Prize who told her that she did not seem to 'know the facts!' was correct; it was 'precisely the case'.[51] Overall, the faculty, Mrs Johnson, Miss Lodge, Miss Pearson and 'even Mr Smith' were impressed with her and just before Christmas in 1896 asked her to 'stop up' for another year. This was an enormous boost to her confidence and a great relief because the prospect of returning home had been like a 'cloud hanging over me before it burst'.[52] Louisa Jebb gave her permission, and Eglantyne began to think that she might have a future as a scholar or a don. She certainly did 'not want to endanger the success of [her] future work by cutting short [her] training'.[53]

In her second year Eglantyne moved to Lady Margaret Hall, where she caught the attention of the principal of the college, Miss Elizabeth Wordsworth, who dominated her imagination for the next couple of years. Wordsworth, the great-niece of the poet and daughter of the Bishop of Lincoln, was a biblical scholar, a poet and a novelist. Her interest in higher education for women 'owed nothing to feminist principles, and everything to her conviction that well-educated women would be better wives and mothers and more useful members of the Church of England'.[54] Eglantyne shared Wordsworth's devotion to the traditions of the Church and she was not bothered, as some women were, by Wordsworth's conservative views on votes for women. Eglantyne took to heart Wordsworth's belief that women must strive for emotional independence and, ideally, financial self-reliance. Wordsworth had named the Oxford women's residence after Lady Margaret Beaufort, a late-medieval noblewoman who was a 'gentlewoman, a scholar and a saint; and after having been three times married she took a vow of celibacy'. Wordsworth asked: 'What more could be expected of any woman?' When Lady Fredrick Cavendish first toured Lady Margaret Hall, however, she remarked that the place looked 'like a lady who had made a dowdy marriage'.[55]

Eleanor Lodge, said that 'no one who was under [Wordsworth] will look back at their time in College without thinking of her Sunday evening addresses, full of humour as well as edification; of talks in her room and parties after Chapel'.[56] Fundraising was an important part of Wordsworth's duties as principal of the college in the 1890s, and she often chose women students to accompany her on visits to Oxford notables. Eglantyne was invited because her uncle was Sir Richard Jebb, the famous professor of Greek at Cambridge, and a supporter of higher education for women.[57] After one such visit, Eglantyne described the rainy walk home sharing a broken umbrella with Wordsworth, who gave her some ideas for an essay on Hobbes and the 'tendencies of modern life'. Eglantyne told Kempe how Wordsworth went into a 'disquisition on modern life in general!...She dilated...on selfishness as being the most prominent failing of the present generation and she traced it partly to the growth of scepticism as regards a future life. I had never before seen the force of "Let us eat and drink for tomorrow we die," as applied to contemporary history. Oh dear, how interrupted I am!'[58] Eglantyne was only too happy to assist Wordsworth with the fundraising work of the college, but she wanted to make her own mark on university life.

Mitchell suggests that in the late nineteenth century, college supplied 'an imaginative framework that let a girl reconceptualize her sense of life's potential'.[59] The inspiring and idiosyncratic Miss Wordsworth fascinated Eglantyne, who studied her mannerisms and tried to emulate her eccentricities, even though extreme and advanced behaviour in young women was highly worrying to the late-Victorian mind-set.[60] To try out her new persona, Eglantyne told Dorothy Kempe, she had 'taken to wandering out into the park in the middle of the morning in order to think', just as Miss Wordsworth did. Eglantyne wrote, 'Miss Wordsworth says she does not think. Her thoughts rush into her head all of a sudden. That is what it is to have genius. When one rakes by main force one's thoughts together from different corners of one's brain, by reasoning, deducting and questioning, the result is not half so satisfactory, the nail does not get hit on the head with such a sharp, concise rap'.[61] Eglantyne's free flowing approach to intellectual discourse did not impress her tutors. Marriott objected to her 'generalizations' and 'defects', which he told her about in 'an unusually definite way',[62] and Miss Pearson told her she was like an 'overgrown colt' because her work was 'scrambled and hurried'.[63]

Eglantyne did not have much success when she tried out her 'experimental philosophy' with her fellow undergraduates either.[64] After reading Henry David Thoreau's *Walden*, in 1897, she attempted her own experiment in simple living, which consisted of taking some furniture out of her room in order to demonstrate the futility of 'luxuries' and 'expenditures...I have not really simplified [my room] half as much as I should have liked' she admitted and the reaction of the other students was disappointing. Noting the bare floor, a neighbour merely inquired: 'Did I think it unsanitary, or was it that the maids did not brush it enough?(!)'.[65] Although Eglantyne loved to mock the 'freshers' for being 'terribly fresh', she took the responsibilities of an upperclassman seriously and tried to mentor them during cocoa parties in her room.[66] She told Kempe, 'One pokes them, (mentally, I mean) sticks pins into them, caresses them, smoothes them, tries to amuse them or interest them or sympathize with them, tries alternately agreeing with them and disagreeing with them, pleasing them, annoying them, flattering them, puzzling them, encouraging them...it is no good...They remain passive lumps of human clay'.[67] In third year she laughed at the group she called 'the dress-and-tea party set, who quote Shakespeare, turning their "my's" into "me's" and have photographs of actors on their chimney pieces and are devoted admirers of Burne Jones' pictures'. Eglantyne loved every minute and wrote Oxford is 'my Jerusalem'.[68]

Wordsworth encouraged Lady Margaret Hall students to 'walk, row, play tennis and hockey and to ride bicycles because she did not want to impose more restrictions than the strict conventions of the period required'.[69] In true new-woman form, Eglantyne participated fully in everything that college life had to offer. She joined the Women's Inter-Collegiate Debating Society, which taught public speaking, how to listen to their opponent's argument and present one's own position.[70] These were skills that Eglantyne would use later in all her social and voluntary action work, especially fundraising and negotiating projects on behalf of the Save the Children Fund. She was proud of her athletic ability and was an accomplished horsewoman and avid cyclist, and university life gave her the chance to play a number of team sports that were new to girls who had been educated at home. Her first athletic goal was to play hockey for Lady Margaret, which had had a team since 1891.[71] Eglantyne bought a hockey stick and resolved to 'play twelve times and then one more thing will be done!' She liked hockey because 'people show a very elementary side of human nature when they play hockey, one feels as though one were touching the original man! As for my play, there is only one thing wrong about it, namely that I can never hit the ball'.[72] Lady Margaret was the first women's college to have a boat on the Cherwell River. Eglantyne grew up boating and fishing on lakes in Ellesmere and Northern Wales, and after a few brief lessons, Miss Pearson qualified her in rowing. She was modest about her natural talents: 'Miss Pearson must have been subject to some strange hallucination...for she told me how <u>well</u> I steered [the rapids]. I cannot make it out, unless my conversation at the time was so entertaining that it obliterated the memory of the various thorn bushes into which the boat ran at headlong speed'.[73]

Oxford did not convert Eglantyne to the great causes of women's suffrage or socialism as it did Evelyn Gunter, or Fight the Famine Council members, Maude Royden and Kathleen Courtney, who were a term behind her. In fact, Eglantyne remained politically conservative and a moderate liberal feminist. Nevertheless, her horizons were widened by the experience of university life and the influence of the older generation of female mentors and dons she was encountering. Duty and service were the buzzwords of university subculture and young women like Eglantyne looked for ways to embrace them. Although wealthy girls like Eglantyne were not expected to earn an income, they understood the importance of finding some sort of purposeful work in order to be what they called, 'of use'.[74] Eglantyne considered a range of career 'choices' including scholar, nurse, teacher and social worker fought for by earlier feminists.

In the late 1890s the question whether women should follow the same academic courses, attend the same lectures and sit the same examinations as men students was dividing the university community.[75] Dorothy Kempe was living in London in 1897; she sent Eglantyne some newspaper clippings on the subject of degrees for women. Eglantyne replied, 'The newspapers made me so angry'. The reason was that she was 'rather against' the idea of degrees for women:

> [T]he higher education of women is of too recent a growth, for us to be quite sure as yet what we do and what we don't want. If we bound ourselves down to it, it would probably prevent forever the possible development of a separate and perhaps better system of our own. We are in such a hurry. But what annoys me so intensely is that…They talk as if we were actually ousting the men, or only going to lectures in order to imitate <u>them!</u> When our presence cannot and does not affect them in the slightest degree. I do not think that they ought to be 'dog in the manger' about our taking a share (not away from them) in educational advantages wh. cannot be had elsewhere and which mean so very much to us. But I hope that all the feeling about it will pass when they see that we have no immediate intention of burying the undergraduates beneath the ruins of their colleges! I often wonder what one wld have done if one hadn't Oxford in one's life…Cld I a few years ago have pictured the vast fields which are (so easily) opened out to one here, I do not know <u>what</u> I shld have done. I never somehow had pictured to myself such a blissful paradise of books, books, books.[76]

Eglantyne was complacent about degrees for women but not about women's right to be a part of the university community as students or staff, so her reaction to the discovery that Mary Talbot, a young don she admired, had chosen to leave it all behind to marry the Reverend

Winfrid Oldfield Burrows, principal of the Leeds Clergy School, should not come as a surprise. University women were expected to resign from their positions once they became engaged and when the rumour reached the ears of the 'Crickets' that Talbot was engaged and not returning, Eglantyne was upset by the 'mournful news.' She felt that Talbot had let them down:

> [H]ear me vow an undying and perpetual grudge against Miss Talbot! Why can't she leave marrying and being given in marriage to the world's great motley host of ninnies? There are too few reasonable people...for us to be able to sacrifice one on the alter of matrimony...I made an effigy of [Burrows] out of a candle-end, (I do not know him and so had to invent his personal appearance, which you may be sure I didn't make flattering), and melted him before the fire, and stuck pins into him, as many as I could while he melted'.[77]

If Eglantyne had later married, her reaction and remark might be dismissed as mock hostility. Indeed, it was fashionable among female undergraduates to declare, romantically, that they 'would never marry'.[78] However, since Eglantyne eventually chose not to marry, her views of marriage are worth examining. According to Dyhouse most women tutors and dons did not marry. They subscribed to 'a conservative image of women's work and lives...exemplifying the quintessentially "feminine" virtues of selflessness and service, albeit in the "public" arenas rather than in the confines of family life.'[79] In the areas of academic life where the ego-driven and competitive culture clashed with traditional notions of 'feminine' self-sacrifice and modesty, female academics like Wordsworth emphasized that for them 'learning was not...a form of self-development, it was a form of service to God or country'.[80] We do not know what Eglantyne knew about her own parents' marriage, but she likely suspected that giving up a 'career' had caused her mother to suffer deeply. It is clear from her letters that Eglantyne admired her aunt Louisa Jebb's independence. Oxford opened Eglantyne's eyes to the possibility that marriage was not a woman's only natural destiny. On the day of the Burrow-Talbot wedding she wrote, '[T]he sacrifice is now consummated. Distant as I was from the scene of action, I was yet too near for my own peace of mind, for my vivid imagination painted the events which were taking place till I wished myself at the Antipodes till it was over'.[81]

Through the lectures young undergraduates attended and their contact with people outside of their privileged circles, a new social 'consciousness' rapidly developed amongst young male and female undergraduates.[82]

Outside of academics, three careers, nursing, teaching and social work were the most realistic possibilities for the students at Lady Margaret Hall, especially the ones who would have to support themselves. While Eglantyne was home for the first spring vacation, an Ellesmere friend who had entered nursing invited her to tour a children's hospital. Eglantyne was horrified by what she saw:

> Kathleen also introduced me to one or two other nurses. She shares her bedroom with one and has 2½ hours to herself out of the twenty-four. She has been in a rush of work ever since she started, and I imagine has had rather a hard time of it, though she had not at all changed her mind about her affection for nursing. But just think of it—mewed up all day with nineteen nurses (none of whom, except the head, having ever heard of such a person as King Alfred, I imagine, not that that makes much difference when one has no time for conversation,) nineteen nurses and nine dying babies!!![83]

During her second year, Eglantyne met Charlotte Toynbee, the treasurer of Lady Margaret Hall who introduced her to a new kind of volunteer work called settlement work. In the 1880s, men of the socially elite Oxford and Cambridge university communities, many of whom expected to become politicians, bought houses called 'settlements' in impoverished neighbourhoods where they dispensed food and clothing to the needy and taught basic reading and writing; by 1900 there were about 30 settlements in England.[84] An early founder was Arnold Toynbee, who believed that a cross-class alliance would form between students and workers because, by living in a slum neighbourhood, socially conscious undergraduates could demonstrate for their poor neighbours the obligations as well as the rights of citizenship. The university settlement movement attracted the active participation of private charities, voluntary societies, political parties and students.[85] Robert Humphreys argues that ultimately settlement workers believed that the connections made with labourers would free the workers from 'all vestige of feudalism and custom'. They would 'become like a middle-class in a working-class dress'.[86]

For a young gentleman, proximity to the poor may have been a novel idea, but visits to hospitals, workhouses and the cottages of the poor had always been a part of Victorian girls' socialization and women's charity work. University communities in the 1890s were 'full of women—often the wives of academics—with enthusiasm for social work, for settlements, housing reform, surveys of poverty and educational work amongst the poor.'[87] Female undergraduates followed their example and took up settlement work by either joining the men in their settlement houses or by starting their own. Eglantyne jumped on the bandwagon. In 1897 she spent her Easter vacation at the Oxford University Settlement in Bethnal Green,[88] where she participated in 'the clubs and danced with factory girls, with whom she felt instantly in touch'. Later she told Eglantyne Buxton and Eglantyne Mary Jebb that it had 'been one of the happiest [weeks] in her life' and that she began to 'resent the shackles of caste [and] the artificialities of class distinctions'. When writing *Rebel Daughter*, Buxton and E. M. Jebb told Wilson that it was around this time that Eglantyne became scornful of the Lyth, with its 12 servants, and resolved to 'reduce her own needs to the bare bone to equip herself to be of service'.[89] There is no indication, however, whether she planned to do this through academic social research and writing or through hands-on social work.

Since many settlement workers were interested in working-class children and education, local board schools became the focus of many settlement projects.[90] Settlement workers could see that young children were the key that opened up their parents' home. Charlotte Toynbee thought that enthusiastic young women were perfect candidates for teaching the children of the urban poor and circulated the idea among the students at Lady Margaret Hall. This is significant because, as Purvis points out, 'college educated women avoided teaching in the state-funded, elementary sector because it catered almost exclusively for working-class children'. Many people thought it was not 'genteel' for middle-class women to enter elementary teaching.[91] Toynbee was not the first person to mention teaching to Eglantyne. The previous spring, a student at Girton had invited her to run an elementary school with her, but Eglantyne had politely declined because of the uncertainty of her plans. Like most girls of her background, Eglantyne had never set foot in an elementary school. Her reaction to a Poor Law school she visited in Wales in 1897 was a 'queer sensation…The children looked cleaner than I had been led to expect', but she concluded that 'the whole place [was] rather comic. I think the comic side of a new thing is always the side which strikes one first'.[92] She could not imagine herself as a part of this environment.

In June of 1897, Eglantyne returned to Oxford to prepare for her *viva*. She was examined in Modern History: British India, 1773–1805, General History, 1715–1815 and Modern British History, 1715–1815. She was hoping for a first class degree and an invitation to stay on to do research. Unfortunately, she had taken the month of December off to travel with her brother to Athens, Cairo and Alexandria. She climbed many pyramids, saw many temples and mosques and survived the 'pickpockets', but she also developed conjunctivitis and her eyes bothered her throughout the term slowing down her preparation for the Schools exams. In spite of this, she was convinced that she had read 'up [her] mistakes and weak points' and hoped that she might 'pull' herself 'up a class'. When she received her results, she moaned, '[T]hey gave me no chance...Beautiful. Beautiful Oxford!'[93] Eglantyne had received a disappointing second class degree.

Vera Brittain describes four types of student for whom a second class result is the 'usual fate': the conscientious plodder, the profound rather than scholarly student, the bad examinee and the student who is distracted by extra-curricular activities.[94] Between 1895 and 1897, Eglantyne fit into each of Brittain's ideal types. She had been a conscientious plodder, a profound rather than scholarly student and a bad examinee, and she had been distracted by extra-curricular activities. At Oxford in the 1890s, it was believed that if a student did not receive a 'first' there was little point in continuing. This chapter has shown that at Oxford, Eglantyne encountered the many influential women and discovered the range of careers that were open to women of her class and generation. However, she realized that a 'second' thwarted her dreams of an academic career and possibly the literary ambitions she harboured; still, she accepted her fate. Oxford had taught her that it was her 'duty' to make her mark. The question was, what sort of meaningful work might one do?

4
Ribbons and Trumpets: Toils and Troubles at Teachers College

'[O]ne has to have faith', wrote Eglantyne, still chafing over her disappointing examination results, that 'Heaven will grant to willing hearts the means and opportunities of serving one's fellow man, with or without the arbitrary symbols of success—its ribbons and trumpets'.[1] In the late 1890s, Eleanor Rathbone, who also left Lady Margaret Hall with a disappointing second class degree put her frustrations more bluntly: 'Parliament was shut to us, and practically everything was shut to us...There was nothing to be ambitious about'.[2] Despite her shaken confidence, Eglantyne still believed that she had abilities worth developing and decided to 'make a fresh start'[3] after Oxford. By the 1890s, many ladies' charities and philanthropic 'good works' had evolved into distinct paid occupations in the fields of social work and health care, which required specialized education and training. The interest of well-to-do women in grammar school teaching, which was regarded as a form of social work is an example. This chapter examines Eglantyne's decision to enter teacher training college and the obstacles and hurdles she had to overcome to become a member of the ill-defined group known as the gentlewoman schoolmistress.

For wealthy people, the most common stereotype of the lady teacher was the impoverished gentlewoman governess who had been 'thrown into the world, perhaps at middle age, to work or starve'.[4] The pitiful plight of the forlorn governess was a popular theme in sentimental Victorian art, literature and newspapers.[5] The development of compulsory education for children of the labouring classes in the 1870s and the creation of national schools under the education acts created a demand for middle-class inspectors, superintendents and grammar school teachers. By the 1880s lower-middle-class girls began to enter teachers' colleges, and soon they made up the majority of teachers in

4.1   Eglantyne at Stockwell Teachers College, source: Jebb Family

state-funded board schools.[6] In contrast to the 'gently-nurtured but ill-educated' governesses who were of reduced social status,[7] board school-teachers were drawn from the academically gifted youth of the working classes. Despite the hardship of a long training, teaching was a career, which promised workingwomen the rewards of improved social status, including economic and employment security. To many in the lower-middle classes, the schoolmistress embodied feminine refinement with her clean, dainty clothes and ladylike manners.[8]

Just the same, teaching as a career for all women was a cause that attracted the attention of feminists. Since the 1860s many had been pointing out the constraints and frustrations, which gender ideology imposed on well-to-do women. Together with demands to open the universities to women came demands for more training schools to prepare ladies for careers. Philanthropic women believed that it was their right and duty to help their poor 'sisters' and teaching poor children was a respectable form of charity work. It was a short jump from slum work to the schoolroom, and the recruitment of gentlewoman teachers was the goal of many late-Victorian feminists. One barrier they faced, however, was the 'universal' idea, which continued into the period of the First World War that respectable women should not work for pay. Upper-class women, like the lady volunteers in Tye's Home Arts and Industries Association, coveted their status as 'disinterested amateurs'. They did not teach art for 'profit or gain', but 'disseminated' art education voluntarily 'for the public good and as a means of discharging their duty and authenticating their claims to citizenship'.[9]

Lady volunteers in the local charity offices distinguished themselves from paid staff by the title 'honorary secretary'. Well-to-do girls, whose fathers' could support them, were expected to follow in their mothers' footsteps and not take jobs away from girls who needed them.[10]

One of the many feminists to challenge this ideology was Lady Louisa Hubbard, educationist and founder of Bishop Otter College in 1873, who included women of all ranks in the 'much discussed and often ill treated "woman question"'.[11] She endorsed the recruitment of ladies to board school teaching by ignoring the stigma associated with ladies in paid employment and overlooking the fact that ladies generally left the education of children, including their own, to nursery maids and governesses.[12] She predicted that although ladies would never make up more than four or five per cent of the total teaching population, she was certain that gentlewoman schoolmistresses could work happily alongside their lower-class colleagues, whom she expected to extend 'a kindly hand of fellowship to their new comrades, feeling that their profession was worthy of being adopted by persons from any rank of life'.[13]

In the late 1890s, a large group of women from academic circles dedicated themselves to the 'ideal of service' and used their influence in academic circles to recruit former students to 'new forms of social work' among the poor.[14] Settlement work and working-class children's education were of interest to Elizabeth Wordsworth who was a strong promoter of women's social work; however it was Charlotte Toynbee who first approached Eglantyne about teaching grammar school. Toynbee was like Louisa Hubbard and two members of the London School Board, Alice Weslake and Edith Simcox, who thought that enthusiastic young women 'from cultivated homes' were perfect candidates for teaching the children of the urban poor.[15] In 1882, Weslake and Simcox persuaded socially conscious Gertrude Tuckwell, a parson's daughter, who was 'lured' to London by the image of 'hideous inequalities and destruction',[16] to enrol in Bishop Otter Training College. While at Oxford, Eglantyne and many other women students became caught up in what Seth Koven calls a 'romance' with the slums.[17] In 1898, Toynbee took Eglantyne to visit a Poor Law school in Oxford and pointed out how much needed to be done and pressed Eglantyne to think about enrolling in a teacher training college.

The idea of becoming a teacher was not completely new to Eglantyne. The year before she went up to Oxford, Louisa Jebb read an article about working-class education and agreed 'that there is a very great need for ladies as National Schoolmistresses because of the good of the children's close contact with them'. She told Eglantyne that she thought it 'would be very good' for her: 'Its being rather unremunerative too renders it so much more desirable for those whose object is not money'.[18] By this she meant that Eglantyne would face the same quandary that Tuckwell had to overcome, which was 'a sort of social stigma...attach[ed] to...women who earned their living'.[19] In 1895, Louisa Jebb turned the problem of the teacher's low pay into a good reason why it was suitable for a pin-money girl like Eglantyne, who would not fret over her income. Four years later, when Tye's brother Heneage and wife Geraldine discovered that their niece was thinking about taking up 'elementary school teaching as a career', they 'disapproved' because girls from prosperous land-owning families did not go in for teaching in a board school. Their teenage daughters, on the other hand, felt a 'mingled' sense of 'admiration' and 'astonishment'.[20]

For her part, Eglantyne had serious reservations because she did not know very much about teaching. She told her mother, 'I am very far from saying that I think teaching would be altogether congenial and delightful but...I think it suitable. I mean I might hope to cultivate the necessary qualities for the post, which are lacking in me. You are my pope and if it worries you to think about it, do not think about it at all'. The letter shows that she valued her mother's opinion and only thought of teaching as something 'suitable' to fall back on if her 'capacities' did not 'justify [her] in leading a wholly literary life'. Most importantly, she was aware that to do this work she would have to 'cultivate the necessary qualities' that she did not naturally possess.[21]

In the late nineteenth century the idea of 'vocation' had been used to define all types of social work, including teaching, as a moral mission for the middle- and upper-class women who took it up. The rhetoric of social motherhood constructed philanthropy as a deeply personal source of moral and spiritual agency. This was evident in Florence Nightingale's nursing, Josephine Butler's efforts to reform prostitutes, Wordsworth's approach to college as a means of educating future Anglican mothers and, of course, Mrs Jebb's Home Arts and Industries Association work where she claimed a kinship with Ireland's starving children. 'What *Ireland* needs is mothers,' Tye wrote 'who will stoop to uplift the little children ...giving them that which their own mothers are unable to give, educating, "drawing them forth"'.[22] Although Eglantyne wanted to find meaningful work she had never claimed to have any interest in social motherhood or a 'genuine interest in or love of children'.[23] When she was 14 years old, the Jebb family took a seaside house, which was not far from an elementary school. Eglantyne would go for long walks alone, timing her return to watch the pupils come outside to play. 'Creeping over a convenient sand dune, I used to look down into the playground and gaze till they went away.' Reflecting years later upon this 'form of amusement', she could not remember if watching 'the little wretches' had given her any 'pleasure'. But she was adamant that the 'Dreadful idea of closer acquaintance had never entered my head.'[24]

Why then did Eglantyne decide to go to Stockwell Teacher Training College? After university, she 'fell into a mood of despair' and had no idea what to do next. She returned to the Lyth, where she tried to write a novel, vowing not to 'go more than needful beyond my own experience,' which meant she had to exclude all 'Questions and love making'. When her novel was finished she realized that it was 'a stupid little story...pointless, colourless, childish, limited, forced. Neither invigoratingly cold nor really hot; just tepid, tepid, tepid!' And there were 'no villains'.[25] Oxford had been a liberating experience for her and she was not ready to play the role of daughter-at-home with her widowed mother, at least not yet. Perhaps it was the fact that her mother liked the novel ('unfortunately publishers have not got the same standards as mothers')[26] or her desire to recapture the magic of Oxford, or the voices of her Lady Margaret Hall mentors ringing in her ears, but resolving to take on more of the world, Eglantyne contacted Charlotte Toynbee for advice and began to search for a teacher's college.[27]

A 'lecturer friend' of Toynbee's told Eglantyne not to 'waste [her] time at college'[28] because men and women with university qualifications could head straight into the upper echelons of the profession through positions in fee-paying schools or high schools or secure positions with the School Board Inspectorate, as Eglantyne's father had expected to do in the 1870s.[29] But Eglantyne stated that she was 'finished' with universities; besides she wanted to work with poor children in a grammar school. Suddenly, she became 'frantically impatient' to 'get into <u>some</u> college...all this ought to have been done years ago.'[30] In September, she was accepted at the British and Foreign School Society's College for Women Teachers at Stockwell in south London. Armed with an Oxford second, youthful idealism and absolutely no idea what she was getting herself into, 22-year-old Eglantyne joined the 2,193 women and 1,378 men who were enrolled in 61 residential and day teachers' colleges in the United Kingdom. The yearly output from all teachers colleges in 1899 was 2,500, which was considered to be inadequate to meet the needs of the country at the time.[31]

Unlike the ancient institutions of elite education like Oxford and Cambridge, teacher training colleges first appeared in the early nineteenth century. The formal curriculum was intended to impart to young working people the academic knowledge and pedagogical skills necessary to teach the children of labourers. The exception was Bishop Otter College, which Louisa Hubbard founded specifically to 'attract "ladies", rather than working girls into teaching'.[32] Unlike Bishop Otter and Lady Margaret Hall, Stockwell College did not pride itself on offering a family-like atmosphere suitable for gentlemen's daughters. Rather, the emphasis at Stockwell was vocational, demanding grinding hard work and a rigid decorum with greater stress on becoming a teacher than on learning for its own sake. The informal or hidden curriculum of the college aimed simultaneously to combine higher education and professional training and to 'socialize students' into the 'academic and cultural values of the middle class proper'.[33] Training colleges assumed that because of the low social-class backgrounds of the students,[34] a great deal of resocialization was required; hence the ethos of middle-class life was replicated within the residential college.[35] This was achieved through a highly structured and disciplined two-year residential course requiring a minimum of 150 hours in the practising school. Middle-class tastes and values were written right into the architecture and furnishings of the buildings. The recreation rooms, one Inspector reported, are 'extremely well fitted up with good prints, a library of standard books, a piano, various games such as chess and draughts. It is not easy to over-rate the value of a good recreation room, both for the comfort and enjoyment of the students and for their general improvement'.[36] The successful schoolteacher had been created once the young student had embraced an appreciation of the middle-class standards (though not the actual status) of feminine or masculine respectability and once their lesson plans, practice teaching and work habits reflected an ability to combine a thoughtful well-constructed lesson with contemporary pedagogical theories.

Eglantyne was glad that Stockwell College was not as proper as Bishop Otter or Lady Margaret Hall. The students had a greater degree of freedom and were allowed to go to church alone and there was a really nice library, which was 'often deserted'.[37] The staff consisted of the principal, Miss Lydia Manley, who had been appointed as head teacher in 1884 and promoted to principal in 1892,[38] ten full-time governesses, and the teachers of the 800 pupils in the associated practising schools. There were 120 Queen's Scholarship students living in the college, 40 students in an outside hostel and 16 day students.[39] Apart from a few third-year students, they were strictly divided into junior and senior year. Eglantyne's mother met Manley, whom 'she liked very much', to negotiate the terms of her daughter's residency. Manley admitted Eglantyne as a 'non-governmental student' under Article 115 of the Education Act, which was designed for 'persons who had passed certain University, University Local or equivalents examinations'.[40] Due to her three years at Oxford, Manley told Eglantyne to 'consider [her]self a III year student and pretend to be one'. Eglantyne understood this to mean that, 'while living at the college and sharing its life…the objects and methods of [her] training' would consist largely of 'actual teaching'. Manley was more off-hand when she introduced Eglantyne to the head-girl. She merely said, '"Here is Miss Jebb who has come to stay with us at any rate for <u>some weeks(!)</u> I am sure you will look after her. Take her to tea—at the III Year's table, <u>you know.</u>"' Eglantyne was embarrassed. She saw that 'the bewildered girl did not "know", but understood that she must look as though she did'.[41] It turned out that Eglantyne would have many solitary meals in the large dining hall because she was the only one of the six third-year students who was not away taking specializing training before graduation. Four students were in France improving their French, and one student was at Ealing College for Teachers of the Deaf. Despite efforts to the contrary, the recruitment of gentlewoman schoolmistresses had been largely unsuccessful, making Eglantyne such a novelty that the Inspector, Sir H. E. Oakley, inserted a reference to her in his 1898–1899 annual report for the Ministry of Education: '[A] student who gained a second class in the Oxford final history schools…entered the college under Article 115th'.[42]

With no previous classroom experience by which to judge, Eglantyne was highly impressed by the Froebel methods Stockwell used, such as clay modelling, painting and games and story telling for teaching young children. The kindergarten instructors learned how to teach pupils the alphabet by drawing the letters in sand and to teach counting by arranging sticks.[43] After a month, Eglantyne was still very impressed by how subjects such as science were taught at Stockwell. 'They teach 1000 times better than it is taught elsewhere', she wrote, adding, 'Mr Hutton [her Oxford tutor] taught execrably by comparison'.[44] Regarding the college life, Eglantyne was instantly aware that nothing in her previous experience, especially Oxford, had prepared her for it. On handmade letterhead, inscribed 'Prison', she told Dorothy Kempe, 'the girls are taken straight off' the Queen's Scholarship list; that is, they had been given two-year grants to cover the cost of books, equipment and tuition. Eglantyne noted that 'their number in that list is their college number, and the class order is the order for the dormitories, for the meals and for the classes.

Both the college and the schools strike one as extraordinary examples of the management of numbers. Indeed there is so much organization that one is driven to wonder whether the thing organized does not disappear.'[45]

Before long it dawned upon Eglantyne that teaching might not be the 'congenial and delightful' career which she and Louisa Jebb had envisioned in 1895, nor would it be easy to 'cultivate the necessary qualities' which she lacked to do this work. She tried to be brave, and only Dorothy Kempe, who was doing settlement work in Lambeth at the time, knew how terrified she really was or how hard she had to struggle. Kempe who had left Oxford in 1896 with a third class in English was devoting herself to public service, through unpaid settlement work, which was more usual for women of her social position. Nevertheless, she was intensely interested in Eglantyne's choice of career although she 'doubted her suitability for it'.[46] The only thing Eglantyne had in common with the Stockwell students was that their mothers had also likely visited 'the head and discussed their daughter's future'.[47] Otherwise, the typical Stockwell student was an academically gifted daughter of the labour aristocracy or lower middle class. Whereas Eglantyne's only visit to an elementary school had been out of curiosity, the majority of her classmates, teachers and supervisors were intimately familiar with the culture and routine of that environment and had excelled in it.[48]

Eglantyne's first impression of the Stockwell students and staff in 1898 is interesting when contrasted with her undergraduate life at Lady Margaret Hall two years earlier. Both institutions were led by strong-minded women and developed autonomous female subcultures, their own traditions and *esprit de corps*. At Oxford, under the mentorship of Elizabeth Wordsworth, the women dons, staff and students, Eglantyne embraced the traditions of elite education and particularly enjoyed mentoring the first-year students. Although she dubbed them the 'dress and tea-party set' and mocked their fad for Burne-Jones's art and their affected use of Elizabethan words, she respected them nonetheless. Unlike her Stockwell fellow students, who came from a world which was unfamiliar to Eglantyne, the young ladies of Lady Margaret Hall were from a background that she understood and she tried to encourage them by arranging her room so that they could sit around her fire for cocoa parties and midnight chats. At Stockwell, the tables were turned, so to speak, and Eglantyne was the object of curiosity and controversy.

Under the leadership of Lydia Manley, whose character combined the 'ideal qualities of "large-brained woman and large-hearted man"',[49] a strong female subculture also developed at Stockwell. Some Stockwell girls had been selected as pupil teachers at the age of 12 or 13 and had already completed a five-year apprenticeship in preparation for teachers' college. Others had been drawn from the Queen's scholarship list.[50] Only a privileged few could afford to stay for a third year because any time out of the labour force was an economic hardship for their families. Widdowson argues that young women of this class would have been uncomfortable with prolonged financial dependence. They 'felt rather abnormal being dependent on their families long after their elementary school friends had started earning a living'.[51] Despite the hardship, for most a career as a schoolteacher promised upward mobility, and these girls received encouragement from their families. At Stockwell, these young workingwomen first had the feeling that they were a professional group, and the friendships they made sustained them throughout their professional lives. Stockwell had a college magazine and a flourishing literary society, which was 'carried on with great spirit by the students'. The annual report for training colleges listed outings to 'many places of interest' including 'Sir Edward Burne-Jones' residence. The artist had 'received a party of students with great kindness at his house and studio'.[52]

At Stockwell, Eglantyne was for the first time meeting women below her social position who were not servants. At the Lyth, even the most cantankerous servants had shown deference toward members of the family. Consequently, many members of the elite classes mistook the qualities of servitude for affection. Initially it upset Eglantyne that the staff and students did not extend the 'kindly hand of fellowship' promised by the promoters of gentlewoman schoolmistresses: 'My first shock of absolute astonishment that any one could venture to snub me, has already given way, by frequent repetition of the experience'.[53] Her experience supports Wendy Robinson's assertion that many professional teachers found it offensive that middle-class reformers thought they could meddle in the 'socialization' and 'social life' of pupil teachers.[54] Since the 1870s veteran schoolteachers had been expressing doubts publicly about their new gentlewoman colleagues. In 1873, a 'certificated mistress' claimed that a 'lady by birth and education could never feel at home' in the profession. 'The habits and behaviour...would be a constant torture to her'.[55] Another said that well-to-do ladies were '[un]worthy of being admitted to the honourable profession of a "Certificated schoolmistress" unless they could "forsake the habits" of "unemployed ladies", and give up "conventional usages" of visiting, and the "race of fashion in dress and recreations"'.[56]

Seth Koven says that 'sisterhood is neither sameness nor equality'.[57] It may have been a self-fulfilling prophecy, or it may have been the professional pride of her teachers and class solidarity among the Stockwell girls, but Eglantyne felt like a privileged do-gooder with little to offer and worse, a rebellious rich girl 'slumming' while she waited for marriage. Stockwell girls were under no obligation to be friendly. Lydia Manley did not take an interest in her as Wordsworth had done, and she did not join their literary society or help with the college paper. Consequently, there is no mention of cocoa parties in Eglantyne's room at Stockwell. She told her sister the reason:

> I had expected to find the life rough but I must say the reality startled me...My new friends mostly if not all come from the Elementary Schools, their sisters are 'in business' serving in shops I suppose. They wear aprons and have accents...The Gods be thanked I have a room to myself. The dormitories are like gigantic beehives. The look of them makes a cold shudder run over me.[58]

Her remarks show that she did not appreciate the deeply rooted class boundaries. She was unaware that Stockwell girls would have been offended by her assumption that their sisters served in shops or worse. She did not know that they regarded 'domestic work and shop work' as 'beneath them and...unsuitable for other girls in their families'.[59] She would have been surprised to learn that they thought of themselves as high achievers.[60] To them, Eglantyne was the only student with an 'accent'. What Eglantyne could not avoid seeing, though, was their physical condition:

> [T]he average of health is so much lower here than at Oxford—all these girls have such wretched physiques, some dozen knock up daily...But they get used to going on and doing their work—badly—in spite of ill-health. One wonders how they ever manage to run their schools. One poor girl here has incurable heart disease, which affects her eyes. Yesterday the doctor told her that she must not study, and that nothing could be done for them, she came into the classroom and sobbed.[61]

Despite her privileges the Stockwell girls had one thing that Eglantyne lacked and desperately needed: they appeared to be outstanding teachers. Eglantyne's special status as a 'false third-year' student meant that she began the programme a full two years behind the others. Manley had 'hurled [her] headlong amongst the students'.[62] Every board school-teacher faced some of the same challenges she faced. The payment-by-result system was still in place until the Revised Code of 1900, which meant that a school's operating grant was based on its students' test scores.[63] Teachers were expected to follow the national core curriculum, which was characterized by rote learning, chanting, recitation and drill. Straight away, Eglantyne had to learn to teach 20 subjects. When Miss Birken, the supervising headmistress said, 'I think you had better be starting on subjects beside history'. Eglantyne 'smiled amiably' without mentioning that she had only studied five of the 20 subjects she was expected to teach and since her 'schoolroom days and had made no subsequent additions to [her] knowledge'.[64] She had to know science, algebra and grammar 'up and down and to teach [each] in the approved methods'. Despite her wish to be taken seriously and to succeed, she began using humour as a defense mechanism and incorporated her 'outsider' identity into her persona by comically portraying her 'foreignness' and ineptness at everything. As we have seen, the Jebbs did not have an ear for music. When Eglantyne discovered that she had to master sol-fa, sight-reading, and ear and time tests in order to teach her pupil's music, she told Kempe, she was relieved because 'the music man discovered in me the rudiments of a voice, much in the same way that physiologists discover the rudiments of swimming apparatus in human beings'.[65]

The additional burden borne by all female teachers was inherent in the gendered nature of the elementary school curriculum. Women teachers were expected to teach not only the 3Rs, but also domestic science. They were expected to bring the girls up to the same examination standard as the boys; at the same time they also had to provide full instruction in household management and nutrition.[66] One of Eglantyne's biggest challenges was needlework taught according to the regulations of the Revised Code of 1874, which allotted four hours per week to sewing. This placed extra pressure on female students, who frequently sewed (the board prescribed goal was 12 to 18 stitches per inch!)[67] while the boys did arithmetic. Female student teachers were required to give step-by-step demonstrations from their own needlework samplers, and this caused problems for Eglantyne because she had no talent for it. She had to brush up on the most basic stitches and sit exams in plain sewing, basic shirt pattern making and cutting out. She found it so frustrating that her teacher gave her a 'pinafore to make, because, as she told one of the students, she thought it would "<u>soothe</u>" me!!' She spent her Christmas holidays practising buttonholes, gussets and gathers.[68]

It has been suggested that one of the strongest attractions of settlement and cross-class slum work for the university women like Eglantyne and Dorothy Kempe, who were raised in homes with armies of domestic servants, was the opportunity to become immersed in the prohibited 'dirtiness' of working-class culture and slum life. Many upper-class women regarded this as a literal and symbolic act of independence and adventure.[69] For wealthy girls like Eglantyne who had servants to light fires, cook meals, sweep floors and mend clothes, domestic education had consisted of learning to manage a large household staff, not to work alongside it. The Stockwell girls and their mothers knew how to do these things, 'ladies' like Jebb and Kempe did not. Eglantyne told Dorothy, whose father was Sir John Arrow Kempe, an official in the Treasury, that she had to learn everything about housework, and she was bewildered: 'how to cook, how to wash, how to dress, how to clean, where to live, what to eat, these are only a few of the items the subject seems to include'. Eglantyne described domestic science in detail to Kempe who would have experienced similar challenges in her settlement work in Lambeth, adding, '[Y]ou can guess that I take to the study like a duck to water'.[70]

It is not surprising the Eglantyne did not excel easily at teachers' college. Experienced teachers like Manley could have predicted her difficulties. Eglantyne was very poorly prepared when she entered, and class prejudice prevented her from acquiring a supportive peer group to show her the shortcuts, but this did not temper Manley's harsh criticism: there was 'no humbug in Stockwell'. The staff watched Eglantyne closely; turning up unannounced in her lessons, though it was 'was prearranged'. Eglantyne reacted politely acting 'as though it was an unexpected delight' to find them sitting at the back of her classroom.[71] They regard 'me as a pleasant idiot'; she told Kempe and wondered if her 'embarrassing experiences' were 'not amusing experiments' for the Stockwell staff.[72] She described her own teaching as 'execrable' agreeing with the 'uncompromising' assistant mistress who told her that her lesson was 'very bad.' She 'criticized me till there was really nothing left of me but my bodily presence. I never felt so swept off the face of the globe in my life, as when she took out a sheet of paper on [which] she had written all the stupid questions I had asked during the course of the lesson, and read them to me'.[73] After a lesson late in November another sheet of foolscap appeared, upon which Miss Manley had written her assessment of Eglantyne's lesson. Read to her by an assistant matron, Eglantyne endured it all stoically:

> Miss Manley wanted to know whether your voice always pitched in that key. I said—I thought it was partly nervousness, but wasn't

sure…[S]he asked: cld. you keep such a large class in order if no one was in the room? I said—<u>No</u>, you couldn't. Look here, you made 21 grammatical mistakes in the notes which you dictated…If you wear such thin shoes on these floors you will catch cold. Why didn't you recapitulate? Why do you hesitate when you begin asking questions? Don't do that. Draw your maps with blunt chalk, not pointed…I will not give you a pointer if you fidget with it. You must not loose [sic] the thread of your lesson. Do you see? Go away now.[74]

It was worse than anything she had experienced from her harshest childhood governess or her Oxford professors. 'That is the way they do it here', she told Dorothy Kempe, and 'you sit and listen to a catalogue of your own virtues and vices as though it was a catalogue of goods and chattels'.[75] But she kept on trying to improve.

Since the 1870s, proponents of women in education had 'insisted upon' gentlewomen having at least two years of teacher training to make up for the 'five years preliminary experience' the pupil teachers had as an 'imperative condition of success'.[76] A 'School Inspector' wrote to the *Times* in 1873 that although an 'educated lady' might eventually become an 'excellent teacher', he was 'far from advocating her employment without previous training. Subjects long passed by or neglected as beneath or outside the curriculum of polite education must be well and carefully studied, even if one is "to the manner born"'.[77] Twenty-five years later a different inspector agreed that 'it is not always easy to understand on what ground students are admitted to colleges under Article 115'. In his view, a 115 exemption 'is too frequently applied…though it is perfectly clear…that the students have a special need of the drill and criticism, which they have never apparently had before'.[78] Another inspector said ladies had trouble 'keeping discipline' and 'find it difficult to think of the lesson and keep their eyes on the class at the same time', but he observed that 'this wears off appreciably in six weeks'.[79]

Despite her lack of exposure to state schools, in her third week at Stockwell Eglantyne was invited to dine with Sir John Gorst of the Education Department and a lady sub-inspector named Katharine Bathurst. Eglantyne told Dorothy Kempe that '*a nous trois*' had 'most entertaining discussions'.[80] Since the 1870s the Department had been recruiting inspectors from the 'young men fresh from the university, who had never seen the inside of a public elementary school'.[81] Such men, just like Eglantyne's father, who had tried unsuccessfully in 1872 to get such a position, found it very difficult to get a foot in the door without family connections.[82] Arthur Jebb had complained about the jobbery, bureaucracy and 'outsiders foisted upon the office' by the incompetent Education Department.[83] He hated the 'official slackness and obstinacy' of the Education Office where there was 'great pigheadedness and little work'.[84] Arthur looked at the problem from the perspective of the gentleman of leisure who felt cut off by the new bureaucratic middle class. Over the intervening two decades, new interest groups had arisen who expressed a very different set of concerns. First, highly educated middle-class women were demanding more opportunities for themselves within the Board of Education. Second, by the 1890s male teachers from the lower-middle class were very resentful because the Inspectorate was closed to them. The reason, according to the board, was because of their social backgrounds; even experienced certificated teachers would never be respected as inspectors.[85]

In the late 1890s, Sir John Gorst was responding to public criticism that he had used 'his influence to place in key positions at the board too many men educated at the public schools and the older universities' by setting up a new class of junior school board inspectors.[86] Since Gorst was an intimate acquaintance of Eglantyne's uncle, Sir Richard Jebb and Lady Jebb, by the 1890s the Jebb family must have had the social connections necessary to move up within the ranks of the Education Department. Gorst wanted Bathurst to meet Eglantyne in order to put Eglantyne on to this career track. Bathurst had been appointed to the Lady Inspectorate the preceding year, and over the next decade became renowned for her 'crusading zeal'.[87] Together, they informed Eglantyne that the board was looking for three new Lady Inspectors.

Being either a male or female teacher in the late nineteenth century meant understanding the gender and class constraints on one's position in the profession.[88] All teachers complained loudly about the excessive requirements of the curriculum, the payment-by-results system and the school inspector's 'lack of knowledge, experience and sympathy, of the variety of standards they adopted, and of their class arrogance'.[89] Although the opportunity for promotion did gradually increase for lower-middle-class men in the late nineteenth century, the Inspectorate remained closed to women teachers (until 1905), except in the uncontroversial female areas of the curriculum like examining girls in needlework and cooking.[90] Experienced professional teachers like Lydia Manley and her first assistant, Miss Kimble, had been encountering gender and class obstacles throughout their careers; so it is unlikely that they would have been overly surprised to discover that Gorst had offered an Inspectorship to Eglantyne. For her part, Eglantyne guessed that the offer was based solely on her social position and not her training or talent as a teacher and she declined the position. She was pretty certain that 'the path of righteousness was not that of promotion'.[91]

Eglantyne's letters from her year at Stockwell reveal that before long she felt betrayed by the enthusiastic lady mentors who had talked her into a teaching career. She quickly realized that 'everything which people told me about things here appears to be untrue'. She did not 'find the work...easy or superfluous...Indeed it is absolutely ridiculous for people even to think that I make any sacrifice in coming here'.[92] She grew tired of receiving pamphlets entitled '"Elementary Teaching as a <u>Career</u>!" I'd write one myself—Elementary Teaching as <u>Toil</u>'.[93] When confronted with the natural talent of gifted young women at Stockwell, Eglantyne commented, 'they compel my respect and admiration...I gaze at them with rapt awe'.[94] After only two weeks she told Dorothy, '[M]y creed has grown. I know it has...In making this fresh start...everything has changed—my resources, my standard of happiness, my relations with the people, my desires'.[95] She told her younger sister: 'It is a matter of perpetual wonder to me that these people whom I used to think of as much as lamp-posts—the people one sees in the streets, on stations and who live in villas all the same, on the edge of towns—have really got character, histories and interests and are sometime very capable beings too...They teach me more, more, more than I can say'.[96]

This chapter has shown that once Eglantyne realized that she had entered Stockwell under a false 'banner of superior enlightenment,' she became more determined than ever to succeed. Still, she had reservations and announced: 'I would like to point out how these ladies entering the profession' must consider the 'harmfulness, when they pretend to reform what they fail to understand'.[97] In her final weeks at Stockwell Lydia Manley asked her to show two Newnham students around the college and she agreed. She told Kempe that the first young woman was very interested whereas the second, merely 'gazed' at them 'with a rather puzzled expression' when they 'exchanged the most enthusiastic sentiments about the work.' Eglantyne understood both students' point of view and she realized that Kempe would wonder what had possessed her to permit Miss Manley to use her 'as a decoy duck' to help 'to lure someone else after me into the toils' of grammar school teaching. Eglantyne explained that notwithstanding her own struggles, she was committed to the work and hoped that there would be a 'succession of University girls here at Stockwell, for I see in dreams all that they might do'.[98]

5
'Hewing out my Future in Defiance to my Friends': The Life and Times of a Gentlewoman School Mistress

Eglantyne had entered teacher training college hoping that she might fulfil her 'obligations to [her] fellowman by a little work'.[1] During her final weeks at Stockwell Teacher Training College, she wondered 'how many thousand years one will have to go on preparing...to do work, which perhaps one will never do'.[2] She had remained stoically determined to achieve something at Stockwell and did manage to earn her teacher's certificate. According to her examination results, the subject she knew best was how to cut out and sew a boy's shirt.[3] Thus, in spite of her previous work in history at Oxford University, she was "'<u>conscientiously</u> recommended" as a teacher of the art!!!'[4] By the early twentieth century, the decades-long battle for women's rights had resulted in the opening of some previously forbidden public spheres and social spaces. Together with wider access to higher education and training colleges came opportunities for more middle-class women to pursue careers, notably in the fields of health care, teaching and social work, which were seen as respectable extensions of women's unpaid work in prisons, workhouses and the cottages of the poor. 'Paid or unpaid', Helen Jones argues that teaching, nursing and social work 'reflect[ed] the supposedly caring and sharing side of women's characters'.[5] This chapter examines Eglantyne's brief experience teaching grammar school and suggests that it is only when we look closely at the experiences of individual women that we fully appreciate the historical and biographical intersection of contemporary ideas surrounding professional responsibilities and her generation's sense of duty to their families, to public work and to themselves.

In the spring of 1899, Eglantyne began to search for a teaching position. She copied out her testimonials onto 'regulation foolscap', which she said made her look like an advertisement for a bar of soap. Then

.1   Eglantyne with mother, source: Buxton Family

he set out on her own around the London dockyards and slum
1eighbourhoods 'to see possible schools'. Naturally there was consider-
ble resistance to this at Stockwell, where the staff objected to her
going into a neighbourhood', where one could not 'walk down the

street' without having your 'watch grabbed'.[6] Lydia Manley recom
mended a post in a good London Board School 'with an efficient head
mistress' where she could 'see good work done' and to continue to have
her 'own work supervised'.[7] She also offered her a place in one of
Stockwell's practising schools, but Eglantyne had other ideas: 'Once more
I am hewing out my future in defiance to my friends—at Stockwell they
look very blank at my plans!'[8] Initially, it had not occurred to Eglantyne
that the exciting underbelly of London would not embrace her with open
arms or that even with the shortage of trained teachers she would have
difficulty finding a job. She searched all through May and into June and
pinned her hopes on a post in a 'poor school in Waterloo Road...I am on
tenterhooks to get it, though I suppose I shant'.[9]

Slowly, it dawned upon Eglantyne that she was facing the same sort
of discrimination that she had faced at Stockwell. She assumed that
nobody wanted to bother with her because of her privileged education
and class background: '[I]nstead of giving one one's weapons', per
petual training had only taken 'away one's natural endowment
When I find how long...seems the road—I turn round and wrathfully
abuse Oxford!!!'[10] She said she could not 'get people to...take me
seriously...The headmistresses laugh in my face, which is unkind!'[11] It
is likely that her Oxford education, social status and teaching cer
tificate made her appear simultaneously qualified and ill-qualified, but
she did not feel over-qualified, in fact, her disappointment at Oxford
followed by her mediocre performance at Stockwell had shaken her
confidence: '[M]y own stupidity and incompetence is like a great wall
which I can't surmount. If I had only the ordinary qualifications of the
average person nothing wld. seem impossible'.[12] Whereas Louisa
Hubbard, Charlotte Toynbee and Sir John Gorst had encouraged gen
tlewoman schoolmistresses, the rest of the profession remained guard
edly suspicious. It is also possible that Manley was correct, Eglantyne
may not have been ready to manage a classroom on her own, not because
she was a 'lady' but because she had only a year of training.

After a few months Eglantyne's uncle, James Gilmore, a retired house
master at Marlborough College, where her brothers had been pupils, came
'round', accepted her 'profession in life' and took her to see some schools
He used his influence in town to get her a position as assistant mistress
at St Peter's Church of England School in a lower-working-class neigh
bourhood in the small rural village of Marlborough. It was not the notor
ious London slum she had been hoping for, and the poorest street in
Marlborough was nothing like the destitution in Ireland she had seen
during her mother's Home Arts and Industry Association days; never

theless, Eglantyne, having read about the struggles of the under-funded village schools, believed she might do some good there. Her mother probably consented to Eglantyne's embarking upon this new career for philosophical and practical reasons. She may have been remembering her own 1882 article, 'The Right of Women', where she had instructed the 'aimless' women of leisure to forsake 'the unsatisfying pleasures of an idle, fruitless life' and go forth 'to suffer with the workers of the world'.[13] Tye may have hoped to relive some of the excitement vicariously through her daughter. From a more practical point of view, however, Emily Gilmore had died recently and Tye and Louisa Jebb thought that Eglantyne would be good company for James. The Gilmores did not have children of their own; it seemed natural that his unmarried niece might keep house for him for a while. And so began Eglantyne's teaching career.

In contrast to the popular image of the lonely village schoolmistress and Eglantyne's father's prediction of 1894 that the educated woman would end up 'a teacher at some sad seminary',[14] Eglantyne relished her newly acquired independence. To celebrate she took a trip to the Netherlands with her sister Lil, who had finished her agricultural studies at Newnham and was trying to set up a cooperative dairy at the Lyth. Lil toured the farms while Eglantyne looked in on the village schools. Through her contact with the university settlement movement at Oxford she had learned that what she called 'her work' was more than just a job, it was a brave new social experiment known as slumming. By taking on the challenge of living among and teaching poor children in a grammar school, Eglantyne joined a small army of highly educated charity workers, settlement workers and slum philanthropists whose goal was, by deed and example, to ameliorate the lives of the poor and thus provide a civilizing influence within the slum neighbourhoods. '[T]he slum explorers, reformers and journalists cast off their clothing and with it the constraints though not the privilege of their social status—to gain insight into the poor and themselves'.[15]

Although Eglantyne was not slumming, by the strictest definition of the term, she was conscious of the low social status of an 'impoverished' board schoolteacher, and to conform to it she adopted a life of voluntary self-denial that she assumed could be emulated by the poor.[16] This disappointed her uncle, who was looking forward to 'buying [her] some pretty clothes',[17] and frustrated Lil, who tried to persuade her to buy good dress fabric at '6/11' when Eglantyne found one that cost only '1/3'. Eglantyne placed an order with *Egerton and Burnett's* for what she called her 'universal costume' of '<u>brown</u> and <u>grey</u>,—colours most appropriate to my profession and lot in life'.[18] Her complete schoolmistress wardrobe included 'one winter dress of cheap fabric and a similar one for the summer, one hat, one pair of gloves and one blouse'.[19] She wanted to set an example of respectable femininity and the virtue of simplicity for her pupils, who would learn from her 'that the truest economy is to buy as good material as you can afford'.[20] However, Eglantyne noticed that her pupils saw through her disguise, they behaved differently with her than with the other teachers.

The next step was to find a suitable place to live. Eglantyne wanted to immerse herself in the culture of the people, rather than live with her uncle who was six miles away in Hallam. She got her mother's permission by stressing that it would only be temporary. This was another breach of class and gender boundaries, for single women of Eglantyne's class did not live in lodgings alone; their relations cared for them. This was also unusual for teachers in poor districts. Ellen Ross argues that they lived in 'nicer neighbourhoods' than slums.[21] Eglantyne found an inexpensive room at 57 High Street about 200 yards away from the school and endured 'the poky mustiness...sooty wallpaper, [photographs of] relations on the chimney, horsehair, and so on', but she found her landlady to be 'pleasant, neat and reasonable'.[22] When she announced that to prepare for domestic economy class she would get up in the middle of the night to practice cleaning the grates, she contravened several social rules. She thought she should do it when the 'housemaid was safely out of the way' in order to conceal her foolish ineptitude. She drew the line at cooking for herself, however, and the landlady sent a 'little maid servant' up with meals.[23] Eglantyne invited Charlotte Toynbee and Ruth Wordsworth to observe her set-up, and Uncle James made sure that she was introduced to the distinguished members of Marlborough society.

Eglantyne was not slumming to the extent that she was trying to deceive anyone, but she had made a conscious choice to dress simply and to support herself on her small salary. It should be stressed that slum work was not simply altruism, for the work brought young, socially conscious people together and enabled young women in particular to escape the monotony and surveillance of domestic life. Initially, Eglantyne was truly excited by the adventure. Feminists had failed to recruit many young women of her class to board school teaching; therefore it was regarded as an unconventional choice. During the first weeks of her first term, she spent many weekends in Cambridge with Richard and Caroline Jebb. She described these weekends as being 'back in civilization'. At the Jebbs' social gatherings she met Cambridge University intellectuals, writers and politicians like Leslie Stephens, R. B. Haldane and George

Trevelyan. To them she appeared to be a self-sacrificing young woman who was participating in an important social cause, but she did not fully accept this incongruous characterization of herself because she knew that the work was hard rather than heroic. Although she was proud to be a certificated woman teacher and thought that the low status of a woman teacher was unfair, she could never put aside her own class prejudice long enough to see her colleagues as her equals.

In Eglantyne's assessment the women in her profession had been raised in low social environments and this caused a clash between their characters, that is, their demeanour and behaviour, and their natural intelligence, which in the late nineteenth century was believed to be generally genetic. She hypothesized that 'the character of elementary teachers is usually at a very much lower level...than their brains'.[24] There were notable exceptions to her evolutionary theory, like Miss Arch, whom she described as 'a light slip of a girl, with a pleasant, honest and resolute face, sunburned and healthy looking...Neatly dressed and well mannered, her voice, when low, is almost free from accent'.[25] More startling had been one of her Stockwell teachers who did not conform at all to Eglantyne's 'idea of a board schoolteacher'.[26] Eglantyne could not get over how closely this teacher's tastes and talents resembled those of a cultivated woman: 'able and attractive...devoted to tennis, sailing, cycling: in her holidays, she appears to have travelled over a considerable portion of the globe'. Paradoxically, this teacher had treated Eglantyne like 'an amiable young fool...presenting me periodically with long lists of my faults'. When another teacher intervened because the harsh comments might hurt Eglantyne's feelings, she retorted that she 'would not modify her comments on that account—I might survive or not as I liked'.[27]

Eglantyne's head teacher at St Paul's in Marlborough was a Miss Pullen. Eglantyne greatly admired her superior teaching skills, even though she had 'rough edges...a tongue in her head' and she occasionally 'fled into a temper' and 'stormed' at the children.[28] Eglantyne noticed that her own class was always better behaved after a lesson with Miss Pullen. In the privacy of her diary, Eglantyne revealed how much she appreciated working with Miss Pullen. 'Our friendship progresses a pace every night we talk and dawdle in the evening sunshine, wandering and chattering...I do not know what makes the opening days of a friendship so delightful. Perhaps it is the joy of entering easily into the attitude of hitherto unmastered and unknown personality?'[29] However, no amount of reverse role-playing, empathy and real or imaginary camaraderie could reduce the social distance between Eglantyne and Miss Pullen. Behind her

back, Eglantyne gossiped and invented romantic scenarios about Miss
Pullen's humble background that would have rivalled the work of Char
lotte Bronte or Jane Austin. Ruth Wordsworth and Eglantyne 'wondered
whence came the influence on Miss Pullen's life that has lifted her so far
above the ruin'. She concluded that it was due either to the influence of a
minister named Mr Fergus or an old schoolmaster named Mr Newhook
'It makes one think how angels are sent to guard the innocent, when one
sees how good responds to good and counts the number of good people
who turn up at the right moment to shepherd the lambs of the world'.[30]
Eglantyne was never able to see how her fellow teachers and Stock
well instructors, even those with direct authority over her, could be her
equals. She did acknowledge their influence, however, and in a few
years would also enjoy wielding the narrow range of authority that was
available to women in the field of voluntary committee work when she
trained social workers for the Charity Organization Society.

After the school term began, Eglantyne settled into the routine and
rhythms of the school day. The opponents of gentlewoman school
mistresses in the 1870s had warned that 'our profession is…not one in
which a lady by birth or education could ever feel at home. The habit
and behaviour (especially in low neighbours and some rural districts)
would be a constant torture to her, and there is often even more to
bear from the parents than from the children'.[31] At the same time
great rewards were promised to those who persevered, as the following
anonymous poem that appeared in the *Times*, in 1873 illustrates

> I trust that at no distant day
> many a true gentlewoman may
> walk among her girls
> With praise and mild rebukes,
> Subduing e'en rude village churls
> By her angelic looks;
> Feeling not that she has lost caste,…but that she has chosen an
> honourable and interesting career.[32]

Unlike the Victorian lady child-savers, Eglantyne was not driven to this
work by a commitment to the doctrine of social motherhood. She had no
desire to provide maternal guidance or to extend loving arms and nurture
the children, so she was not personally 'affronted' by the habits and
behaviour of 'rude village churls', although they were an eye opener
for her. Moreover, she did not have any trouble with her pupils, whom
she viewed as steady simple-minded street girls, 'nine out of ten clean

and eight neat'.[33] As their teacher, her job was to criticize, cajole and correct them, but as with the Stockwell students, she could not help observing how grim their lives were and how philosophically they accepted sickness, poverty and even death.

Carolyn Steedman says that poor children have always looked 'wrong' to the middle-class observer: 'tired, dirty, old before their time, their faces showing only an absence of childhood'.[34] At first, Eglantyne was surprised by what she called their 'callousness' and astounding 'indifference to death', but later she began to understand and respect it. One little girl who was 'constitutionally delicate' told her 'with pride that the doctor says she is "a very bad case"'.[35] One morning as a little group of them walked across a street together, Ann Gregory announced calmly: 'Mother is very ill, loike to die'. Eglantyne did not know whether the 'two syllables of "like"' were due to the child's 'emotion or accent, but if to the former, she showed no other feeling at all, but smiled imperturbably'. She recorded this conversation in her diary and in a letter to Dorothy Kempe. 'I am not sure whether it is not a "callousness" I admire…Fanny Penny was telling me she was the youngest of 12 children, another chiming in said they were six, but had been seven but one had died. "None of us have died yet" chimed in a third'.[36]

Like many privileged people who worked among the poor, Eglantyne was mystified by the amount of affection that existed in the children's homes and this amplified the social distance between them.[37] She equated cleanliness with intelligence and moral decency and regarded the village mothers as sloppy, over-sexed and violent-tempered. One pupil's mother told her that every morning upon leaving for school her little daughter cried out, 'Now take care of yourself, Mother, don't let me find you ill when I come back'. Eglantyne was genuinely surprised and somewhat baffled by the child's devotion to the mother, whom Eglantyne described as 'a flighty woman brought up at a public house'. She suspected that the 'daughters seemed to keep their mothers in order'.[38]

Since Eglantyne had never been at school she did not understand schoolgirl culture any better than she had understood her fellow students in the 'gigantic beehive' dormitory at Stockwell. After a pupil named Beatrice Worth was punished for throwing a snowball at a Marlborough College boy, Eglantyne mimicked her 'little airs and graces' and her incessant questioning: '"Is it right"?'[39] Eglantyne's 'little maidservant' told her that she had left St Paul's two years earlier to mind the babies for her mother. She regretted leaving school and could see that her younger sister who stayed on longer would have 'greater advantages'. What she regretted the most was leaving her classmates. She told Eglantyne all about their pranks: '"Miss Crosby, Haraway and Cox's girl had been a four", they sometimes "copied"—Miss Pullen did not like it, but "they had to put up with that"...and they laughed when they were found out'.[40] In her diary she nicknamed one older girl who exasperated her 'Sunday-best' Tilda. Her landlady had engaged Tilda to do some house work, and one Sunday Eglantyne wrote a little description of her:

> ...[T]he variant Sunday-best Tilda, entertained me with such an exhib ition of instinctive conversational power, that once more I lamented that she was not born into the highest circles of society! I never before met a child who enquired so gracefully into your concerns and fluttered with such dexterity into such a variety of topics, and all with the self-possession and modesty of a well-trained girl of twenty. Pity Tilda's Sunday best appears so rarely, and that her week-day wear of character is that of a slum child: beautiful, slovenly, slow, inaccurate tom-boyish fascinating Tilda, the whole of her talent lies in the voc ation of a society luminary. She would enjoy herself madly, bring all the world to her feet, distinguish herself in the midst of it all by her generosity and kindness, be as easily entertained as she herself would entertain splendidly, would love and be loved to the end of her days—and Tilda will grow up a washerwoman—exercise a bane ful influence on sundry young men, make her home miserable by her untidiness, idleness, and want of concentration, and die an ugly ill-tempered, half-starved, old harridan.[41]

Through observing the realities of life for working-class women, Eglan tyne began to understand the position of girls and young women of her own social class better. As a child, she had written imaginative stories about a little girl who defied her governess and ran away into the forest with a boy named Jack; such narratives, Steedman argues, are literary experiments where little girls enact the roles they expect to play as adult women.[42] By 1900 Eglantyne had spent almost two years deeply immersed in the lives of working-class girls and lower-middle-class professional women and genuinely admired and respected their courage. She developed a great deal of sympathy for her pupils and the teachers whose lives were punctuated by the rhythms of the terms, low salaries and poor health; yet in her writing she constantly returned to the theme of her distance from them. After Eglantyne left teaching she became a social investigator for the Charity Organization Society and this 'female consciousness' informed the chapter she wrote in her study of Cambridge charities. She was speaking from the heart, in 1906, when she wrote

> It is one thing to be told that the girls in the poorer classes are exposed to temptations and dangers comparatively unknown to their more educated and more safeguarded sisters; it is quite another thing to know this truth in the sordid, pathetic, tragic details of the ruined lives of individuals…It is probably no exaggeration to say that…the majority of women and girls in the wealthier and better educated classes live in…a fool's paradise to one who has passed outside the barriers which usually confine them.[43]

Eglantyne was acutely aware of the narrow-mindedness of the privileged women of her own class and generation, she never lost it herself. She pointed out that the wealthy classes are 'blind' to the fact that working-class girls 'live in danger where we live in comparative security'.[44] In contrast to the unsupervised lives of labouring women was the surveillance of the privileged young women she called the 'Susie's of Life' of her own social class. Eglantyne noted that one thing all women had in common was trying to 'please her mother.' In a short essay that is part of her private Marlborough writing in 1899, Eglantyne condemned the rigid roles that girls of her own class were expected to play:

> There is one type of girl and only one, which generally speaking passes—everywhere like the British sovereign. This is not the case with men…There are a few elementary qualities which universal consent would judge essential…but beyond these, there are a number of possible ideals not mutually exclusive…We do not grumble at the men we meet today, because ones acquaintances of yesterday were darker or fairer, taller or shorter. But come to girls! Who does not know the girl, whom [sic] all girls must be? No one can help knowing her, because all self-respecting girls masquerade in her clothes. The girl is not necessarily pretty, but she is good looking. She is self-contained and well dressed, cheerful, amiable, loving, her sympathies are guided by *savoir faire*, and her manner of life by the wishes of her parents. This ideal with a few variations seems to have held good for many centuries, with some modifications to meet the particular demand of different classes and societies…Poor Susie trying to be grown up and to play the daughter at home and to practice the small arts and please her mother! I am indeed to think that we like many kinds of men, because there are many uses for them. For girls—lately there has been only one

use. The ideal domestic character has been made into the ideal for the whole female sex. The Susie's of Life, who should try their strength on stern methodological work, who should help to open up new countries [and] solve scientific problems…are condemned by hook or crook to turn themselves into dainty ornaments of the drawing room and they are judged by the success with which they accomplish this exercise in gymnastics.[45]

Was Eglantyne feeling the pressure to be grown up? Was she feeling guilty about not wanting to 'play the daughter at home' for her widowed mother? Was there talk of her finding a husband? These questions cannot be answered, but we can see that Eglantyne thought there was a genera-tion gap between the 'struggling beginners' of her generation and the self-educated 'women of the past' who were the pioneers of the battle for women's rights, her mentors at Oxford, her mother and her aunts. It was their vision of emancipation, duty and service that put the girls of Eglantyne's generation into the trenches, working in hospitals, schools and settlement houses. In her diary she wrote that older women, whom she called 'women of the past…say they envy us our education and the opportunities that have been denied to them'. She had no wish to 'dis-illusion' them, but she doubted that they fully understood the sacrifice, hard work and 'anxieties' of an 'independent life' and she pointed out the downside, the difficulties, the shocks and struggles of a professional life.

Envy our arduous work a day hammering at books? Well, let it be, we are glad of any error which makes her feel a faint degree of respect for us—the fallen angels. The woman of the past…is permeated to her fingers tips with the highest and best culture of the world…Thus, when straight from this undeniably hot and dusty world we come into the giant presence of one of these women of the past, we under-stand how men in olden days regarded women as superior and almost angelic beings…[W]e cannot help contrasting our own nervous, eager, excitable habit of minds with their consistent, impenetrable repose. We might, we think have grown into such women, if we had lived as they, in a sort of cultured seclusion, surveying a rather picturesque world from a comfortable window seat. But now alas, it is no longer possible!…We the struggling beginners, trying to adapt our inherited natures to an altered order.[46]

At this point it would be tempting to argue that Eglantyne's girlhood delight in rehabilitating broken dolls, the primordial smell of Irish poverty, dancing with the factory girls at the Bethnal Green settlement, her discoveries at Stockwell, her infatuation with her work among poor children in Marlborough would eventually culminate in the founding of the Save the Children Fund and becoming a great humanitarian, but this would be too easy. The opponents of the gentlewoman schoolmistress who warned that 'a lady could never feel at home' in a grammar school were partly correct. Eglantyne did have difficulty coming to terms with her contradictory attitudes towards her pupils, her profession and her personal goals. Despite her best efforts to sharpen her pupils' intellect, she doubted that any had any real academic gifts. The exceptions were Madge Taylor, with her 'phenomenal' notebook and 'beautiful writing [and] no trespassing ink', and Alice Williamson, whose writing book evolved from 'a dreadful confusion of bad writing and blots' to the best in the class. Eglantyne took this as a hopeful sign of her teaching virtuosity and that Lydia Manley had been wrong about her.[47]

As a young girl, Eglantyne had been a loner. Her girlhood diary shows that she had preferred reading and daydreaming to the bustle of activity of their aunt's workshop. Though she had the friends she wanted at Oxford, she was never part of an active social circle. One of her greatest discoveries at Lady Margaret Hall had been her own room. Eglantyne did not turn her Marlborough flat into a settlement house at the end of the school day and do social work among her pupil's families or in the neighbourhood the way slum teacher Clara Ellen Grant did.[48] After school was out Eglantyne considered herself at liberty to enjoy the pleasures of solitude, but because of her uncle's social position in the town, she was invited to many social engagements when she would rather sit alone in her rooms at 57 High Street. 'For some years I have been wishing to be alone', she wrote, 'I have obtained my wish and the pleasure surpasses all expectation, and I have resorted to doing nothing in order to make the time pass more slowly...I sit over my fire, listening to the rain and the ticking of the clock and the silence'.[49] A month later, she declared, 'the delight of living by oneself grows and increases. Solitary walks, silent meals...[M]y landlady here is so satisfactory and just my cut—manually efficient and with a limited vocabulary'.[50] Unfortunately, her solitude seemed to be disrupted 'at tea-time' when the 'friendly inhabitants of Marlborough' dropped by to invite her to a lecture. Eglantyne made up excuses in order to stay home and 'the instant they are gone...quick! My short skirt and stout stick—and I wander out to cut across the downs to keep my engagement with the setting sun'.[51] Eglantyne wanted to use her spare time to read up on Wiltshire history and archaeology, to cycle for miles in the countryside and attempt to write another novel, but over the months more and more diary entries revealed a distressing secret that she had not yet managed to speak aloud: despite every effort to the contrary, Eglantyne deeply detested hands-on social work, and she deeply detested teaching, which she compared to the tread-wheel, blacking shoes and breaking stones.

For Eglantyne, elementary school teaching was toil. It had taken her over a month to get accustomed to standing all day. After a year she still complained about 'talking even though your throat is sore, standing even though your back aches, and working extra hours if a headache makes you work slowly'.[52] Before the first term began, she had toured the school and found that the buildings were clean and well ventilated, but later she discovered that because of underfunding, the staff had to economize on chalk, needles, coal in the winter, books and maps, though not upon the teacher's time. She spent most of March drawing 'a large map of England…to save the school board 10.6d', and on the coldest days the children had to clap their hands and stomp their feet to prevent from freezing, and so did she. Eglantyne wished that 'the Managers would come by to find us jumping and banging in a deafening tumult in order to stave off instant death'.[53]

After her initial excitement at the chance to teach school and her social experiment subsided, she discovered that there was nothing romantic about this life: '[I]n my childhood, I prayed fervently to be a writer, I will be satisfied now with time to write'. One particularly stormy week began (on Sunday) with: '[T]he prospect of returning to my work tomorrow makes me feel physically ill, my body and heart ache in concert. If I were only going to the dentist tomorrow—but to stand, mutilating scripture to the detriment of inattentive children, I could shed tears over the prospect'. On Wednesday she wrote, 'I can now recollect nothing of the day which is worth recollecting…A day lost. How is this? Was there nothing I might have seen or learnt? What of my work? Nil; the children have learnt nothing either. And so it goes: day after day into vacuum'. The next day was not any better: 'Another day has dropped into silence. I have done 10 hours work today and accomplished nothing. Looking back, I cannot remember anything about it, except the faces of the children'. The next week began with more gloomy thoughts. Sunday night she deliberated, 'Could I have believed that I should have worked over 6 months and still be afraid—yes, literally afraid of my work—afraid. Heaven help me—even now—to master this fear'.[54] Two months later she summed up:

> The causes of my unhappiness were as follows—my hatred of my profession, that fact that it seems to absorb my whole life, leaving

little except its hated self, and my conviction that it did not give me anything back for all it took, and did not, either benefit anyone else. I would give, say ¾ of my life to breaking stones, were I quite convinced that other people were really made happier by it, but to give 9/10 to a work one hates worse then breaking stones and for no good at all that seems cruel, one realizes what a punishment is the treadmill. [55]

Eglantyne believed that the true source of her misery was not the job of teaching itself, but her own inability to do it well: 'I hated it, because I could not do it. I have none of the natural qualities of a teacher. I don't care for children and I don't care for teaching'.[56]

Francesca Wilson was a teacher in the early 1900s. She wrote, '[O]nly those who have faced...a class of unruly children know the depth of shame it is possible to suffer. It is something the victim does not discuss...She does not blame the circumstances, the children, the headmistress, the school; she blames herself...before a class her desire for flight is almost overwhelming'.[57] Wilson described what many teachers feel at some point in their careers. Eglantyne's inexperience before she entered Stockwell, compounded by her lack of peer support may have contributed to her lack of confidence in the classroom; so she convinced herself that she had none of the natural qualities of a teacher. This was not unusual. Steedman's work on teachers' autobiographical writing describes the difficulty some teachers have identifying with working-class children, 'so very unlike themselves and those children they might possibly have one day themselves'.[58] However, Eglantyne would have agreed with Seth Koven's proclamation that dirt 'could not diminish [the] innate goodness' of all of the children.[59] In her first year she said, 'I began to understand a little more the charm of childhood, its freshness, sweetness and happiness'.[60]

Eglantyne was truly enchanted by the bold and defiant little pupils like Fanny and Ann, who one November day, executed a defiant 'war dance in the middle of the High Street' because a big white dog was frightening them. 'Ann Gregory, at the other side, got up an impromptu jig, and floundered about to the bobbing of Fanny's red tam o-shanter'. Fanny confessed 'afterwards she was afraid of him'. Eglantyne always admired courage in others and applauded it warmly. And the little girls returned her affection. On the day of the dog fight, as soon as they noticed her watching them, Ann and Fanny 'came tumbling across the street and beamed up in my face all the way home, and I carried a ray of sunshine into my dark little room'.[61]

In spite of herself and her resolution not to care for the children; as Eglantyne got to know her pupils better she developed a great affection for them. For example, Alice Williamson, whom Eglantyne admitted was 'the first child for whom I have cared two pence', but it was not because of her neat scribbler, there was something more. 'Alice W. has for some time attracted me, in a way no other child ever has.' She described the beginning of their 'friendship' like this: 'I do not like Miss Pullen any the less because she has a tongue in her head, but just occasionally she fled into a temper, which makes me feel a little bit queer'. One day in the classroom, shortly after Eglantyne arrived, Miss Pullen 'suddenly began to storm at a child' during a sewing lesson. 'I was sitting down with Alice standing beside me, showing her something. My heart seemed to beat a little more slowly, but I was not aware of having even changed colour'. Eight-year-old Alice must have been watching Eglantyne closely and seen that despite her cheap brown dress and unfamiliar accent and manners, Miss Jebb was a thing apart, a superior, a lady. When Miss Pullen began shouting irately at one pupil, Eglantyne 'looked up' and was quite startled to see Alice's flushed bright pink cheeks. 'I met her big blue eyes full, they were fixed upon me...It flashed across me that somehow or other the little child had seen what I felt.' Poor Alice was ashamed of Miss Pullen's coarse behaviour and by extension her own rough mother and her future self. Alice was aware that their harsh language and rough manners were an affront to a person of quality like 'Miss Jebb'; no number of tidy note-books could conceal the inevitable. Eglantyne was ashamed too, but for different reasons. She knew that her St Peter's girls would grow up to become 'rough girls' of the washerwomen class like their downtrodden mothers.[62] Eglantyne lacked the tools as a teacher and a woman to save them. 'I wonder' she asked her diary, 'whether it will be possible for Alice not to deteriorate. I would rather she died'.[63]

Eglantyne began to worry about the moral well being of the other pupils too, and at the end of term discovered that she was 'sorry to lose most of my old girls—even the difficult Tilda', who quickly exchanged her school smock for a servant's uniform. Eglantyne did not write anything explicit about the sexual vulnerability of her pupils, but to many women of the elite classes, cleanliness was linked to sexual purity and explicit in her descriptions of their slovenly demeanour and dirty clothes. One evening she noticed two young girls wandering on the road ahead of her, they turned out to be Tilda and her friend Florence Tarent, a younger 'girl of tow-colour locks, an absolute absence of principle and a bliss to thieving, unredeemed by any conspicuous traits of character. The two glided along together in their trampled-down shoes and ragged clothes…looking like two young birds of prey, their dark plumage ruffled after combat'.[64] Shortly after the next term began, she bumped into Florence again and they walked to school together. Florence having had her 'last fling in the delights of the wicked world', surprised Eglantyne. She looked 'reformed' in her white starch apron and said she was ready to do her lessons. Eglantyne realized that she had underestimated her. Florence was eager for Miss Jebb to teach her something and Eglantyne learned a great deal from Florence and the others in return. She described the contradictions of a teacher's role perfectly when she wrote:

> I seem to scold them all day long in school, it doesn't seem to do any good, neither [does it] make any difference to their affection. When I open my door in the morning…I am greeted by the howls and shrieks of a little company who fall upon me with inarticulate sounds resembling those of pigs when they see their food coming. Does it make a strange far-down feeling between us now, that I dislike school more than they?[65]

Although Eglantyne detested teaching, she remained convinced that it was her life's work until her career ended abruptly because her mother insisted that she quit. Eglantyne never told Tye about her struggles at Stockwell or St Peter's, nevertheless, Tye suddenly called a halt to her career and even offered to pay for a substitute teacher to replace her.[66] What had happened? Tye had initially supported Eglantyne's 'work', but perhaps later she began to worry that it had gone too far. As passionate as Tye had been about her Home Arts and Industries work, she had never let it take over her life completely. Tye knew that Ruth Wordsworth doubted Eglantyne's suitability for teaching[67] and so did Dorothy Kempe. Ruth said that when Eglantyne 'chose to behave and dress as such' she could be 'a dazzlingly lovely woman'.[68] Her comment implies that Eglantyne was misbehaving by not allowing Uncle James to parade her amongst the Marlborough locals and he may have supported this assessment. He may even have heard gossip from the Marlborough locals who had seen the strange new schoolmistress tramping around alone in the moonlight. This would have been considered abnormal behaviour for any respectable young lady, but even more reprehensible for the schoolmistress, whose moral standards were expected to be beyond question. Tye insisted that a doctor examine Eglantyne, he confirmed that her health (health also meant mental health at the turn of the century)[69] was at risk and he predicted that she might break down completely.

It has been said that 'being a woman and being a teacher' means understanding oneself in relation to the historical and biographical intersection of contemporary ideas surrounding professional responsibilities and cultural expectations about women's duties toward their families, to public life and to themselves.[70] This chapter has shown that while Eglantyne was conscious of the conventions and restriction imposed upon women of her background, she regarded herself as a modern young woman who could bend the rules in order to do meaningful social work among the poor. However, in 1900 mothers had a great deal of authority over their daughters. Tye had been a widow for six years, Dorothy was about to enter Newnham College; not wanting to be alone at the Lyth, Tye decided to move to Cambridge to be closer to her brother Richard. She desired a companion and selected Eglantyne to fill the dreaded role of daughter-at-home. Eglantyne abruptly realized that she had overlooked one important part of her social experiment—'the idea that it didn't make any difference to me what people thought or said.' She told Kempe, 'I can only blame myself'. By the time she realized that her mother was serious about her quitting her work she 'was too much overcome by surprise and vexation to combat the idea…I did not understand how I could ever have allowed it to happen…I ought to have been able to find a way—stuck to my work somehow. Not that I was getting to care for it any more, (indeed it was getting worse)…I have not only been beaten in the battle—I have been found sleeping at my post'.[71] Eglantyne protested and insisted she was in fine health, but she knew that she had little choice. The young woman who had written so defiantly about the 'Susie's of Life' was wanted at home.

6
Matchmaking Matrons and the Misread Maidens of the Cambridge Charity Organization Society

Less than two years after leaving her teaching post in Marlborough, Eglantyne announced that she had 'set up a new amusement', that 'sandwiched' between 'tea parties, calls and at homes', she had begun going as a 'visitor' to Cambridge Charity Organization Society meetings.[1] The Charity Organization Society (COS) had been founded in 1869 by two philanthropic reformers, Charles Bosanquet and Charles Steward Loch, who believed that the undeserving poor and professional beggars had no reason to commit themselves to an honest day's work when they could survive suitably well on hand-outs. The COS took upon itself the responsibility of combining and co-ordinating the efforts of old Victorian charities with the new state provisions under the Poor Law by making sure that the services did not duplicate each other. Its other goal was to reduce the widespread abuse of philanthropic agencies, which Organizationists believed occurred when the wily and cunning poor hoodwinked local charities.[2] In 1902, Eglantyne was not interested in catching paupers; she was interested in studying the people who studied poverty. The COS meetings entertained her. 'The people who are on the committee amuse me—and the cases amuse me still more'.[3] Like a *Punch* satirist ridiculing the upper-class response to the plight of paupers,[4] Eglantyne mocked the diamonds on the 'very white fingers' of the honorary secretary's hands. 'Case after case read, case after case ticked off, a jotting in the account book, an entry in the journal, then the flare of the gay light in the dark ugly room, the earnest faces coming out of the shadows, stories of drunkenness, debt, disease: one goes on then to the next tea party'.[5]

This chapter shows that while Eglantyne's previous participation in settlement work, her university education, college training and time spent among the poor in Marlborough had expanded her 'moral imagination',[6]

SCOTT &
WILKINSON
CAMBRIDGE

6.1   Eglantyne at Charity Organization Society, source: Jebb Family

she re-entered social work cautiously and for personal reasons. With the support of a number of Cambridge COS women, Eglantyne returned to public work, not as a hands-on social worker, but as a social investigator. At the COS she deepened her commitment to an ethos of professionalism in women's social work and assembled a group of volunteers, charity organizers and teachers to work on her *Cambridge Survey* of poverty. By 1907, Eglantyne was becoming a prominent social investigator, committee administrator and regarded as a mentor to a new generation of lady volunteers.

After Arthur Jebb died, Eglantyne's mother said she would stay on at 'the Lyth and make a home for the children…When the boys [were] at college and the girls at Newnham or in London pursuing their studies of different kinds, she would travel or visit friends'.[7] Her eldest son

Richard married Ethel Lewthwaite in September 1900 and the couple spent the remainder of the year travelling. Richard had inherited the Lyth from his father and planned to take it over when they returned. There is no hint of animosity between Tye, her son or this new wife, but a month after the wedding Tye leased a house in Cambridge. Dorothy went away to boarding school at Bournemouth in order to prepare for Newnham and by December Tye was pressuring Eglantyne to give up teaching and live with her in Cambridge.[8]

Tye chose Cambridge to be closer to her brother Sir Richard Jebb and his American wife, Lady Caroline Jebb. Caroline Slemmer (née Reynolds) was the daughter of an English clergyman who had immigrated to the United States in the 1820s.[9] In 1870, 'Carrie' was the widow of a Civil War lieutenant. After travelling in France and Switzerland she settled down for an extended stay with her cousin in Cambridge. At the time the 30-year-old widow was described as possessing a 'Titianesque beauty'.[10] After her arrival in Cambridge, it was said that 'every marriageable man proposed to her; three in one day, including the Vice-Chancellor'. When someone asked if it was true that three proposals made were in the same room, she replied coyly, 'Oh no, that is absurd; two were in the garden.'[11]

In 1870, one of the most eligible bachelors in Cambridge was 29-year-old Richard Claverhouse Jebb, fellow of Trinity. He confessed that he fell in love with Carrie the instant he saw her. For her part, she had 'disliked him from the first'.[12] It took Jebb three years to persuade her to marry him. The wedding took place at the Lyth on 18 August 1874. Lady Jebb had been hesitant about marrying a Cambridge professor, but once she had made the commitment, she devoted herself wholly to her husband and his career. She told her sister in the United States: 'We get on very well together, chiefly I must say, because I have so little sensitive *amour prefere*. But then, he has enough for both, and more would overwhelm the family'.[13] Caroline took over her husband's finances and imposed limits on his drinking to get him out of debt and in so doing 'cured him of both faults'.[14] She also learned to give formal dinner parties and to seat the guests in accordance with university protocol: 'the Heads of Houses ranked by the dates of the foundation of their colleges'.[15]

Tye and Arthur had doubts about the match between the dazzling socialite and the shy scholar until Arthur attended one of the couple's first dinner parties. Among the guests were the scholars Henry Sedgwick, Henry and Helen Fawcett and Hallam Tennyson. Arthur reported back to Tye that Carrie instantly won him over with her charm, grace and beauty. 'We were just 12 at dinner...Carrie came well into the front under the stimulus of a male audience...everyone seemed *bien content*...My

American sister walked straight into my affections. She called me *Arthur* in a gentle purring murmur and took pains to introduce me'.[16] Five years later Arthur still considered Carrie to be a 'perfect hostess... [S]he is a woman of whom any man might be proud—tender and true—and her Americanism, so far from being a blemish, is as refreshing as a sea breeze'.[17] Tye, however, remained jealously unconvinced of her beloved brother's happiness and was relieved when he told her 'how lonely he & Carrie often felt—and how much he looked forward to the companionship of my children'. She wrote in her dairy, 'we assured each other of how we should all always cling together all the days of our life'.[18]

The decision to remain strictly within the family circle or socially isolated had direct effects on the lives of girls and unmarried daughters.[19] In Shropshire and Marlborough Eglantyne had lived quietly and had never really been in society. Once in Cambridge, Tye was counting upon her sister-in-law, who was at the centre of university social and cultural life, to introduce Eglantyne to the right people. Lady Jebb took on Eglantyne as her new protégé and introduced her to Cambridge society. Eglantyne was very grateful to her aunt who did 'so much...which nobody but herself would think of'.[20] In 1901, she was 25 years old and regarded by many people as 'extraordinarily beautiful'. The honorary secretary of the COS, Florence Keynes, recalled her 'red gold hair...and a white rose complexion'. Her name '"Eglantyne" suited her so well'.[21] Ruth Wordsworth described her as the

> very ideal of the Burne-Jones beauty and...a Rossetti model too... with more animation and variety of mood...with a queer mixture of extreme shyness and dignified poise...also at that time sometimes 'ruthless'...even to her friends, and rather cruelly snubbing to young men suffering from conceit, though she was exquisitely gracious to the unhappy or awkward, and could be as witty among the courtly dons of Oxford as any famous dame down the centuries.[22]

Dorothy Jebb said that her sister's 'brilliance and charm...soon made her a most popular member of University society'.[23]

Eglantyne welcomed the attention because she had arrived in Cambridge feeling glum. Her commitment to public work had gone beyond that of most young women of her class and generation, and she felt bitter towards dubious do-gooders and Lady Bountifuls who blindly devoted their lives to clearing up social problems they did not fully understand. Eglantyne no longer believed that she had anything to offer 'the horrid, dusty, noisy, pitiable world of human affairs—ugh'! Rather than become an advocate for the poor, Eglantyne resolved to 'do nothing at all'. She travelled in Wales with Lil and spent two months in Germany with her sister Dorothy and uncle, Heneage Jebb. She visited Mrs Toynbee and kept insisting that she would never again 'get near' social work or 'touch it...How it jangles and creaks, and grinds one up! How glad I am no longer to be involved in the vain attempt to help in the machinery of society!'.[24]

To fill her days, Eglantyne enrolled in a course on biblical scholarship and attended lectures at the college. In doing so, she met an exciting youthful generation of college dons who impressed her with the importance of their research. At a Trinity College at-home, one scholar spoke to her of his work in New Guinea and Uganda, another lectured her on the 'savage' Papuans and another 'drew aside' a 'bit of the veil from off the Great Lakes'.[25] Eglantyne enjoyed the attention: '[S]uddenly in those bare rooms crowded with people, the world seemed to sweep back upon my gaze...You know the feeling, when you have long been cold and somebody rubs you warm...It seems odd that when you have failed yourself you should yet take such delight in...people who have done things and succeeded'.[26] Everyone was pleased except the puritanical Dorothy Jebb, who said that under Lady Jebb's tutelage her sister had become caught up in the whirl of Cambridge society and was behaving like a 'flighty young woman'.[27]

Eglantyne's life soon consisted of more than at-homes and riding parties. Lady Jebb was prominent among the other faculty wives who were working for a number of local charities. The 'COS model of charity cum social work'[28] had caught on, and by 1893 there were 25 COS offices around the United Kingdom. From the beginning the university was involved in COS work. In 1880, Henry Sidgwick, Professor of Moral and Political Philosophy and Fellow of Trinity College, took up the cause for Cambridge.[29] College representatives and their wives and adult daughters sat on most sub-committees, reviewed decisions in co-operation with the Poor Law Guardians, acted as trustees for the ratepayers, approved subscriptions and provided grants and loans for temporary relief.[30] The COS ideal was to make charity precise, rational and scientific by creating a central umbrella agency which would organize and co-ordinate all governmental and voluntary resources available in a region. It required that all applicants for aid apply through its local offices. COS social workers, both paid workers and volunteers, were carefully trained to investigate applicants, or 'cases', and to verify the legitimacy of each claim to ensure that they were not 'double- or even triple-dipping in the welfare coffers'.[31]

In the 1920s Eglantyne would adapt this model to international relief work in the Save the Children Fund.

Lady Jebb gave the COS and other worthy causes a great deal of her money and time. As such, she was one of the women whom Lynn Hollen Lees calls the 'foot soldiers' in all forms of charity work.[32] In the early twentieth century, philanthropy and unpaid social work were still regarded as a form of serious work for middle- and upper-class women, and due to the removal of restrictions under local government acts, women were standing for municipal elections and working more closely than before within local government agencies like school boards and poor law guardians. Like their Victorian predecessors, Edwardian women were attracted to charity work for a number of reasons. A strong religious impulse to help the poor motivated some women; whereas others were motivated by an interest in politics and social questions. Also, there were those who felt the need to escape the confinements of domesticity or life at home. They were joined by a new group of 'slum travellers', identified by Ellen Ross as well-trained paid professionals such as nurses, social workers, teachers and elected school board members. There were also a few 'artists, journalists and social investigators' who 'tramped through the streets and alleys, chronicling poverty'.[33]

In 1901 Lady Jebb put Eglantyne to work for her most pressing concern, the Women's Memorial Fund for Queen Victoria, which the Ladies' Discussion Society had organized to raise money to build a monument to the late Queen in Cambridge. The Memorial Fund put Lady Jebb in touch with a group of university women who were not part of her COS group and she said 'it was a very great pleasure to meet in business and work with ladies I have before only met occasionally in calling and dining. Another side of character came out in them and me...To me it was interesting to find energy and method in those who before had seemed insignificant'.[34] Eglantyne soon discovered that she also enjoyed visiting professors' wives in their homes. She joked that she and Lady Jebb looked 'like a Bishop and his secretary' as she, laden with papers, trudged along from house to house behind her aunt. Their 'victims', she said, were the wives of the Trinity fellows, who understood that it would be imprudent to turn away such an important woman as Lady Jebb. Eglantyne was intrigued with the way her aunt 'laid the case before the different "mistresses" of the colleges and persuaded them to collect. Cambridge is an old-fashioned place—so many said they must first ask their husbands—their husbands graciously gave permission'.[35] By watching Lady Jebb, Eglantyne observed the important roles which prominent women played in raising money for charitable causes. She also observed that women in different walks of life brought different skills and abilities to philanthropy. She remembered this lesson years later when she set up the Save the Children Fund.

The COS was not Lady Jebb's only good cause. In 1886, Lady Darwin and 'a good many ladies' who were 'anxious to solve some of the social problems of the day' formed the Cambridge Ladies Discussion Society (CLDS). Its aim was 'to leave things a little better than they found them'.[36] Lady Jebb was in charge of nominating new members and she proposed Eglantyne and her mother. The CLDS raised money for many COS projects like the Convalescent Home for Surgical Cases; it administered a fund for feeble-minded girls[37] and started the University Settlement House.[38] The CLDS was largely made up of mothers, daughters and matrons of the Cambridge elite, whose method of self-education was to invite experts to Girton College to read papers on any branch of work or social problem they wished to understand a little better.[39] Over the years the ladies hosted impressive speakers like Margaret Llewelyn Davis, Millicent Fawcett and Beatrice and Sydney Webb. In 1897, 'the stage as a career for women' was rejected as 'not a very appropriate subject'.[40] In 1906 they asked Tye to provide a detailed account of the origins of the Home Arts and Industries Association, which had just celebrated its twenty-first anniversary.[41] Even though Eglantyne had resolved to keep away from 'human affairs', contact with these women brought her back in touch with the important issues of the day, and by 1904 her name appears on numerous CLDS and COS organizing committees.

Edwardian philanthropy was one way in which wives and daughters of the upper classes promoted themselves and was a respectable way for well-bred young ladies to meet and make connections with eligible young men. As the daughter of a Shropshire landowner and niece of a famous professor, 25-year-old Eglantyne was the perfect age for marriage and would have seemed like a suitable match for a young gentleman. It was Tye's responsibility to put her daughter forward and she may have been hoping that her sister-in-law's society connections would serve this purpose. Lady Jebb had orchestrated matches between many girls from good families and Cambridge dons, including her American niece, Maude DuPay and Charles Darwin's son George Darwin. Their daughter, Gwen Darwin described Lady Jebb's matchmaking side with gentle humour in her autobiography *Period Piece* (1952), but said privately that Jebb reminded her of 'Chaucer's Wife of Bath'. Gwen and her cousin Nora Darwin shared a 'horror of Lady Jebb'. Gwen said:

> I think she was sensually quite cold—she said to me once 'Of course <u>men</u> are so much for all that sort of thing, but <u>I</u> think it such a bore.' What she cared for was attention, admiration, flattery and

power (the power of arranging 'matches')...When you have been a professional beauty all your life, it seems the most important thing in life; and you can't live without the interest and power of your fascination over men....[42]

It appeared that Lady Jebb had hopes for Eglantyne and Marcus Southwell Dimsdale, a 41-year-old Cambridge don, whom she first introduced to Eglantyne in 1898. In Eglantyne's letters to her mother she mentioned cycling with Mr Dimsdale. Thirteen year-old Gwen Darwin was one of their chaperons and remembered stopping to gather wild flowers for Eglantyne to take back to Lady Margaret Hall.[43] His name appeared in a letter to Dorothy Kempe a few years later. They had been riding together and Eglantyne said, 'Mr. Dimsdale...is always a trump card, from his knowledge of hedges, gaps in hedges, distances, nature of soil, ditches, flowers, views, history and last, but not least, horses, his own being matchless and a delight to look upon'.[44] This time their chaperon was Goldsworthy Lowes Dickenson. Eglantyne was happy that no other women showed up to ride that day. She 'prefer[red] the masculine contingent' because women tired too quickly and she could 'never feel absolutely certain that they wont tumble off and hurt themselves, and, (worst of all) they are apt, at half-past three when we are six or seven miles from home, to discover suddenly that they must be back by four'.[45]

Francesca Wilson learned about Dimsdale while researching *Rebel Daughter,* though she did not reveal his identity in her book. She was told by Eglantyne Mary Jebb and Eglantyne Buxton that Eglantyne was 'in love' with him and that waiting for 'the young man' to declare himself added to the thrill of the parties and picnics. 'It was a slow-ripening friendship', and no one knew about it except her sister Dorothy because in those days 'well-bred women...hid these things in their hearts'.[46] Lady Jebb said marriage proposals and cast-off lovers were topics ladies never bragged about. In her own case, she found that 'it only makes those old maids hate me and try to detract from me, and offers are the last things to boast about...To make people envy you is far on the road to making them hate you'.[47] Margaret Keynes said that Eglantyne received many proposals in her Cambridge period, but was so 'unselfconscious' that they came as a 'disturbing surprise' because she 'hated to hurt'.[48] There is nothing in Eglantyne's private papers to suggest that Dimsdale was in love with Eglantyne or that he knew of the depth of her feelings toward him. Nevertheless, Dorothy told her daughter that Eglantyne 'suffered' deeply when the engagement of Dimsdale to Elisabeth Philips was announced.[49]

The sexual politics of proposals and disappointments in the late-Victorian and early-Edwardian eras weighed heavily in the biographies of numerous spinsters and maiden aunts, who by the end of the nineteenth century were also called 'redundant' women.[50] Dorothy Buxton told her daughter all the details of Eglantyne's 'disappointment'. She explained that 'there was the old-fashioned idea that there was one person destined for you—and that it was morally right to give yourself up in love to that one person...To turn to other men would have implied that her love had not been genuine'.[51] In Eglantyne's semi-autobiographical novel, 'The Ring Fence', after Angela is jilted by her lover, she concludes 'that having loved once, she could never love again'. Eglantyne wrote that Angela 'had a picture [of herself] in her mind [as] the beautiful girl, secretly heartbroken, making everybody happy around her, inconsolable, yet winning universal gratitude and admiration'.[52]

Dorothy Buxton also told her daughter that Eglantyne was so distraught by Dimsdale's marriage, that once, after meeting the couple 'she rushed out of the house in the direction of Madingley, [her] mind obsessed with a picture of the ditch; as she rushed along an inner voice kept telling her that if she went that way she would never come back'.[53] Dorothy said the only thing that prevented Eglantyne from 'drowning herself was the recollection that it was Mrs Alfred Marshall's at-home day'.[54] This romantic narrative sounds exaggerated, but it also appears in 'The Ring Fence', which suggests either that it was true, or that Dorothy read it there, and imagined it to be drawn from Eglantyne's own experience. In the novel, Eglantyne writes that when Angela discovered that her lover Hugh had married Freda, a former settlement worker: 'She fell to sobbing—frightful, delirious sobbing with few tears. It was as well that the shock to her physical system thus convulsed her, for it blurred for the moment her faculties...A frantic wish came over her to find some precipice down which to fling herself,—for to face the future seemed beyond possibility. Shattered as she was, however, she was incapable of retaining the same thought for two minutes together or of acting on any one of her disordered impulses'.[55]

The 'cultural link' forged in the late nineteenth century between 'disappointment' and social work achieved the 'status of conventional wisdom in the decades ahead.'[56] Olive Schreiner and Beatrice Potter are cited as examples of women who were drawn into slum work so as to heal their broken hearts. Unquestionably, the sex lives of slum workers, social reformers and youth workers were commented upon, and scandals regarding 'queer men' and 'odd women' were common.[57] For her

part, Eglantyne made no secret of the fact that she returned to the
world of 'human affairs' in order to fill a 'missing link' in her life.[58]
Despite her reservations, over the next five years, she became more
involved with the COS committees than she ever thought she would,
but her work took her on a different path than previously. She did not
want to do hands-on social work directly with poor children, in schools
or in settlement houses, but followed a pattern of public work set by
Beatrice Webb, who disliked house-to-house visits, finding the 'smell,
dirt and brutality' of slum life unbearable.[59]

Shortly after arriving in Cambridge, Eglantyne began attending
lectures on political economy by Mary Marshall, whom she regarded as
'a very undoubtedly sane and sage middle-aged woman'.[60] Mary Paley
Marshall had been one of the first five women at Girton College in
1874, where she received good results in the Moral Sciences Tripos and
had become a resident lecturer.[61] Impressed with Eglantyne's essays,
qualifications and experience, Marshal had been pressing her to take
up more serious philanthropic work. One afternoon after tea with
Marshall, Eglantyne broached the subject of doing some work for the
COS; however she confessed that she still felt like a failure after the
Marlborough experience. '[H]aving always failed in what I attempted
I had come to the conclusion I would do nothing'. 'Never mind!'
Marshall replied 'in a very sympathetic voice...That does happen to
people:—you mayn't be any worse!!' To encourage her, Marshall told
Eglantyne she had gathered from her essays that she could write and
'thought that this might be turned to account'. When Eglantyne
protested that she could not add sums, Marshall countered, 'Adam
Smith could not count and yet he made an epoch. You must make an
epoch too'.[62] In this way, Eglantyne was persuaded to see Florence
Keynes, the honorary secretary of the COS about some work with the
Society.[63]

Keynes was impressed with Eglantyne's credentials and appointed
her to the Social Bureau.[64] In the early 1900s, Cambridge was in the
midst of an industrial slump which was causing a great deal of poverty
and unemployment. The COS was inundated with applications for
relief and needed someone to do a comprehensive study of the social
and industrial conditions of the city and evaluate what could be done
by local charities. Eglantyne agreed to conduct the survey, which they
wanted 'done immediately', so she 'cut her summer holiday short and
got down to work'.[65] Since she never undertook a challenge until she
felt properly trained, she accordingly prepared herself for her new
career as social investigator by studying political, social and economic

subjects. It was a rocky road from grammar schoolteacher to amateur sociologist, but Eglantyne approached it as an intellectual challenge. Nonetheless, she found that economics 'was dull as last week's bread' and the 'international exchange' was even worse. Inwardly, she was 'smiling all over at the idea' and she told Kempe, 'of course it means... beginning the fight over again'. It is unclear whether she meant that she was fighting her own 'self-doubt' or social inequality in Cambridge, but she was happy about a new beginning, 'a lot more preparatory work and another doubtful issue...but there!!'[66] As a social investigator she was able to study and write about the conditions which produced poverty without interacting directly with the poor.

By working 'ten and eleven hours a day', Eglantyne assembled a team of over a dozen experienced women social workers, charity organizers and a few clergymen and set up meetings with representatives of local and national charities and social welfare organizations, the opinion of the poor does not appear to have been invited. Nor did they realize the magnitude of the project until a London social worker told them that a 'digest' of charities was a good preliminary step, but it 'is very laborious and could not be done in under several years'!!! Eglantyne's sub-committee had 'pledged' to complete theirs by the end of November'.[67]

Eglantyne wrote a few original contextual chapters, co-ordinated the statistical and factual information provided by volunteers and added the final editorial polish so that it would meet the high standards which Marshall and Keynes set for COS publications. In late 1904 she produced *Cambridge: A Brief Study in Social Questions* followed by a smaller abridged pamphlet called *Cambridge Register of Educational, Economic, Philanthropic, and other Agencies for Promoting Self-Help and Mutual Help in the Town and Neighbourhood.* Eglantyne modelled her survey upon the classic Victorian studies of urban poverty by Henry Mayhew and Charles Booth. Like Mayhew's *London's Labor and the London Poor,* she divided the Cambridge labour force into those who *cannot* work, those who *will not* work and the unemployed able-bodied in search of work. From Booth she borrowed the idea of a map, which indicated poverty in districts according to the rent paid by residents.[68] By the early twentieth century, late-Victorian evangelical philanthropy had gone out of fashion and been replaced by a more environmental-eugenic analysis of social problems which was more appealing to Chartists and Trade Unionists.[69] Following this framework, Eglantyne offered multifaceted environmental explanations, which outlined the historical origins of the unemployment, health and sanitation crises in the New Town, which had resulted in a century of misery for the inhabitants.[70] She realized that Cambridge lacked the notorious over-crowded slums of larger cities; its inadequate sewage and sanitation problems had been caused in the 1840s by poor urban planning. In her effort to explain poverty and pauperism scientifically, she concluded that 'heap[s] of refuse which accumulated in the courts' and the fetid stagnant air and the typhoid, scarlet fever, smallpox and cholera it caused were the 'natural results of the conditions in the town'.[71]

Ross argues that in contrast with men's empirical surveys of poverty, 'pathos was perhaps the most powerful of the specifically feminized style of fictional and nonfiction slum writing. It structured a "fem-inized epistemology of sympathy."'[72] In her survey, Eglantyne drew heavily on her personal encounters with the working class while train-ing at Stockwell College and teaching in Marlborough. She emphasized that only those who 'knew' the 'facts' could 'know' the poor.[73] For Eglantyne the problem was emotional, but her analysis, driven solely by COS's ideology, upheld the principles of thorough primary research, analysis and efficient scientific case work, which condemned indis-criminate charity, the improvident early marriages of the poor, drunk-enness and gambling, maternal ignorance and the lack of productive leisure and recreational activities.

Eglantyne's most insightful arguments harkened back to the late-Victorian child-saving ideal of saving the child in danger before he or she became a danger to others.[74] She wrote, 'the Charity Organizationist knows how hopeless it is to expect thrift and industry from those who have squandered away their youth'.[75] She said that energy must be directed toward the moral and industrial education of young people. 'Girls who can find no better happiness than that of parading the streets in their best clothes grow up into women who spend their day gossiping on their doorsteps or in reading penny novelettes. The boys who loaf at the street corners grow up into men who spend their evenings in the public houses'.[76] In the case of boys Eglantyne recommended training schemes for school leavers, so they could avoid low wages and dead-end unskilled labour later in life. Their personal improvement could be achieved through joining youth clubs like the Boys' Brigade and taking Bible classes for self-improvement and moral independence. Finally, team sports would inculcate a 'manly and Christian type of character…and drill and discipline on military lines'.[77]

On behalf of the girls, for the first time in her public writing, Eglantyne invoked the rhetoric of sisterhood in her chapter entitled 'Work amongst Girls'. Cambridge lacked the large factories that created the rough independent girl labourers whose lives were well documented in London, Manchester and Birmingham before 1900.[78] In Cambridge, girls from poor families reared in overcrowded slum-like housing left school at 14 and went either into shops or service, where they had to survive on low wages and endure long hours of monotonous labour. Their wages were either turned over to their parents or squandered on 'smart hat[s]' and 'showy dress'.[79] In the 'rush of working life', Eglantyne observed that these 'girls feel that nobody cares for them'.[80] Before long they began to suffer from ill health, nervousness and over-strain or to yearn for freedom and were easily led astray. 'Her whole being craves recreation…so she gets it wherever she can, and the street is the natural place…Thus…a dangerous freedom alternates with work'.[81] In her special plea for girls, Eglantyne called upon wealthy women to 'link hands with their sisters'.[82]

While training at Stockwell, the hardworking pupil-teachers had impressed Eglantyne, and at Marlborough she had seen how anxious her pupils like Alice Williamson and Florence Tarent had been to improve. In her chapter on girls, Eglantyne laid out her model of 'new' girlhood for working-class girls, which emphasized the innate personal strength and courage she had observed while living and working amongst them. Ambition was generally regarded as shamefully unfeminine in middle-class girls, but at university it had been advantageous and cultivated. At Lady Margaret Hall women students 'were proud of each other's gifts'.[83] To enable working-class girls to improve themselves, Eglantyne recommended the YWCA, Girls' Friendly Societies, Church Guilds and Girls' Registries for the 'kindling' of 'ambition' and fostering of a competitive ethos among members.[84] She maintained that girls who trained hard earned better wages and would not be driven by the hardship of low pay to early marriages. To that end, she stressed the importance of working girls having friends of their own class. 'Lady friends' might hold up a high standard to them', but they could never do as much as good girl friends of their own standing, for these have a yet stronger influence'.[85] Eglantyne concluded, '[G]irls will not so readily contract early and improvident marriages when they have girl friends and many interests in their lives'.[86]

The Charity Organization Society was not evangelical like many traditional 'faith based charities'. Prochaska argues that it 'saw religious enthusiasm as an impediment to charitable efficiency'. Charity Organizationists stressed that 'social science would produce the religion of charity without the sectarianism of religion'.[87] Eglantyne did not subscribe to this feature of COS theory and warned Florence Keynes she intended to write a 'pious ending' for her survey.[88] She told Keynes, 'when I think how revolting piety is to most of my friends…Wouldn't it be a good plan to have little red flags, stuck in the margin…as a warning…of where to skip?'[89] Eglantyne concluded her chapter on girls with the observation that 'secular clubs can do some good in making girls lives happier and better, but experienced social workers know that religion is their only real safeguard, when they are brought face to face with the worst difficulties and dangers to which their circumstances may expose them'.[90] Eglantyne was very proud of the final 274-page monograph, and Florence Keynes overlooked the 'piety', which crept in.

The *Cambridge Survey* created a stir in Cambridge and established Eglantyne's reputation as a valuable member of the COS, her contribution was acknowledged in the annual reports of 1904 and 1905 and in the press.[91] Her move into voluntary social work had been made possible through a network of supportive Cambridge friends, relatives and matrons who recognized her training and aptitude for social research and thought she might be good at training new recruits. After completing the *Cambridge Survey*, Eglantyne was appointed honorary secretary of the committee 'to train personal [sic] who are willing to assist in particular branches of COS work'.[92] Eglantyne accepted the challenge of instructing women of her own class, a task that suited her temperament.

All her life she had watched other women closely: the Lady Margaret freshers, the Stockwell pupil-teachers and Lydia Manley, and her little girls at St Peter's Parish School and Miss Pullen. She had written about the 'Susies of Life' and the 'women of the past', and she greatly admired powerful women like Wordsworth, Toynbee, Lady Jebb, Mitchell and Keynes. At the same time that she accepted her new position on the COS volunteer training committee she took on another teaching challenge as well. In 1903 she offered to tutor her two teenage cousins. Years later, Eglantyne Mary described it as a 'really dynamic episode [which] probably changed the whole course of our lives'. She and her sister Geraldine confessed that they were Eglantyne's poor 'imperfectly educated' cousins. To help Heneage Jebb's family, Eglantyne offered to tutor two of his daughters in history and English just as Aunt Louisa had done for her family. Geraldine said, '[W]e were hardly known to her…I don't know what induced her to make this extraordinarily generous offer'.[93] Eglantyne took them to see castles and battlefields, gave them books, set essay questions for them, provided Geraldine with riding lessons and bought her the 'first really good clothes she had ever had'.[94] Eglantyne also persuaded their father to send them to university.[95] Geraldine remembered the 'experiences' as 'among the most enchanting memories of my life.'[96]

The women who came of age in the 1880s and 1890s were the beneficiaries of higher education but found their ambitions stifled by legal
restrictions, professional bans, social conventions and family obligations;[97] however there were cracks in philanthropic societies as Winifred
Knox discovered upon leaving Lady Margaret Hall in the late 1890s. She
said that settlements, charity societies and clubs were 'crying for well-
educated, reliable, voluntary workers…with the shelter and financial
backing of her home'.[98] In the early 1900s, Eglantyne met many such
women at the COS, women like herself who were using philanthropy to
fill gaps in their lives. They were just as sceptical as she was about how
their work could solve the problems of poverty, pauperism and moral
decay in 'outcast' Cambridge; however she trained them in COS case
work methods. Her cousin by marriage, Gwen Darwin said she could
not 'bear to just be a young lady living at home and waiting for someone to come and marry her as most girls are…I feel I can't really settle
yet…O O O why wasn't I a man and why haven't I to earn my living'.
She concluded that there was 'nothing to be done except ask Eglantyne
if she could be any good as a clerk under her'.[99] Darwin illustrated the
Booth maps for the *Cambridge Survey*. In 1906 Florence Keynes gave
Eglantyne her 22-year-old daughter Margaret to train. At first Eglantyne
found Margaret 'too nervous' to do very much. She must have reminded
Eglantyne of herself at Stockwell because Eglantyne said, 'knowing how
miserable she must be feeling I am only using her to do the easier
things'.[100] Many years later Margaret said that it was due to Eglantyne's
encouragement that 'I [began to] believe in myself'.[101]

Edwardian volunteers had to contend with the public perception of
themselves as voyeuristic and self-interested do-gooders.[102] Darwin, a
struggling artist, is a typical case. Although she never tried to conceal
her boredom around the COS office she felt like a hypocrite. She wrote:
'I feel I can't really settle yet…everything seems to make me more and
more socialistic—if anyone can be a socialist, who is wearing a silk
blouse'.[103] Unlike Darwin, Margaret Keynes began to enjoy working in
the Boys' Registry but she did have misgivings. She recalled trying to
convince a poor widow that her family should be able to survive on
one boy's wages of four shillings a week. The mother thought it necessary to inform Margaret that 10/6 was not much for '3 of us, for coal
and boots and everything'.[104] This was the year that Margaret's father
gave her 200 pounds for her Christmas present.[105] Margaret tried to
assure the poor mother, that she understood, however, she later reflected,
'here we were in this comfortable drawing room and they went away
thanking me for my kindness…I am always having selfish, discontented

thoughts for myself'.[106] Nevertheless, Margaret faced the physical dangers of social work undaunted. She told Eglantyne that Detective Marsh had been by to see if she 'wanted protection from a woman whom I have frustrated in her effort to get her stepbrother back and who is given to assault'![107]

This chapter has shown that soon after arriving in Cambridge Eglantyne was to be drawn back into the world of human affairs, albeit cautiously, at first by watching and listening to Mrs Keynes read 'her brief reduction of the miseries of life on the other side of the line'.[108] Later she discovered new talents. Her effectiveness as mentor to new social workers lay in her ability to understand the anxiety felt by other young well-educated women who 'feel they have no place in the world'.[109] She described it in a fictional account in 'The Ring Fence' when a young lady named 'Clarissa' told her parents that she wished to take up a little meaningful social work. 'Not all good families approved of their daughters doing social work'. Clarissa's father objected: 'No daughter of mine shall be a social worker'. He was afraid of what it might lead to. 'There were lots of girls to mess about among the poor, without Clarissa doing it too'.[110] Her mother chimed in: '"Parties, popularity and a rich marriage" was all that Clarissa needed'.[111] By the twentieth century, the Lady Bountiful had become a stereotype, and Edwardian social workers had to contend with the public perception of themselves as do-gooders and dowdies; nevertheless, between 1903 and 1910, Eglantyne put her own stamp on Cambridge social work and was content to keep doing it, until her mother announced that she wished to live abroad for her heath. This was a great disappointment to everyone. Gwen Darwin told her sister that she 'like[d] Eglantyne so very much' because she has 'a sense of humour, which saves her from the kind of hopeless philanthropicalness of most good ladies'.[112]

7
Honour thy Mother: Duty vs *'Free Unsheltered Life Fraught with Pitfalls and Danger'*[1]

A hotel like this is for the rich what the workhouse is for the poor…the gathering point for the aimless and shiftless'.[2] This is how Eglantyne described the fashionable Swiss hotel where she and her mother were living in 1911. As for the guests who were having their health cures, she said she preferred 'the sick rich people…to the others who if not idle by nature are nearly always made so by the circumstances of their life'.[3] Eglantyne's uncle, Sir Richard Jebb died in 1905 and a few years later Lady Jebb returned to America; shortly thereafter, Eglantyne's mother lost all interest in Cambridge and began making plans to live abroad. Even though Eglantyne was deeply involved with Charity Organization Society work, Mrs Jebb expected her to accompany her. Grudgingly, Eglantyne resigned from her committees and spent the next three years touring European watering holes. She quickly grew weary of the hotels and the exasperating guests. Her only diversions was the novel she was writing and daily letters to Margaret Keynes, who had become her closest friend. Margaret assured Eglantyne that writing her novel would make 'time… pass quickly'[4] and pleaded with her 'not to sacrifice her life to her mother'.[5]

This chapter shows that despite expanding career opportunities for women in the fields of education, health care and social services, never marrying did not free all women to pursue them. In the early 1900s, the cultural expectation was still in place that a daughter's duties toward their parents must come before her duties to public life or herself. Unmarried women, like Eglantyne, were expected to remain at home under the supervision of their parents, in the role of what was called daughter-at-home.[6] While Eglantyne's mother imposed limitations on her career and constraints upon her friendship with Margaret, voluntary social work offered Eglantyne and Margaret the pleasures of friendship, the possibility for adventure and an escape, for a time, from the constraints of domesticity.

7.1   Margaret Keynes and Eglantyne, source: Buxton Family

Martha Vicinus argues that the compensation which unpaid social work offered unmarried women in the late nineteenth and early twentieth centuries was a network of friends, which she says was 'seen as completing a life's work, as validating the decision not to marry, to have a career, to [have] a wider sphere than one's immediate family'. Never marrying, however, did not free all women of their domestic responsibilities. Carole Dyhouse has observed that some biographers, autobiographers and novelists paint pictures of unmarried daughters 'chafing' in positions 'as daughter-at-home' while others provide examples of 'saintly girls' who renounced all claims to 'lives of their own'. It is difficult to know how they really felt about it.

The social position of unmarried daughters, especially those like Eglantyne, who were over 30, the age when marriage 'ceases to be probability or possibility'[9] was the subject of public discussion in the *Times* in 1909. The debate began when one reader asked: 'Have not the

arents of daughters...some claim to have their homes brightened by
younger generation...and to have the pleasures and benefit arising
rom the education and accomplishments for which they have paid?'[10]
This 'bad and ugly' way of commodifying the emotional tie between
parents and daughters exposed the painful reality which had faced
generations of unmarried women, namely the 'heroic self-sacrifice' of
devot[ing] the best years of their life...to the care of aging and invalid
parents'.[11] Eleanor Gordon and Gwyneth Nair argue that the early
wentieth century produced an 'increasing band of women' for whom
he dependent role of daughter-at-home and marriage was 'either an
nterference or an impossibility'.[12]

The *Times* rebuttal came from feminists who focused on the 'misunder-
tandings and frictions' which developed between parents and unmarried
daughters.[13] One letter writer put it plainly: 'Many parents expect it as a
ight and never realize they are ruining their daughter's life'.[14] The suf-
ragette Elizabeth Garrett Anderson, offered a range of solutions to
prevent daughters over 30 from growing 'a little faded outside' and 'drab-
olored within.'[15] The most radical was to give them a 'small allowance'
nd let them move out as their brothers and married sisters had done.[16]
The idea of giving an unmarried daughter her financial independence
vas outrageous to many conservative readers. Their solutions included
ld chestnuts like Sunday school teaching, visiting the poor and emigra-
ion, because 'there was abundant scope for gentlewomen trained as
eachers or nurses in the Canadian North-West'.[17] A 'Sexagenarian
Mother' said the state of affairs in the country was 'deplorable'. Owing to
he selfishness of unmarried daughters who had neglected their respons-
bilities, too many elderly parents were forced to hire secretaries and companions. '*Punch*'s sarcasm of the early days of woman's rights is truer than
ver now: "Father is blind and mother's an invalid, so I am going out as a
urse."'[18]

Mrs Jebb had been suffering from *maladies imaginaries* since the 1880s.
ince beginning her work with the Charity Organization Society in 1903,
glantyne had learned how to balance her pressing committee work,
vriting and meeting schedules with her mother's needs, which included
ntertaining houseguests, hostessing at-homes, managing Tye's financial
ccounts and dressmakers' appointments, reading to her in the evening
nd supervising the construction of a new house. By 1906, Eglantyne
vas developing her own health problems. Her Cambridge diary lists
er committee work and speeches to community groups, and describes
ycling four and six miles a day to meetings and feeling increasingly 'tired
nd depressed'.[19] In June she saw Dr Drake, who diagnosed her severe

headaches, sleeping difficulties and dark moods as the symptoms o
thyroid disease. He prescribed a 'strong tonic' and told Eglantyne no
to 'go down to the office more than once a day' or 'bicycle more tha1
4 miles daily when working or go out more than 1 evening a week'.[20]

Eglantyne was too busy to heed Drake's advice. She interpreted one da
in the office as a morning at the Education Bureau and an afternoon a
the COS. To cut back she tried writing her reports at home, but he
headaches and worries about 'failures at work' caused her to 'muddl
things'.[21] She tried sleeping outdoors to cure her insomnia but continue
to feel tired and had difficulty eating.[22] Her mother was not of very mucl
help. Tye struck many people as a 'rather shadowy figure'.[23] Lady Jeb1
had known her for 13 years before she felt 'a sisterly feeling toward Tye
She thought her sister-in-law was 'pampered and spoiled'[24] and ha
become very dependent upon Eglantyne's domestic services. We d
not know what sort of allowance she gave, but Eglantyne kept track o
every penny and often walked and bicycled 'too far' because she coul
not 'afford hansoms'.[25] In the evenings Eglantyne had to read to Tye
Between June and October she read Somerset Maugham's *The Bishop*
Apron, John Galsworthy's *Man of Property*, David Hume's political essays
Samuel Pepys's essay on contracts, John Keats's early poems and Lad
Caroline Jebb's newly published widow-biography of 'Uncle Dick's life
Tye's review was: 'No comment'! Eglantyne confessed that she wa
relieved on the evenings when her mother was out 'because she coul
work late and have the next day free'.[26]

Extant Save the Children Fund monographs vigorously emphasiz
Eglantyne's devotion to her mother, but they do not show how com
plicated their relationship was or how deeply Eglantyne was trouble
by having given up Charity Organization Society work. Tye moved t
Cambridge to be closer to her brother and sister-in-law. After Dick die
and Carrie went back to the United States, it was not the same, so Ty
decided that she and Eglantyne should go abroad for medical treat
ment. Though Eglantyne did not want to go, she realized she had t
comply with her mother's wishes.[27] In 1909 they began a three-yea
tour of the fashionable spas of Switzerland, Austria and Italy, an experi
ence which Eglantyne found odious. Her only diversion was the nove
she decided to write and letters from Margaret Keynes, who had becom
her most cherished friend. Surviving letters and other accounts by th
Jebb and Keynes families and friends show that between 1908 and 1913
Eglantyne and Margaret formed an intimate friendship. This friendship i
difficult to describe because Margaret burned Eglantyne's 'most intimat
letters' by the time she died in 1928.[28] In 1967 Dorothy Buxton's so1

)avid destroyed many more of Eglantyne and Margaret's letters. In 1956, 1owever, Dorothy Buxton transcribed the majority of Margaret's letters nto an old *Boots Scribbling Diary*. Together with Francesca Wilson's esearch notes, what survives shows that Margaret and Eglantyne shared deep emotional attachment. However, their time together, and plans or the future were constrained by their positions as unmarried daughters- t-home and their mothers' expectations of them.

The pre-World War One era was the heyday for passionate friendships mong women. Susan Pedersen argues that 'new women' formed close motional bonds with one another and felt free to devote themselves ully to public work in a way that married women did not.[29] Vicinus's tudy of women's friendships show that voluntary social work opened up he chance to have a wider sphere of acquaintances than one's immediate amily.[30] The historical and social construction of women's friendships rovides many competing explanations of the exact nature of their inti- nacy. Shelia Jeffreys' study of women's letters and diaries shows that narried and unmarried women had passionate friendships which ncluded declarations of love, nights spent in bed together, a sharing of kisses and intimacies and declarations of lifelong devotion, without xciting the least 'adverse comment'.[31] To understand the nature of this ntimacy, Vicinus finds it best to place same-sex relationships on a con- inuum to encompass multiple forms of relationships, flowing from non- sexual (passionate, devout, intense) to homo-affective to homoerotic sexual intimacy.[32] Judith Bennett, however, suggests more controversially hat we consider women's desire for personal autonomy and inde-)endence to be 'lesbian-like' behaviour.[33] The reasons for the naming controversy are numerous and draw upon Michael Foucault's assertion hat the history of sexuality is merely the history of what has been said about sex.[34] On the one side, Olive Banks said that passionate friendships lid not involve erotic genital or other sexual manifestations; so they were 'not lesbian in any conscious sense'.[35] Jeffreys claims that before the sexological category of "lesbian" was named as such, by Havelock Ellis and others, women involved in passionate friendships did not identify hemselves as lesbians'.[36] Christine Bolt focuses on the wider political mplications of the medico-moral shift, pointing out that just when the numbers of unmarried women seeking access to higher education and professional employment was increasing, the '"experts" sexualized and discredited singlehood'.[37]

Margaret was the 23-year-old only daughter of Florence Keynes (née Brown), honorary secretary of the Charity Organization Society and John Neville Keynes, a Cambridge University professor. She grew up in the shadow of her brilliant brothers, John Maynard and Geoffrey, who went to Eton and Rugby and then on to Cambridge. Florence and John met when Florence was a student at Newnham in 1878; they were strong believers in the university education of women. Until Margaret went away to Wycombe Abbey in 1899, a German governess taught her at home. She loved painting and handicrafts, gardening and her five years at boarding school.[38] However, her mother assessed the experiment as only 'partly successful' and the education of her unscholarly daughter was 'a problem'.[39] According to John Maynard Keynes's biographer, Margaret was 'packed off to Germany' because she had failed her exams.[40] The acquisition of a foreign language was still considered a feminine accomplishment, and the Keyneses believed that total immersion in a culture was necessary. Margaret was sent to live with the impoverished family of the Baroness von Bissing, who lived in the Lutheran town, Wittenberg, where there was 'wailing in the streets' when the 'whole town went into mourning on All Soul's Day'. A local philanthropist threw buns to the three pauper families who occupied the ground floor of the Baroness' house. The other lodger was a madman, 'who in a fit…had once attacked his wife.' Margaret was miserable and for six months begged to come home early.[41] Uncertain of what else to do with her daughter, Florence asked Eglantyne to train Margaret in social work and afterwards to find her something to do in the Boys' Employment Registry.

It has been observed that philanthropy and social welfare work created an environment where like-minded women formed close intimate communities.[42] At the COS Margaret encountered an impressive group of distinguished committeewomen, lady volunteers and unmarried daughters who were anxiously pursuing 'very busy philanthropic lives' doing 'the world's most necessary unpaid work'.[43] Their formidable leader was Florence Keynes, whom Maynard's Bloomsbury friends called 'Good Mother Keynes'.[44] She expected her 'shy and gauche' daughter to display the same propensity for social work that she did.[45] In 1907, the COS was setting up an employment registry for school leavers. Eglantyne spent three weeks in London observing similar projects there, and the Cambridge COS followed her recommendations and appointed her honorary secretary of the Boys' Registry.[46] Eglantyne was looking for volunteers to collect the names of school leavers and interview parents, headmasters and tradesmen to help boys find suitable employment matches in local businesses.[47] Margaret was very anxious to do well and Eglantyne found it endearing. She told Dorothy Kempe, '[Margaret] changes colour and assents in a great hurry to everything I tell her to do'. Eglantyne was 'angry' however because Mrs Keynes always expressed 'surprise in front of her' whenever Margaret performed a task well.[48] At the COS Margaret and Eglantyne developed a deep admiration for each other. Margaret said it began by her 'adoration of a beautiful and witty woman nine years her senior'.[49] The letters they wrote to each other after Eglantyne and Mrs Jebb left for Europe show that their friendship blossomed into love.

It is said that in the nineteenth century letter writing was elevated to an art and the letters of this letter writing generation are as intimate as conversations. Their personal letters 'mould and mirror' the fluidity of their relationships.[50] Eglantyne and Margaret wrote to each other frequently after Eglantyne left the COS. In 1910 their 'mutual' Christmas gift was to send each other a letter a day. After the first year Margaret told Eglantyne that 'it never seems too often' to write.[51] After the second year she called it a 'present that goes on getting nicer and nicer'.[52] Eglantyne's surviving letters to Margaret are full of descriptions of hotels, churches and historic ruins; reports of Tye's health; and updates on the progress of the novel she was writing. Margaret's letters contain gossip about Cambridge friends, news about Mrs Keynes's political career, admonitions to Eglantyne to drink a lot of milk and Ovaltine, and her encouraging suggestions for Eglantyne's writing.

Margaret said that although she and Eglantyne were very 'different' they were 'in perfect sympathy'.[53] Since writing the *Cambridge Survey*, Eglantyne's commitment to social work had drifted towards social policy, whereas Margaret liked face-to-face social work. She thought the University is so taken up with preparing for life' whereas town was 'infinitely more alive'. She said, 'I like…life itself'.[54] Even though Eglantyne was hundreds of miles away, Margaret continued to consult her on COS policy decisions as if she were still in the next office. When faced with a challenge, she told Eglantyne, 'I try and think what you would do'.[55] When Margaret was nervous about addressing the Newnham Settlement Society, she remembered how 'you made yourself do your best…so I ought to be able to make myself do it'.[56] Eglantyne proofread a pamphlet Margaret wrote called *The Problem of Boy Labour*, which the COS published in 1911 and which John Maynard Keynes thought was 'extraordinarily good'.[57] Margaret also kept Eglantyne up to date on the progress of old registry boys like the Barnardo boy 'who stabbed his mother with a fork'.[58] She also introduced new boys like the apprentice who 'lost his fingers in a machine.' Margaret suspected that his family was trying to get his 'compensation for themselves' and she was determined to stop them.[59] Despite being a 'pocket-money' social worker,

Margaret was so dedicated that people teased her because her only 'topic of conversation' was the COS.[60]

Eglantyne and Margaret were liberals in their politics and their feminism. Margaret cheered Lloyd George's 'magnificent audacious' National Insurance Scheme from the Ladies' Gallery in the House of Commons because it would 'affect clearly the welfare of millions'. She marched with the suffragettes and while sympathetic, she drew the line at militancy. She asked Eglantyne, 'Isn't L. George splendid about the women? I don't think the militants did much harm this time as no one has paid much attention to them'.[61] Margaret and Eglantyne were very critical of the rigid education of middle-class girls. Margaret was 'exasperated' because her 17-year-old cousin's mail was controlled at her high school and she could not go out alone. 'Worst of all she doesn't mind!...all the great wonderful stir and life e.g. the people, their interests, hopes, mean almost nothing to her'. Margaret's mother told her she was 'exaggerating'.[62] At the time, Margaret did not see marriage as essential to a woman's life: '[Many] women of leisure...are miserable' or 'feel worthless' at the 'thought of remaining single...but I don't'.[63] Eglantyne had commented extensively on marriage in her fiction in her *Cambridge Survey*. She was acutely conscious of the restrictions marriage and family life imposed on women and girls of all social classes.

Eglantyne and Margaret's letters also contain protestations of love and commitment to each other's careers. They regarded the separation imposed upon them by Mrs Jebb as temporary, and they hoped some day to live and work together.[64] Margaret wrote: '[Y]ou said I might be frightened at the seriousness with which you took my words when I told you I belonged to you. No, that didn't frighten me; what...frightened me was the thought that you might not want me...[Y]ou gave proof to me and I trust you...[S]ometimes it seems too wonderful to be true'.[65] After returning from a visit with Eglantyne in April 1911, Margaret called it the most perfect fortnight of her life. 'To see...the real true, beautiful you has only increased my devotion...[and] desire to serve you, the most perfect friend and comrade in the world'. When their Cambridge friends asked if Eglantyne was coming back, Margaret said, 'I sadly shake my head, and sigh...I can see you lying in bed on your back like a carved figure and looking very beautiful'![66] Margaret explained that her 'love...is a very healthy feeling. No bad elements in it now...nothing you could tell me could shake my faith in you... It's like resting on a rock to have you to love and who loves me'.[67] Margaret described 'the sense of security gained by each other's love' and wondered if they could live together someday?[68] Eglantyne replied that she had never felt this way about 'anyone before':

> ...I really, seriously don't believe that I should be able to live without you; I might endure for a little, doing work which didn't interest me, but I don't believe I could have any happiness. I should be counting the moments till I died, the world would have nothing left in it to hold me back, without you it would seem simply impossible to live. This is strange and foolish! – I wish it were not so; it cannot be good, but I do not know how to help it! I suppose I must just wait, and hope that the natural healthiness of affection will some day assert itself, and I shall come to love you better and therefore less dependently.[69]

After a visit to Italy late in 1912, Margaret wrote, '[Y]our face is the most beautiful one in the world and the nicest to kiss and kiss...but it meant leaving—always the misery—of parting. Someday we wont any more, not for one single night'.[70] These were not merely affectionate words; they reveal a plan that would enable them to be together. Eglantyne, who was determined to keep working, decided the best way to do so was to write a successful novel. Margaret believed in Eglantyne's literary gifts and hoped that if Eglantyne had a modicum of success, her mother would allow her to pursue a serious writing career in England. Whenever Eglantyne felt ill or had doubts, Margaret reminded her that 'George Elliot had the greatest difficulty in making herself write her early novels'.[71] 'You have so much to express', Margaret assured her, 'I know you can do what other pple [people] can't do...—doing in the sense of telling'.[72] Margaret was worried that if Eglantyne was 'always abroad she would lose touch with home affairs and lose touch with the things about which she writes'. She thought Eglantyne's writing 'required that [you] be infused with the needs of modern England...[you] had a store of it to take away but [it] need[s] replenishing frequently.'[73] Margaret kept pressing Eglantyne to hire a companion or a Swiss maid to look after Mrs Jebb. She said Mrs Jebb had to 'get used to having someone' besides Eglantyne. 'In every partnership there must be give and take so it must be in yours and your mothers...You've stayed months longer than you wanted to so if she wants to stay months longer still she must get another companion'.[74] She begged Eglantyne not to permit herself to be 'permanently exiled'.[75]

Eglantyne wanted to make the study of social question the subject of her novel. She had never joined the suffragettes or any socialist

organizations, but since her teenage years she had been trying to overcome the class privileges which taught young people of her class and
generation to feel superior to the servants and townspeople.[76] Her
private writing reveals that she had grown to despise the artificialities
of class, which were represented to her by the Lyth. Even though she
felt uncomfortable rubbing shoulders with those outside her social
class, her experiences in settlement work, grammar school teaching
and COS training had enabled her to submerge herself in the lives of
the poor and the lives of the philanthropic women who tried to help
them. From her hotel rooms in Switzerland and Italy in 1911 and
1912, Eglantyne poured her heart into a 1,098-page novel called 'The
Ring Fence', which explored the lives of two young women: a social
worker and a leisured daughter-at-home. She felt invigorated. In her
diary on 10 November 1911, she wrote, 'I am writing now at the novel
in a fever, frantically…so that I can scarcely put my pen down night
and day. I only leave off writing to write letters instead, also I read to
mother for about two hours every day and I only leave off to read to
myself: Shakespeare and the newspapers. I've read twelve novels since
we came abroad'.[77]

Fictional accounts of social work written by women at the time show
how public work led to personal growth, intense emotional experiences and opportunities for leadership. Moreover, according to Seth
Koven, writing about poverty enabled women writers to envisage and
explore the 'slums, dirt and cross-class relationships'.[78] Eglantyne's
'Ring Fence' was like a slum novel in that it contained detailed descriptions of rural poverty, the filth and squalor of cottage interiors and the
suffering of mothers and children. Many of her characters express
harsh criticisms of the various late-nineteenth century social and economic programmes intended to mitigate poverty and inequality. Ellen
Ross suggests that the appeal of slum novels for women writers was
that they allowed their authors to depict the 'trials and tribulations of
strong, intelligent and independent female slum reformers'.[79]

The setting of 'The Ring Fence' was Branston-le-Roy, which was really
Ellesmere in the 1890s. The two semi-orphan female protagonists,
Frieda Jones and Angela Langham, represent opposite extremes of late-
Victorian womanhood. Angela is a beautiful penniless ward whose
social position depends upon making a suitable marriage. She is devastated when she discovers that her lover, Hugh Overton, has proposed
to a former settlement worker, motherless, Frieda Jones, the daughter
of a nonconformist socialist draper who recently inherited the manorial
estate and fortune, which Hugh had hoped for.

It is not a Cinderella story. Mr Jones' great expectation turned out to be the downfall of many characters. Angela is almost driven to suicide upon discovering that Hugh and Frieda are married, but instead, she altruistically befriends Frieda and teaches her how to dress, do her hair and behave like an elegant lady. After her father's death, Frieda and Hugh try to carry on his reformist design to convert the manor house into a workingmen's college and the estate into a self-sufficient co-operative temperance colony. Complications arise when Frieda, who had developed phthisis while doing settlement work in London, is sent to Australia to restore her health. In her absence, Hugh is seduced by visions of luxury, wealth and power and his socialist ideals crumble. He secretly takes control of Frieda's inheritance, exploits the tenants and allows the pig-headed elite to cheat the ratepayers and mismanage the local school. When Frieda discovers the deception, their marriage deteriorates and they grow to despise each other.

'The Ring Fence' is a complicated saga in which the stock characters and plotlines, secret alliances, eponymous heroines, deathbed promises, medieval curses, unrequited love and murder—are borrowed from the nineteenth-century classics. Many of the 48 chapters are wonderfully well written, but overall the novel is a didactic attack on upper-class hypocrisy and sectarian prejudice. At one point, one of the characters declares the 'egoism' of the upper-classes 'eats into its heart like a canker…the men were domestic tyrants and the women querulous and discounted'.[80] Eglantyne's attempt to liberate the workers, rather than being revolutionary, is restricted to an endorsement of COS social policy, including self-help, friendly societies, youth clubs, temperance and small land holdings.[81] Then from the vantage point of the twenty-first century the most interesting theme is her attack on what some nineteenth-century feminists called the sexual slavery of women in marriage.

According to Koven, 'novels register not just what can be said, but also what cannot be said…[or] fully understood by contemporaries. Novels can give us access to cultural attitudes—fantasies—about urban dirt and female sexual desire'.[82] 'The Ring Fence' is not an autobiography, Eglantyne was writing autobiographically, however, her letters suggest that she was unaware of the similarities between her characters and the events in her own family. For example, Hugh's refusal to allow Frieda to continue her social work parallels both Arthur Jebb's insistence that Eglantyne's mother resign from the Home Arts and Industrial Association and also Tye's more recent insistence that Eglantyne give up social work. Like Eglantyne, Angela is forced to live an idle life abroad with her step-mother, who lets their estate. They are both miserable and lonely. Frieda however is the heroine who rebels. Unlike Tye, who submitted to Arthur's authority, Frieda defies Hugh and continues her ameliorative work among the poor. Hugh says 'a wife's place in the evening is at home'[83] and he belittles her for ruining her 'complexion' distributing 'socialist tracts'.[84]

In one chapter, the fashionable dinner guests agree that no man 'wants to have in his home a standing reminder of the wretchedness of the outer world?...A woman's first duty to her husband is to make him forget his duty to his neighbour'.[85] When a young lady named Clarissa announces that she would like to take up charity work, a sympathetic older woman recommends that she take up photography, collect plates or knit ties instead: 'I like interests which draw you closer to other people, instead of cutting you off from them...That's the worst of social work. Once you take it up you are lost to society'. The lady cautioned Clarissa, 'no girl goes in for it who can ever hope to marry...The men in our neighborhood all say they wont marry social workers'.[86]

Frieda's friends watch her 'slowly succumbing beneath the burden which Hugh has placed upon her, the gradual extinction of her hopes, the crushing out of her joy and interest in life'.[87] Frieda realizes that Hugh has 'no idea how much he hurts her by sinning against her natural ideals. It would have hurt her less if he had beat her, but he understood that beating hurt; he did not understand that this did too'.[88] Frieda admits that she has 'failed in her duty as a wife', but resolved to push onward in the 'loneliness' of public work:

> Slowly she raised her head, proudly her eyes met [Hugh's]. As something visible and tangible the truth seemed to lie between them, the truth which was to bring misery and havoc into their severed lives. In that moment they recognized it and they recognized also each other. They seemed to know each other as never before, and in their first intimacy they became strangers. More than strangers—enemies. The truth which lay between them was like a glove which he had thrown down for her to pick up. They would fight. And each knew the other would never give in.[89]

The significance of the novel for Eglantyne's biography is that it constitutes the longest subjective account available of her life to 1911. At various points in 'The Ring Fence' each of the central female characters feels trapped by their obligations to men, their silly ambitious mothers and the social conventions which force women to observe the world from behind a ring fence. A Freudian would argue that Frieda and

Angela represent both sides of Eglantyne's unconscious. At the moment of writing, she was sublimating her hostility toward her mother while exploring the courageous impulse it would take to stand up for herself. At numerous points in 'The Ring Fence', Eglantyne describes the all-consuming loneliness she was feeling and her 'passionate hunger' for 'joy' and 'pleasure'.[90]

Margaret was pleased with the early chapters. She read them to her mother who was also 'delighted' with them; 'you are a genius' Margaret told Eglantyne.[91] However, as more chapters arrived, Margaret grew increasingly disturbed about the content. When Eglantyne told her that she was 'in sight of finishing' her novel, Margaret told her not to 'let anyone read isolated chapters and to get the next book started'.[92] Years later she told Dorothy Buxton that she had thought the problem with 'The Ring Fence' was that it was 'conventional and propagandist. There was so much of life that Eglantyne "did not see"...hence life was described as Eglantyne thought it should be, not as it was'.[93] We do not know what Tye or Eglantyne's brother Dick who had taken over the Lyth thought of 'The Ring Fence', but Lil's husband, Roland Wilkins who was a civil servant, said it was 'depressing'.[94] In contrast, Dorothy Buxton admired it and saved a copy. After Eglantyne's death she showed it to the novelist and Save the Children Fund volunteer, Ethel Sidgwick, with a view to getting it published. Sidgwick guessed that 'heaps of it must have been straight from life'. Regarding its literary merit, however, she thought some of the 'minor characters were worthy of George Elliot. She was reminded of Dorothea of *Middlemarch*', but overall it was 'about twice too long for any publisher to look at' and 'out of date'.[95]

In *After the Victorians*, Peter Mandler and Susan Pedersen argue that the reexamination of bourgeois marriage in the late 1890s led to improved legal rights for wives and gave married women who wished to assert it, greater autonomy. However, a daughter's role still meant meeting uncomplainingly the demands of aging parents. 'Love could sweeten duty, of course'.[96] In her biography of Eleanor Rathbone, Pedersen asserts that female partnerships were unique because, unlike marriage, they were organized to foster, and not to undermine, women's political and social ambitions.[97] This may have been the case for independent women like Eleanor Rathbone and Elizabeth Macadam, but Margaret and Eglantyne were not emancipated. Their relationship was played out under the watchful gaze of their mothers. The *Times* debate on 'unmarried daughters' demonstrates there were mothers in 1909 who would not offer their unmarried daughters more liberty than the house to herself 'one evening a week for an "At Home"'[98] or the promise not to interfere with 'correspondence, expenditure or amusements'. A liberal minded mother could arrange 'flexible meal times' but must always show a 'cordial interest' in everything her daughter did.[99] One *Times* writer pointed out that society regarded unmarried women over 30 as a 'sort of waste product.'[100] Writing a successful novel was Eglantyne's only chance at achieving independence and a life with Margaret. She had done her best, but she would have agreed with Virginia Woolf's assertion that 'art could not be founded on selflessness, and that one of the tasks of the woman writer was "killing the Angel of the House"'.[101]

By 1911, Eglantyne's siblings were all married and Margaret had much less freedom than her brothers, who lived in flats on their own. Mrs Keynes took more than a 'cordial' interest in her activities and friends; and made it clear to Margaret that she disapproved of Margaret's and Eglantyne's constant letter writing. She remarked, 'What a lot of time Eglantyne wastes in writing to you!' Margaret replied defensively, 'I don't think anything could be a waste of time that gives as much pleasure as your letters give me'.[102] On 6 December 1911, Margaret described going to an 'at home' (horrid thing) with her mother because sometimes she says [people] don't know she has a daughter!'[103] There was an awkward silence around the subject of sex in the Keynes's household. In the 1910s Maynard was having a love affair with the artist Duncan Grant, and he was worried that his mother would discover his 'sexual tastes'.[104] Margaret seems to have had some understanding of male homosexuality, for she teased Maynard and Geoffrey when their mother was listening. Maynard was embarrassed when Margaret said, 'I expect you know lots of men you wouldn't mind marrying, don't you?'[105] While preparing for a fancy dress party, she said, 'I think you had better go as Oscar Wilde'. Maynard told Duncan that he 'turned with a dreadful start only to find her addressing Geoffrey and to hear my mother saying, "Oh that would be a horrid thing to do". But the females can't keep off the subject'.[106] On 11 October Maynard told Duncan that he had 'a dreadful conversation on Sunday with my mother and Margaret about marriage, and had practically to admit to them what I was. How much they grasped I don't know'.[107]

It was Margaret's grandmother who noticed how absorbed Margaret was with Eglantyne. She said Margaret seemed 'to belong' to Eglantyne 'as much as to mother and she thinks she ought to be hurt—but I've asked her and she's not!!! I like belonging just to you two and unless I marry I will never belong to anyone else as well'.[108] However, on 4 August 1912, Florence Keynes had 'a conversation' with Margaret about 'getting married'. Margaret told Eglantyne her mother 'would rather like her to'.

Margaret assured her mother that Eglantyne 'wouldn't stop my marrying', but Mrs Keynes was not persuaded and feared that their 'closeness' might make Margaret 'less inclined'. Margaret tried to assure her mother that the opposite was the case. She thought her friend would make it 'easier for me to marry someone really eligible'.[109] Eglantyne and Margaret were planning a trip to Ireland at the time and suddenly Good Mother Keynes announced that she intended to go along as their chaperon.

Margaret's letters show their plans to be together depended on Eglantyne's mother and she thought Mrs Jebb knew 'how much we want to be together and will help us'.[110] Though Margaret was annoyed, because their short vacation plans always seemed to be upset by Mrs Jebb's sudden relapses. Once travel arrangements were well underway, Mrs Jebb would abruptly announce that she was too ill to do without Eglantyne. In February 1912, Margaret offered to go to Switzerland for two months to do 'some reading aloud' to Mrs Jebb so that Eglantyne could finish her novel.[111] Eglantyne's sisters were busy with their own young families, but they still complained that Margaret seemed to 'monopolize' Eglantyne.[112] Despite these obstacles Eglantyne and Margaret were looking for some work to do together and planning to get a flat in Kensington, and in December 1912 they found something to do that interested them.

Their new project had nothing to do with finding employment for school leavers or writing novels. In fact, 'The Ring Fence' was back from a publisher, who thought it was too long, and Eglantyne did not have the heart to cut it down. Rather than writing another 'never-to-be-published novel' Eglantyne and Margaret decided to help Eglantyne's brother-in-law Charlie Buxton and his brother Noel Buxton in their work collecting money on behalf of Bulgarian refugees for the Macedonian Relief Fund they had recently founded. Margaret and Eglantyne began making travel plans to inspect Buxton's refugee hospital in Monastir. Eglantyne told her mother she wanted to carry on this work alongside Margaret and Mrs Jebb had agreed.[113] Then, two weeks later, Eglantyne received a letter from her sister Emily, who was living with her husband and 14-year-old son in Ireland. In the letter Emily offered to take over the full-time care of Tye, which would make Eglantyne the freest from domestic restraint that she had been since Marlborough; but rather than jump at the chance to set up with Margaret, Eglantyne pulled back.

There is no indication that Eglantyne discussed Emily's offer with Margaret before she refused it. She told Emily it was 'very nice and sensible' of her 'to take the line that unmarried women should not be turned into domestic drudges.' But she thought that Emily had gone 'a little too far in pitying' her because she did not have a career:

> [T]here are bachelors of both sexes who continue to pass through life without ever incurring any responsibility for particular individuals, but I am not quite sure whether either they or their work for the world is really the better for it...I admit I have failed a good deal up till now...at present in our unsettled state, without a home and mother ill, it is quite out of the question to do both...and I do honestly think...I should have no one to blame but myself.[114]

Why did Eglantyne choose this moment to pull away from the life she had been planning with Margaret? Eglantyne was 39 years old and defined herself as bachelor. There is no indication that she saw herself as having 'failed' because she did not have a husband or children like her sisters, although they may have seen her this way. Her letter to Emily makes two things clear. First, she considered it her duty to look after her mother; and second, not to do so would be a sign of failure. If this seems surprising, perhaps Emily's offer made her realize that with Margaret she was facing yet another possibly dependent relationship with a whole new set of sacrifices. Suddenly, she knew exactly what she wanted to do. 'Look after Mother & do my work'. Without mentioning Margaret she told Emily, 'Mother is reasonable and sincerely anxious that I should work. I have only to establish her in a small house where she has everything she wants, where people can come and see her and to insist on her having a secretary and if I am resolved enough there is no sufficient reason why I shouldn't get my own way'.[115] That is why Eglantyne chose her independence over Margaret. To all intents and purposes, she used the culturally acceptable notion of 'duty' between mother and daughter as an excuse to pull away. At the time it may have felt like a victory, but Eglantyne did not realized that in the long run she would lose Margaret's devotion.

Margaret was 27 years old and under pressure from her mother to get married.[116] In 1912 Mrs Keynes was very busy with her social and political work. She had been elected to the Cambridge town council in 1911, served on numerous sanitation and public-health committees, and was very active with the National Council of Women.[117] It seems, however, that in December she took a break from her work to do some matchmaking. Two weeks before Emily's offer to take over the care of Mrs Jebb, Margaret met Archibald Vivian Hill and his sister Muriel, who were having tea with Mrs Keynes at her home in Harvey Road;

they 'stayed some time'.[118] Archibald Hill was a physiologist who had recently taken up Cambridge COS work. Margaret noticed that her mother seemed to have 'a particular affection' for Hill, who suddenly was at the house a lot and his name began turning up in many letters to Eglantyne: 'Mr. A. V. Hill is depressed with a cold...Perhaps I will ask him to tea'?[119] She told Eglantyne that she had advised him to give up his COS work 'at once' because 'he longs to do research'.[120] She told her that Hill wanted her to go to tea on Monday but her mother did not think it 'would be proper!' Margaret was insulted, 'having for yrs built up the character of being a prig, I might now benefit by being allowed to do as unconventional things as I like'.[121] She told Eglantyne about the fun she had riding in Hill's 'side car' and how much she wanted her 'to get to know him. The fact is, L, he seems to admire yr P a good deal and it rather frightens me. At the same time I like being with him. I suppose it is always nice being with ppl who appreciate you more than you deserve. He writes that I don't know what good it does him being allowed to converse with my good self!! Of course it may just be his friendly ways. Do you think I am silly darling'?[122]

What Margaret did not tell Eglantyne right away was that on 23 January 1913 A. V. Hill had proposed to her. The details of the event were recounted to Duncan Grant by John Maynard Keynes, who stopped by the house to see his mother and inadvertently walked in on the couple just after Margaret had rejected Hill's marriage proposal: 'Marg was really calm and collected', but the 'poor young man was practically in tears...and had extraordinarily the appearance of having had his face bashed in...Tea had just been served and their chairs were drawn up by the fire...He was a pitiable sight...Indeed it's not his fault that's responsible, but the fact that Margaret is more deeply entangled than ever in a Sapphistic affair'.[123]

It is not known exactly what Maynard knew about Margaret and Eglantyne's relationship, but he had 'rather a prejudice against' Sapphism.[124] His own love affair with Duncan Grant did not become public knowledge during his lifetime, though the fact that their letters were 'carefully preserved', suggests that they knew some day it would be. Keynes's biographer, Sir Robert Skidelsky states that whereas today gay-rights activists expect 'acceptance', Keynes and his Cambridge Apostle's generation considered the love of young men to be a superior form of love. They believed 'that women were inferior—in mind and body'. They saw love and sex from an ethical point of view. If 'love should be attached only to worthy objects, then love of young men was ethically better than love of women'. 'Higher Sodomy' was thus an 'ethical position' not merely 'a sexual or emotional preference'.[125] Maynard called sodomy 'the passionate love of comrades'.[126] It trumped Sapphism. He told Duncan, '[Y]our cousin Marjorie [Strachey] seems to Saphinize rather openly with Ray [Rachel Costelloe], but these females always behave as if they had nothing to conceal'.[127] Whatever his philosophical position, in 1913 Maynard valued discretion and he asked Duncan to 'make a secret of Margaret's affair'.[128]

Faderman says that while there were exceptions, even 'women from wealthy families who loved other women generally...still suffered under tremendous and often inescapable pressure to marry'.[129] Margaret must have told her mother of Hill's proposal and been urged to accept it, for three weeks later, Maynard told Grant that Margaret was 'duly engaged to Mr A. V. Hill'.[130] Margaret knew that she should tell Eglantyne about Hill's proposal in person and the following day wrote that she was 'tickler anxious' for her to come, but stated no reason.[131] Once the news was 'public and official' Maynard told Grant that Margaret was in the 'highest state of elation, the family well satisfied, and even the Sapphist not notably obstreperous. "She's much too sensible" Margt. said to me "to make a fuss"'.[132] Hastily plans were made for a June wedding. Margaret and Eglantyne promised each other that the marriage would not disrupt their friendship. Two days after the engagement was announced, Eglantyne wrote a letter to Margaret that revealed her true feelings.

> One thing I was absolutely determined to run no risk of doing—I would not 'hang about you' by which I meant, interfere however slightly or remotely, with claims which must admittedly come first, and a long way first...only 2 courses remained open, to go away, or to deepen our friendship...I began to tend toward the first, because I found that the second might be asking too much of you. I wondered whether I had any business, considering the strength of your feelings and the way in which the whole current of your being must now set...[133]

Eglantyne accepted Margaret's decision to marry and understood that other 'claims' upon Margaret's 'being' had to do with a desire for children. Eglantyne was not interested in playing 'Auntie Eglantyne' to the four Hill babies born during the war years. Margaret was disappointed because her letters suggest that she thought that Eglantyne had abandoned her. She wrote, 'You never write to me now but I know you are probably busy. The only thing is you always will be busy in future, I expect your letters will be further and further in between'.[134]

How does Margaret's and Eglantyne's friendship fit within the history of sexuality and women's biography?[135] Eglantyne died in 1928, the same year that Radclyffe Hall's *Well of Loneliness* was published. Hall's novel depicts a same-sex relationship between two English women who meet while serving in an ambulance corps. Hall explores the relationship using Richard von Kraft-Ebing and Havelock Ellis's congenital theories of 'sexual inversion'. One woman, Stephen was born 'homosexual' a 'true invert', whereas Mary was a 'pseudo-homosexual' (or *faute de mieux*). Their relationship was fraught by social ostracism and isolation and ends with Mary's marriage. Hall portrays same-sex love as biologically determined and created by God, she makes an explicit plea for toleration. Stephen says: 'give us also the right to our existence'.[136] The book was considered obscene and banned in England. Laura Doan says the publicity around the censorship trial brought women's intimate friendships out of the shadows and created for the first time, a single and identifiable 'image' of the lesbian.[137] Afterward the attitude towards women's intimate friendships underwent a reversal because of the microscope of sexology and the 'new science of naming and managing errant sexual ways',[138] which defined friendships between women as abnormal, deviant or shameful in a way that they had not been when Margaret and Eglantyne were together.

When Eglantyne died in 1928, the Save the Children Fund executive approached Margaret, as Jebb's oldest friend, for her memories of their esteemed founder. In the post-*Well* climate, Margaret may have become uneasy and self-conscious. She was, after all, the wife of a Nobel Prize winning professor at the University College of London. In the flappable 1920s she may have wanted to conceal an association with lesbianism. When Dorothy Buxton interviewed her for *The White Flame* in 1929, Margaret assured her that Eglantyne's most intimate letters had been burned. Margaretta Jolly says that, 'nowhere is the vitality of a letter clearer than when it is burned.'[139] Margaret was reluctant to say anything about her own feelings. What she did say was that her marriage to Hill was a 'great blow' to Eglantyne. She thought that Eglantyne had 'become *too dependent* on her...and was convinced that it was in the nature of an obsession'. She told Buxton she used to read Eglantyne's letters to her other friends and they asked her 'chaffingly, "how much of that do you really feel?"'[140]

In *The White Flame* all that Dorothy said of her sister's love life was that 'an intense desire to be of service left her no peace. Balls and parties, her beloved pursuit of riding, the manifold enjoyments offered by the exercise of her literary gifts—these were exchanged for laborious social work and intensive study'.[141] Among family and friends, Dorothy clarified her sister's 'intense desires' by revealing the relationship with Marcus Dimsdale (who committed suicide in 1919).[142] It was a plausible heterosexual explanation, which moved the spotlight off Margaret Keynes and explained Eglantyne's return to social work, which was still a suitable activity for respectable highly educated women in the early 1900s.

Eglantyne and Margaret's friendship was still a source of controversy within their families 40 years later.[143] Between the 1930s and 1960s the boundaries between homosexual and heterosexual behaviour became even tighter. Because of the medico-moral discourses of 1950s, sexual intercourse came to be considered essential to the physical and psychological functioning of mature adults and those who opted out were thought to run a grave mental health risk.[144] By the time the three 'spinsters'—Eglantyne Mary Jebb, aged 78, Francesca Wilson, aged 79 and Eglantyne Buxton, aged 61—began working on *Rebel Daughter* in 1965, sexological discourse and conventions had long since placed never married women like themselves on the defensive. When *Rebel Daughter* appeared in the sexually charged albeit homophobic 1960s, Eglantyne Mary was satisfied with it, but the younger-generation Buxton, was horrified because to the 'modern mind', the friendship suggested that 'EJ was a lesbian'. It bothered her because 'to many people it is very very discrediting'. Buxton loved her aunt and wanted to protect her from the cruel jokes and prurient publicity. She stuck to her mother's explanation that her aunt had been 'overwhelmingly' in love with a man. According to Buxton, in the Victorian and Edwardian periods a '"grand passion" was a familiar phenomenon; a girl would have a "passion" for another, often an older woman. It was a passing phase' and girlish crush, which ended with Margaret's marriage.[145] By privileging Margaret's 'normal' feminine transition to heterosexual marriage and motherhood over Eglantyne's sexually dubious desire for independence and a career, Buxton tried to vindicate them both. Margaret's marriage was proof that they were both heterosexual. In Buxton's assessment, Eglantyne 'had great concern and friendship' for Margaret, 'her immense capacity for feeling—had to find an outlet somehow'. She concluded: 'that seems to me to account for it'.[146]

When Mrs Patrick Campbell asked George Bernard Shaw for permission to publish his love letters, Shaw refused, saying, 'I am not going to play horse to your Godiva'. With this thought in mind, in 1965, Wilson sought legal advice and permission from the 81-year-old Margaret Keynes Hill to quote from her letters in *Rebel Daughter* and they met twice to discuss it. Margaret confirmed that she and Eglantyne had had a 'passionate friendship', which began when they met at the COS. She seemed to Wilson to be 'very proud' and only asked 'to take out 2 or 3 sentences' which 'might be "misunderstood" by her 17 grandchildren'.[147] Eglantyne and Margaret remained life long friends, but the marriage to Hill was the end of their love story. Their lives quickly moved in opposite directions. This chapter has shown that voluntary social work opened up a friendship network to women, but not marrying did not make Eglantyne independent or free to do her work. Nevertheless, as we have seen, in the end, she did not sacrifice her life for her mother. We do not know if Mrs Jebb was disturbed by what Eglantyne wrote in 'The Ring Fence' or what she thought of the *Times* correspondent who said, 'Let parents remember that their daughters have the same aspirations as themselves, the same longings and the hopes they once had',[148] but with Tye's encouragement in 1913, Eglantyne travelled alone to the Balkans and inspected refugee camps and hospitals for the Macedonian Relief Fund and it marked the beginning of a new direction in her life.

8
The Sisters and Social Action

On 15 May 1919, it was announced in the press that Eglantyne Jebb and a suffragette named Barbara Ayrton Gould of the Women's International League for Peace and Freedom (WILPF) had been arrested in Trafalgar Square for handing out leaflets demanding that the government end the blockade of the Central Powers. The *Times* published an article headed 'Raise the Blockade Leaflets' and the *Daily Herald* reprinted copies of the leaflets and a photograph of Jebb and Ayrton Gould standing in the street outside of the Mansion House Police Court, where they had been summoned to appear on charges of violating the Defence of the Realm Act. Eglantyne's leaflet included a photograph of a starving Austrian baby and the statement: 'Millions of children are suffering in health, thousands actually dying: we must save them, but we can only do so if we put aside political animosities and unite...[T]o save them is more important than...boundaries, indemnities, or any political question.'[1] Her leaflet announced that a new charity called the Save the Children Fund (SCF) would be launched at an upcoming Fight the Famine Council (FFC) rally at Albert Hall.[2] This chapter focuses on Eglantyne's life between 1913 and 1919; it shows that she was increasingly drawn to direct-action organizations and to people, including her sisters, who were combining their personal, spiritual and political ideologies with meaningful voluntary social action.

According to Leila Rupp the First World War 'energized' women.[3] Indeed, Frank Prochaska's, *Women and Philanthropy*, shows that while Victorian women trod cautiously around the political side of their work, this was no longer necessary in the twentieth century. Local and international women's suffrage societies had been run along the lines established by nineteenth century philanthropic institutions, and the fundraising, bookkeeping, committee work methods were adopted by Edwardian suffragists.[4] By 1900 many women's voluntary organizations

8.1   Mansion House Court, evidence for the prosecution, source: Jebb Family

were so entrenched in political issues that voluntary action and social action were inseparable in their minds.[5] They took full advantage of new opportunities in municipal agencies and hoped to influence government policy directly.[6] Many women, the Jebb sisters included, were protesting, lobbying and campaigning for social and political causes. After Eglantyne returned to England, her mother found a house in Sussex, 'Miss Taylor' was engaged to serve as her companion and Eglantyne was much freer to work and resume her writing. From then on, her life became much more entwined with the lives and work of her sisters, Louisa (Lil) Wilkins and Dorothy Buxton.

Julia Parker identifies 'close family connections' as one of the features that several prominent Victorian women had in common. By this she means families who shared an interest in the 'problems of the world' and their 'duty and right' to 'take part in public affairs'.[7] Parker's observation can be applied to the Jebb family. In charity organizations 'sisterhood' was both figurative and literal in many late-Victorian voluntary agencies. Some Anglican charities took names like Sisters of Charity, Sisters of the People and Sisters of the Poor. Some charity workers were really sisters, the most famous examples being the McMillan and Potter sisters.[8] Eglantyne and Lil and even more so, Eglantyne and Dorothy are candidates for the list because the later partnership led to the formation of the first international children's rights charity.

Dorothy Jebb left the Lyth in 1900 to pursue higher education, and after a year at a boarding school in Bournemouth, she followed in Lil's footsteps to Newnham College to read politics and economics. Dorothy, who had inherited a strong sense of social justice from her mother, joined the Women's University Settlement. And having inherited from her father a passion for debating, she joined the Political Debating Society. The Newnham debaters became proficient at presenting mock bills, thereby preparing themselves for the political work many women of this generation would do. Dorothy's chief debating rival was Mary Agnes Hamilton, who stood against her as Liberal Party leader. Hamilton recalled that 'D.F.'s fiery' speeches were 'narrow, fanatical and unrealistic' and D.F. was not 'a co-operator'. She had a 'tendency to a one-eyed line of her own'. Hamilton had no 'regrets in beating Dorothy', but she wanted her in her '"Cabinet"'.[9] Other people's opinions of Dorothy are informative. Her tutor, John Maynard Keynes, considered her intelligence to be 'exceptional'.[10] Years later her children would describe her as 'terrifying in an argument.'[11] After 15 years of marriage, her husband, Charles Roden Buxton, said of his wife, 'she would mould this world of ours if she could, nay break it and recast it...She has made her brain a keen sword and kept it sharp. She is a fighter on our human battle-ground...She is a bringer of discomfort—so people think, and rightly think.'[12]

In the early 1900s Cambridge University women were conscious that they would have choices that were unknown to their mother's generation, but the topics of religion and sex were still taboo. The Newnham students were 'all blankly ignorant about sex and its manifestations'. Hamilton said they 'made up for this' by talking about love and politics 'a great deal'.[13] In 1902 Dorothy met Charlie Buxton, a 29-year-old Liberal Party hopeful who had been a student of Sir Richard Jebb's at Trinity College. He came from an influential English brewing family. His great-grandfather had introduced a bill to emancipate slaves of Great Britain in 1833. His Quaker great-grandmother was a sister of Elizabeth Fry.[14] At Trinity Charlie was president of the student union and enjoyed amateur theatricals and hunting until he grasped that blood sports were 'repugnant'.[15] He supported women's access to university. In the *Cambridge Review* he questioned 'why the advantages of education... should be allowed to every nationality, every creed, every colour under heaven, but denied to their own sisters'.[16] After leaving Trinity with a first in the Classical Tripos, Charles went to Australia, where his father was Governor. When he failed to get a fellowship his plans for an academic career vanished, his health broke and the doctors sent him to the Riviera to recover. From there he went to Texas and worked on a cattle ranch for

.2   Charles and Dorothy Buxton, source: Buxton Family

six months. When the 'ex-Texas Cowboy',[17] as the press later dubbed him, returned to London in 1901, he began working for the Liberal Party, read for the Bar and gave lectures on English literature at a workingmen's college.

There will always be some people, like Arthur T. Jebb, for whom the 'angel of the house' connotes a golden age, but many progressive highly educated Edwardians saw 'the angel' as the a symbol of oppressed womanhood, 'trapped in the gilded cage of Victorian male domination'.[18] Many Edwardian couples wished to replace the Victorian ideal with an 'equally close but egalitarian model of private life' resembling a companionate socialist or feminist comradeship where participants were free to become autonomous human beings.[19] By the early twentieth century Sidney Webb and Beatrice Potter, Bernard Bosanquet and Helen Dendy, and Fredrick and Emmeline Pethick-Lawrence were setting an example of the new marriage ideal amongst settlement workers. These couples combined their companionate ideals with like-minded intellectual and political pursuits and social activism.[20] In 1902 Charlie took at break to help his suffragist-Newnham sister Victoria organize a 'Trinity-Newnham reading party' in the Lake District. The guests included prominent young lecturers and student-intellectuals of all political stripes, including Dorothy Jebb.[21] Charlie and Dorothy quickly discovered that they shared a love of poetry and the Liberal Party. Shortly afterwards, Charlie dedicated his life to politics, poetry and Dorothy.

Hamilton said that Dorothy and 'her young man' were very interesting to the voyeuristic Newnham clique, who were relieved that 'there was no uncomfortable evidence of physical passion' between them.[22] The late 1890s was a period of 'self-consciousness and frankness' in discussions of the marriage question in '"advanced" circles'.[23] Newnham women agreed that the ideal marriage should epitomize 'mutual dedication and dedication to high goals and ideals'. They approved of the Buxton-Jebb match because of their commitment to 'high ideals and good works'.[24] Dorothy told Hamilton that there was only one subject upon which she and Charlie disagreed. She was a 'militant materialist' and he a 'deeply sincere and reverent Christian', so Hamilton assumed Dorothy meant religion, but she did not. The 'bone of contention' was Old Age Pensions. Dorothy was distressed because Charlie was in favour of a 'non-contributory scheme' and she intended to 'convert him'.[25]

Charlie and Dorothy devoted their lives to social justice and humanitarian causes. Charlie called Dorothy his 'Dear Comrade'. Like Fred Pethick-Lawrence who promised Emmeline that he would never put his interest or career before hers,[26] Charlie vowed he would never 'try to sweep a woman from her own unfettered judgments'. A sentiment like this would have astonished his late father-in-law in 1886, but Charlie meant it. He was as committed to Dorothy's work as he was to his own. He told her, 'Sometimes I think we are showing our-selves wiser and stronger than other people. Sometimes I think we are heaping up ramparts of sand against the contemptuous, the irresistible flooding of the sea'.[27] From the outset, Eglantyne liked Charlie very much. He had also engaged in social experiments sojourning among the poor as she had done while teaching in Marlborough. In the 1890s, Charlie's elder brother Noel had fallen under the influence of the settlement movement and conducted 'slumming' experiments.[28] Noel and Charlie dressed up in their oldest clothes and spent evenings loitering about pubs and common lodging-houses near the Buxton's brewery, 'where a vast common frying-pan' formed 'a link' between the wealthy Buxton brothers and the 'working-people they wanted to know'.[29]

It was through supporting Charlie's early election campaigns that Eglantyne abandoned her 'romantic Toryism'.[30] She joined the Liberal Party around 1906, became honorary secretary of the Liberal Political Education Committee and campaigned hard to get Charlie and the Cambridge candidate, Stanley Owen Buckmaster elected. After two attempts Charlie got into Parliament in 1910. To assist the Liberals and Charlie's campaign, Eglantyne wrote a 'Manual of Prayers' that was used by party members and supporters.[31] Her contributions to the elec-tion campaign resulted in her introduction to the wider Liberal Party. An article in the *Cambridge Independent Press* on 8 July 1910 reported that 'Miss Jebb made her first appearance on a Liberal platform

> ...when she spoke with great earnestness and eloquence on behalf of Mr Buckmaster...Never had educational work been so thoroughly done in Cambridge as during the last 6 months, and this happy result is owning to Miss Jebb more than anybody else...Miss Jebb lost her father before she began to take an interest in politics, and grew up a Conservative...Miss Jebb in describing her conversion, says, 'I was a long time realising that social reform on the part of the conservatives is like charity in the hands of a Lady Bountiful—everything to be made nice and pleasant, but the "upper class" is to be respected and obeyed. The corruption at elections first opened my eyes, and I came to believe that no social reform could be of use which did not promote the independence of the people.'[32]

In the 'official history' of the Save the Children Fund, *The Right of the Child*, Eglantyne's co-worker Edward Fuller explains that when war broke out in the Balkans, Jebb heard the ancient cry 'come over to Macedonia and help us!' She reportedly rushed to Greece 'to help bring relief to the civilian victims of war'.[33] Fuller's simplistic account of what actually happened shows that Eglantyne continued the Macedonian Relief Fund fundraising work she had been doing for Charlie Buxton early in 1913 but without Margaret Keynes, who lost interest in it after she met Archibald Hill.[34] In 1912, Charlie was appointed as Secretary of the Land Enquiry; however, his longer-term interest, which he shared with Noel, was the political rights and cultures of small nations. As advocates of internationalism, the Buxtons supported the independence struggles in Wales, Ireland, in South Africa (on behalf of the Boers) and above all, the Balkans, where they believed the Turks were oppressing the Macedonians. In 1902, Noel and Charlie created the Balkan Committee, and after the insurrection of 1903, they formed the Macedonian Relief Fund (MRF) to help refugees.[35]

Through Charlie, Eglantyne became interested in questions of national identity and she was struck by the difficulties she faced when she tried to raise money for the MRF because the money was going to people outside the country. She was also astonished by how much more money had been given by 'non-conformist Christians' than by members of the Church of England.[36] At the Charity Organization Society she had learned a great deal about co-ordinating charitable initiatives. She suggested to the MRF executive that they should try organizing some 'non-party meetings…with facilities for earmarking donations for the Turks' because it would enable 'people of every shade of opinion' to donate 'not on political but on purely humanitarian grounds'. This 'would afford… the political parties to co-operate for once'.[37] The First Balkans War had recently ended, and the Serbs were victorious. The Turks had been driven out of Greece, but the treatment of the civilians on both sides was callous.[38] In February, Charlie asked Eglantyne to go to Macedonia to survey the MRF hospital and recommend how the funds might be better spent. Eglantyne spent the first two weeks of March 1913 touring refugee hospitals in Monastir, shown around by the English nurses who cared for the 'stricken multitudes'.[39] It was the first time she had witnessed the suffering of people under the privations of war and she was 'very glad' to 'have had this practical experience of starting relief, because now I really feel I know a little bit how it is done'.[40]

Although Eglantyne had been sent to Macedonia to report on the administration of aid to the Muslim and Christian refugees, her attention was caught by the work of the English nurses who ran the hospitals. She had been familiar with women's hospital work since her

Lady Margaret Hall days, but it had never appealed to her. After touring a hospital in 1897 she had said she could not imagine being 'mewed up' all day with 'nurses...dying babies' and 'no time for conversation'.[41] By 1913 her attitude had changed: 'My first feeling [on surveying a ward] was a sense of home'. She admired the chief agent, Miss MacQueen, who was with the Queen's Jubilee Nurses. MacQueen told Eglantyne how she had crossed the mountains on horseback 'through mud, over rocks...[I]t was fearsome in places' to reach the men, women and children in the 'ransacked villages'.[42] Eglantyne was impressed by her courage. When she returned to England she wrote a report called 'The Barbarous Balkans' for the *Brown Book, Lady Margaret Hall Chronicle* (1913) and a newspaper article 'Where War Has Been: Lady's Work in Macedonia'.[43] It began with the line, 'thinking of mice and hoping for jam' and proceeded to describe the 'prosaic suffering' of the non-combatant victims who faced 'the slow torture of gradual starvation...influenza, bronchitis, typhoid fever and smallpox...[A] continuous stream of refugees flooded the roads'.[44] Eglantyne did not know it then, but this was the first of hundreds of descriptions of destitution, poverty and suffering that she was to write over the next 15 years. She constructed her plea for funds around the Charity Organization Society principle that the best way to help 'destitute refugees' to make a 'fresh start' and go back to a 'self-supporting life' was to help them to return to their villages. She told her readers that 'repatriation should appeal to all lovers of sound charity'.[45]

By the time Eglantyne became involved with the Macedonian relief work, it had been almost three years since she had done any public speaking; however, in May and June she travelled around Scotland and England giving lectures on Macedonia to help raise money for the refugees. In a letter to Margaret she described how she had 'trudged from house to house all day' with little money at the end to show for it.[46] In her next letter she said that while sitting at dinner she had watched a suffragette address a crowd of hundreds. From the dining room window of the Old Waverly Hotel in Edinburgh, she 'could just see through the gathering darkness the outline of her graceful figure swaying between two fluttering flags'. When the suffragette 'turned her face...the lamplight showed its pallor.' Eglantyne was so moved that she went out into the street just 'in time to hear her defend militancy'. Eglantyne told Margaret that she had never seen 'anything like the coolness' with which the suffragette 'smashed up and trampled on every objection'. Without realizing what she was doing Eglantyne bought a copy of the 'condemned paper—"the Suffragette"'. She did not support militancy of any kind, but the 'exhausted' suffragette on the road outside her hotel whose 'marvellous' speech had 'gripped and dominated' the 'hostile audience'[47] stimulated Eglantyne's imagination just as the courageous English nurses in Macedonia had done. Eglantyne was beginning to see new possibilities for herself in the work other women were doing for social and political causes, and this included her sister Lil who had become a 'tireless advocate' of the Co-operative Small Holdings Society.[48]

In 1902, Rider Haggard wrote that 'nothing concerning the future of the land excited so much controversy' and 'animated discussion' as the size of farms and the best method of profitable agriculture.[49] One of the leading proponents of the smallholdings and co-operative movements was Louisa Wilkins, who by 1913 was living in London with her husband Roland and two daughters. In 1892 their aunt accurately predicted that Lil would be successful at Newnham. One of the first English women to take an agricultural diploma, she emerged with a strong moral conviction that English agriculture needed to be reformed. When Charlie Buxton joined the Land Enquiry office he encouraged Lil to take her ideas, which were regarded as a 'rash political experiment',[50] into the political sphere. In 1907 Lil wrote an influential book based upon a three-year of study for the Co-operative Holdings Association called the *Small Holdings of England: A Survey of Various Systems* and she was called to testify before the Select Committee on the Small holdings and Allotments Act.[51] In the early 1900s the alternative agriculture movement wanted to bring men and women back to the land by applying the doctrine of self-help to voluntary co-operative organizations. Lil's survey included interviews with large landowners who had successfully converted their vast estates into smallholdings so that agricultural labours and families could gradually take over grain and livestock production and eventually become freeholders, what Horace Pluckett called, 'peasant proprietors'.[52] Lil's survey described how to set up co-operative benefit societies, equipment co-ops, credit banks, cow and pig clubs, profitable market gardens and allotment societies. The benefit for agricultural labourers was that they 'became their own masters'.[53] She cited the Parish of Friskney as an example of successful land reform. In Friskney she could only find a 'few widows' receiving 'parish relief' and saw 'practically no drunkards'.[54] Lil concluded that once the working classes had a stake in smallholdings and co-operative enterprises, 'Thrifty hard working populations' would be 'empowered to benefit their own by self-help'. This would 'bring men back into the land [and]...raise the level of cottages...because people refuse to live in the tumbled down cottages they would otherwise have been compelled to put up with'.[55]

All of the Jebb sisters supported alternative methods of landowning and the co-operative movement.[56] Dorothy Kempe said that Eglantyne fell in love with the co-operative movement.[57] This explains why Eglantyne's 'The Ring Fence' was much more than a dense saga of love and hate, duty and loyalty, patronage and power in landed aristocratic families. In 'The Ring Fence', Eglantyne wanted to provide a fictional account of Lil's intensive factual survey. This is why her villains are cruel landlords who starve the overworked labourers and why her heroes are composite portraits of the real reformist landowners—Harris, Bligh, Freyer, Eyre and Lord Harrowby—whom Lil interviewed in her survey. In 'The Ring Fence', Eglantyne describes exactly how an enlightened landlord could break up his vast estate and create smallholdings. She further advanced Lil's position by recommending that the manor house be converted into a workingmen's college and the gatehouse to a people's archaeological museum. Like her previous *Cambridge Survey*, 'The Ring Fence' drew on primary social scientific research to promote her strong moral conviction, in this case, that the co-operative movement 'was a gateway to human regeneration' and the foundation of the 'new moral and economic order'.[58]

In 1913 Lil was on the executive of the Agricultural Organization Society (AOS), which promoted the ideals of the new rural society, the training of women for careers in agriculture, market gardening and co-operative food production.[59] Lil asked Eglantyne to take over the editorship of the newsletter, *The Plough*. Although Eglantyne was still working for Macedonian relief, she agreed; however, she decided to ask for a salary.[60] The reason for the salary was not just because she wanted an income. Eglantyne had begun to regard the overwork of unpaid women by benevolent agencies as a form of exploitation. She told Margaret, who was still volunteering for the COS that 'we ought to take a strong stand' about getting paid for our work. She added, 'One of the reasons why I contemplated asking the AOS to pay me, is that it would place me in a position to organize one department at least of the AOS in which people won't be overworked'.[61]

Eglantyne was given a salary of 125 pounds a year. She took over *The Plough* in September, and by March 1914 described herself as 'not only the editor but the entire staff...journalist, clerks, typists, office boy, all rolled into one'.[62] One of the first people she met at the office was Henry Lionel Pilkington, a 56-year-old army officer who had been decorated for service in South Africa, the West Indies and Australia.

Pilkington and his wife were both prominent in the Irish co-operative movement. He wrote articles on rural development under the pseudo nym 'Patrick Perterras'.[63] His wife, Ellice Pilkington, the daughter of Sir John Esmonde, was the 'most gifted and energetic' founder of United Irishwomen (1910), a 'nonpolitical' association committed to stem ming the emigration of rural Irish women by improving agricultura life, and for Ellice Pilkington this meant Home Rule.[64] In 1914, Eglan tyne told her friend Maud Holgate that Pilkington's wife had gone insane and been 'confined' as 'incurable' to an asylum.[65] Eglantyne was instantly attracted to Colonel Pilkington. She described him as 'very gentle, courteous and witty...zealous hard working and capable.. public-spirited'. She told Dorothy Kempe that he was going to be her 'chief ally and helper'.[66] Therefore, she was deeply saddened when Pilkington suddenly died from septic pneumonia on 6 March 1914. She told her friends that she felt as if she had lost an 'old and intimate friend', which she admitted was strange because she 'really did not know him so very well'. They had only just discovered that they had the 'same politics...till a few days ago...we had always thought the other was an enthusiastic Conservative!'[67]

Margaret was too wrapped up in the excitement of her first pregnancy and plans for the baby due in June to grasp how deeply Pilkington's death was troubling Eglantyne. She merely responded, '[I]t is fearfully bad luck to have lost your best contributor, but another may turn up to take his place'.[68] Margaret's off-handed reply that someone 'may turn up' was both ironic and prophetic, because Eglantyne had withheld a crucial piece of information about her relationship with Pilkington. Maud Holgate, an old friend from Lady Margaret Hall, was staying with Eglantyne at the time and Eglantyne told Holgate that Pilkington's spirit had appeared to her and she was communicating with it. Holgate over heard these conversations and was alarmed because Eglantyne 'began to allot a special time daily (about two hours) in her bedroom to talk'.[69] She said that Eglantyne seemed to 'live for the daily talk and all that it meant to her'.[70] She begged her to stop, but Eglantyne refused to discuss it. Every evening Eglantyne carefully transcribed her conservations with Pilkington's ghost into a journal she labelled 'Conversations with a Departed Friend', which within two weeks exceeded 50 typed pages.[71]

Eglantyne's interest in the spiritual world was not recent. Since her brother Gamul's death in 1896, she had felt in touch with the spirit world.[72] Many people in Lady Jebb's Cambridge social circle had been associated with Henry Sidgwick's Society of Psychical Research, which made psychic 'investigations' of paranormal phenomenon. Eglantyne had enjoyed hearing accounts of the 'spiritual séances' at the Sidgwicks ady Jebb said the professors were 'as anxious to believe as infants'. She thought psychic research was 'arrant nonsense' however it was amusing to watch 'these great geniuses' look for truth in a 'millstone'.[73] Eglantyne's Marlborough diary contains an account of an afternoon talking about Anna Kingsford, mysticism and spiritualism with friends.[74] Dorothy Buxton did not share this interest and was very alarmed to discover the 'Conversations with a Departed Friend' among Eglantyne's old papers. In 1933 she wrote to Holgate suggesting that 'nothing should ever be made public' concerning the episode. Holgate agreed and said it was unlikely that Eglantyne had spoken to anyone except her about the 'conversations'.[75] Holgate was wrong. Eglantyne discussed her psychic experiences, which occurred when she was 'feverish', with many people who thought that her premonitions were 'unusual psychic instincts'.[76] Florence Keynes had first come across Eglantyne's 'second sightedness' in Drogheda when their tour was cut short because Eglantyne 'got into an extremely nervous condition…[She] seemed to get back into the troubled atmosphere of the sack of Drogheda. E. said: "I cant bear it". The place is full of ghosts'.[77] Dorothy Kempe knew of Eglantyne's 'Conversations with the Dead'. Eglantyne once told her about meeting a 'distressed' woman on a train. She could not have known that the woman had recently 'lost her sister'. Nevertheless 'presently' Eglantyne saw a 'standing figure' in the coach who 'conveyed to her the message…"speak to her". Then it vanished'. Eglantyne was convinced that the 'standing figure' was her fellow traveller's dead sister. She delivered her 'message of comfort to her companion.'[78]

There is a rational explanation for Eglantyne's reaction to Pilkington's death that must be considered alongside the possibility that she was in direct communication with the spirit world'.[79] A series of emotionally painful events had occurred in her life over the previous 12 months. In spite of her conviction that it was her duty to look after her mother, she had hired Miss Taylor as Tye's companion, a decision that probably provoked stronger feelings of guilt than she anticipated. In addition, there were major delays with Tye's house in Sussex, and in February 1914 they were forced to spend three months in Locarno, where they could live cheaply, while they waited for the house. The trip started badly. Eglantyne was not looking forward to three months in 'exile' with her mother. She told Margaret, 'Mother is hating the place, she says that her room is shaped like a coffin. It is pouring with rain and I really don't know where else we are to go'.[80] It was in Lacarno that the news of Pilkington's death reached Eglantyne.

In addition to her worries about her mother, Eglantyne was also dealing with the new direction her seven-year relationship with Margaret had taken. Margaret's marriage had been a 'great blow' to Eglantyne. She loved Margaret 'more than anyone else in the world'.[81] If she was having second thoughts about her own part in initially altering the nature of their friendship, the news of Margaret's pregnancy only three months after her wedding, signalled that it was too late to go back. Margaret said Eglantyne 'was obsessed with the idea of death and always terrified that (Margaret) would die'.[82] Pregnancy was still dangerous in 1914, and Pilkington's sudden death when Margaret was six months pregnant may have reawakened Eglantyne's fear that Margaret might die too, and irrationally, that her own selfishness had put her beloved friend's life in danger.

Eglantyne was aware that she had disrupted many people's lives for her 'work', which was central to her self-identity, and she was prepared to sacrifice a great deal more for it; however, her work was not going well in 1914 either. She had planned to do her AOS work in Switzerland but the 'fatigue of travelling' made it difficult to concentrate and reawakened old anxieties of failure.[83] She felt guilty about abandoning her co-workers for so long because everyone around her was overworked, especially at the MRF. She believed that she was needed in the office. Many MRF members who had been eyewitnesses to the great human suffering the wars caused in 1912 and 1913 were 'very much distressed' when the fighting began again in February 1914. Many people on the MRF committee had put their personal and professional lives on hold to help the region's dispossessed, but the end of the ceasefire caused some to wonder if the Turks, Albanians, Bulgarians and Greeks 'invest[ed] too much in regard to the "sacred right" of "nationality"'. In COS terms, the 'refugees' were exhibiting a weak commitment to what old Charity Organizationists called self-help and were showing themselves to be 'unworthy' recipients of MRF charity. Eglantyne said she no longer knew who to 'feel most sorry for', and some members of the MRF were 'sick to death of the whole concern'.[84] Morale was low at the AOS as well. Eglantyne had a tendency to 'idealize' people and only saw what she wanted to see in them.[85] In a few short months she had begun to idealize Colonel Pilkington, whom she regarded as a 'very distinguished man in mind and bearing'.[86] She thought he was doing great work in the world, just like she wanted to do. And she had finally found a friend who was going to help her. Pilkington's untimely death was too much to bear.

On top of all of these stressful life events, Eglantyne had been suffering from a slowly progressing thyroid disease for a decade. Adult hypothyroidism, or 'myxedema', was first identified in 1874 and linked in 1888 to 'delusions and hallucinations', a connection still made in 1940 when the term 'myxedema madness' entered the medical literature.[87] The association stuck because impaired thyroid functioning mimics many indicators of mental illness. Since 1906 the only treatment Eglantyne had received for her mood disorders and depression, which were caused, at least in part, by her malfunctioning thyroid were fresh air, controlled diet and bed-rest. News of Pilkington's death did not trigger a florid psychosis, for Eglantyne's letters show that she continued to work and write coherently, however the shock did trigger some disengagement from reality.

News of a sudden or tragic death, according to Freudians, may result in severe fear anxiety, with psychosis and projections. Communication with ghosts is a way to cling to the object of loss. Once the person deals with their fear the apparitional symptoms disappear. Eglantyne's reaction to Pilkington's death and the nature of her bereavement can be made clearer to the modern reader by reference to Dr Elisabeth Kubler-Ross's five stages of grief: denial, bargaining, anger, depression and acceptance.[88] Eglantyne's letters to Margaret and Dorothy Kempe show that she was not in denial, for when the AOS asked her to write Pilkington's obituary she did so immediately. She knew she suffered from depression[89] and she was certainly angry, but at whom and about what? Pilkington's death triggered deep feelings of loss, but so did Margaret's pregnancy. Since the wedding Eglantyne had received numerous letters from Margaret gushing with details of her new and happy life: '[Vivian] is a delightful travelling companion, considerate and thoughtful...[I am] very lucky...[I've] got the best husband in the world, having already the best friend and the best parents and brothers...It gets better and better and I couldn't have a more perfect lover...it is impossible to imagine a man who would be more considerate to a woman than V is to me...I shall be very well looked after! Mother gets on excellently with Mrs. Hill and Muriel.' In December 1913, Margaret wrote, '[W]hen you get here...there will be [a baby] to nurse, to amuse and take out and you will love that!! Poor dear put-upon Auntie Eglantyne'.[90]

Kubler-Ross's theory suggests that Pilkington's sudden death and the appearance of his ghost represents the 'bargaining' stage of grief. In 1914, Eglantyne was frustrated by her work, lonely, jealous, sick, 'exiled' again with her mother, and grieving the loss of two treasured friendships; but rather than lash out at Mrs Jebb, Margaret or Pilkington, Eglantyne projected her anger toward the AOS and social work. Her final 'conversations' with Pilkington enabled her to move onward and accept his death by giving her one last chance to get the help he had promised her. In her 'conversations' she asked him all the questions she could about the Board of Agriculture, divine love and redemption, consciousness, the condition of life after death, Galileo and the psychic world, and Home Rule.[91] In the 'conversations' Pilkington assured her that he was not sad or suffering. In the obituary she wrote for him, she lashed out at unpaid social work for contributing to his death. She told Margaret that the AOS was not going to like her obituary because she had 'made no secret of the responsibility the AOS had incurred by overworking him…It is often said when women breakdown in doing social work, that if men were concerned they would never be so foolish. But place them under similar circumstance and they are every bit as bad, every bit.'[92] Once she felt that she had got justice for Pilkington, she was able to give up his ghost.[93]

In 1933 Maud Holgate assured Dorothy that Eglantyne's 'conversations' were a sign 'leading her to be indeed a hand of God's will and to be used by him for great work'. Holgate interpreted this work as the Save the Children Fund.[94] But Eglantyne's physical health did not improve much, and when the First World War began she was too ill to sign up for war work. Her letters describe the 'clashing of bombs' and watching out for 'Zeppelins' and morning greetings to the maid, when instead of saying, 'what a beautiful day, we are not going to have drop of rain, you say…what a beautiful night! Not a single bomb'.[95] Eglantyne's thyroid disease had been progressing, and despite almost year of bed rest she had goitre surgery and radium treatment in 1916. Her 'doctor at the Radium Institute' believed 'in mountain air for goitre cases, when recovery sets in'.[96] Eglantyne spent many months at a cottage in Scotland; Charlotte Toynbee kept her company. She also visited her sister Emily in Ireland.

In the autumn of 1917 Eglantyne was well enough to join the Buxton household in London. The foundation of Charlie and Dorothy's lives was their strong Christian socialist ideals. Like many of their compatriots amongst the 'intellectual aristocracy' of the Liberal Party 'the personal became political'.[97] They were renowned for practising what they preached and had self-consciously rejected the 'comforts and privileges of their class and childhoods, especially the large country houses and numerous servants.[98] Their first flat was in a working-class neighbourhood of Kennington Terrace close to Trinity Mission, where they did their settlement work, and the workingman's college where Charlie taught. They further demonstrated their ideals by doing most of their own house work and never taking taxis. A nephew, Bernard de Bunsen, recalled that the Buxton's always stayed in 'the cheapest, the least attractive, if not the grubbiest hotels they could find, on principle'.[99] Though neither Charlie nor Dorothy was what the Edwardians called 'child lovers', they had two children. Eglantyne Roden Buxton was born in 1906, and David in 1910. The whole family loved the outdoors and camping, but the children were frequently left to their own devices.[100]

By 1914 Dorothy was a committed pacifist, and within weeks of the outbreak of the war she gave up their house to German refugees and rented a flat for her family in Hampstead Garden.[101] She soon became so 'horrified by the language of jingoism' in the mainstream British press, especially the dehumanization of the German people, that she took up journalism herself.[102] She feared that wartime propaganda would only prolong the war and make a genuine peace settlement impossible. To give the public a more balanced view, she began translating articles from the foreign newspapers in order to show the effect the war was having on the civilians; she published them anonymously as circulars. In August 1915 she decided to send them to *Cambridge Magazine*,[103] which was the largest circulating university weekly in England between 1916 and 1920.[104] The chief editor was Charles Kay Ogden, a charismatic young intellectual and pacifist. Ogden offered Dorothy a weekly column called 'Notes from the Foreign Press',[105] which they launched in the 28 October 1916 issue. It soon became known that 'Mrs C. R. Buxton' was the editor. When the importation of many foreign papers was banned under the Defence of the Realm Act, Charlie used his influence with Lloyd George to get Dorothy a special licence from the Board of Trade to continue importing banned papers.[106] The papers 'arrived through the letterbox' of Buxton's Hampstead flat where Eglantyne had a bed-sit.[107]

In the *Right of the Child*, Edward Fuller says the First World War 'brought with it conditions quite different from those of earlier wars. It was no longer possible for civilians like Miss Jebb in Macedonia, or—half a century earlier—Henri Dunant, the founder of the Red Cross, at Solferino, to wander at will behind the lines, succouring the victims. Eglantyne had to content herself with fighting her part of the battle from her desk in London'.[108] This is a typical example of SCF hyperbole and of Fuller's tendency to attribute Dorothy's motivations to Eglantyne. In the 1950s Dorothy objected to his sidelining of her role, reminding Fuller that she was the Jebb sister behind the *Cambridge Magazine*. It was she rather than Eglantyne who 'felt that the greatest service she could render was to make known to the British people the terrible things which were taking place in the war-stricken lands'.[109] What is true is that Eglantyne helped organize volunteers and translate articles. Due to efforts of their girlhood foreign governesses, Eglantyne and Dorothy were still fairly fluent in French and German. Eglantyne applied what she had learned training volunteers at the COS to the 'large staff of public minded...

specialists in Russian, Scandinavian and Italian' who offered to help. They each had to 'read one important daily paper, cut out and mark and label the most important articles, give short summaries of most important ones.' Eglantyne told an Italian specialist that the papers arrived on Wednesday and had to be sent off by us by Friday, making the work 'a little heavy in the middle of the week'.[110] David Buxton, who was a small boy at the time, remembered watching bundles of newspapers fall through the letterbox and the 'hive of industry in the editorial office—namely the large attic room in our Golders Green house'.[111] David was also struck by the contrast between his mother and his aunt's personalities. His mother was 'a formidable person...rather lacking in a sense of humour', whereas his aunt seemed to 'attract people to her'. She had a 'vivid personality...charismatic...and a sense of humour which allowed her to laugh at herself'.[112]

Between 1916 and 1918 Dorothy and her team of volunteers gleaned over 200 newspapers for 'pertinent material'.[113] Ogden admitted that 'Notes From the Foreign Press' likely escalated war tensions as evidenced by the number of readers who cancelled their subscriptions, the withdrawal of advertisers and the personal harassment of everyone involved. One subscriber complained that *Cambridge Magazine* was a 'perverted intelligence'.[114] Another letter arrived on black-bordered stationary from a grieving reader who called Buxton's column 'pro-German poison'.[115] On 11 November 1918 the *Cambridge Magazine* office was raided and Ogden's bookstore was bombed as an Armistice Day gesture of loyalty to Britain.[116] The Buxton household became associated with pacifism, which to some meant they were unpatriotic. Charlie caused uproar at a Friends' meeting in 1916 when his speech, entitled 'The War: Problems of Settlement', was interrupted by 'the hoots and hollers' of a delegate with the Anti-German Union. One heckler yelled, 'You're trying to preach pro-Germanism under the cloak of religion. You're a traitor...you ought to be hung by the neck.' Charlie's attacker began singing 'God Save the King' and the audience joined in heartily. A journalist reported that Mr Buxton sang along too in a 'demonstration of loyalty'.[117]

Cambridge Magazine also received many letters of support. William Cadbury donated five pounds and wrote that the 'translations were... invaluable to anyone whose mind is not closed to instruction'.[118] C. Franklin Angus of the Indian YMCA wrote that 'Mrs. Buxton's selection' was 'quite invaluable, esp. as the Indian papers publish nothing from enemy sources'. He was 'surprised' that she had 'been allowed to go on for so long'.[119] Even unsympathetic readers agreed that 'Foreign Notes' was 'broadening'. One wrote, 'I disagree with your magazine...and get fairly wrathful every Tuesday when I get it... I hope to kill a few Germans before the war ends and in any case don't think life is worth living unless and until Russian Militarism is destroyed. By the same token, I would always support the freedom of the press. We are fighting against Tyranny'.[120]

As an active working mother in wartime, Dorothy performed the same juggling act as other working mothers. In contrast to some women of her class, however, she did not turn her children over to her unmarried sister or a governess, for unlike the spinster aunts of old, Eglantyne had not joined the Buxton household to perform unpaid childcare services. In fact, her nephew David did not think that his aunt seemed interested in 'individual children'.[121] Instead, as Tye had done in her Home Arts and Industries Association days, Dorothy included her children in her work. Ogden tried to ease her burden by sending four-year-old David some books. When Dorothy thanked him, she added, 'David has flu or some mysterious complaint (temp 104) and these books are most comforting. It makes it possible for me to scrape though my work. He wants me all the time, but [books] are a good substitute! The CM...as you may have noticed shows symptoms of flu too'.[122] In another letter she told Ogden about 'trying' to revise a 'translation in the train with my children one on each side of me. They are insufferable'.[123] She sent them to 'excellent' Sussex friends 'for a whole week' to get her 'longed for full day alone at home'.[124] After the war the Buxton children were sent to learn French at a boarding school in Geneva. Soon afterward, the father of one of the pupils threatened to withdraw his child upon discovering that the Buxtons had 'contaminated' his child with 'their subversive internationalist views'.[125]

Dorothy kept editorial control of 'Foreign Notes' until December 1918. She told Ogden that she 'never thought' she would 'find other work that seemed even more urgent',[126] but when she heard the vindictive terms of the Armistice she knew the moment had come to move on. In *The Right of the Child*, Fuller says that Eglantyne's 'motives in founding the SCF were dominated by her sense of the one-ness of mankind',[127] but obviously the SCF had a more complicated beginning. In 1918, Charlie, like many intellectuals, Quakers and Fabians, broke with the Liberals completely and he and Dorothy joined the Independent Labour Party. The same year, their frustration at the Church of England's stance on the war led them to join the Society of Friends.[128] Eglantyne was a pacifist. In autumn 1918 the Austrians and Bulgarians asked for a ceasefire and wanted to begin peace negotiations, but much to the Buxton household's horror the Allies continued the food blockade. Neither did the Allies call off the blockade when the German Kaiser fled to the Netherlands in October, but continued it to the spring of 1919. When the terms of the Treaty of Versailles were announced in the summer of 1919, Charlie felt that the treaty and its 'repercussions had betrayed the dead of every land', he said: 'The Treaties and post war policy alike had played fast and loose with human life; they had mocked at "the war to end war"'.[129]

In an effort to do something to help fight the famine that was crippling Europe, they assembled a group of friends, writers, intellectuals and political allies, including Charlie's brother Noel Roden Buxton, Lord Parmoor, Lady Courtney, Leonard Woolf, Jerome K. Jerome and John Maynard Keynes, who formed a lobby group called the Fight the Famine Council (FFC). The Quaker suffragette Marion Ellis (soon to become Lady Parmoor) and Eglantyne agreed to serve as honorary secretaries. By the first public meeting, the FFC members included 13 bishops, several deans and numerous politicians who agreed to pressure the government to negotiate a non-vindictive peace, end the economic blockade and support Woodrow Wilson's plans for a League of Nations.[130]

Dorothy emerged as head strategist of the Fight the Famine Council.[131] She was a member of the Women's Labour Federation and the Women's International League (WIL), which was the British branch of the Women's International League for Peace and Freedom, formed at an international congress in The Hague in 1915 by a number of members of the National Union of Women's Suffrage Societies who objected to Emmeline Pankhurst's suggestion that feminist organizations support the war effort. The Legaue's immediate objective was to try 'to stop the war' and push for permanent international disarmament.[132] In March 1919 Dorothy asked the WILPF who were feeling 'disillusioned' by their own organization's ineffectiveness, to help the FFC raise money, which they agreed to do, but the League's executive made it clear that they were a political organization and that they did not want to get sidetracked by relief work.[133] The FFC and WIL joint-committees planned a public march in Trafalgar Square to convey their condemnation of the blockade to Winston Churchill and they sent deputations to urge Lord Robert Cecil, Minister of the Blockade from 1916 to 1918, to permit Germany to import food and raw materials to alleviate suffering.[134]

The whole time, Dorothy had been wondering how the British people would accept an appeal on behalf of the starving children of central Europe. In February 1919 she had the idea, which she discussed with Eglantyne, of forming a special council of the FFC called the Save the

Children Fund, which would raise money to send directly to the children of Central Europe. Knowing that the Women's International League was planning a meeting in Zurich in May, they asked delegates to collect '<u>Facts</u>, <u>Photos</u>, and <u>Cinema Films</u>' to help promote the SCF. Dorothy told the delegates that 'the rescue of the children of Europe is the first duty of the women's movement at the present time'.[135] In a separate letter of appeal to the British public Dorothy said she had 'talked to people straight back from Germany and Austria, the whole thing is a nightmare to me'. She asked them to take a 'collection box' for starving children. Dorothy and Eglantyne were planning to launch the SCF at a public meeting at the Albert Hall on 19 May.[136] While everyone was at the Zurich meeting, Barbara Ayrton Gould and Eglantyne decided to pass out some handbills in Trafalgar Square to promote the Albert Hall meeting; which is what they were doing that Sunday in early May when they were arrested and charged with violating the Defence of the Realm Act. Since the war was over they had not seen any reason to submit their leaflets to the Leaflets Department of the Press Bureau.[137]

Their case was heard on 15 May 1919 at Mansion House Police Court. The charges were serious. Sir Archibald Bodkin, for the prosecution, said that the maximum possible penalty was five pounds for each copy of the leaflet, of which 7,000 had been distributed.[138] William Francis Moss represented the Labour Party because the National Labour Press, which had printed the leaflets, was also charged. Moss said he did not believe the handbills were anti-war propaganda. He knew of the Fight the Famine Council, which included half a dozen bishops and other 'law-abiding citizens, who would not ask him to print anything that was contrary to the welfare of the Realm'.[139]

Barbara Ayrton Gould was also not intimidated by the arrest. She had been active in the militant suffragette's window-breaking campaign of 1912 and had spent a short time in Holloway prison because she had refused bail.[140] Many members of the WIL were well known to the authorities; in fact, their office had recently been raided and numerous publications and handbills were confiscated.[141] When a delegation of League members appeared at the courthouse to watch the trial, they were refused entry.[142] Ayrton Gould's leaflet said: 'What does Britain stand for? Starving Babies, Torturing Women, Killing the Old? These things are being done to-day in Britain's name all over Europe'.[143] Ayrton Gould taunted the court saying 'what is written I stand for'. Even though the League promised to raise money to pay her fine, she insisted that she would not compromise. She would go 'to prison as a protest'.[144]

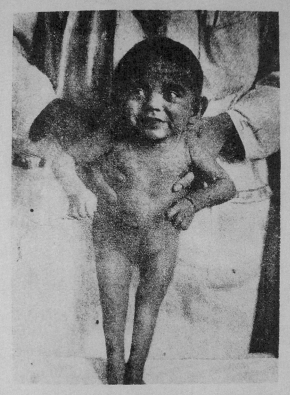

A

STARVING BABY

This child is 2½ years old, and its weight is only 12 lb. 2 oz.
The normal weight of a child of this age is 28 lb. 2 oz.
The size of the child's head is out of all proportion
to its body, because through starvation its body and its
limbs have not developed.
There are millions of such children starving to-day.

**The only way to bring real help to starving Europe is
TO RESTORE FREE INTERCOURSE BETWEEN
THE NATIONS AND ALLOW THE STARVING
COUNTRIES TO FEED THEMSELVES.**

National Labour Press Ltd. 8&10 Johnson's Court. Fleet Street, London, E.C. 4

8.3   Early Save the Children leaflet, source: Jebb Family

Eglantyne's leaflet was considered to be more egregious because of the photograph of a starving baby. Her text read:

A
Starving Baby
This child is 2½ years old, and its weight is only 12 lbs. 2 oz.
The normal weight of a child of this age is 28 lbs. 2 oz.
The size of the child's head is out of all proportion to its body, because through starvation its body and its limbs have not developed.
There are millions of such children starving to-day.
The only way to bring real help to starving Europe is
TO RESTORE FREE INTERCOURSE BETWEEN
THE NATIONS AND ALLOW THE STARVING
COUNTRIES TO FEED THEMSELVES[145]

Eglantyne had never before been implicated in a criminal charge and was conciliatory before the magistrate. She stressed that she had prepared her leaflet without the knowledge of the FFC. While apologizing for having implicated the Labour Press, she insisted she 'had not broken the law'. Nevertheless, the magistrate found them guilty and fined the National Labour Press 80 pounds and Eglantyne and Ayrton Gould five pounds each or they faced eleven days imprisonment. They were given a week to appeal or pay. They both paid their fines and Eglantyne also contributed 60 pounds toward the printer's fine.[146] Eglantyne wrote to her mother immediately after leaving the police office: 'I am still at large', adding that the 'police inspector had tea with me' and on the way out she had the cheek to ask the prosecutor 'for a subscription'. She sensed that the magistrate had sympathized with her 'misguided zeal'. Everyone in the FFC and WILPF told her that the fine was the 'equivalent to victory'.[147]
Dorothy was already famous for her political 'stunts' and was delighted with her sister's arrest.[148] A week later, Dorothy introduced her Albert Hall speech by waving a tin of condensed milk in the air. Over the audience's 'tremulous' applause, she shrieked, '[T]here is more practical morality in this tin than in all the creeds'.[149] It was soon clear to the FFC that the trial and public rallies organized to embarrass the authorities had brought the SCF into the public eye; it occurred to them all that Dorothy was on to something. The first thing Eglantyne learned from her court appearance was the efficacy of controversy in a social movement. It gave her the authority to pick up her pen and send a protest letter to the *Daily News*. In it she pointed out the irony that

her 'prosecution' had taken place at the same time as Edith Cavell's funeral. In 1915, Cavell, an English military nurse, had helped 300 French soldiers to escape from a German prison camp in Belgium. Despite the public outcry, Cavell was executed by a German firing squad.[150] After a prolonged battle the British government succeeded in having Cavell's corpse repatriated to England; a public memorial service was held at Westminster Abbey at the same afternoon as Eglantyne's trial. Quoting Cavell, Eglantyne wrote, 'Let us have no hatred nor bitterness toward anyone'. By linking Cavell's heroism, her martyrdom and innocence with the image of the children the SCF was trying to save, Eglantyne invited her readers to put Cavell's 'teaching into practical effect by rescuing the perishing children'.[151]

Eglantyne united the memory of a heroic 'saver of life' with the Save the Children Fund, which she called the 'greatest life-saving movement the world has ever seen'.[152] Within weeks of the arrest, the humility she displayed in court quickly dissipated and with no small sense of bravado, she described her prosecution in the following terms.

> Recently I was prosecuted for not having submitted to the Censor a leaflet with a photo of a starving child…What I regret is this—that if such a simple humanitarian document is to be regarded as 'a leaflet likely to be used for propagandist purposes in relation to the present war', then the implication is that the starvation of children is a war weapon still in use, and that the relief of their suffering is a political and not, as I contend, a purely humanitarian object…Workers are weary of conflict. They resent attacks upon themselves, upon the Army, upon the Governments, upon other classes…They say to me, 'We will give you money for the starving children, and go on giving it, if only we can be sure that the food really reaches them', but they think it more important to relieve the famine than to listen to diatribes about the responsibility for it. This is an attitude, which ought to be readily understood, especially by women, doctors, and ministers of religion. I appeal to my fellow-countrymen to make this view prevail, and to insist on public and private effort.[153]

Dorothy Buxton's name is listed as the first honorary secretary of the Save the Children Fund; however, she 'had many strings to her bow' and was more interested in 'making a demonstration of international solidarity' than in 'child welfare work'.[154] Likewise, the Women's International League for Peace and Freedom refused to get sidetracked by philanthropy. Many members of the FFC were prominent political figures and feared that their reputations would taint the appeal of the SCF. The question arose: who then, could run the Save the Children Fund? The position of honorary secretary required a person of high social standing and no public association with unpatriotic causes. On the face of it, apart from her recent court appearance, Eglantyne had no notoriety. Since leaving the Charity Organization Society she had not been much in the public eye. Although she joined the Liberal Party in 1910, her activities had been minimal; her considerable work for *Cambridge Magazine*, the Macedonian Relief Fund and the Agriculture Organization Society had been behind the scenes. What Eglantyne lacked, however, was respect for the ethos of 'charity work'. She had always wrestled with guilt over elite privilege. Having witnessed grinding poverty in Marlborough, she had tried to cast off the 'shackles' of privilege by working among the children of the 'washerwoman class'; and yet she described hands-on social work as worse than 'breaking stones'. Later, with the COS, she criticized class snobbery and the cold hand of charity. By the time she was working for the MRF and the AOS she regarded unpaid social work as exploitation. She revealed her feelings in 'The Ring Fence' where she wrote: 'A ridiculous word—charity...we know that charity cloaks a multitude of sins'.[155]

Why, then, did Eglantyne take on the leadership of the SCF? Katie Pickles argues that the repatriation of Edith Cavell's corpse in 1919 represented victory and triumph to the British people, but also the collective loss of millions who had 'done their duty' during the fighting.[156] In the aftermath of the war and the shadow of the blockade, many British voluntary action agencies took on a political aspect that was attractive to Eglantyne. This chapter has shown how Eglantyne got from Macedonian refugee hospital on the shores of the 'furiously' rampaging Dragor River in 1913 to the steps of Mansion House in London.[157] She was increasingly drawn to direct-action organizations and to people, who were combining their personal, spiritual and political ideologies with meaningful voluntary social action. In 1919 it dawned upon her that a Save the Children charity might give her a way to carry forward the rebuilding of Europe, by literally and symbolically saving 'enemy children' who were the most innocent victims of unthinking patriotism. For Eglantyne, the Save the Children Fund was more than just a charity; it was an agency to unite voluntary social action and with 'world-wide responsibility' and she 'put her heart and soul into it'.[158]

9

'A Perfect Jungle of Intrigues, Suspicion and Hypocrisies': The Early Save the Children Fund in Time of Crisis

'We have been attacked,' Eglantyne Jebb told a Save the Children Fund volunteer, Victoria de Bunsen in 1922. We 'probably shall continue to be attacked so bitterly and insidiously from outside; we must not let the forces which are against us disrupt us internally'. Eglantyne was describing the 'mental anguish' the exhausted 'little band' of volunteers felt as they struggled to raise money for the world's children.[1] The end of the war did not bring stability to Europe, and children continued 'dying of hunger and want' in the 'war zones' of Europe.[2] The Fight the Famine Council had formed the SCF to take over famine relief so that they could focus directly on lobbying the government to restore trade relations in Central Europe and support Woodrow Wilson's proposals for a League of Nations. By 1920, despite the controversy surrounding it, the SCF caught on in some quarters and garnered wide cross-class appeal. This chapter shows that after the war many British men and women renewed their interest in voluntary action. The SCF gave Eglantyne a way to make use of her interest in social questions and her talent for committee work and provided an outlet for her writing. It also enabled her to challenge government policy and to create controversy, which was a long-standing prerogative of women's philanthropic work. By 1921, there were SCF national committees in 12 different countries. Eglantyne announced that 'the movement had grown much too large...to be able to stop it'.[3]

   To run the SCF Eglantyne drew upon everything she had learned in the Charity Organization Society, Macedonian Relief Fund, Agriculture Organization Society, Fight the Famine Council and Women's International League. When she agreed to take over the fund, everyone involved expected it to last about six months. Her plan, insofar as she made one, was to adapt to international children's aid the time-tested COS methods of scientific social work, self-help and mutual aid. The

The Soviet's Intermediary in Famine Relief Work Arrives in London

Dr. Nansen, the famous explorer, who is acting as intermediary between the Moscow Government and the various foreign Governments, arrived in London last week-end in connection with the international scheme for the relief of famine-stricken Russia. Here he is seen on arrival at Victoria with Lord Weardale of the " Save the Children Fund " (on left), Mrs. Snowden, and Miss E. Jebb, the honorary secretary of the fund

9.1   Eglantyne and Russian Famine Delegation, source: Jebb Family

prestige of the Charity Organization Society had slipped by 1919; however, Eglantyne knew its ideology would still appeal to potential donors. She announced that the role of the SCF was to apply to 'the realm of international philanthropy some of the high ideals, which animated the pioneers of the Charity Organization Society, in the realm of domestic charity in England, half a century earlier'.[4] In effect, she formed partnerships with existing voluntary agencies like the Red Cross and Society of Friends and provided temporary grants to orphanages and children's hospitals until local government agencies were able to take over.

There was nothing new about a children's charity in 1920. Throughout the 1800s it had been 'relatively easy to tap the pockets of the public by a sentimental appeal' on behalf of destitute girls and boys.[5] Due to the missionary zeal of philanthropists like Mary Carpenter, Lord Shaftesbury,

Dr Barnardo and the Society for the Prevention of Cruelty to Children, an elaborate network of voluntary child welfare agencies, homes, ragged school programmes and emigration schemes had evolved. By 1900, the state had passed legislation to cover many areas of child welfare that had previously been served by child-savers and private philanthropy. For example, the decade-long lobbying for a higher standard of child health and education and the fear of juvenile delinquency resulted in a number of pieces of legislation, which embodied the principle of the best interest of the child. The partnership between the child-savers and state agencies resulted in the Reformatory and Industrial School Acts of the 1850s and 1890s, the Education Acts of the 1870s, the Children's Acts of the 1880s and the Infant Life Protection Acts of the 1900s.[6] Owing to the economic rise of Germany and the United States in the 1890s, the findings of eugenics societies and royal commissions and the military humiliation which accompanied the Boer War, politicians, feminists and reformers concluded that a nation which ignored the needs of children, its greatest natural resource, did so at its own risk.[7]

By the early twentieth century, public and voluntary sectors recognized that British children had a right to protection from the most extreme consequences of poverty, ignorance, vice and cruelty. The public was used to charities' sentimental appeals for money for local needy children, but the idea of a charity or official body helping the needy children of Britain's war enemies, which is exactly what the SCF pledged to do, sparked fury in some sectors. Immediately after the Armistice, David Lloyd George, anxious to keep himself and his coalition in power, held a general election in which an appeal was made to the worst passions of the electorate. Slogans like 'Hang the Kaiser', and 'We'll squeeze Germany till the pips squeak' were effective. The coalition won its majority; the blockade of enemy countries continued and so did the demonstrations, street riots and strikes against shortages of food and housing, and mass unemployment. There was also unprecedented inflation, and in 1919 an influenza epidemic killed hundreds of thousands. These problems were the most severe in Germany, Austria and Hungary. This was the environment within which Eglantyne began to set up the national infrastructure of the SCF. When she announced that the SCF was planning to send aid to the children in Central Europe regardless of race or creed, she had her work cut out for her.

The FFC registered the SCF under the War Charities Act in May 1919 and almost immediately 'disassociated' itself in order make the SCF appear independent of all outside 'economic or political influences'.[8] The division of labour was simple. The FFC would continue lobbying against the blockade and economic clauses in the Peace Treaty, which prevented 'international reconciliation'.[9] It would demand the restoration of trade, business and development throughout Europe and the re-establishment of credit to Germany and throw its support behind the League of Nations. This put the SCF at liberty to concentrate on getting urgently needed food and medical aid to starving children.[10] By using the symbol of the innocent suffering child, Dominique Marshall asserts that Eglantyne wanted to accomplish for the children of war enemies what the Red Cross had been doing for wounded soldiers since 1864, that is, gain the sympathy of the public.[11]

Eglantyne knew the most urgent order of business was to hire competent staff to run the office and assemble an influential executive to attract high-status benefactors, patrons and donors to begin the campaign. She drew upon her vast experience in COS 'social work methods' to train staff and volunteers and set up committees.[12] On 7 February 1920 the first SCF office opened in a building scheduled for demolition on Golden Square. The staff was told that their employment would depend on the expected short 'life' of the SCF.[13] A year later the SCF office moved to 42 Langham Street. The ground floor was used for interviewing prospective donors, volunteers and clients; a postal dispatch; and a switchboard. The real work was done upstairs. Every day throughout 1921, 1,000 to 1,500 donations and requests for assistance arrived from regions in Armenia, Serbia, Germany, Czechoslovakia, Russia, Switzerland, France and Poland. They were piled in bundles of 100, filed into dress boxes and stacked along a wall until some second-hand index boxes were bought and an alphabetical indexing system set up. The office staff included clerks and a dozen typists, the executive council, general and managing secretaries, and many lady volunteers, who were easily distinguished from the paid-staff because 'they always wore their hats' in the office. Squeezed tightly around a trestle table, the ladies sorted the mail. If anyone had a difficult question about the geographical location of a request, one of the office girls took the letter back to her 'boarding-house…in the hope that one of the many residents would know the answer'.[14]

Amidst the pandemonium of the office, a teenage office worker called 'Miss Lawrence' noticed 'a tall slim person…who always wore a brown dress' and she soon discovered this individual was 'the founder'. Lawrence was 'impressed by [Miss Jebb's] wonderful face and kindly manner'. Eglantyne often had to travel to Geneva, and an early indication of her unwillingness to dress or act the part of the Lady Bountiful is that she 'carried' her 'luggage…in a ruck-sack on her back', which struck Lawrence as peculiar for a highborn lady.[15] From her COS and Macedonian work, Eglantyne knew exactly the sort of people she wanted to represent the SCF as patrons, fundraisers, and executive and council members. She told Grace Vulliamy of Lady Muriel Paget's Missions in Eastern Europe that she was not looking for 'any one who is merely a "Society name"'.[16] She needed people whose names were known 'for war work or philanthropic work', and not just their social standing. The first president of the SCF was a Liberal and former member of the FFC, Philip James Stanhope (Lord Weardale). All appeals for aid were made under his name[17] until he died suddenly in 1922. The next president was a Conservative, the Duke of Atoll, who had been the president of the Scottish branch of the SCF. Not until Lord Noel Buxton took over from 1931 to 1948 did the SCF have a Labour president.[18]

Eglantyne found it difficult to dissociate the SCF from political controversy. Although she was too practical to be idealistic about charity work, she believed that the SCF was unique and that one way to mute partisan political attacks was to recruit followers of every creed. Consequently, the SCF became very popular with many feminists, socialists and pacifists who might otherwise have dismissed relief work as simply a palliative.[19] Even hard-line feminists like Helena Swanwick, who was adamant that women stay out of charity work, made an exception for the SCF and tolerated her members doing SCF work, 'either in other organizations, or as individuals'.[20] People on the political right, however, were worried that the reputations of many volunteers could actually hurt the philanthropic goals of the SCF. When a man from the Exeter SCF discovered that Mary Sheepshanks, Maude Royden and Kathleen Courtney of the Women's International League for Peace and Freedom were touring the country for starving children, he was 'horrified' by the 'extraordinary instance of crooked thinking'. He wondered how pacifists could induce 'people of the Jingo-persuasions, with money and influence, to feel sympathy towards the suffering little ones…[N]othing will be done for the children by the rich, that is by the only people who, by giving, can help them'.[21]

Critics on the left complained that Eglantyne 'appeared too optimistic' in her selection of patrons, and some thought that she had made some major miscalculations.[22] In her rush to appear non-partisan, she invited war ministers and 'blockaders' to sit on the executive. This was unacceptable to Quakers and pacifists like Douglas Parsons and Emily Hobhouse, who wrote angry letters protesting the appointment of Lord Robert Cecil, former Minister of the Blockade, as patron in 1921.[23] Eglantyne also had to stifle a rumour that Margaret Lloyd George was a vice-president.[24] A socialist, who could not believe that 'individuals whose inhuman and cold blooded actions have caused the Fund to be formed' were working for it as 'honorary officials', pointed out, '[I]f those who feel as acutely for children will associate...with their destroyers what can we expect of the ordinary man in the street! It is as if a murderer were to head the public subscription list for a coffin for his victims'.[25] Eglantyne was practical about the SCF but idealistic about human nature. She believed that the SCF was the only 'body' in England 'which can bring about the co-operation between English capitalists and socialists, but the difficulty of the task is great'.[26]

In the *Road to Wigan Pier,* George Orwell observes that progressive political movements have in common 'the really disquieting—prevalence of cranks'. These organizations 'draw towards them with magnetic force every fruit-juice drinker, nudist, sandal-wearer, sex-manic, Quaker, "Nature Cure" quack, pacifist and feminist in England'.[27] Orwell was referring to English socialists in the 1930s; he might have made a similar remark if he had seen the earliest supporters of the SCF in 1920. Dorothy certainly did. She said, 'When [Eglantyne] and I first started the SCF in March 1919 we were both idealists, with <u>no</u> experience to qualify us for dealing with <u>people</u>. We collected about us both on our committee and as officers of the fund the queerest collection of <u>cranks, fools</u> and <u>vassals</u>...that could well be imagined'.[28] Eglantyne seemed to find such people amusing; for she had described the philanthropist-type in 'The Ring Fence'. One of her characters said that philanthropists were all 'rampant socialists with all sorts of mad notions'. His wife chimed in, '[T]eetotalers, non-smokers, non-conformists, radicals'. She could never bring herself to mouth the 'more offensive name of socialist'.[29] As honorary secretary of the SCF, however, Eglantyne ignored the positive and negative attention her patrons and fundraisers attracted and kept pushing for wider representation.

Geoffrey Finlayson has said that a crucial feature of post-Armistice voluntary social work was national duty, patriotism, reconciliation and 'making religion relevant'.[30] Eglantyne would have agreed completely. She felt that 'if every minister of religion became a propagandist for the children...what might we not do'.[31] She wanted to established inter-faith joint committees and appealed to the compassion of leaders of national churches, who she thought should see it as their sacred duty to give money to the needy, whoever and wherever they may be. In summer of 1919, she approached Randall Davidson, the Archbishop of Canterbury, who flatly refused to make an appeal on behalf of the SCF. Undeterred, even though there were no Roman Catholics on the SCF council at the time, Eglantyne drafted a letter to the Pope and found

14 eminent people to sign it.[32] Much to everyone's astonishment, she and the new SCF honorary treasurer, Dr Hector Munro, an eccentric socialist-feminist doctor whose Munro Medical Corps was doing relief work in Belgium,[33] were granted a 20-minute audience at the Vatican with Pope Benedict XV on 27 December 1919. This was a coup for an obscure British charity with no achievements to its name and no Roman Catholics on the executive.

Once the meeting was announced, the sectarian fighting and lobbying of various religious and philanthropic interest groups began in earnest. Dorothy thought this was because they had 'seen a vision of the Pope's millions'.[34] Following COS principles of 'working through existing organizations',[35] Eglantyne wanted to persuade the Swiss Comité International de Secours aux Enfants to form a joint sub-committee as the Friends Emergency and War Victims Relief Committee, Acton Lodge, the International Committee of the Red Cross and the British Committee for Relief in Poland had done.[36] Eglantyne and Dorothy did not know very much about the Comité, which was a Roman Catholic charity, or realize that it had other ideas. Soon after approaching it, Dorothy concluded that the directors were 'men of doubtful outlook and qualification' who only wanted money. She said 'our work is cut out for us to extricate ourselves...from a dangerous situation'.[37] Eglantyne was terrified that their hard work would be 'unfixed' by the 'folly of mankind'.[38] She managed to disentangle the SCF from the Comité before she attended her meeting with the Pope. She later wrote a detailed account of the meeting, which lasted over two hours, and which Edward Fuller published:

> Our audience with the Pope...had the oddest beginning. As we left the antechamber, where we had been waiting, the man who was showing us the way turned to us with violent gesticulations, shouting out voluble Italian in which I only distinguished the work 'Come'. Then he turned around again and, to my utter amazement, took to his heels and ran. He was wearing a flowing purple garment, which blew out all round him as he ran. There was nothing for it but to run too. Grasping my mantilla I ran after him, through one gorgeous antechamber after another, where groups of soldiers and gentlemen-in-waiting turned to look. At last through an open door he turned with a wild wave of his hands. Precipitating myself in his wake, I perceived a small lonely figure like a ghost standing stock still in the vast room, and recollecting that popes always wear white I dropped on one knee...[39]

The Pope promised to issue an encyclical; *Paterno Iam Diu* for the children of Europe was delivered in 24 November 1919 and one year later, on

1 December another encyclical, *Annus Iam Plenus,* was issued. It reaffirmed the commitment and again mentioned the Save the Children Fund by name.[40] The first encyclical resulted in donations totalling 25,000 pounds. When the Archbishop of Canterbury learned that the pontiff had endorsed the SCF, he had the idea of using Holy Innocents' Day (28 December) as 'a common Sunday', when simultaneous collections for children would be made in churches of all denominations.[41] Eglantyne loved the idea and quickly went on to secure the patronage of the Archbishop of Wales, the Chief Rabbi of England, the Church of Scotland and other Protestant denominations and the Orthodox churches. She also tried to extend the SCF's influence by establishing links with other spiritual communities such as the Theosophists and the Bahais. With SCF funding, Dr Armstrong Smith of the Theosophists ran the Acton Lodge relief camps in Vienna and Austria and Lady Blomfield of the London Baha'i ran workrooms in Budapest.[42]

According to Robert Humphries, an old trick of COS members was to 'infiltrate the committees of other charitable institutions'.[43] Eglantyne tried this with the British Red Cross but was unsuccessful because the Red Cross refused to see why they should help the SCF raise money when the SCF could be raising money for them. In the long run this turned out to be good for the SCF because it forced Eglantyne to look elsewhere for an ally further afield. In September 1919 she arranged a meeting with Frederic Ferrière of the International Committee of the Red Cross (ICRC) who had created the Central Prisoners of War Agency.[44] She explained to Ferrière that she wanted to create a neutral international centre for the administration of child welfare. The Geneva-based International Committee of the Red Cross was also looking for ways to work more closely with the new League of Nations.[45] In November with Ferrière's support the ICRC took three unusual steps. It offered the SCF its 'patronage', it consented 'to receive the funds' on the SCF's behalf and it allowed the SCF to retain 'independence of appeal and independence of allocation'.[46] The patronage of the ICRC enabled Eglantyne to create an international 'central agency', which she called the Save the Children Fund International Union (SCIU). The patronage of the ICRC led to a new round of negotiations about where the SCIU headquarters should be located. Eglantyne and her new ally in the ICRC, Ferrière's niece, Suzanne Ferrière, whom Eglantyne called her 'understudy' and 'international sister'[47] wanted the SCIU to be in Geneva close to the ICRC and the League of Nations, whose patronage Eglantyne wanted to secure next. There was fierce opposition to this decision in Berne.

One of the first lessons the Jebb sisters learned in Switzerland was that denominationalism was not confined to England. Eglantyne said, 'I suppose it is everywhere!!!'.[48] In a letter to her Aunt Louisa, Dorothy described the 'unprecedented ethical venture in trying to unite all the creeds and all the parties for the saving of the children'; it revealed that saving children came 'second in most minds to their personal, party or religious prejudices'.[49] Eglantyne thought that an agency based in Berne would defeat the Pope's 'humane intentions'.[50] She did not want the SCF to look like a Roman Catholic charity. She faced the 'unenviable task to strike a balance between RC's suspicions of Prot's and Prot's suspicions of RCs; between German philes and German phobes; between the Bernese who are jealous of Geneva, and the Genovese who are jealous of Berne, and so on'.[51] She was successful. On 29 November 1919 a memorandum was sent to London, which announced that the 'SCF should forthwith open an office in Geneva'.[52] Eglantyne's temperament turned out to be perfectly suited to international diplomatic negotiations. Dorothy was impressed by how her 'beautiful darling saint' of a sister could represent herself as having only a 'lofty pure and disinterested purpose' amidst the 'perfect jungle of intrigues, suspicion and hypocrisies'.[53] However, Eglantyne was aware that she had aroused 'the antagonisms of so many pillagers and highwaymen that the whole scheme may be wrecked by being too good for the wicked world'. She told her aunt Louisa Jebb, '[T]he intrigues, which have gone on about money, are beyond belief—no one seems to think of the good of the children'.[54]

Leila Rupp observes that the League of Nations was particularly 'enticing to women'. Although the door 'to the diplomatic corps within countries' had been closed to them, the Covenant of the League of Nations promised to be different.[55] The League of Nations represented several causes dear to the hearts of internationalists and humanitarians, including the setting up of an international court of justice; provisions against arms trafficking and slavery; support for the Red Cross and because it established the International Labour Organization.[56] The FFC and the Buxton-Jebb household regarded the 'Covenant' as 'the one redeeming feature' of the Peace Conference. Charlie Buxton liked it because it contained mechanisms for handling international disputes between countries, thereby decreasing the need to resort to violence.[57] Feminist internationalists expected the League to promote the status of women.[58] Eglantyne liked it because under Article 24 it had pledged to work closely with, and promote co-operation with, various voluntary organizations. She wanted the SCF to shed its British national identity, which was one reason why she set up her SCIU in Geneva, the city the Women's International League called 'the little city, so full of traditions of noble internationalism'.[59] An alliance with the League in Geneva would be the SCF's best chance of improving the status of children and by extension the prestige of the SCIU. Eglantyne had a right to be optimistic, despite the controversies; by 1920 several international SCF branches had opened in South Africa, New Zealand, Australia and Canada. They were sending relief, in the form of food, new and used clothing, drugs, cod liver oil and money to the SCF office in London, which forwarded it to feeding kitchens, hospitals, sanatoria, refugee centres and orphanages.

Sociologists who study how social problems are framed have observed that charities develop 'vocabularies for giving'. These vocabularies are the terms, concepts, ideas and definitions that audiences use to justify why they should care about a problem and why they should part with their hard-earned money to support someone they are never likely to meet.[60] In the case of the SCF, Eglantyne's first task was to present the suffering children of Britain's war enemies as worthy recipients of charity, and not, as one potential donor said, 'enemies who will raise up again and kill us 25 years hence!'[61] Her foundational claim was that hungry children living in various countries around the world, regardless of the nature of the regime in power, were in fact 'the world's children' and deserving of aid, medical care and education. Drawing upon the Victorian child-saving rhetoric of childhood innocence (save the child in danger before he or she became a danger to others), Eglantyne responded to people who criticized her object by quoting George Bernard Shaw who said, 'I have no enemies under the age of seven'.[62]

In 1921 Dorothy Buxton officially returned to her Labour Party work and Eglantyne and L. B. Golden, the Anglo-Russian general secretary she hired from Lady Muriel Paget's Mission, took over the task of overseeing the SCF's fundraising machine.[63] Following the time tested fundraising strategies used by other successful charities, Eglantyne and her volunteers appealed to the British public through the press, posters, platform lectures and lantern-slides. SCF's achievements were announced in the annual reports, which listed the names of distinguished donors, sizable donations and general financial standing. A monthly magazine called *The Record of the Save the Children Fund* was also started in October 1920. By 1921, the circulation was over 5,000. In July 1922 it became a quarterly and the name was changed to *The World's Children: A Quarterly Journal of Child Care and Protection Considered from an International Standpoint*. The SCIU published its own report called the *Bulletin*.

Since the late nineteenth century the voluntary sector had exhibited a voracious appetite for facts,[64] and the SCF was no exception. In 1925, all references to the SCF were removed from the title of *The World's Children*; henceforth all references to the SCF appeared as news items. Most issues opened with 'an emotionally riveting grabber'[65] and eye-witness accounts of ghastly events in the lives of a particular starving child. These news articles humanized the child-victims (parents, especially fathers were rarely mentioned). The 'facts' and statistics offered the proof of the seriousness of a famine, drought or disaster.[66] One SCF critic at the *Daily Express* observed that the fund thought only 'in terms of millions'.[67]

The SCF became early masters of the use of visual images by using new and old technologies. Before and after photographs and films provided melodramatic journalistic accounts of starvation and rescue. A typical set of photographs was 'The Deadly Contrast'. The caption under the 'before' and 'after' panels respectively entitled, 'Found Dead' and 'Saved'. The right balance between hope and despair was however difficult to manage. In 1924 the London Tube Railways office informed Eglantyne that the fund's illustrated poster had been rejected as unsuitable for display on the grounds that it was 'too gruesome'.[68] Describing what would today be called 'compassion fatigue', L. B. Golden summed up for the executive committee, the first decade of the fund's advertising campaigns, in the following terms:

> Advertising—publicity, to be effective, must be adjusted to the needs of the moment…the advertisements…were written with the express idea that if the reader were sufficiently interested to read to the end he was unable to resist the appeal and send a donation. It was impossible to make these advertisements more full of horror: the highest point was sounded and it was not possible to go higher, with the result that public sympathy was gradually worn away and the ads brought in little or no return…The ratio of returns to cost of advertising was steadily going down…but if it is possible to invent a totally new form of advertisement it might pull.[69]

Eglantyne and her colleagues went further than other charities to establish the SCF's reputation as the leading authority on famine relief and its ability to deliver aid to starving children. Eglantyne and Dorothy shocked SCF supporters and opponents when they hired the *Daily Mail's* press agent Ernest Hamilton to do public relations. This was unprecedented among respectable British charities. Hamilton could not see why he could not 'adapt to the needs of philanthropy methods which had hitherto been reserved for the publicizing of patent medicines'. Saying that 'every picture tells a story', he 'introduced crude line drawings of agonized, screaming women clutching to their breasts ghastly skeletons of children whom the British public were urged to save from otherwise certain death'.[70] In 1921, the Jebb sisters commissioned George H. Mews, also of the *Daily Mirror*, to make one of the first film documentaries of the Russian famine to convey the urgency to potential donors. Mews's film was shown over 300 times in 1923 and proved to be an 'excellent method of propaganda'. Screening brought 60,000 pounds directly to the SCF.[71]

Eglantyne encouraged large fundraising campaigns. She did not think the film documentaries or placing double-column full-page advertisements in major British papers was too expensive.[72] They tapped her 'flare for publicity'.[73] She was not bothered by the fact that her modern methods upset traditionalists like the Quaker philanthropist Emily Hobhouse, who complained that 'many people besides myself had a strong feeling that there had…been a tendency in the SC Fund toward a change of policy…great names…[and] a desire for big offices and consequent heavy expenditures'.[74] Eglantyne disagreed. She thought that 'Mr Golden and Mr Hamilton our press agent, had done wonders with regard to our own organization'.[75] She was a spiritual woman but her background with the COS taught her that faith alone could not run a dependable and efficient charity. She wrote: 'the new charity…must be scientific and possess the same thoroughness, the same intelligence as are to be found in the best commercial and industrial enterprises'.[76]

Eglantyne realized that a variety of propaganda techniques were necessary because donors, however generous, are not likely to go on repeating their gifts. One idea was her child 'Adoption Scheme' whereby adults and school children could 'adopt' a starving child for two shillings a week. The SCF staff matched prospective foster-parents with child refugees in the orphanages and refugee camps in Austria, France, Germany and Hungary and from among Russians 'scattered throughout Europe'.[77] In exchange for the food the selected children were given, it was hoped that a 'correspondence would spring up between the child and the foster parents which would be fruitful for good'.[78] At Easter in 1921, children in a Nuremberg refugee camp were told 'they had been adopted by English families'. A prepared text was read over the camp loudspeaker informing child refugees that the food they were eating which they must not share with other children was sent by their new English families: 'You yourself only are to eat the provisions…So you must answer their letters politely and nicely and thank them for all that you receive'.[79]

Nearly every issue of *The World's Children* repeated the assertion that the SCF was non-sectarian and non-political. And yet, ironically, rhetorical strategies and appeals quoted scripture and celebrated the natural generosity of the British and Britain's position as a world leader. In the previous century the Shaftesbury Society and Dr Barnardo had appealed to Christians to reach out, metaphorically, to help slum children who were like 'imaginary' heathens and savages.[80] The SCF was asking donors to send aid to the 'real' children of Africa, China and India who may not share their donor's religious beliefs. Eglantyne appealed to both logic and self-interest when she said that some day 'these babes whom we have snatched from the jaws of death will be citizens. They will never forget that when they had only grass and the bark of trees to eat, British men and women came to them with open arms, fed them and helped them...not for the sake of reward, or concession or repayment of loans, or political hopes, but because the Master said "Feed my Lambs"'.[81]

Eglantyne was also aware that the world was shrinking in the aftermath of the First World War. She pointed out that health problems and diseases in countries far away from England's shores could afflict Britain. In the 15 January 1922 issue of *The Record*, she wrote, '[I]t has passed almost into a commonplace of post-war relief work that if the relief of suffering, disease ridden humanity on the continent were neglected, even Britain's geographical insularity would not preserve her from the possibility of a scourge analogous to the Black Death of the fourteenth century'.[82] In what amounts to an early recognition of a globally interconnected world, Eglantyne argued that Britons could ill afford to think that developments in far-off places were irrelevant to British society. Using Russia as an example, The *Record* informed its readers that

...there is another and deeper sense in which we must realize that the fate of these children in Russia is our concern. At present, it may be argued that Russia is not only geographically but culturally remote from us, but it is reasonable to assume that a great change is dawning in both these spheres. Western culture is making extraordinary progress in Russia and we have only to recall the establishment within the past few days, of a regular air service between Berlin and Moscow to realize how geographical distance is being annihilated by the hand of modern science and commercial enterprise. Now all this means that we cannot, even if we would, ignore the children of

Russia for they are destined to play an important part, for good or ill, in the future of Europe and of the world.[83]

The SCF had a wide cross-class appeal, but the fact that so many people donated to it does not mean that they always shared its philosophy. Frank Prochaska has observed that 'charity can turn privilege into virtues and propel people into good works who have little goodness in them'.[84] On 16 May 1922, a foster-mother complained about their adopted son, Johann Bednerz. She had received a 'nice little letter from him' but she was displeased because 'we have given her a Jew'.[85]

When the SCF was first formed, Fredrick Pethick-Lawrence, a fund supporter, told the Jebb sisters they would be lucky to raise 100 pounds. He was wrong. By 1922 they had in fact raised 700,000 pounds, and by the time the fifth annual report for 1924 went to press they had raised 1,895,064 pounds. Pethick-Lawrence was correct however, about how difficult it would be to raise money. In the early 1920s, the SCF staff and volunteers faced continued criticism from the COS for creating yet another children's charity. The Society of Friends and the Red Cross did not always agree with SCF policies, and the press and public alleged that the SCF was feeding the enemy's children while British children went hungry. One potential contributor said flatly that she would not send a donation to starving children because she did 'not desire their recovery...[O]nly half-hearted patriots would wish to relieve enemies whose conduct had disgraced them'.[86]

Eglantyne's first big campaign after the blockade crisis had passed was the Russian famine.[87] When she announced her plan to send aid to the child victims of the famine, she encountered opposition from Russian émigrés and the wider British public, who thought that to feed Russian children was to fuel Bolshevism and the Red Army. Eglantyne told Suzanne Ferrière there were people in England 'who would rather die than support the Bolsheviks'.[88] In 1921, a frightened 'flag-seller' returned her collection box to the office because 'unkind people' at the Henley Regatta 'threatened to put her into the river' for helping Russian children. Unemployed workers picketed the SCF office 'for the same reason'.[89] When Lady Norah Bentinck was asked to approach people on behalf of the SCF, she replied that few would give English money 'to the foreign and largely "Bolshie"...who will only rise up and kill us again 25 years hence'.[90] Eglantyne observed anti-Bolshevik feelings within the SCF executive as well, where only a few were 'genuinely neutral'. Personally, she was also struggling to view the 'matter without bias'.[91] She replied to one critic's comment that spare English money 'had better be spent on those Britons who have suffered by the war'[92] by developing a policy that every local branch set up a home committee to collect money for needy children in their community Critics called her 'home committee' a 'camouflage'.[93]

Despite this hostile political climate and the fact that the SCF was already running relief programmes in Armenia, Austria, the Baltic countries, China, Turkey, Hungry, Finland, France, Germany, Poland and Romania; Eglantyne still wanted to send relief to Russia. In summer of 1921 Fridtjof Nansen the Norwegian explorer and diplomat whom the League of Nations had recently appointed High Commissioner for Russian Relief, came to an agreement with the Russian government for Europeans to provide relief to Russia. Almost immediately the International Red Cross, the Society of Friends and the League of Red Cross Societies invited Nansen to a meeting in Geneva. It was Eglantyne's 'cherished hope' that the SCIU would also be invited and thereby become an 'integral' part of 'combined national' and 'international action'.[94] She used her contacts within the International Red Cross to get the SCIU invited to the meeting where the International Committee for Russian Relief was formed. After consulting with Russian authorities, on 28 August 1921, Nansen gave the SCF responsibility for the relief of children in the province of Saratov, along the banks of the Volga, 'in the heart of the Russian famine zone'.[95] This was a turning point in the brief history of the SCF because until then it had always worked through other agencies. Its Russian aid campaign was the first time it sent relief on its own, and that aroused the wrath of SCF critics.

On 7 September 1921, Eglantyne instructed the SCIU to send a ship load of supplies to Russian children in the Volga region, where crops had been destroyed by drought. Within a year the SCF was running 1,450 kitchens and feeding 300,000 children per day in the Russian province of Saratov.[96] The articles Eglantyne and sympathetic SCF relief workers wrote in *The Record* show they realized that for the campaign to be successful they had to persuade people to think of the famine as a natural phenomenon rather than a result of misguided Bolshevik policies. They also had to get donors to send money to them rather than to the Society of Friends or the British Red Cross, which were also working in Russia. Moreover, donors had to believe that giving money directly to Russian children would not be bolstering the Red Army. This explains why SCF articles always avoided discussions of who, or what, was to blame for a famine. In the case of Russia *The Record* made no reference to Lenin's earlier attack on the *kulaks* he Bolshevik confiscation of food, the devastating effects of the irst World War, the civil war in Russia, or the Allied blockade of Russia.[97] It was an effective campaign, for by the summer of 1922, he SCF had collected 484,000 pounds in support of famine relief in Russia.[98]

Early in 1921 the SCF became a victim of its own publicity when the *Daily Express* became aware of the large amount of money the SCF ad sent to Russia.[99] With a circulation of approximately 400,000 in 919 and 793,000 by 1922, the *Daily Express* was a force to be reckoned vith in British conservative public opinion.[100] The paper's owner, the Canadian financier Max Aitken (Lord Beaverbrook) and the editor-n-chief, R. D. Blumenfeld, a founder of the Anti-Socialist Union, both eared the spread of communism in Britain and elsewhere. Beaverbrook vould not tolerate 'attacks on the Empire, advocacy of socialism or of [British] involvement in Eastern Europe'.[101] The activities of the SCF ;ave them the opportunity to promote their views. From September 921 to the spring of 1922, the *Daily Express* published 56 articles riticizing the SCF's involvement in Russia.

The *Daily Express* quickly caught on to the SCF's rhetorical strategy of using big numbers to portray the scale of the Russian famine and ccused them of exaggeration.[102] To further discredit the SCF, The *Daily Express* also published photographs of life in Russian cities.[103] Beaverbrook owned *The Pathé Gazette* and he began producing docu-mentary-type silent newsreels and still photographs of, for example, a well-filled shop window in Moscow' and cheerily robust Russian hildren with the caption 'do these children look as though they need British food?'[104] The SCF wrote rebuttals, which appeared as letters o the editor in the *Times, Manchester Guardian* and *Daily Mail*. They pointed out that Saratov was over 500 miles from Moscow. However, .glantyne was concerned that the *Daily Express's* attacks were dam-aging her charity's reputation and she sent a long personal letter to Blumenfeld where she offered to send a representative of the News-paper Proprietors' Association to Saratov to settle the matter of whe-her the famine was 'real'. She told Beaverbrook that Britain, as a world eader, must join other world leaders who were sending aid to Russia. The United States had undertaken to feed 1,000,000 Russian children, the French government had voted 6,000,000 francs, the Pope had allocated ,000,000 lira in support of famine relief in Russia and Sweden had equipped a sizable Red Cross mission in Russia. If she was hoodwinking he British public then so too were these governments deceiving their respective electorates.[105]

The *Daily Express* augmented their assault by focusing next on des‐
titute children in England. One article carried the headline 'While ou
hospitals are starving, thousands of pounds diverted to Russia, bitte
irony, tragedy of closed wards'.[106] The paper added a personal direc
attack on the Archbishop of Canterbury who had become a member o
the SCF executive council. Blumenfeld asked: '[W]hat is the Archbisho
doing in his own province'? He challenged the Archbishop to 'wal
alone through the slums of Lambeth that lie within the shadow of hi
palace. He would see...enough to make an Englishman believe tha
charity must begin at home'.[107] The *Daily Express* set up its own charit
for Cornish miners and published the names of contributors in orde
to appear more transparent about its activities than the SCF. In 192
Eglantyne and the Irish suffragette and novelist Charlotte Despard ha
started an Irish branch of the SCF. The Jebbs being long time sup
porters of Home Rule, the *Daily Express* suggested that the only loca
children the SCF seemed to be helping were 'the children of Sinn Fein
an enemy within.[108]

The *Daily Express's* third angle of attack was on the large amount th
SCF spent on fundraising propaganda. Like other leaders of charities
Eglantyne was sensitive to the criticism that too much money was use
to sustain the organization rather than going to people in need.[109] A
SCF executive meetings, *Daily Express* articles were read, discussed a
length and pasted into a scrapbook. Realizing they had to reply pub
licly to the allegations of misspending and misrepresentation, Eglantyn
sought legal advice.[110] The executive committee was advised to allo
the *Daily Express,* through a third-party accounting firm, access thei
books. The resulting investigation, which took place in January 1922
showed that the SCF's expenses were not out of line with those o
other charities like the Society of Friends.[111] The *Daily Express* ignore
this and turned to attacking the Labour Party, but not before takin
one last shot at the SCF. In April 1923, the *Daily Express* published
cynical piece under the heading 'Save the Tractor' in which it claime
that SCF money for famine relief had been spent on American-mad
tractors for Russian collective farms.[112] The editorial accompanyin
'Save the Tractor' closed with the wish: '[W]e hope now to have hear
the last of the "Save the Children" Fund'.[113]

The editors of The *Daily Express* were not alone in hoping they ha
heard the last of the SCF. Between inter-agency bickering and problem
with the press, few people would have blamed Eglantyne if she ha
decided to retire, but instead the SCF shifted its main relief effort
toward children in Greece. To raise funds the SCF made a film called

The Tragedy of the Near East, which described the 'burning of Smyrna' and the millions of refugees who fled mainland Turkey; overwhelming Greece with refugees. By 1924 the SCF was feeding 27,000 children in Greece a day.[114] It also began working more closely with local governments, and one way they did this was setting up permanent 'model villages' for refugees. According to Fuller the 'villages' would be 'showcases for SCF work'.[115] In November 1925, 50 refugees were settled in the new SCF-built village in Bulgaria; King Boris inaugurated it on 21 November 1926. The village was named 'Atolovo' in honour of the SCF's second past-president, Lord Atoll. The SCF then began building a second refugee village in October 1926 in Albania. In a rare moment of vanity, Eglantyne permitted them to name it *Xhebana,* pronounced 'Jebbana' after her.[116] She probably regretted this decision shortly afterward because suddenly other executive members wanted villages to be named after them too. It seems that Noel Buxton was dissatisfied with the plans for his model village; he referred to it sarcastically as his 'West End garden-city in Bulgaria!!' His sister, Victoria de Bunsen asked Eglantyne, '[W]hy can't his be unhampered by Atoll's?...since "Atolovo"... why not Noel-ovo!!'[117]

Finlayson argues that during the First World War the voluntary sector focused its extensive philanthropic effort within Britain on the needs of families and the troops. In the aftermath of the war, the destruction and devastation created new opportunities for charities to work in closer cooperation with local and international government agencies.[118] This chapter has shown that Eglantyne's first four years as leader of the SCF taught her that there would always be a political subtext to relief work. She admitted that the fund supported 'any government anywhere, under which we are working' if the government shows concern about child welfare.[119] In September 1924, she synthesized everything she had learned about fundraising in a confidential report to her executive council, entitled 'Nonproductive Stunts'. The first lesson was that a charity was all about the money and how to get more. Some fundraising campaigns produced money that did not pass through SCF account books, and some stunts produced nothing at all.[120] One 'type of stunt', which would never bring any money directly to SCF was the League of Nations, to which Eglantyne pledged her unconditional support. Eglantyne regarded an alliance with the League as the SCF's best chance to build a genuinely international movement. In 1924, she announced, [T]he moment ha[s] come...when we can no longer...conduct only relief actions. If we wish...to go on working for the children where need is indeed so great...[we must] evoke a co-operative effort of the nations to safeguard their own children on constructive rather than on charitable lines'.[121] The way Eglantyne set up the national and international SCF infrastructure, her fundraising strategies and early struggles with press and popular opinion illustrate the development of her commitment to internationalism and her desire to 'rouse her contemporaries to full responsibility for the world's children'.[122]

10

'Internationalization' of Charity in Peacetime: Declaring the Rights of the Child

I think the lessons flashed upon one in moments of
ecstasy are never really measured until learned afresh
from the turmoil and toil of practical affairs.[1]

The world looks for greatness in the persons of soldiers, rulers and revolutionaries' wrote Nina Boyle, a 'valiant suffragette' who volunteered for the Save the Children Fund for 22 years.[2] When her friend Eglantyne Jebb died, she predicted that Eglantyne's name, like that of Josephine Butler's, would 'be blessed by generations unborn'.[3] Eglantyne had not set out to run a charity, let alone a children's charity; in fact, she 'hated the Lady Bountiful' image and insisted that 'the SCF must never go as a philanthropist from outside preaching about how local people ought to look after their children and doling out charity'.[4] She believed that the SCF movement was 'an expression of an international ideal', namely world peace.[5] Nevertheless in the ensuing decade, she grew into the role of humanitarian advocate and developed the first international child welfare organization dedicated to voluntary social action. In *Writing a Women's Life,* Carolyn Heilburn studied the autobiographies of women who accepted new challenges later in life. She offers Virginia Woolf, Kathie Kollwitz, Florence Nightingale and Beatrice Webb as examples of women who displayed 'new attitudes and new courage' in middle age;[6] the same may be said for Eglantyne Jebb. This chapter examines Jebb's final work for the SCF from 1924 until her death in 1928 and how she built up the Save the Children International Union, its links with the League of Nations, and her collaboration on the Declarations of the Rights of the Child, which marked the beginning of international thinking about children's rights and the special role of the social worker in the new international field of child welfare.

Lafayette Ltd.

10.1   Eglantyne with Save the Children, source: Jebb Family

As honorary secretary of the SCF and vice-president of the SCIU, Eglar
tyne tackled the strenuous work of travelling and addressing meetings i
order to collect money, as she had done earlier with the Macedonia

elief Fund. Many aspects of the work overwhelmed her, but she did it to
et an example to those 'friends who seemed to shirk this disagreeable
vork'.[7] Eglantyne was basically an *ideas* person who hated public speak-
ng. She used to say 'her friends told her that [she] appealed for money so
adly that it positively pained them to hear her do it'.[8] Like many early-
wentieth-century spiritualists and theosophists, Eglantyne discarded the
onventional bourgeois dress code. She was aware that the English upper
lasses believed that one's character was reflected by the style and quality
f one's clothes. In her fiction she depicted the 'amused pity' that fine
adies felt for the 'sorry spinsters' who appeared in good society in their
hread-bare' dresses.[9] Just the same, Eglantyne rejected the role of Lady
ountiful and along with it the large feather hats and crystal beading on
he gowns worn by some 'smart socialist-types' and other 'dashing
vomen of the world' who hid 'their sins under a mass of fine feathers'.[10]
nstead, she opted for a plain 'gown of Franciscan brown' and a large
piscopal cross, which hung by a 'silk ribbon at her breast'.[11] The effect
vas enhanced by her hair, which had turned from 'flaming gold' to
nowy white.[12] A Hungarian SCF worker described her as a 'frail...most
thereal figure'.[13] Transforming her appearance served two purposes.
: was a challenge to the fashionably dressed women of her class. She
sked 'what possible justification can there be for spending even, say
00 a year upon clothing...[when] multitudes of children...went about in
irty, cast-off rags'?[14] In addition her self-effacing clothes enabled her to
reate a persona, which kept people at a distance and helped conceal the
neasiness she at times felt for being 'such a charlatan'.[15]

 It was not only the psychological pressures of administering an inter-
ational children's aid organization that overwhelmed Eglantyne. She
vas in poor health: her thyroid disease had progressed, and the cardiac
pecialist told her that 'thyroid trouble originated from emotional
train...worry more than anything else' causes 'over action of the
land' and 'affects the heart'.[16] From the beginning, it was apparent to
he SCF executive committee that they would have to organize a great
eal of the work around Miss Jebb's health. When she looked very
l, L. B. Golden burst out, 'You must drink milk three times a day'.[17]
n a confidential letter to Suzanne Ferrière, he wrote '[B]etween our-
elves...we are so very anxious about Miss Jebb...Could you please do
our best to get her to take a few days rest, say 4 or 5 away from <u>any</u>
vork whatsoever'?[18] Eglantyne's doctor limited the 'amount of letter
vriting' she was allowed to do, but this only increased her frustra-
on.[19] In addition to her SCF work, Eglantyne was overseeing the care
f her bedridden mother and Louisa Jebb, who were both in their late

70s and 'very feeble'. Eglantyne told Margaret Keynes she sometime dreamed 'of our all crossing the border together—all three of us! Fc the doctor doesn't encourage me much about the state of my ow health'.[20]

Eglantyne's doctor, hoping to avoid a second goitre operation, pre scribed a three-pronged treatment: six weeks of bed rest, a carefull controlled diet of 'fish, plain meat, potatoes, fresh beans, lots of butte cream and milk, weak tea, malt and cod liver oil' and 'psycho-analys treatment', which he told her could be 'useful'.[21] Eglantyne and he circle of friends were absorbed in mind-cure therapies like New Though Christian Science and nature cures.[22] They would have ignored his fina recommendation. Eglantyne blamed Colonel Pilkington's death on ove work and gave her office staff a three-week annual holiday for 'rest an rejuvenation' at a time when most workers felt lucky to get seven days. In 1922, she urged Victoria de Bunsen to 'have the rest cure at Malvern because the Russian famine was 'only the beginning of trouble'.[24] For he own health, Eglantyne tried New Thought techniques and accepte the faith healer's argument that spiritual forces played a strong rol in scientific healing. In 1918 she had kept a 'Dream Diary' where sh recorded sleeping and waking experiments as part of self-healing.[25] Bt she found it ineffective and concluded that while the 'Eddyism c Eddyites...is aggravating...Christian Science as a possible workin hypothesis is...more helpful than anything I have read on New Though lines'.[26]

Early in her Save the Children Fund work she began to believe herse to be the instrument through which the fund served God. She believe that it could inspire 'suffering humanity with hope...in perhaps i darkest hour'. A small group of her co-workers, including Victoria d Bunsen, believed this too. Eglantyne encouraged them all to 'persever at all costs'. If it was 'the will of God' to 'serve in other directions, ind viduals will be called away'.[27] Francesca Wilson says that there 'was som thing mystical and profoundly Christian in the conviction'.[28] In the 192(and 1930s, she had observed it among other relief workers, whose fait she described as 'a conviction that it was outrageous to believe in Christ one did not live according to his teachings'.[29] Some of Eglantyne's close friends believed that her profound spirituality was the cause of her alarm ing physical transformation. Florence Keynes said she seemed like 'a thin apart'.[30] Her sister Emily noticed that she had become 'more spirit tha flesh'.[31] Dorothy observed that 'everybody who comes in contact wit her gets inspired and they all worship her'.[32] In 1924 she said that 'peopl speak of her with baited breath almost as if she was a spirit come straigl rom heaven'.[33] Dorothy was rather baffled by Eglantyne's 'powers' but he appreciated how a charismatic leader helped the cause. Eglantyne's loctor realized that insisting upon her complete 'withdrawal' from the vork to which she was so deeply committed could 'lead to more trou-le than it relieved'.[34] After years of treating her, he characterized her unusual psychic gifts', withdrawal and 'black pessimistic moods, when he hit out in prose or verse against apathy and indifference'[35] as psycho-ogical impairments indicating depression and possibly mania (as in her antic writing).[36] When he told her that 'psycho-analysis treatment' had een 'useful' in 'mild cases' of thyroid disease, he was perhaps gently ncouraging her to seek a more scientific approach to her health than rayer.[37]

For her part, Eglantyne kept her sense of humour and joked about her brown uniform' and 'monastic attire'. She thanked Margaret for ending her a pair of urgently needed 'dark stockings', which arrived ust in time' to prevent her from wearing her 'light coloured stockings' nd thereby 'introducing a startling incongruence into my monastic ttire'.[38] In September 1921, she described her appearance at a typical undraising event:

> I started down in to the hotel drawing room expecting to meet a few friends...and there was the room full of smart people in evening dress...I tried to hide...my brown uniform is so dreadfully grubby now and I fear getting ragged as well. Just as the music was over and the people were going away...I was told to address them, because 'some of those poor people had never heard me'. I arose in my brown uniform, spoke dreadfully badly...The people in evening dress hurried up to thank me with tears in their eyes...I know I am only talking about '<u>wool</u>' and that the only reason why this is not known is because it is fashionable for the moment to make a fuss over me. [39]

As the Armistice crisis subsided, questions arose concerning the role he SCF would play in peacetime. As industrial unrest swept England in he early 1920s, Eglantyne watched as poverty, in all its forms, become a entral issue across the political spectrum; it was almost impossible she aid, 'to gain a hearing for a purely humanitarian cause in the midst of he political strife'.[40] On the left, the dream of a welfare state supplanted he earlier Charity Organization Society individualist approach to welfare. ike other charities, the SCF was under attack from 'intellectuals and ocialists', who assumed that because charities had traditionally worked

within the existing capitalist socioeconomic structures, charity worker
approved of social divisions between the haves and the have-nots.
One of the SCF's socialist volunteers said that she dealt with the con
tradictions by putting aside her 'principles' while working for the 'pal
liative' SCF. She said she had lived all her 'life among the workin
class' and always resisted 'schemes' that 'afford means of bolsterin
up political oppressors...and perpetuate the very evils they are sup
posed to be attacking. I ignored these arguments when I worked fo
the fund...I think my life long devotion to children conquered m
reasons.'[42] Eglantyne noted the 'one fact which seems to stan
out...Labour in this country is more and more recognizing that charit
is only a palliative and economic reconstruction.'[43]

Charity work was under attack from feminists too. In 1882 Eglantyne'
mother had written that 'no government with its paid officials' could d
the work of a 'strong network' of women. To Mrs Jebb the work of th
women of the Home Arts and Industry Association was 'as beautifu
as the spider's fairy web...brightened by the women's faith and lov
and hope'.[44] By World War I, a new generation of feminists were crit
icizing women's charity work. Helen Swanwick, president of the Women'
International League for Peace and Freedom thought it impeded th
emancipation of women. For her, charity work signified 'surrenderin,
to the age-old notion that women had no concern in public life except t
wipe up the mess made by men'. She said that except for a few leader
and organizers, charity work 'required only jog-trot feminine capacitie
and had no permanent effect on policy'.[45] Swanwick, did however, mak
an exception for the SCF because of its focus on children.

Like Eglantyne, Nina Boyle understood the purpose of the SCF mor
broadly. Boyle stated clearly that her work for the fund had nothin,
whatsoever to do with concern for children. She freely admitted tha
she did not 'sentimentalize unduly over "the child"...My sympathie
are deeply enlisted for the mother, its proper and natural guardian
To me, the working-class mother is the pathetic figure, the marty
to our civilization'. For two decades Boyle kept a vigilant eye on th
SCF's status of women and girls committees, notably, infanticide in
China, child marriage in India, baby farming and traffic in women
In her view, the 'work of the Save the Children movement touche
all other movements for social betterment. Sociologists, educationists
scientists, politicians, as well as philanthropists, join hands with u
somewhere'.[46] In the post-war period many progressive political an
charitable organizations encouraged close co-operation on a range o
issues.[47] For Boyle and other volunteers, SCF work was part of a life

long personal commitment to fight against the impact of poverty on women. In the 1920s the membership lists for the FFC and SCF included the names of many of the better-known British feminists and female politicians, including, Katherine Courtney, Mary Macarthur, Maude Royden, Olive Schreiner, Margaret Llewelyn Davis, Muriel Paget, Edith Picton Turbervill, Ethel Snowden, Cynthia Mosley, Duchess of Atholl, Maria Ogilvie Gordon, Emmeline Pethick-Lawrence, Susan Lawrence, Charlotte Despard and Catharine Marshall.

A great deal of charity work, especially children's charities, required the support of local municipalities and government agencies. Geoffrey Finlayson asserts that this is because the war, in fact, created opportunities for new charities due to the League of Nation's pledge to co-operate with voluntary organizations.[48] The Paris Peace Conference of 1919 established new relief organizations for central and eastern Europe in co-operation with the International Committee of the Red Cross (ICRC), and a little later, under Articles 23 and 24, the League of Nations.[49] Finlayson suggests that the Save the Children International Union with its objective of providing aid to all children regardless of race or creed is an example of the League actually fulfilling one of its obligations to children and charity. He adds that the SCIU and the other voluntary agencies the League promoted represent three things: the 'internationalization of charity,' the ability of the voluntary sector to adapt to new 'circumstances and challenges' and 'its tendency to create more organizations with similar objectives'.[50]

As we have seen, the Save the Children Fund had been formed as an emergency measure to aid the child victims of war, but with the backing of prominent British pacifists, intellectuals, humanitarians and feminists it took on an international dimension and became a 'machine' with a life of its own. By 1922 the SCF had drifted into two parts: the London office and the umbrella SCIU in Geneva. The London office raised a great deal of money for local children and oversaw the work of the local branches and home committees which were formed in 1920 in response to the criticism that they were feeding only 'enemy children' while British children were in need. In order to blunt such criticism it became a condition for membership that every local branch also support local children in need. SCF annual reports assured the public that it kept the 'home fund' and 'foreign fund' entirely separate.[51] British home committees proved to be enormously successful in developing co-operative relations with local women's groups, government agencies and trade unions. There were SCF representatives at the annual general meetings of the National Council of Women (NCW) and the National League for Health, Maternity and Child

Welfare. Their joint projects included child welfare centres for mother and grants to nurseries, crèches and children's homes.[52] The SC and the National Union of Teachers distributed boots, milk and semi medicinal food to needy children.[53] In exchange, local SCF project received funding from the Miners' Children Fund, National Counci for the Unmarried Mother and her Child, Women's League of Servic for Motherhood and the Women's Freedom League Settlement.[54] Durin, the miner's strike in 1926 Lady Astor broadcast a general appeal fo milk for children in north and south Wales and over 9,000 pounds wa collected.[55] The scope of the work confirms that newly enfranchisec women did not turn their backs on local charities.[56] SCF annual report show that of the 14 women MPs who entered the House of Common in June 1929, only two had no recorded involvement in SCF causes One of the MPs was Edith Picton Turbervill, who was led to the Labou Party by 'social and philanthropic work'. She said, 'I came to th conclusion...that fundamental changes in law were necessary to obtai better conditions of life for people'.[57]

Eglantyne was more of an educationalists and social scientist than philanthropist; as a result she was not interested in limiting her worl to running a 'money box' charity or giving handouts like a 'patron izing' old-fashioned charity.[58] As leader of the SCF, she was far mor interested in the SCIU, which oversaw international fieldwork unde the patronage of the ICRC.[59] The COS model entailed the preventior of pauperism and promotion of independence by helping children anc their mothers by giving small grants and temporary relief to soups kit chens, orphanages, children's hospitals and day nurseries until suck time as local authorities and administrative bodies were in a positior to take over. The SCF's first projects had been in Armenia, Hungry Czechoslovakia and Russia. SCF aid was sent to projects that had beer established during the war by the Society of Friends and various women': hospital corps.[60] As vice-president of the SCIU, Eglantyne worked closely with Quaker feminists like Edith Pye, Hilda Clark and Ruth Fry, who were all members of the Women's International League with Dorothy Buxton.[61] In 1919 Eglantyne was co-opted to the Friends' Emergency anc War Victims Relief Committee that enabled her to channel money fo children in Friends' Relief camps in central and Eastern Europe. In Polanc the SCF sent relief to the Friend's Relief 'soup kitchens,' run by Ruth Fry who described her 'kitchen' as a 'tiny wattle hut containing a boiler anc fire and perhaps thirty barefoot children seated outside'. One of her goal: was to help the village health nurse to 'teach the mothers not to feec delicate children on black bread.'[62] Moreover, in the 1920s, Eglantyne invited a number of Quaker feminists to work for the SCF. Edith Pye and Alice Clark established SCF refugee hospitals in Vienna and other parts of central Europe.[63]

By providing grants to women's relief projects, Eglantyne helped shape her own career and also the careers of a sizable number of individuals, thus extending traditional women's foreign missionary work into the developing field of professional medical relief work. Evelina Haverfield was an international aid worker with strong militant suffragette credentials. A founding member of the Women's Emergency Corps, she had paid her own way to Serbia and joined up with Dr Elsie Inglis, a suffragette and founder of the Scottish Women's Hospitals (SWH).[64] During the winter of 1919–20, Haverfield and her partner, Vera Holme used SCF funds to re-organize orphanages at Uzince and established the Haverfield Home at Bayna Bachta.[65] When the war ended, many Scottish Women's Hospitals staff were determined to remain overseas to help rebuild Europe and to continue demonstrating their commitment to international peace. Dr Isabel Emslie also a member of the National Union of Women's Suffrage Societies, joined up with the Lady Muriel Paget's Mission in Russia.[66] Another SWH surgeon in Serbia, Katharine Macphail remained overseas, depending on SCF grants to support her Anglo-Serbian Children's Belgrade Hospital.[67] Macphail later became a vice-president of the Save the Children Fund.

Since 1920 tensions had developed between the London and Geneva offices.[68] Eglantyne's goal had been to make the SCIU the centre of the international child-saving movement. She did not want it to encounter the same problems that the Red Cross had experienced which seemed to her to be 'split in two;' the ICRC having all 'moral authority' and the national branches 'all the money'.[69] However, this is what seems to have happened between the SCF and SCIU. Both sides found it difficult to operate by means of telegrams, letters and sub-committee reports, and the London office was reluctant to make decisions with Eglantyne away in Geneva. Before long, angry letters began to arrive from field-workers and volunteers who demanded to know 'who is on the Committee, occupying its principle posts and guiding its policy both spiritual and material?'[70] From the point of view of the London office, the Geneva office should have been moved back to England after the Russian famine crisis.[71] Members of the Social Section Committee of the League of Nations agreed. Dominique Marshall says that many delegates thought that 'once the emergency work of famine relief became less pressing...the organization had become unfocused.' League of Nations' staff thought the SCIU was 'inefficient and useless'.[72] Eglantyne was disappointed because the 'English side' had become 'really only interested in dispensing relief' to home committee projects and she feared that the international movement would 'gradually peter out' if it cut its ties with the League of Nations.[73] But rather than wind up the SCIU, she devised a plan to rejuvenate the movement, expand its international influence and the profile of the fund and formalize its role in peacetime. This entailed doing more than dispensing charity and paying lip service to the idea of 'mutual help'.[74] Eglantyne picked up an idea that was circulating at the time, that the Save the Children International Union should claim certain 'universal' rights for children.[75]

From a financial point of view, interest in the international child-saving movement was waning in the early 1920s, and membership in the SCIU needed to increase if it was going to survive. To boast interest in it Eglantyne decided that the SCIU should draft a children's charter. The writing of what would become known as the Declaration of the Rights of the Child, or indeed, the 'child's *Magna Carta*' has become legendary within the history of the Save the Children Fund.[76] Various versions of the story go that 'one cloudless summer Sunday in 1922', Eglantyne packed 'her rucksack with a frugal meal and set off alone for her favorite spot in Mont Saleve'. She climbed to the summit and 'looked out over Geneva and its lake, there in silence she drafted what is now known as the Declaration of Geneva'.[77] Like most things associated with early SCF history, it was of course, more complicated. The drafting of the charter involved meticulous research and the labour of many highly trained people representing numerous child welfare organizations. In the decades that followed, the children's charter, which began as a publicity stunt to promote the SCIU, acquired a great deal of political and cultural significance. In 1924, Eglantyne's children's charter was adopted by the League of Nations and became the basis of the United Nations Declaration in 1948. Today, children's rights activists regard it as 'the first comprehensive internationalist instrument' devoted to protecting children, who are often the first victims of human rights violations'.[78] Brian Milne says Jebb's Declaration of Geneva symbolizes the end of the 'prehistory of children's rights'.[79]

Eglantyne had a mental picture of how the charter should be framed and the principles it should embody. She wanted it to include a universal declaration of rights, a legislative code and a definition of the duties of parents, private organizations and the state. Apart from this, individual countries would be encouraged to identify their own 'black spots' and draw up their own codes to reflect the needs of their own children. The final charters would be submitted to the SCIU for ratification.[80] In July 1922 Eglantyne scribbled down a version of her 'code for children' for her own reference and in September struck a sub-committee with Victoria de Bunsen as chair. For most of 1923 de Bunsen's working group consulted medial doctors, teachers and representatives of various national and international organizations to elicit their ideas concerning the 'minimum standard of child well being throughout the world'.[81] At the time the idea of constructing a children's rights charter was not entirely original, for similar documents had been attempted years earlier by voluntary and state organizations, notably, the Shaftesbury Society, the Ragged School Union and the Independent Labour Party. It was not until de Bunsen's sub-committee had nearly finished its first draft that de Bunsen was informed that the powerful International Council of Women (ICW) had 'been devoting its attention...to the development of a Charter' since 1920.[82]

The importance of the International Council of Women taking an interest in children's rights was not lost on Victoria de Bunsen. In 1919 the ICW held the distinction of being the oldest transnational women's organization. Its roots lay in many of the nineteenth-century mixed-gender social movements, including abolitionism, socialism, pacifism, temperance and moral reform. Leila Rupp says that the cross-national character of these causes brought conservatives, liberals and radicals together and a variety of connections were forged among the women, creating what social movement scholars call a 'preexisting communications network'.[83] The first international women's congress was held in Paris in 1879. Elizabeth Cady Stanton and Susan B. Anthony in Washington organized the second meeting in 1888. They called upon 'all women of light and learning' in trades, professions, suffrage, temperance and moral purity societies, peace organizations and literary clubs to participate.[84] The result was the formation of the International Council of Women. Its president from 1899 to 1902, from 1914 to 1920 and again from 1922 to 1936 was Lady Ishbel, Marchioness of Aberdeen and Temair.[85]

With the restoration of peace in 1919, women in ICW member countries were given some new political rights and responsibilities, which the ICW had been fighting for.[86] Rupp asserts that waves 'of enfranchisement freed women's energies' for international peace work, and the League of Nations seemed a promising place to begin promoting their status and concerns.[87] Like other women's groups, the activities of the ICW had been greatly disrupted during the war. In September Lady Aberdeen began planning her first post-war conference in Oslo for November 1920. Her long-term goal was to revitalize the ICW and obtain a clause in the League of Nations covenant opening positions to women. But before she could begin, she had to heal the war wounds that had penetrated her own organization. Some British members, for example, shuddered at the idea of resuming comradeship with 'the hateful Germans'.[88] Needing a reason to hold the first post-war meeting, Lady Aberdeen thought that focusing on children would depoliticize the war and remind the delegates of their symbolic power as protectors of future generations. '[H]ad not Wilson himself' she asked, 'called the ICW the "mothers of the new world"?'[89] After the 300 delegates from 26 countries had approved her suggestion that they write a children's charter, the Child Welfare Committee was appointed to carry out an inquiry in different countries on the conditions of child life. The final document, called 'The Children's Charter', summed up in 51 clauses and seven categories what women in member countries considered necessary for normal child development and the measures state agencies must take to bring them about.[90] Maria Ogilvie Gordon wrote a paper called 'The Children's Charter' to read at the Maternity and Child Welfare Conference, 'The Call of the Children' planned for October 1923. In anticipation of the launch of the charter, in April 1923, Grace Abbot, Chief of the Children's Bureau in Washington, 'expressed the hope that the international standard of child welfare outlined would be generally adopted, and that it might become the subject of international rivalry'. It was ready to be presented and adopted at the annual meeting of the International Council of Women in Copenhagen in May 1925.[91]

There is no direct evidence that Eglantyne deliberately set out to take over the ICW's children's charter idea or to antagonize Lady Aberdeen, but her actions may be an illustration of what Ruth Wordsword called Eglantyne's ability to be 'ruthless…even to her friends'.[92] While rejecting the role of the grand Lady Bountiful for herself and mocking society women's philanthropy, Eglantyne recognized the importance of such women to an organization. One of the first women she approached for the SCF was Lady Muriel Paget, who was called the 'pioneer of charity balls' because of the way she 'stormed London' in 1905 raising money for Southwark Invalid Kitchens.[93] During the war, Paget founded the Anglo-Russian Hospitals, and after demobilization she redirected her resources to SCF relief projects. Another important wealthy benefactor was Rozsika von Wertheimstein, the Hungarian wife of the wealthy English banker Charles Rothschild, whose substantial donations included paying the staffs' salaries at an SCF industrial school for girls in Budapest.[94] Equally important was Lady Sara Blomfield, known in the Baha'i community as *Sitarih Khanum*, who infused the SCF with her 'oneness of mankind' spiritual theology and her material wealth.[95]

The *grande dame* of the International Council of Women was Lady Aberdeen. She and Lord Aberdeen were not only patrons of the SCF; they backed the donation of the enormous sum of 5,000 pounds in 1920 and Lady Aberdeen brought Scotland into the SCF family.[96] There is evidence that Eglantyne already new about Lady's Aberdeen's charter when she appointed de Bunsen's committee. One month after Lady Aberdeen's ICW meeting in Oslo, she wrote to Eglantyne in her capacity as president of the ICW, asking if the SCF would help the ICW's national councils 'follow up' the charter resolution.[97] There had always been good relations between the SCF, the ICW and the local National Council of Women of Great Britain (NCWGB); many SCF members did volunteer work for the SCF and sat on numerous joint sub-committees. From the beginning, the NCW council minutes 'call[ed] attention to the admirable work...being done by the SCF'.[98] Obviously, Lady Aberdeen was disgruntled to discover that de Bunsen was drafting a charter for the SCIU to promote.[99] She refused to let it supplant her charter and insisted that they all come 'to an understanding regarding the form of the Children's Charter to be ultimately adopted'. She informed de Bunsen she had been 'anxious for common action all along'.[100] Lady Aberdeen had only minor objections to the 'arrangement and phraseology' of de Bunsen's charter. She asked that a clause for interdenominational religious instruction in the schools be inserted and that de Bunsen's suggestion 'that children should learn an international language' be deleted because it was 'opposed to ICW policy'.[101] Otherwise, Lady Aberdeen could find nothing to prevent the charters from being combined, and she graciously proposed 'co-operation' so as not to 'confuse' people. However, she reminded de Bunsen that 'in several countries our Councils have disbanded their committees and have just accepted our Charter'.[102]

Clearly, if Eglantyne wanted the SCF's name to be associated with a children's charter, she would have to co-operate with Lady Aberdeen; however, this was difficult for two reasons. Hugh Cunningham observes that by the 1920s it was the view of many voluntary organizations that 'the interests of the children and the interests of the state were the same'.[103] It is not surprising; therefore, that the focus of the ICW's charter was on what the state should do for children. Eglantyne was resistant to state intervention in areas she had claimed for SCF's model of co-operative mutual aid. And she thought the ICW's draft was too 'socialistic.' She said if 'we wanted a Charter summing up the duties of the state toward children...I imagine that a series of legislative enactments would carry it out',[104] but she made a distinction between feminist charters that appealed to state legislation and a humanitarian charter, which Prochaska would say embodied 'the values and principles of active citizenship'.[105] Eglantyne envisaged a charter that appealed to 'everyone who came into contact with children. That included parents, teachers and voluntary societies of every nation, 'not only to governments'. She said 'it is not much use passing laws unless the whole community is endeavouring to carry out the principle underlying them'.[106]

The second problem facing Eglantyne was de Bunsen's draft did not reflect her own point of view either. She thought she had missed the point to such a degree that she preferred 'Lady Aberdeen's Charter to ours'.[107] de Bunsen's draft contained 15 clauses and dozens of sub-clauses concerning practical rights like health care, adequate housing, wholesome food, education, vocational training, welfare and legal protection, all of which Eglantyne supported. However, it also had numerous additional sub-clauses, which Eglantyne regarded as 'puerile'.[108] Eglantyne wanted an irrefutable universally valid document that would appeal to a wide international audience, not a list of sublime privileges like the 'right to share in mankind's heritage of beauty...sunshine... contact with nature...to protect animal and plant life...to be taught to contribute to the beauty of the world...to hear good music and take part in pageantry'.[109] She knew this would not fly in poorer countries and was frustrated because the 'great point to be realized is that <u>relief alone cannot save children</u>. If we really want to save them we must...stimulate a new outlook such as will render it impossible to go on spending money, which is needed for children for education, on unremunerative luxuries and amusements'.[110] For the time being her hands were tied. At a joint meeting on 27 June 1924, the ICW and the SCF agreed to co-operate and they struck a small sub-committee to finalize a common charter. Victoria de Bunsen and Jeanette Halford represented the fund and Maria Ogilvie Gordon and Elsie Zimmern of the Maternity and Child Welfare Committee represented the ICW. Eglantyne's last hope was that her allies in the union office in Geneva would act as though they had considered the charter and then 'turn it down'!![111]

In February 1923 Eglantyne arrived in Geneva with a mandate to present the composite charter to the union.[112] She was expected to put forward the collaborative version of the charter, which consisted of 44 clauses, which set forth the needs of the child from conception to young adulthood and society's responsibility to provide for them. Former SCF archivist, Rodney Breen suggests that Eglantyne was acting upon her own initiative when she presented the SCF-IWC charter in two parts, the first being a preamble she had inserted based upon the children's code' she had written around 1922; and the second being the composite charter. The SCIU executive council liked both parts. Eglantyne's preamble became known as the Declaration of the Rights of the Child, or Declaration of Geneva.[113] It began with the now famous phrase, 'Mankind owes to the Child the best that it has to give…beyond and above all considerations of race, nationality, or creed'. There followed five concise children's rights: to the means of material, moral and spiritual development; to special help when hungry, sick, disabled or orphaned; to first call on relief in distress; not to be economically exploited; and to an upbringing that instills a sense of responsibility toward society. In Jebb's view, the first clauses dealt with what the community owes to the child and the final clauses with what the child in future life owes to the community, therefore it contained the principle of mutual aid and social responsibility that she had long advocated.[114]

The charter and declaration were accepted by the SCIU on 28 February 1924 and the declaration was translated into 36 languages and sent to the League of Nations delegates for study and endorsement.[115] Initially it was called the 'Children's Charter of the League of Nations' and presented as an international collaborative document and not the work of any single individual or organization.[116] Later it was attributed solely to Eglantyne whereas her most important contribution was using her influence to get it approved by the League of Nations.[117] Susan Pedersen argues that securing the League's backing of the declaration was a most striking example of humanitarian entrepreneurialism'.[118] For Eglantyne had an existing network of influence within the League of Nation's Child Welfare Committee that Lady Aberdeen's International Council of Women lacked. Many League members and delegates had been among the first SCIU executive members and supporters, notably, Giuseppe Motta, who was president of the League of Nations Assembly in 1924.[119] The motion by the Hungarian delegate Count Albert Apponyi to have the declaration approved by the general assembly was taken forward. Etienne Clouzot, SCIU member and secretary of the ICRC, and Eglantyne's brother-in-law, C. R. Buxton, of the British Delegation pressed British delegates to persuade their friends and foes to support the motion. The Declaration of the Rights of the Child was adopted at the fifth assembly of the League of Nations at a meeting on 26 September 1924. From that point onward, the history of the non-binding Geneva Declaration became a matter of public record.[120] By 1930 it had been signed by the prime ministers of Great Britain, Canada, Australia, New Zealand and South Africa and by the chief delegates of the Irish Free State and India.[121] In 1946 Eglantyne's original five 'rights' were expanded to seven and given the approval of United Nations. It was approved by the General Assembly again in 1959.

For the next couple of years the SCF and the ICW busied themselves with publicizing the charter. Lady Aberdeen and Eglantyne shared speaking engagements at national and international conferences on children welfare.[122] In May 1925 they organized a highly publicized dedication service at St Martin-in-the-Field, where 200 English representatives signed the Declaration of Geneva.[123] Shortly after, the ICW left child-saving behind and turned its efforts back to improving the status of women in the international arena, leaving the SCIU more or less alone to promote the charter. The charter gave the union the membership boost it needed. Under Eglantyne's leadership it was reconceptualized as a *palais des enfants*; the SCIU became a clearing-house for academic developments in scientific child study and welfare[124] and took on an educative role by commissioning child welfare studies, reports, fact packs and pamphlets and publishing books, like Edward Fuller's *International Yearbook of Child Care and Protection* (in 1928). For the remainder of the decade *The World's Children* published a wide range of research dealing with scientific child study, mental hygiene, innovations in pedagogy, juvenile delinquency and its new focus on children in Africa, India and China. The future of the SCIU seemed to be secure for the time being.[125]

In 1925 Eglantyne's position with the SCIU and League of Nations Child Welfare Committee led to her appointment as an assessor to the League of Nations Advisory Committee on the Traffic of Women and Protection of Children. She served on the legal committee, which examined the repatriation of alien children and the provision of relief in the temporary country of residence. She described the honour as one of the ways 'the SCF movement is brought into close relation with the work of the League of Nations'.[126] It was the highpoint in her public career, but she was frustrated by the slowness of the bureaucracy of international diplomacy. There was also a problem with the League's inability to enforce recommendations. Since her Charity Organization Society days she had maintained that 'scientific collection of data' was the only 'possible basis for a scientific world-policy of child saving' however, it was of 'little value for the League to undertake investigations and to accumulate information if the results obtained are to remain of mere academic interest...[T]he foundations of a house are of little use unless the house is built. It is for us social workers to build the house'.[127] A more personal achievement was being granted special permission on 14 August 1924, by the consistory in the Protestant Cathedral of St Peters in Geneva, to give a sermon on the subject of the

Declaration of Geneva, which was a rare privilege for a woman. Eglantyne called her sermon 'The Claims of the Children'. Addressing a crowd of 500 people, she began by asking the congregation to pray for the 'children of God...neglected, exploited, starved, persecuted, tortured, their innocent minds have been poisoned and their white souls dragged through the vilest mud.'[128] From the podium she said:

> ...Look across the world and see the suffering of the children. Think of the handicapped children in many lands who are born with tendencies to hereditary disease, who are brought up in overcrowded and insanity hovels...Think of the children with rickets and tuberculosis. Think of the wastrels who will never do a good day's work; the cripples who will never know the normal joys of life; the feeble-minded children, born perhaps into a sub-human existence...Think of the children in alien countries who are denied hospital treatment or schooling. Think of little girls in China, the binding of whose tender feet causes them years of pain...Think of the child marriages of the East, and their terrible consequences, both to the victims and to their offspring. Think of the child slavery, which still exists... Think of the children in certain parts of America who...are subjected to such heavy toil...Think of what happens in England [where children]...are thrown on to the labour markets, without a dog's chance of a decent existence...We excuse ourselves by saying we have not money enough to save the children. But so long as the world had money enough for cigarettes and cinema and numbers of little pleasure and comforts, it has money enough for the saving of child life...Think of the refugee children in Greece...Think of the orphans of Armenia...Finally, let us think of the children throughout the world who have been degraded and brutalized by their suffering, the children who are cruel to animals, cruel to each other, and who, before the years of childhood are passed, are already old in vice.[129]

Since beginning the SCF, Eglantyne had done a great deal of her administrative and fundraising work while travelling to Geneva and trying to spend time at her mother's home in Sussex and with Louisa Jebb in the Shropshire village of Lee. It was Emily who noticed that Mrs Jebb 'lived vicariously, there in her bed' through Eglantyne's work. She 'craves for E's frequent letters about people and doings, and she exists largely in her pride of her. She insists on E's distant foreign trips...I cannot conceal from myself that others and I often tend to bore her'![130] It meant a great deal to Eglantyne to be able to nurse her mother and Aunt Louisa and to have been at their bedsides when they died in November and December of 1925 respectively.[131] She told Suzanne Ferrière, '[F]or many years I have dreaded separation from my mother, who was such a companion to me, but now that the apparent separation comes...I do not feel separate at all'.[132] However, four months later, the 'strain imposed' by her mother and aunt's illnesses had hit her and she admitted that unless 'I can recover my health now and get my heart healthy now, I shall have illness and weakness for the rest of my life'.[133] She asked Suzanne to arrange 'several months rest' for her. Suzanne found her a room in Lausanne, Switzerland, which Eglantyne said would be 'quite prefect' for her 'Trappist life'.[134]

Eglantyne's final home was Switzerland where she tried to continue shoring up the prestige of the SCIU. She began learning Esperanto and Chinese and wrote a great deal of poetry and travelled for the fund when she could. Her health continued to be poor; her 'travelling companions' duties included carrying her 'off a channel steamer on a stretcher to acting as a lay audience at a rehearsal of a forthcoming speech, in a *wagon-lit*'.[135] A relief worker in Salonika recalled how 'he first met her carried ashore by her friends, utterly exhausted; yet she at once heard his report and said, "Tomorrow morning at 9:30 we start for Macedonia". When he turned incredulous eyes toward her companions, he saw in their faces she would carry out her plan'.[136] Because of her precarious health, Eglantyne was communicating to a greater extent with the international child welfare movement through her writing. Her articles in the *World's Children* show what she thought and wrote increasingly about a new world order. By 1927 she was more philosophically opposed than ever to one-sided charity, which she equated with alms giving and, sadly, the work of the London office. She envisaged a commonwealth of social institutions that made contributions to international 'social work' not 'charity work'.[137] Eglantyne felt that the London office's control of the purse strings put the SCIU at a 'psychological disadvantage' and she was uncertain of the executive's commitment to the union.[138] She was right to be concerned because many of the new volunteers in the London office, during the period referred to in the United Kingdom as the 'war on want', wanted to confine their work to local projects for local children.[139] After Eglantyne died they held a special meeting to consider the future of the umbrella organization, and it was only out of loyalty to her memory that L. B. Golden convinced them to keep it open. In 1946, however, the SCIU merged with the International Association for the Promotion of Child

Welfare founded in Brussels in 1921 and became the International Union for Child Welfare, based in Belgium. Save the Children's international work continued from London.[140]

In 1927 Eglantyne wrote a series of articles for the *World's Children*, in which she laid out her philosophy of mutual aid and international social responsibility. Her philosophy of 'modern relief work' can be divided into two main areas: child welfare and education. '[P]overty is the great enemy of children', and the SCF must work toward its extinction. Child poverty 'makes children suffer and stunts the race of which they are the parents'. Ideally the role of the government would be to enhance the 'human economy' through better labour relations and the use of technology to 'improve the means of production…to eliminate waste and diminish the expense of distribution…reorganize industry, adjust profits to services and effect a more equitable distribution of wealth'.[141] The larger educative role of the SCF was to teach a new generation to abide by and apply the principles laid out in the Declaration of Geneva. To that end, Eglantyne called for an education system for working-class children that would use Froebel's and Montessori's methods. New education must 'aim at developing not so much the receptive capacity as the creative abilities of the children'. They should be 'taught to do things rather than to read about them, to make them instead of talking of them'.[142] She used the SCF workrooms in Budapest as examples of all that could be achieved. In a curious choice of words for a humanitarian, she said, 'The African savage, no less than the child of the European city slum must make his choice, and it is for us who believe we have seen the light to help him to make a wise choice'. In workrooms, Eglantyne explained,

> we have a method of relief which can really attain the object with which relief should always be given…that of placing the recipient beyond the need of further help…If we are prepared to accept the immediate cost of helping destitute children on constructive lines, we should later on effect incalculable savings on the money we spend on hospitals, asylums, prisons and other institutions which are filled with the failure and the misfits.[143]

In the autumn 1928, when the London and Geneva offices joined together to plan an international conference on 'the African child', Eglantyne was too ill to help, but she followed their progress with interest. She told Margaret Keynes the conference would 'emphasise our fundamental principle—that mankind as a whole is responsible for the world as a whole, and that the people of every race should unite to get rid of such evils as child slavery, premature marriage, child labour and neglect and starvation of children'.[144] Eglantyne believed there was a special role for the social worker in the new international field of child welfare.[145] Twenty days before she died she dictated her last article for the *World's Children*; in it she said: '[S]ocial workers all over the globe should feel that they are laying the foundation for the civilization of the future...Many obstacles to peace and mutual aid will disappear...once we have realized that the world is a common home and that we are called upon to do our share in making it a real home for all the races—beautiful, orderly and rich in opportunity for all'.[146]

In July 1928 Eglantyne was admitted to a nursing home in Geneva and then moved to a hospital for goitre surgery. Her heart being too weak to withstand the whole operation at once, it was done in three stages with only a local anaesthetic. Everyone was optimistic of a full recovery, and her spirits were high. She continued her SCF work from her hospital bed by dictating letters to her nurse and a Danish girl who was hired to type. On 12 December Eglantyne wrote to her friend, Mrs Radcliffe, telling her about reading Katherine Mayo's *Mother India*. Eglantyne had become very interested in India's child welfare policy, especially child marriage and age-of-consent laws. She told Radcliffe that she was trying to get 'closer unity between workers in India and England'. She thought she could persuade Mahatma Ghandi and Rabindranath Tagore to promote the fund.[147] A week later Emily Jebb received a telephone call from Geneva telling her that Eglantyne had suffered a stroke. She had been unusually well all week, but on Thursday at dinner suddenly leaned forward and lost consciousness. The doctor gave Eglantyne a '20% chance of life' and performed an operation. She survived but 'began to sink soon after'.[148]

When news of Eglantyne's death on 17 December 1928 was announced letters, flowers and tributes from around the world flooded the offices of the Save the Children International Union.[149] Under her leadership, by 1928 the SCF organization had raised over 4,000,000 pounds and had national committees in 40 countries around the world. Many member countries had drafted their own children's charters signifying their commitment to upholding the Declaration of the Rights of the Child.[150] It was Eglantyne's wish to be buried in Geneva, a city that had meant so much to her and although it was difficult for her brother and sisters to comply with this, she was buried there in St George's Cemetery. A few friends and dignitaries from the League of Nations, the Red Cross and International Labour Organization attended her small funeral in Geneva.

At the same time in London a memorial service was held at St Martin's-in-the-Field.[151] This chapter has shown that while Eglantyne had not set out to run a charity, let alone a children's charity; in the ensuing decade she grew into the role of child's rights advocate. Her final work for the SCF exemplifies how her collaboration on the Declaration of the Rights of the Child marked the beginning of international thinking about children's rights and the special role of the social worker in the new international field of child welfare. Eglantyne had been prepared for a fight when she took on the SCF. For almost a decade she fought the press and public opinion because she believed that a scientific rather than sentimental charity could be the 'expression of an international ideal and help the <u>consciousness</u> of world unity to grow'.[152]

Epilogue: The Legacy of a *Rebel Daughter* and Early Save the Children Women

In the mid-1960s Eglantyne Roden Buxton jotted down 'a few points' for what she hoped would be the definitive biography of her aunt, Eglantyne Jebb. It had been 35 years since her death and Buxton thought the 'steps' by which the Save the Children Fund had been founded and 'put on the map' would make a 'striking story'. Of course she realized that 'only the first few years' of the fund would come into the book because her aunt died a few years after she and Dorothy Buxton founded it. Nonetheless, she thought 'Miss Jebb's life can stand up to being treated with complete historical objectivity'. After all, she had been a 'significant and exhilarating personality'.[1] With the help of Eglantyne Mary Jebb, Buxton asked Francesca Wilson to write the book. Buxton was satisfied that Wilson, (then 78), was not 'too old'. She had been a teacher, a social worker and a relief worker in the 1920s and 1930s and seemed very vigorous, 'on the spot and sympathetic'.[2] But when the biography appeared, Buxton quickly changed her mind. She was disappointed and her criticisms were many. She called Wilson's *Rebel Daughter* 'a waste of an opportunity' and an 'utter failure'. Wilson's attempt to examine Jebb's life 'historically and sociologically' looked to Buxton to be 'padded out with material about people...not relevant to EJ's life'. The finished product was 'like a broken statue with the head missing'.[3] Though Wilson defended her approach and Eglantyne Mary Jebb was 'well satisfied' with the book, Buxton felt betrayed.[4]

It has been said that 'who is known and honoured' in biographies 'has depended to a great extent on the accident of what has been written about them in their lifetime or shortly afterwards'.[5] After Jebb's death the Save the Children International Union attempted to secure a Nobel Peace Prize in her memory. To improve their chances, Dorothy Buxton and the SCF executive decided to play up the non-denominational apolitical side of the SCF and represent Eglantyne as sole founder of the SCF.[6] When the nomination failed, they turned the nomination notes into a couple of short monographs, which were sold as fundraisers in the 1930s and 1940s. They portrayed Jebb as virgin martyr; the SCF's 'white flame' whose 'apostolic spirit' has 'lighted our path'.[7] Eglantyne Buxton had always objected to this 'plaster saint'[8] representation of her aunt and had hoped to rectify it with Wilson's *Rebel Daughter*.

Biographies are cultural products that reflect the political and social climate in which the author and reader find themselves.[9] In the 1960s the quarrel over *Rebel Daughter* illustrates what modern feminist biographers like Ros Pesman call the unstable intersections and boundaries between biography and autobiography or 'how women tell stories about their own lives and those of others'.[10] Though Wilson did not explore the feminist roots of the SCF in *Rebel Daughter*, her biography shows her awareness that the achievement of greatness is usually the result of collective efforts, political networks and patterns of social embeddedness. According to Stanley it is the biographer's responsibility to illuminate the 'networks of relationships in the subject's life' and 'the role of social processes in producing and changing what 'a self consists of'.[11] What looked like 'padding out' to Buxton was really Stanley's 'kaleidoscope' casting around, reflecting new images and possibilities, new people and directions for Eglantyne.

In *Writing Women's Lives*, Carolyn Heilburn observes that supportive female networks, especially for middle-aged women, mean the 'end of fantasy' and the 'beginning of work and adventure'.[12] For modern readers, Jebb's life story illustrates the familiar hard and heroic struggle to accommodate the demands of family, the search for adult intimacy and the acceptance of new challenges and possibilities. Since childhood, Eglantyne encountered many women who influenced the direction of her voluntary social work career. She took inspiration from the work other women, including her sisters, were doing for social and political causes. At Lady Margaret Hall, Stockwell Teacher College, while teaching in Marlborough and at the Charity Organization Society she acquired a deep respect for the ethos of professionalism in social work. Even though she personally disliked hands-on social work, she was drawn into the lives and predicaments of the working-class women and girls; and she wrote sympathetically about their courage. Long before she took over the Save the Children Fund, she had contributed to social work as a teacher, a committeewoman, a social investigator and mentor of a new generation of social workers.

Women's history and biography show that it is only when we look closely at the experience of individual women in 'careers' that we fully appreciate the intersection of contemporary ideas surrounding professional responsibility, marriage and family duties. By looking at the late-Victorian and Edwardian marriages of Mr and Mrs Jebb, Sir Richard Jebb and Caroline Jebb and Charlie and Dorothy Buxton this book has shown that charity work gave married women opportunities beyond domesticity. At the same time, Eglantyne's decision not to marry did not free her from domestic responsibilities. She spent most of her adult life struggling to balance her sense of duty toward her mother, her desire for personal autonomy and her health problems against her need for a satisfying career. Voluntary social work offered her the pleasure of the companionship of like-minded women and a chance to display her talents and leadership skills and to write about social issues.

By the end of the First World War, Eglantyne had been drawn toward direct-action organizations like the Macedonian Relief Fund, the Agricultural Organization Society, Fight the Famine Council and the Women's International League for Peace and Freedom, and to people who were combining their personal, spiritual and political ideologies with meaningful national and international humanitarian and political work; this led her to take over the leadership of the Save the Children Fund and the Save the Children International Union. By following Stanley's 'anti-spotlight' approach to biography, this study has used Eglantyne's life as a lens through which to view at the history of women's voluntary social work in action. Although Eglantyne Buxton would have preferred biographers to keep the spotlight on Eglantyne, an exclusive focus on the subject alone obscures the part which women's networks played in Eglantyne's life and her belief that the 'far-reaching' work of building a new civilization for future generations must fall to women, and above all to women social workers.[13]

What women actually did in voluntary social work depended upon their social position and personal inclination. The First World War caused tensions within many political organizations including the women's movement. Some prominent suffragists insisted that women's full financial and personal participation in the war effort would be an opportunity to prove their capabilities and patriotism. Others, like the Quakers and the Women's International League for Peace and Freedom, engaged in relief work during the war as a demonstration of pacifism and international solidarity. After the war, women of all political creeds took advantage of new opportunities in municipal agencies, hoping to influence government policy directly.[14] Many women, the Jebb sisters included, were found protesting, lobbying and campaigning for social, political and humanitarian causes.[15] In 1919 when the opportunity to run the SCF presented itself, Eglantyne decided to focus her efforts on international children's aid. She discovered that giving aid to children regardless of race or creed made the fund extremely appealing to feminists, pacifists and the labour movement.[16] The SCF helped shape not only Jebb's own career but also the careers of a sizable number of women by providing opportunities and grants to relief projects.

What did working for the SCF mean to the women who were founding members of the general council and volunteers in the early 1920s? When Eglantyne took over the fund she had over 20 years' experience with voluntary-action organizations. When applying the professional ethos of the COS to international charity work, she insisted that rigorous investigative casework had to be done before relief was dispensed and projects had to be carefully monitored. To that end she called upon women from all walks of life as medical relief workers, fundraisers and project investigators. In doing so, she gave them the opportunity to display their talent, experience and intelligence and to travel abroad. To do the hands-on relief work, that is, running refugee camps and orphanages, Eglantyne used many women with strong feminist credentials. In 1919 Buxton used her acquaintances in the Society of Friends to make connections with projects run by Edith Pye, Hilda Clark and Ruth Fry in Vienna, Armenia, Hungary and Czechoslovakia. Eglantyne extended SCF influence by forming links among women prominent in private charities and the work they were doing in Poland, Romania, Slovakia, Crimea and the Baltics. Most notable was Lady Paget's Mission in Russia, which was the first British medical unit to enter Russia after the war.[17] During the war, Dr Hector Munro had engaged a large number of women doctors when the British War Office was still refusing to authorize women to go overseas. Susan Raitt described him as far keener on women's rights than most of the women were.[18] Munro joined the SCF executive and put Eglantyne in touch with many women doctors from the Women's Emergency Corps and Scottish Women's Hospitals, including Dr Elsie Inglis who distinguished herself by forming an all-women unit of doctors, nurses, orderlies, and ambulance chauffeurs and mechanics to serve at the front, thus proving women's battlefield capabilities.[19] When the war ended, many SWH staff, including Dr Katharine Macphail were determined to remain overseas to help rebuild Europe and to continue to demonstrate their commitment to international peace. Macphail depended on SCF aid to run her Anglo-Serbian Children's Belgrade Hospital.[20] She ran the hospital until 1941, when the German army took British residents as prisoners of war and repatriated her. She worked in the SCF London offices until returning to Belgrade in 1945.[2] The SCF enabled a number of medical women to further their career after the war and expanded women's relief work beyond their traditional contribution as missionaries.

In addition to engaging women for SCF medical projects, Eglantyne used women from other walks of life to do investigative work, publicity and propaganda work to promote the fund. The early influence upon late-Victorian girls of foreign governesses, language teachers, map studies in the schoolroom and travel diaries produced wanderlust in many well-to-do women who, in fantasy and reality, felt destined to explore the far reaches of the empire. Many women with the money to travel were inspired by lectures on the philanthropic initiatives in far-away places like India and Siam which were popular topics with ladies' associations and discussion societies. Victoria de Bunsen drew on her travels by horseback from Turkey to Baghdad in her work on behalf of Turkish children.[22] SCF volunteers were comfortable with the world beyond England's shores. The idea of travelling to the continent to inspect and report on SCF relief camps held the same romantic appeal for some educated middle- and upper-class women which local slum work held for others. The SCF sent many well-known women to do investigative work for the fund, just as Eglantyne had done for the Macedonian Relief Fund in 1913. The novelists Ethel Sidgwick and Henrietta Leslie travelled to famine areas to survey conditions. Charlotte Despard set up the Irish Save the Children Fund and went to South America on a 'propaganda mission' in 1924.[23] Edith Tucker went to Germany to visit SCF orphanages.[24] Geraldine Cooke, who had been a member of the National Women Suffrage Union, inspected work shops in Saratov.[25] Margaret Darnley Naylor published her 'eyewitness account of SCF work in Greece and Macedonia'.[26]

Many women, newly enfranchised, were just beginning their political careers, and the services they offered to the SCF enhanced their personal public profiles and the child welfare programmes of their respective political parties. Prominent female members of parliament from across the political spectrum served on SCF committees and promoted the fund. They included Lady Astor of the Conservative Party; Edith Picton Turbervill, Ethel Bentham, Susan Lawrence, Lady Cynthia Mosley and Margaret Bondfield of the Labour Party; and Violet Markham of the Liberal Party. Katherine Atholl was a Conservative MP and her husband was president of the SCF. Vera Brittain was once asked why so few militant suffragettes stood for election in 1918? She answered that 'hunger strikes

tension, persistent work, and physical onslaughts had left many Suffragettes with impaired health and diminished energy. They felt that the
next stage in the journey...must be carried on by women with fresh
vitality'.[27] The Fight the Famine Council and SCF membership lists
show that many suffragettes and feminists began volunteering for the
fund in the 1920s and 1930s. Although some had officially retired from
public life they devoted a great deal of energy to SCF causes. Emmeline
Pethick-Lawrence who had been imprisoned for her part in suffrage
campaigns volunteered for the SCF for over a decade. Similarity, SCF
volunteers Charlotte Despard and Nina Boyle supported militant suffrage campaigns and the Six Point Group. Louise Creighton, who had
been prominent in the social purity movement, was a member of the
National Union of Women Workers. Margaret Llewelyn Davis was
the General Secretary of the Women's Co-operative Guild in 1920 and
active on SCF home children committees. Many SCF women were
elderly when they travelled abroad for the fund. Despard was 73 when
she went to Hungary; Lady Sara Blomfield was 61 in 1921 when she
began her Industrial School for Hungarian girls and was still active in
the SCF when she died in 1940. Boyle volunteered for 22 years and
died in 1943 at the age of 78. Dorothy Buxton, who never retired from
the political side of relief work, kept her honorary place on the SCF
executive council until her death at the age of 82.

But the SCF was not just the playground of wealthy and well-known
women. Women from all walks of life made their mark on the SCF. As
well as the prominent women and wealthy patrons like Lady Aberdeen,
Lady Mosley and Rozsika Rothschild, there were paid women office
workers, typists, stenographers and secretaries like 'Miss E. Lawrence'
whose first job was with SCF in 1920 when she was a teenager earning
30 shillings a week. Her hours were supposed to be from 9.30 to 5.30,
but she had to be prepared to stay until 8.00, the latest a 'respectable
firm' would permit a 'young person' to say.[28] Lawrence saw the SCF as
a good prospect for someone like herself. Her remarks in an interview
in the late 1950s suggest that although there was a feminist consciousness in the SCF, it was not utopian. The lady volunteers always wore
their hats in the office and the 'better-off' folk went out for a meal
while 'the rest nibbled sandwiches' at their desks. On one occasion
Lawrence and a co-worker ran 'across the road' to a shop without their
hats, they were called back to 'put them back on' because they were never
to leave the office looking carelessly dressed'. A few weeks earlier, 'a misguided' girl came to work 'wearing a short-sleeved jumper (...just coming
into fashion)'. The 'lady in charge' made her wear her coat 'for the rest of

the day' with a warning never to come to work in a 'vest-like garmen again'.[29] Despite the poor pay, long hours without overtime and the management's disapproval of 'flapper' couture, it was a good job an Miss E. Lawrence was still a member of the SCF staff 36 years later.

Many SCF investigators, relief workers and volunteers adapted tech niques used in the late-Victorian genre of travel writing and 'domesti lady-slum investigative reports'[30] in their reports on relief camps, souf kitchens and orphanages. Whether they were Christians, Theosophists Baha'i, Jews or Salvation Army, socialists, Conservatives, Liberals o Labour, they worked side by side on the same projects to improve the status of women and children. Their essays, short stories, and article were published in *The World's Children*. Publishing the opinions o prominent British women was good propaganda for two reasons. First it gave the fund an occasion to question the foreign policies of the British government indirectly. Second, writing by women volunteer mobilized readers to action in support of specific policies and causes.[31]

Contributions to *The World's Children* reveal that neither persona ambition, nor public admiration nor a 'masquerade' could protect vol unteers from the profound physical and spiritual exhaustion which international children's aid work caused. SCF women's writing was no merely propaganda. Field inspectors and relief workers were tormente by visions of the devastation they witnessed in war-torn regions Reflecting upon the 'terrible situation of the child population through out large areas of Central Europe', on 11 May 1919, Dorothy Buxtor wrote, 'The whole thing is a nightmare to me, from which I can neve escape'.[32] Emily Hobhouse was 'horrified by the conditions of childrer in Leipzig'.[33] In Hungary in the summer of 1920, Charlotte Despar 'saw newborn babies sleeping on course sacking made of paper fibre and a general, sickening absence of the "decencies of life"'.[34] The mili tant suffragist and hunger striker Evelyn Sharp, an eyewitness to the devastation in Vienna, Germany and Russia, explained that her worl in devastated Europe was an extension of her lifelong commitment tc feminist politics. 'The worst of having been a suffragette is that, eve afterwards, you think public work cannot be worth doing unless it i the most unpleasant task you can find to put your hand to'.[35] In the summer of 1920, Ethel Snowden attended the first SCF council meeting and gave lectures on SCF projects, and in 1921 visited Vienna anc Budapest on behalf of the fund. She wrote articles for *The World' Children* describing the 'unimaginable' suffering of women and chil dren. 'Petrograd and Moscow are likely to become cities of the dead'. Ir one article she wrote, '[T]he special terrors for women in childbirth are unnameable. Lack of doctors and nurses, medicines and surgical instruments, linen for bandages, sheets for beds and soap for cleanliness is responsible…The horror of it'![36] Edith Picton-Turbervill tried to raise an awareness of the self-sacrifices made by SCF workers. She wrote a tribute to the workers who regularly went without food and slept on station platforms' *en route* to their destinations.[37] Eglantyne was haunted for years by the fear that the SCF would not have the money to meet its commitments. 'My attempts to collect money had been in the nature of a suicidal obsession,' she wrote in 1928. She said that from the time they started the SCF, 'whenever I went across a bridge or a high landing on a staircase, I heard a voice saying to me, "Throw yourself down, throw yourself down"…I had no intention however of obeying the suggestion, it simply made me react, brace myself, and go straight on.'[38]

The first generations of SCF volunteers were affluent, well-educated 'new women' who were comfortable using their social status to assert themselves and to lobby for children's rights. However, their international child-saving efforts must be considered in the context of 'maternal imperialism' in the 1920s. From a South Asian perspective, western women were divided into 'bad' women, who were muckrakers, social reformers and missionaries bent on christianizing and civilizing indigenous peoples, and 'good' women, who embraced theosophy or Hinduism and raised funds for worthy causes like hospitals and schools and supported Home Rule.[39] The SCF recruited women in both of these categories.

The relationship between fundraisers and the recipients of funds is complex. Eglantyne and other SCF women used *The World's Children*, speeches and film presentations as an opportunity to speak out on what they regarded as injustice and hypocrisy. In 'high-flown' deeply personal language they revealed a belief, which was shared by many educated western women, which was that, they were in the best moral position to save the world's children.[40] Although SCF women's benevolent motivations were sincere and heartfelt, their strongly emotive fundraising appeals reveal an inherent chauvinism, which some women, including Eglantyne had never been able to overcome. Operating from the perspective of early twentieth-century environmentalism and eugenics, it was difficult for SCF women to see non-European childhood in other than negative terms. Eglantyne's speeches and essays ring loudly with sensational ethnocentric stereotypes and severely critical descriptions of customs and cultural practices she had never observed. In her speeches one finds references to African 'savages', 'semi-oriental' women, wayward Hungarian girls and the 'feeble-minded children' who are a 'social menace'.[41] There is also the standard elite classes' disapproval o working-class leisure activities like smoking, gambling and the cinema. She wrote of the 'problem' of education among the 'native races o Africa'. She criticized child labour in China and Persia.[43] Her condemn ation of child marriage was based on information from Katherine Mayo *Mother India*, which later caused 'scandal' for its ill-informed portrayal o India's backwardness.[44] Ironically, Eglantyne saved her harshest criticis for English state schools. She said the curriculum encouraged an inheren British chauvinism, which taught children to 'distrust' or 'despise fo eigners'.[45] As we have seen, the Declaration of the Rights of the Child wa supposed to save children by educating them to western ideals even if meant first convincing them that they needed to be saved.

In 1979 the International Year of the Child was made possible by century of work by international relief agencies on behalf of children i Europe, Africa, India and Asia, which originated with Jebb's Declaratio of the Rights of the Child. Since then it has become commonplace t speak about 'the world's children'. The ideology of the child-centre society gives the 'interests of the child' a prominent place within th policy and practices of legal, medical and educational institutions, bu critics, scholars and activists have long argued that the concept o 'the world's children' unites 'our' children and 'their' children only t reveal the vast differences between them. Between 1920 and 1970 th SCF became notorious for its contentious fundraising propaganda and it exploitative pictures of suffering and starving children.[46] Eglantyne woul not have recognized that her own fundraising rhetoric was perpetuating dangerous form of nationalism, for the FFC and SCF were formed to brea down the fear that they were 'saving foreign children' who would 'rise u and kill us again'.[47]

Dominique Marshall argues that donors to children's charities wantec and volunteers delivered, images of the intense suffering of innocen children at the hands of evil enemies, thus reinforcing xenophobia an enhancing the isolationist elements of nationalism, which remaine very close to the surface in the 1920s and 1930.[48] Yet, Eglantyne's child saving narratives from 1926 and 1928 drew the most negative stereo types of people of her own social class and culture. Her poem 'Th Amoeba' was a 'savage attack' on the values of 'a Christian gentleman and 'society's parasites who profit from, or wilfully ignore the suffering imposed upon children by industrialism and war.[49] Her poem 'Murde and accompanying essay, 'A Note to a Murder' was directed at the igno rance of 'charming ladies in dainty dresses…[T]he darling little pet insulting those they slay'.[50] Though highly racialised, fund ideology an ounding principles indicate awareness that local problems require local olutions.

By ousting the Lady Bountiful, Eglantyne made the SCF different rom other children's charities and state agencies because she insisted, [T]he SCF must <u>never</u> preach about how local people ought to look ifter their children'.[51] She carried forward lessons learned at Lady Margaret Hall, at Stockwell and with the COS, which was that elite ady outsiders must realize their 'harmfulness, when they pretend to eform what they fail to understand'.[52] For almost a decade Eglantyne upervised the training of numerous relief workers, and it was her lirective that teachers be selected for their linguistic abilities. Five years ifter Eglantyne died, Julia Vajkai a long-time Hungarian volunteer, who vas vice-president of the SCIU, recalled Jebb's plan to train Chinese social vorkers to do their own child welfare work in China and her policy that educational work should not be started by anyone but a native person vho had the most intimate knowledge not only of the situation but also he racial qualities and defects as well as of the traditions of a country'.[53]

Eglantyne's philosophy of social responsibility reflected the style of the ate-Victorian rational-scientific needs-based Charity Organization Society ocial work. She believed that the role of international charity was to >rovide temporary emergency assistance until local governments were in i position to take over. From then on, parents, professionals and polit-cians had collective responsibly for child welfare, which was a child's ight. Eglantyne's philosophy of global co-operation and international nutual aid seems like common sense to many people today, but in the l920s it was controversial and could be put into practice only by influ-ential politicians and diplomats. Today, Eglantyne Jebb and the modern *Save the Children* hold prominent positions alongside influential NGOs ike Oxfam, Amnesty International and Greenpeace and in academic tudies of the globalization of charity work.

Eglantyne's programme for international children's aid was feminist n practice. As honorary secretary of the SCF and vice-president of the iCIU, she gave newly enfranchised women a chance to see first-hand he consequences of war, and many volunteers continued to educate hemselves about child famine and poverty and to deepen their inter-est in politics while working as healers and social workers in regions levastated by war. Another important function of charity work served >y the SCF was to create a sphere of friendship and a supportive net-vork for married and single women. International children's aid work :ntailed making connections with committeewomen around the country ind the world, and it brought women together around issues intended to improve their own lives and the lives of others. Surviving SCF committee minutes, field reports and 'confidential' correspondence reveal that intimate bonds existed between many SCF women. They used personal names, inquired about one another's families, stayed at one another's flats, shared travel expenses and exchanged advice on heath cures. Eglantyne called SCF women her 'international sisters'.[54]

When Eglantyne died, her colleagues, many of whom were among her closest friends, remembered her with admiration. Sidgwick said 'Eglantyne Jebb saw her ideal very simply; justice first, justice to the helpless and then common sense'.[55] Boyle predicted that she would become known as 'one of the greatest international philanthropists'.[56] There are three parts to Eglantyne's legacy: her contributions to children's right, to philanthropy and to social work. Children's charters were not unique in the 1920s, but it is significant that it was Eglantyne's version that was adopted by the League of Nations and adopted by the United Nations. Modern children's rights activists continue to regard Eglantyne's original five principles as foundational.[57]

Biography is written in response to the political and social climate in which the biographers find themselves. In response to the question what can modern readers learn from life writing about women of the past? Eglantyne Jebb was a highly educated member of the English elite. She was not a scholar or an intellectual, but a vivid interpreter of world events. She had visions of social action rather than concrete economic theories or political philosophies. She was a shrewd judge of people, a skilful administrator, capable committeewoman and persuasive public speaker with a flare for publicity. She was driven by a profound sense of duty that came from her faith, upbringing and education. She was self-absorbed and reclusive but not shy. She was a loner with a stunning charisma, who never fully appreciated the effect she had upon those around her, yet she inspired deep devotion and loyalty. Her dislike for hands-on social work and sentimental child-saving rhetoric does not diminish her. Since the 1980s voluntary action, with its emphasis on feminism, consciousness-raising, ethical organizing and social justice has come back into fashion.[58] The Lady Bountiful has been reenergized; however, the charity ladies of old, who did good-works among the poor without analysing the systemic causes of poverty would be unrecognisable to the modern business women, royalty and celebrities who lead or figurehead international NGOs today. From the distance of decades, Eglantyne would applaud their professional ethos.

Appendix 1: Women Founders of the Save the Children Fund: General Council Members (1920–1939)

The Marchioness of Aberdeen and Temair	1920–1938
Mrs. Francis Acland	1920–1921
Lady Acton	1920–1921
Mrs. S. A. Barnett, C.B.E.	1920–1921
Miss Ethel Bentham., M.D.	1920–1930
Catherine Booth	1920–1938
Miss C. Nina Boyle	1920–1938
Lady Brunner	1920–1938
Mrs. C. R. Buxton	1920–1938
Lady Cantlie	1920–1921
Miss Castelloe	1920
The Lady Florence Cecil	1920–1921
Miss Magda Coe	1920–1938
Mrs. Creighton	1920
Miss M. Llewellyn Davies	1920–1921
Mrs. de Bunsen	1920–1938
Muriel, Countess de la Warr	1920–1921
Mrs. C. Despard	1920
Miss M. E. Durham	1920–1921
Lady Fletcher	1920–1921
Mrs. Franklin	1920–1921
Mrs. A. Ruth Fry	1920
Mrs. Margaret Lloyd George, O.B.E.	1920–1921
Mrs. Ogilvie Gordon, D. Sc., Ph.D., F.L.S.	1920–1921
Mrs. Ernest Gowers	1920–1921
Mrs. E. Hood	1920–1921
Miss Eglantyne Jebb	1920–1928
Mrs. Pethick Lawrence	1920–1938
Mrs. A. Sarah Lawrence, L.C.C.	1920–1921
Mrs. Lindley	1920–1938
Mrs. E. M. H. Lloyd	1920–1938
Lady Emily Lutyens	1920–1921
Lady Lyttelton	1920–1938
Mrs. E. H. Major	1920–1921
Miss Violet Markham	1920–1938
Lady Maurice	1920–1938
Mrs. McKenna	1920–1938

Lady Scott Moncrieff	1920–1938
The Dutchess of Norfolk	1920–1921
Miss Oldham	1920–1932
Muriel Paget	1920–1937
Lady Palmer	1920–1938
Miss E. Picton–Turbervill, O.B.E.	1920–1921
The Countess of Plymouth	1920–1921
The Dutchess of Portland	1920–1921
Mrs. Walter Roch	1920–1921
Mrs. Charles Rothchild	1920–1938
Lady Rumbold	1929–1938
Mrs. C.P. Sanger	1920–1938
The Countess of Selborne	1920–1921
Mrs. Philip Snowden	1920–1938
Mrs. Harold Spender	1920–1921
Lady Sykes	1920–1921
Mrs. Stephen Tallente	1920–1921
Mrs. George Trevelyan	1920–1938
Miss Jane Walker, M.D., L.R.C.P.	1920–1921
Miss M. P. Willcocks	1920–1921
Miss Ethel Williams, M.D.	1920–1938
Lady Blomfield	1922–1938
Miss Yolande de Ternant	1922–1938
Miss Jeanette Halford	1922–1938
Miss Ethel Sidgwick	1922–1938
Mrs. Thompson	1922–1932
The Lady Weardale	1923–1932
Mrs. Henrietta Leslie	1924–1938
Mrs. G.M. Morier	1924–1938
Lady Cynthia Mosley	1924–1931
Miss Grace C. Vulliamy, C.B.E.	1924–1938
Mlle. Suzanne Ferrière	1926–1937
Edith Tucker	1929–1938
Mrs. M. T. Anderson	1929–1938
Dr Stella Churchill	1929–1939
Miss Annie W. Cooke	1929–1939
Miss Geraldine Cooke	1929–1932
Mrs. de Lafont	1929–1932
Mrs. Edgar Dugdale	1929–1938
Mrs. E. M. Pye	1929 1931–1936
Lady Nora Bentinck	1930–1938
The Countess Beauchamp	1932–1938
Mrs. Horace Farquharson	1931–1938
Adelaide Anderson	1932–1936
Mosa Anderson	1932–1938
Lady Young	1932–1938
Miss C. Lambert	1934 1936–1938
Mrs. Gilbert Ponsonby	1936–1938
Mrs. Gladys Skelton	1936–1938

Notes

1 Save the Children Fund (SCF) Archive, London, Gardiner Papers, Eglantyne Jebb (EJ) to Dorothy Kempe, Letter 162, October 1900, p. 37.
2 Jebb Family Papers, private collection (JFP); E. Jebb, 'The Ring Fence', pp. 71–72 (Unpublished Novel, 1912).
3 Ibid.
4 Ibid., pp. 248–249.
5 Ibid., p. 555.
6 Ibid., p. 805.
7 S. Koven, *Slumming, Sexual and Social Politics in Victorian London*, (Princeton: Princeton University Press, 2004). In 1893 Louisa Hubbard and Angela Burdett-Coutts did a survey that estimated that about 500,000 women were 'continuously and semi-professionally employed in philanthropy. Additionally, 20,000 supported themselves as 'paid officials' in charitable societies. These figures do not include the 20,000 nurses, 5,000 women in religious orders, and 200,000 members of the Mother's Unions, which did a considerable amount of charity work and over 10,000 women who collected money for missionary societies. See: F. Prochaska, *Women and Philanthropy in Nineteenth-Century England*, p. 224 (Oxford: Clarendon Press, 1980). Parker makes a distinction between two kinds of philanthropy, and so does Maria Luddy. The first kind is simply fundraising and distributing aid. Luddy calls this 'benevolent'. It is simply doing 'good work' within an organization for local people. The second type of philanthropy is more complex. It deals with the impulse itself. For Parker it entails the philosophy, intellect and spirit behind the effort. For women it goes beyond benevolent fundraising to an exercise of women's right to freedom, occupation and independent life devoted to public matters. In Parker's view it was work that women had a right and duty to take part in. J. Parker, *Women and Welfare*, pp. 29–31 (New York: St. Martin's Press, 1989). Luddy focuses on the reformist agenda in her definition of the second type of philanthropy. She argues that women's philanthropic work led to public and political action and campaigns. Reformist philanthropic work was powerful; it required ameliorative social action and a change of consciousness. M. Luddy, *Women and Philanthropy in Nineteenth-Century Ireland*, p. 5 (Cambridge: Cambridge University Press, 1995). In the late-nineteenth century well-to-do women were not expected to find paid work, and very few were prepared for it. Women who did have to support themselves also did unpaid charity work. I do not make a distinction between paid and unpaid social work, because the women themselves did not make this distinction. Women in unpaid social work regarded it as their profession.
8 *Daily Herald*, 16 May 1919.
9 F. Prochaska, *Schools of Citizenship: Charity and Civic Virtue*, p. 5 (London: Civitas: Institute for the Study of Civil Society, 2002).

10　Ibid., pp. 3, 6.

11　A. Platt, *The Child-Savers: The Invention of Delinquency* (Chicago: Chicag University Press, 1969).

12　J. Donzelot, *The Policing of Families*, p. 16, trans. R. Hurley (London: Hutchir son, 1979).

13　L. Mahood, *Policing Gender, Class and Family, Britain, 1850–1940*, p. 7 (Londor University College London, 1995).

14　'Great Army of Busybodies', in Prochaska, *Schools of Citizenship*, pp. 1–6.

15　S. Koven, *Slumming*, pp. 14, 187–188; J. Peterson, *Family, Love and Work in tl Lives of Victorian Gentlewoman*, p. 136 (Bloomington: Indiana University Pres 1989). The character-type originated in George Farquhar's 1707 play *The Beau Stratagem*. Lady Bountiful is a gracious gentlewoman whom everyone praise for her generosity and benevolence. She 'is a constant cornucopia; she give freely and unaffectedly whatever she has'. She heals the sick neighbou without ever dispensing money or realizing that she is being fooled by the false complaints. Eric Rothstein, *George Farquhar*, p. 152 (University of Cal fornia, Berkeley, 1967). McCarthy describes the stereotype as a 'stock figure i the gallery of feminine stereotypes' albeit she created a parallel power structu to that used by men through philanthropy and charity work. K. McCarth (ed.) *Lady Bountiful Revisited: Women Philanthropy and Power*, p. ix (New Jerse' Rutgers University Press, 1990).

16　SCF, Gardiner Papers, EJ to Dorothy Kempe, Letter 233, 24 November 190:

17　Jebb, 'The Ring Fence', p. 556.

18　C. Steedman, *Childhood, Culture and Class in Britain: Margaret McMillan*, p. (New Jersey: Rutgers University Press, 1990).

19　D. F. Buxton and E. Fuller *The White Flame*, p. 20 (Toronto: The Weardal Press, Ltd., 1931).

20　E. Fuller, *The Right of the Children* (London, Victor Gollancz, 1951 K. Freeman, *If Any Man Build, Let Him Build on a Sure Foundation* (Londor Save the Children Fund, 1965); R. Symonds, *Far Above Rubies: The Wome Uncommemorated by the Church of England* (Leominster: Gracewing, 1993).

21　Buxton Family Papers (BFP), E. Buxton, 'Eglantyne's Notes on Eglantyne Jeb Mostly Prompted by the Inadequacies of Francesca Wilson's *Rebel Daughter* n.d., p. 19.

22　Buxton was 22 when Jebb died. She had vivid memories of her. She tol Wilson, 'with her one seemed to breathe a freer air.' F. Wilson, *Rebel Daughte of a Country House: The Life of Eglantyne Jebb, Founder of the Save the Childre Fund*, p. 220 (London: Allen & Unwin, 1967). At Oxford in the 1920s on of Buxton's lecturers used the SCF as an example of an organization tha contributed to internationalism. Buxton 'was thrilled that SCF was notice in the academic world'. BFP, E. Buxton, 'Notes for a Possible Biography c Miss Eglantyne Jebb', pp. 1–2.

23　BFP, E. Buxton, 'Eglantyne's Notes on Eglantyne Jebb', p. 12.

24　Geraldine Jebb C.E.B. (1886–1959) was Principal of Bedford College from 193 to 1951. Eglantyne Mary Jebb C.E.B. (1889–1978) was the Principal of th Froebel Institute from 1932 to 1955. See obituary: 'Miss E. M. Jebb, *Time.* 11 May 1978; F. Wilson, *Gem Jebb: A Portrait by Francesca Wilson*, Bedfor College [n.d.]; Royal Holloway, University of London Archives (BC RF141/1/1 E. J. Jebb, *A Personal Memoir of her Sister* [n.d.]; Royal Holloway, University c London Archives (BC RF141/1/1).

5 F. Wilson, *In the Margins of Chaos: Recollections of Relief Work in and Between Three Wars* (London: John Murray, 1944); F. Wilson, *Aftermath: France, Germany, Austria, Yugoslavia, 1945 and 1946* (Harmondsworth: Penguin Books, 1947); F. Wilson, *They Came as Strangers: The Story of Refugees in Britain* (London: Hamilton, 1959). See obituary: 'Miss Francesca Wilson', *Times*, 22 April 1981, *Contemporary Authors*, vol. 103, 1982, p. 549.

6 Wilson, *Rebel Daughter*, p. 83; BFP, Francesca Wilson to David Buxton, 7 August 1967.

7 *Church Times*, 10 November 1967.

8 *Sunday Times* review summarized by Wilson in a letter to David Buxton. BFP, Wilson to David Buxton, 7 August 1967.

9 *Daily Telegraph*, 17 August 1967.

10 Buxton told her brother, 'I wrote several times to Cousin Eglantyne about my dissatisfaction'. Nevertheless, she was still reluctant to hurt Wilson's feelings. BFP, E. Buxton to David Buxton, 11 June 1967. After the book appeared, Buxton wrote a 25-page critique, which David Buxton entitled, 'Eglantyne's Notes on Eglantyne Jebb, Mostly Prompted by the Inadequacies of Francesca Wilson's *Rebel Daughter*'.

1 BFP, Wilson to Eglantyne Mary Jebb, 3 July 1970. By 1969, 1608 copies of *Rebel Daughter* had been sold.

2 S. Mitchell, *Frances Power Cobbe* (Charlottesville: University of Virginia Press, 2004), p. 4; M. Myall, '"Only be ye strong and very courageous": The Militant Suffragism of Lady Constance Lytton', *Women's History Review*, 7:1 (1998), p. 62; T. Vammen, 'Forum: Modern English Auto/biography and Gender', *Gender and History*, 2:1 (1990), p. 17.

3 E. Ross (ed.) *Slum Travelers: Ladies and London Poverty, 1860–1920*, p. 28 (Berkeley: University of California Press, 2007).

4 S. Hewa and D. H. Stapleton (eds) *Globalization, Philanthropy, and Civil Society: Toward a New Political Culture in the Twenty-First Century*, p. 118 (New York: Springer, 2005). Save the Children currently has a branch in 27 countries, which work on projects in over 115 countries around the world.

5 L. H. Lees, *The Solidarities of Strangers: The English Poor Laws and the People, 1700–1948*, pp. 268–269 (Cambridge and New York: Cambridge University Press, 1998).

36 Prochaska, *Women and Philanthropy*, p. 7.

37 Brian Harrison, 'Philanthropy and the Victorians', *Victorian Studies*, June, 1966, p. 360.

38 Ibid., pp. 357, 360.

39 Parker, *Women and Welfare*, pp. 11–13, 27.

40 Luddy, *Women and Philanthropy*, p. 218.

41 L. Mahood, 'Feminists, Politics and Children's Charity: The Formation of the Save the Children Fund', *Voluntary Action*, 5 (2002), pp. 71–88.

42 Ross, *Slum Travelers*, p. 23; Koven, *Slumming*, pp. 183–184, 187.

43 L. Stanley, *The Auto/Biographical I: Theory and Practice of Feminist Auto/Biography*, p. 234 (Manchester: Manchester University Press, 1992).

44 L. Stanley, 'Biography as Microscope or Kaleidoscope? The Case of "Power" in Hanna Cullwick's Relationship with Arthur Munby', *Women's Studies International Forum*, 10:1 (1987), p. 21.

45 Ibid., p. 19.

46 Ibid., p. 21

47   J. Lepore, 'Historians Who Love too Much: Reflections on Microhistory and Biography', *Journal of American History*, 88:1, 2001, p. 126.
48   Mills identified three key questions that the researcher should ask when using the sociological imagination: 1) What is the structure of a particular society and how does it differ from other varieties of social order? 2) Where does this society stand in human history and what are its essential features? 3) What varieties of women and men live in this society and in this period, and what is happening to them? C. W. Mills, 'The Promise', in C. W. Mills, *The Sociological Imagination*, pp. 3–8 (Oxford: Oxford University Press, 2000).
49   Gorham argues that 'historical biography continues to engage reader because it offers us intimate knowledge of another personality and another period, and that knowledge allows us to know ourselves and our own period better'. D. Gorham, *Vera Brittain: A Feminist Life*, pp. 5–6 (Oxford: Blackwell, 1996).
50   Ross, *Slum Travelers*, pp. 5, 28.
51   B. Haslam, *From Suffrage to Internationalism: The Political Evolution of Three British Feminists, 1908–1939*, p. 17 (New York: Peter Lang, 1999).
52   Prochaska, *Women and Philanthropy*, p. 222.
53   M. Vicinus, *Independent Women: Work and Community for Single Women 1850–1920*, p. 158 (London: Virago Press, 1985). See also: M. Vicinus, *Intimate Friends: Women Who Loved Women, 1778–1928* (Chicago: The University of Chicago Press, 2004).
54   C. Steedman, *Childhood, Culture and Class in Britain: Margaret McMillan* pp. 5–6 (New Jersey: Rutgers University Press, 1990).
55   J. Purvis, *Emmeline Pankhurst: A Biography*, p. 6 (London: Routledge, 2002).
56   R. Pesman, 'Autobiography, Biography and Ford Madox Ford's Women' *Women's History Review*, 8:4 (1999), p. 655 and L. Stanley, 'Mimesis, Metaphor and Representation: Holding Out an Olive Branch to Emergent Schreiner canon', *Women's History Review*, 10:1 (2001), p. 28.
57   Lepore, 'Historians Who Love too Much', p. 129.
58   See Barbara Caine's essay on feminist autobiography in: M. Spongberg, B. Caine, A. Curthoys (eds) *Companion to Women's Historical Writing* pp. 193–203 (London: Palgave, 2005).
59   BFP, Dorothy Frances Buxton, Talk With Margaret Hill, 10 October 1929 p. 6.
60   C. Clay, *British Women Writers, 1914–1945: Professional Work and Friendship* pp. 30–31 (Hampshire: Ashgate Publishing Limited, 2006).
61   M. Jolly, *In Love and Struggle*, p. 19 (New York: Columbia University Press 2008).
62   Ibid., p. 207.

Chapter 1

  1   Jebb Family Papers (JFP), Eglantyne Louisa Jebb Diary, 25 December 1882. Eglantyne Louisa Jebb (1845–1925) will be referred to as 'Tye' and 'Mrs Jebb' throughout this book to distinguish her from her daughter Eglantyne Jebb.
  2   JFP, E. L. Jebb, *The Rights of Women* (Leaflet), 1882, p. 2. Reprinted from the *Temperance Visitor*, 1882.

3 D. T. Andrew, *Philanthropy and Police: London Charity in the Eighteenth Century*, p. 202 (Princeton: Princeton University Press, 1989).
4 G. Finlayson, *Citizen, State, and Social Welfare in Britain 1830–1990* (Oxford: Clarendon Press, 1994).
5 E. Jebb, 'The Ring Fence' (unpublished novel, 1912), p. 204.
6 Sophia Smith Collection (SSC), Box 1, File 1–18, Caroline Jebb to mother and sisters, 20 August 1874.
7 JFP, E. Ussher, Jebb Family History (unpublished manuscript, c. 1930), p. 11.
8 F. Wilson, *Rebel Daughter of a Country House: The Life of Eglantyne Jebb, Founder of the Save the Children Fund*, p. 26 (London: Allen & Unwin, 1967).
9 SSC, Box 1, File 1–18, Caroline Jebb to mother and sisters, 20 August 1874, Caroline Jebb to Lealie, 19 Jan 1889.
10 *Liverpool Mercury*, Issue 7249, 18 April 1871.
11 JFP, Ussher, Jebb Family History, pp. 1–2.
12 JFP, Eglantyne Louisa Jebb Diary, 18 September 1882.
13 JFP, Ussher, Jebb Family History, pp. 11–12.
14 Ibid., p. 13, Caroline Jebb had a different impression. She said, 'having three children in three years has been rather much for her looks'. Tye was seven months pregnant when Caroline wrote this. SSC, Box 1, File 1–18, Caroline Jebb to mother and sisters, 20 Aug 1874.
15 L. Davidoff, M. Doolittle, J. Fink and K. Holden, *The Family Story: Blood, Contract and Intimacy, 1830–1960* (London and New York: Longman, 1999), p. 135.
16 Sutherland, G. *Policy-making in Elementary Education, 1870–1895*, p. 56 (Oxford: Oxford University Press, 1973).
17 Ibid., pp. 56–57, 58.
18 JFP, Arthur Trevor Jebb (ATJ) to Eglantyne Louisa Jebb (ELJ), 16 May 1873.
19 Ibid., 23 September 1873.
20 Ibid.
21 Ibid., 16 September 1875.
22 Ibid., 24 September 1873.
23 Ibid., 16 May 1873.
24 Ibid., 7 June 1873.
25 Ibid., 28 May 1873.
26 Ibid., 24 May 1873.
27 Ibid., 20 June 1873.
28 Ibid., 30 August 1873.
29 M. Bobbitt, *With Dearest Love To All: The Life and Letters of Lady Jebb*, p. 164 (Chicago: Regency, 1960).
30 JFP, ATJ to ELJ, 20 June 1873.
31 Ibid., 14 June 1873. Ibid., 7 June 1873.
32 Davidoff, et al, *The Family Story*, p. 18.
33 JFP, ATJ to ELJ, 16 September 1875.
34 Ibid., 20 May 1883.
35 Ibid., 28 September 1876.
36 Ibid., 19 July 1880.
37 Ibid., 5 July 1882.
38 Ibid.

39 Ibid., 3 May 1883.
40 Ibid., 20 May 1883.
41 J. E. C. Harrison, *Late Victorian Britain, 1875–1901*, pp. 38, 40 (London Fontana Press, 1990).
42 SSC, Box 1, File 1–18, Caroline Jebb to Lealie, 19 January 1889.
43 G. Finlayson, *Citizen, State*, p. 59.
44 Harrison, *Late Victorian Britain*, pp. 38, 40.
45 S. Smiles, *Self-Help*, pp. 1, 5–7, 294 (London: John Murray, 1905); L. H. Lees *The Solidarities of Strangers: The English Poor Laws and the People, 1700–1948* p. 233 (Cambridge and New York: Cambridge University Press, 1998); Finlayson, *Citizen, State*, pp. 19–20; K. Fieldson, 'Samuel Smiles and Self-Help' *Victorian Studies*, pp. 158–159 (xii December 1968).
46 Finlayson, *Citizen, State*, p. 24.
47 'Letter to the Editor', *London Times*, 7 April 1888. Lees stated tha 'Although overseers in the eighteenth and early nineteenth centuries had rarely tried to coerce kin to support elderly paupers, many guardian moved aggressively to do so, particularly after 1870'. Lees, *The Solidaritie. of Strangers*, p. 173.
48 JFP, Ussher, Jebb Family History, p. 3.
49 In 1920 Eglantyne's brother Richard Jebb was living at The Lyth and involvee with the Provident Society and hospital. JFP, EJ to ELJ, 3 November 1920.
50 Jeanne Peterson stressed that this stereotype was only appropriate for the wives and daughters of clergyman with incomes well above 200 pounds a year. M. J. Peterson, 'No Angel in the House: The Victorian Myth and the Paget Women', *The American Historical Review*, 89:3, 1984, p. 677.
51 Wilson, *Rebel Daughter*, p. 25.
52 SSC, Box 1, File 1–18, Caroline Jebb to mother and sisters, 20 August 1874
53 Bobbitt, *With Dearest Love To All*, pp. 116–117, 164–165.
54 SSC, Box 1, File 1–18, Caroline Jebb to Dearest Sister, 16 February 1894.
55 *Freeman's Journal and Daily Commercial Advisor*, Dublin, Ireland, 19 May 1870. For more on the stereotype see: J. A. Banks and O. Banks *Feminisn and Family Planning in Victorian England*, pp. 58–70 (Liverpool: Liverpoo University Press, 1965); J. Murray, *Strong Minded Women & Other Lost Voice: from 19th Century England* (New York: Pantheon Books, 1982); D. Gorham *The Victorian Girl and the Feminine Ideal* (Bloomington: Indiana University Press, 1982); L. Davidoff, *Best Circles: Society and Etiquette and the Season* (London: Croom Helm, 1973).
56 JFP, Eglantyne Louisa Jebb Diary, 20 September 1882.
57 Wilson, *Rebel Daughter*, p. 30.
58 JFP, E. L. Jebb, 'Handwork for Children', *The Nineteenth Century*, p. 610 (October 1882); E. L. Jebb, *The Home Arts and Industries Association*, n.d., p. 1.
59 C. G. Leland, *The Minor Arts: Porcelain Painting, Wood-carving, Stencilling, Modelling, Mosaic Work, Etc.*, p. 11 (London: Macmillan, 1880).
60 A. Anderson, 'Victorian High Society and Social Duty: The Promotion of "Recreative Learning and Voluntary Teaching"', *History of Education*, 31:4 (2002), pp. 321–322.
61 JFP, E. L. Jebb, *The Home Arts and Industries*, p. 87. Reprint from *Cheltenham Examiner*, 15 December 1885.
62 Finlayson, *Citizen, State*, p. 73.

63 Hanna Moore quoted in P. Hollis, *Women in Public: The Women's Movement*, p. 223 (London: George Unwin, 1979).
64 J. Donzelot, *The Policing of Families*, trans. R. Hurley, p. 16 (New York: Random House, 1979). 'Whatever the motives, good deeds were done. Landowners could be paternalistic toward their tenants'; Finlayson, *Citizen, State*, p. 54.
65 E. Yeo, 'Social Motherhood and the Sexual Communion of Labour in British Social Science, 1850–1950', *Women's History Review*, 1:1, (1992), pp. 63–68.
66 Anderson, 'Victorian High Society', pp. 311, 315.
67 Jebb, *The Home Arts and Industries Association*, p. 86.
68 JFP, E. L. Jebb, *The Home Arts and Industries Association*, n.d., p. 1.
69 Jebb, *The Home Arts and Industries Association*, p. 84.
70 J. Parker, *Women and Welfare*, pp. 11–13 (New York: St. Martin's Press, 1989).
71 JFP, Eglantyne Louisa Jebb Diary, 1 August 1882.
72 Ibid., 19 July 1882.
73 'supplying by their ready-witted ingenuity, their compassionate tenderness, their courageous and self-forgetting sympathy, their genius for the graciously recreative side of life...that which the stronger and sterner sex may sometimes find themselves...in need'. JFP, E. Jebb, *The Rights of Women*, p. 1, JFP, Eglantyne Louisa Jebb Diary, 28 September 1882.
74 JPF, Eglantyne Louisa Jebb, Diary I (1 July 1882–September 1882); Diary II (20 October 1882–1 June 1883); Diary III (28 October 1883–31 May 1883).
75 Ibid., 3 August 1882.
76 Ibid., 25 August 1882.
77 Ibid., 17 August 1882.
78 V. Glendinning, A *Suppressed Cry: Life and Death of a Quaker Daughter*, p. 6 (London: Routledge & Kegan Paul, 1969).
79 Personal correspondence with Lionel Jebb, 16 July 2008.
80 JFP, Eglantyne Louisa Jebb Diary, 20 September 1882.
81 Davidoff, *The Best Circle*, p. 42.
82 Ibid., pp. 42–43. J. Peterson, *Family, Love and Work*, pp. 133, 139 (Indianapolis: Indianapolis University Press, 1989).
83 JFP, Eglantyne Louisa Jebb Diary, 24 September 1882.
84 B. Harrison, 'Philanthropy and the Victorian', *Victorian Studies*, June 1966, pp. 364–365.
85 The first annual meeting took place in 1884. The chair was taken by founding president, Lord Brownlow, Anderson, 'Victorian High Society', p. 323, Jebb, *The Home Arts and Industries Association*, p. 91.
86 JFP, Eglantyne Louisa Jebb Diary, 29 August 1882.
87 Ibid., Sunday August 1882.
88 Ibid., 5 September 1882.
89 JFP, E. L. Jebb, *Memorandum to Government: Respecting the Establishment of Home and Village Industries in Ireland*, 1886, p. 2.
90 JFP, Eglantyne Louisa Jebb Diary, 5 September 1882.
91 In the 1880s the Irish Home Rule campaign demanded self-government and national autonomy for Ireland. ELJ was sympathetic. BFP, D. F. Buxton, Interview with Mrs Florence Keynes, May 1929, p. 2.
92 Jebb, *Memorandum to Government*, p. 3.
93 A. O'Day, *Irish Home Rule, 1867–1921*, pp. 154–158 (Manchester: Manchester University Press, 1998); W. B. Owen, 'O'Brien, Charlotte Grace (1845–1909)',

rev. Marie-Louise Legg, Oxford Dictionary of National Biography (Oxford University Press, 2004) [http://www.oxforddnb.com.subzero.lib.uoguelph.ca/view/article/35276, accessed 12 September 2007].

94 M. Luddy, *Women and Philanthropy in Nineteenth-Century Ireland*, p. 218 (Cambridge: Cambridge University Press, 1995).

95 L. B. Tanner (ed.), *Voices From Women's Liberation* (New York: New American Library, 1970); D. Spender, *Man Made Language,* 2nd edition (New York: Routledge, 1985).

96 JFP, Eglantyne Louisa Jebb Diary, 19 September 1882.

97 Ibid., 30 August 1882.

98 JFP, ATJ to ELJ, 25 October 1883.

99 F. Prochaska, *Women and Philanthropy in Nineteenth-Century England*, p. 227 (Oxford: Clarendon Press, 1980).

100 JFP, ATJ to ELJ, 20 May 1883.

101 JFP, ATJ to ELJ, 16 October 1883.

102 Ibid., 3 May 1883.

103 Lees, *The Solidarities of Strangers*, p. 241.

104 JFP, Eglantyne Louisa Jebb Diary, Thursday September 1883.

105 SSC, Box 1, File 1–18, Caroline Jebb to sister 15 December 1874.

106 JFP, Eglantyne Louisa Jebb Diary, 28 October 1883.

107 Ibid.

108 Prochaska, *Women and Philanthropy*, p. 222.

109 For accounts of these marriage see: J. Lewis, *Women and Social Action in Victorian and Edwardian England* (Stanford, Stanford University Press, 1991); A. McBriar, *An Edwardian Mixed Doubles: The Bosanquet versus The Webbs* (Oxford, Clarendon Press, 1987).

110 JFP, Ussher, Jebb Family History, p. 33.

111 R. Brandon, *The New Women and the Old Men: Love, Sex and the Woman Question*, pp. 250–251 (London: Secker & Warburg, 1990).

112 Charitable activities were not taken to excess or put before domestic responsibilities. See: M. Abbott, *Family Ties: English Families 1540–1920*, p. 34 (London and New York: Routledge, 1993); Davidoff, *The Best Circles*, p. 57.

113 Tye exhibits this impulse in her diary. JFP, Eglantyne Louisa Jebb Diary, 28 October 1883. Burstyn says 'The subordinate position portrayed in Genesis and the Epistles called for self-restrain from women. They had to suffer silently whatever misfortunes life held in store...Tied to the home with little variety of experience to divert thoughts, women dwelt on misfortune in a way unknown and often unsuspected by the more active partners. In this atmosphere self-denial came to be preached as a virtue on itself.' J. Burstyn, *Victorian Education and the Ideal of Womanhood*, p. 105 (London: Croom Helm, 1980).

114 Jebb, *The Rights of Women*, p. 1.

115 Letter refers Mrs Jebb's resignation. JFP, Letter from ELJ to Miss Baha, 29 February 1884; Eglantyne Louisa Jebb Diary, 16 June 1886; Ibid., 18 June 1886. Ibid., 20 June 1886.

116 SSC, Caroline Jebb to Pollie, 23 September 1887. Tye's obituary said, 'It was owing to her strenuous activities that Mrs Jebb's health broke down, and she was never able to resume any direct part in public work'. JFP, 'Obituary', *Oswestry Adviser*, 11 November 1925.

117 Parker, *Women and Welfare,* p. 190.
118 E. Gordon and G. Nair, *Public Lives: Women, Family and Society in Victorian Britain*, p. 88 (New Haven and London: Yale University Press, 2003).
119 JFP, Ussher, Jebb Family History, p. 7.
120 Ibid.
121 Ibid., p. 1.
122 JFP, Eglantyne Louisa Jebb Diary, 25 December 1882.
123 JFP, ELJ to Louisa Wilkins, c. 1921.
124 Jebb, *The Rights of Women*, p. 1.
125 JFP, Ussher, Jebb Family History, p. 15.
126 JFP, ELJ to Louisa Wilkins, c. 1921. Emily published *The Trail of the Black and Tans* (Ireland: Talbot Press, 1921) under the pseudonym 'The Hurler in the Ditch'.

Chapter 2

1 Jebb Family Papers (JFP), Eglantyne Jebb Diary, May 1886.
2 A. Fletcher, *Growing Up in England: The Experience of Childhood, 1600–1914*, p. 283 (New Haven: Yale University Press, 2008).
3 C. Steedman, *The Tidy House*, p. 76 (London: Virago Press Limited, 1982).
4 F. Wilson, *Rebel Daughter of a Country House: The Life of Eglantyne Jebb, Founder of the Save the Children Fund*, p. 23 (London: Allen & Unwin, 1967).
5 JFP, Eglantyne Jebb Diary, 3 April 1886.
6 M. Abbott, *Family Ties: English Families 1540–1920*, p. 176 (London and New York: Routledge, 1993).
7 JFP, Eglantyne Jebb Dairy, January 1887.
8 JFP, Dorothy Jebb to Richard Jebb, n.d.
9 JFP, Emily Jebb Diary, 4 August 1886.
10 Ibid., 24 August 1885.
11 Fletcher, *Growing Up in England*, p. 10.
12 C. Dyhouse, *Girls Growing Up in Late Victorian and Edwardian England*, p. 3 (Boston: Routledge and Kegan Paul Ltd., 1981).
13 Mitchell argues that the 'imaginary' new girl culture broke down after the First World War. S. Mitchell, *The New Girl*, pp. 3, 173 (New York: Columbia University Press, 1995); D. Gorham, *The Victorian Girl and the Feminine Ideal* (Bloomington: Indiana University Press, 1982). Caine suggests that girlhood and femininity were redefined in the 1880s and 1890s in response to 'worrying changes in behaviour'. She argues that 'The Girl of the Period', whose behaviour caused such distress in the late 1870s was followed by a debate about the 'Revolt of Daughters' in the late 1880s. Both fell into disuse in the 1890s, when the 'new woman' appeared. B. Caine, *English Feminism, 1780–1980*, p. 134 (Oxford: Oxford University Press, 1997).
14 L. Broughton and H. Rogers, *Gender and Fatherhood in the Nineteenth Century*, p. 6. (London: Palgrave, 2007); J. Tosh, *A Man's Place: Masculinity and the Middle-Class Home in Victorian England* (New Haven: Yale University Press, 1999).
15 Fletcher, *Growing Up in England*, p. 48.
16 JFP, Arthur Jebb to Eglantyne Louisa Jebb (ELJ), 12 July 1877.
17 Ibid., 4 July 1882.

18 'young realists who paid him scant heed until they saw the characteristically absent-minded look leave his face and watched, with breathless anticipation, his lips silently move, until he gave out couplet or verse about one of us, witty end complete'. JFP, E. Ussher, Jebb Family History, p. 6 (Unpublished Manuscript, c.1930).

19 S. Margaretson, *Victorian High Society*, p. 94 (New York: Homes and Myers, 1980).

20 L. Davidoff, *The Family Story: Blood, Contract and Intimacy, 1830–1960*, p. 115 (New York: Longman, 1999).

21 L. Davidoff, *The Best Circles: Society, Etiquette and the Season*, p. 40 (London: Croom Helm, 1973).

22 JFP, Arthur Jebb to ELJ, 4 July 1882.

23 F. Wilson, *Rebel Daughter*, p. 11.

24 JFP, Ussher, Jebb Family History, pp. 5–6, 36–37.

25 JFP, Eglantyne Jebb Diary, January 1887.

26 E. Ross (ed.) *Slum Travelers: Ladies and London Poverty, 1860–1920*, p. 20 (Berkeley: University of California Press, 2007); L. Davidoff and C. Hall *Family Fortunes: Men and Women of the English Middle Class, 1780–1850* (London: The University of Chicago Press, 1987); Tosh, *A Man's Place*, pp. 34–39, 146–150.

27 T. L. Broughton and H. Rogers (eds), *Gender and Fatherhood in the Nineteenth Century*, p. 16 (New York: Palgrave Macmillan, 2007).

28 Fletcher, *Growing Up in England*, p. 29.

29 JFP, Ussher, Jebb Family History, p. 36.

30 Fletcher, *Growing Up in England*, p. 308; P. Jalland, *Death in the Victorian Family* (New York: Oxford University Press, 1996).

31 JFP, Eglantyne Jebb Diary, 17 June 1886.

32 JFP, Ussher, Family History, pp. 33–34.

33 JFP, Eglantyne Jebb Diary, April 1893.

34 Emily added the brackets. JFP, Ussher, Jebb Family History, p. 34.

35 C. Steedman, *The Tidy House*, p. 76.

36 JFP, Ussher, Jebb Family History, p. 36. The Lyth was passed on to his eldest son, Richard Jebb (1874–1953), and is still in the family today.

37 Dyhouse, *Girls Growing Up*, pp. 3–4.

38 JFP, Ussher, Jebb Family History, p. 7.

39 E. Jebb, 'The Ring Fence', p. 203.

40 JFP, Ussher, Jebb Family History, p. 7.

41 JFP, Eglantyne Louisa Jebb Diary, 13 August 1882.

42 Davidoff, *The Best Circles*, p. 46.

43 A. Anderson, 'Victorian High Society and Social Duty: The Promotion of "Recreative Learning and Voluntary Teaching"', *History of Education*, 31:4 (2002), pp. 313, 333.

44 JFP, Eglantyne Louisa Jebb Diary, 5 September 1882.

45 JFP, Eglantyne Jebb Diary, 2 July 1886.

46 Ibid., 3 July 1886.

47 JFP, Eglantyne Louisa Jebb Diary, May 1866.

48 JFP, Eglantyne Jebb Diary, 17 June 1886.

49 JFP, Eglantyne Louisa Jebb Diary, 1882.

50 JFP, Dorothy Jebb Diary, 7 June 1890.

51 JFP, Eglantyne Jebb Diary, 30 March 1886.

52 JFP, Emily Jebb Diary, 19 August 1886.
53 Dyhouse, *Girls Growing Up*, p. 20.
54 Sophia Smith Collection (SSC), Box 1, Folder 1–17, Caroline Jebb to Pollie, 23 September 1887.
55 JFP, Jebb, 'The Ring Fence', pp. 239, 296–238, 304, Buxton Family Papers, Buxton, Eglantyne's Notes on Eglantyne Jebb (Dictated by EJ), p. 1.
56 Wilson, *Rebel Daughter*, p. 23.
57 Steedman, *Tidy House*, p. 69.
58 JFP, Ussher, Jebb Family History, p. 29.
59 JFP, 'Briarland Recorder', (September 1889–February 1890), (March 1890–August 1891), (August 1891–March 1892).
60 JFP, Ussher, Jebb Family History, p. 22.
61 D. Gorham, *The Victorian Girl*, p. 4.
62 JFP, D. F. Buxton, Description of Heddie Kastler, p. 1.
63 Ibid.
64 Ibid., p. 2.
65 JFP, Dorothy Buxton to Miss Pullen, 1 April 1935.
66 JFP, Eglantyne Jebb Diary, 17 June 1886.
67 JFP, EJ to Gamul Jebb, 19 October 1890.
68 Ibid.
69 JFP, Ussher, Jebb Family History, pp. 25–26.
70 Ibid., p. 4.
71 Ibid.
72 M. J. Peterson, *Family, Love, and Work in the Lives of Victorian Gentlewomen*, p. 41 (Indianapolis: Indiana University Press, 1989).
73 JFP, Ussher, Jebb Family History, p. 5.
74 JFP, Emily Jebb Diary, 8 May 1887.
75 JFP, Ussher, Jebb Family History, p. 4.
76 JFP, Emily Jebb Diary, 5 August 1885.
77 Dyhouse, *Girls Growing Up*, p. 3.
78 Peterson, *Family, Love, and Work*, p. 41.
79 JFP, Eglantyne Jebb Diary, 21 June 1886.
80 Steedman, *The Tidy House*, p. 77.
81 J. Burstyn, *Victorian Education and the Ideal of Womanhood*, p. 105 (London: Croom Helm, 1980).
82 JFP, Arthur Jebb to Eglantyne Louisa Jebb, 4 October 1891.
83 Save the Children Fund (SCF) Archive, Gardiner Papers, Eglantyne Jebb to Dorothy Kempe, Letter 45, 18 June 1898, p. 42.
84 Steedman, *The Tidy House*, p. 81.
85 JFP, Eglantyne Jebb Diary, 4 April 1886.
86 Ibid., 4 March 1886.
87 JFP, Emily Jebb Diary, 14–19 August 1885.
88 Wilson, *Rebel Daughter*, p. 12.
89 JFP, Dorothy Jebb Diary, 13 June 1891.
90 JFP, Emily Jebb Diary, 18 August 1885.
91 Ibid., 21 August 1886.
92 JFP, Eglantyne Jebb Diary, 5 January 1887.
93 Ibid., 12 September 1886.
94 JFP, Emily Jebb Diary, 8 May 1886; 12 September 1886.

95 JFP, EJ to ELJ, October 1892.
96 Steedman argues that it is possible to use little girl's diaries 'in much the same way as spoken language had been used to reconstruct the theories they evolved in order to become a part of a particular society in a particular place and time'. Steedman, *Tidy House*, p. 75.
97 JFP, Ussher, Jebb Family History, p. 15.
98 SSC, Caroline Jebb to Pollie, 23 September 1887.
99 JFP, EJ to ELJ, 15 January 1890.
100 E. O. Hellerstein, L. P. Hume and K. M. Offen (eds) *Victorian Women: A Documentary Account of Women's Lives in Nineteenth-century England, France, and the United States*, p. 21 (Stanford: Stanford University Press, 1981).
101 J. Parker, *Women and Welfare*, p. 188 (New York: St. Martin's Press, 1989).

Chapter 3

1 F. Wilson, *Rebel Daughter of a Country House: The Life of Eglantyne Jebb, Founder of the Save the Children Fund*, p. 57 (London: Allen & Unwin, 1967).
2 C. Dyhouse, *No Distinction of Sex? Women in British Universities, 1870–1939*, p. 12 (London: University College Press, 1995).
3 Wilson, *Rebel Daughter*, p. 51.
4 M. Hilton, and P. Hirsch (eds) *Practical Visionaries: Women, Education and Social Progress, 1790–1930*, p. 10 (London: Longman, 2000).
5 S. Mitchell, *The New Girl*, p. 49 (New York: Columbia University Press, 1995).
6 Ibid., p. 50. M. A. Hamilton, *Remembering My Good Friends*, p. 37 (London: Jonathon Cape Ltd., 1944); J. Purvis, *A History of Women's Education in England*, p. 112 (Milton Keynes: Open University Press, 1991).
7 E. Lodge, 'Growth', in G. Bailey (ed.) *Lady Margaret Hall*, pp. 60–92, 74 (England: Oxford University Press, 1923). June Purvis argues that nearly all of the early women students at Cambridge had encountered opposition and disapproval from their friends and families. J. Purvis, *A History of Women's Education*, p. 113 (Milton Keynes: Open University Press, 1991); Sally Mitchell calculates that not more than a few thousand women had been students as Oxford or Cambridge by 1915; S. Mitchell, *The New Girl*, p. 49.
8 Save the Children Fund (SCF), Archive, Dorothy Gardiner Papers (GP), Eglantyne Jebb (EJ) to Dorothy Kempe (DK), Letter 45 [Spring 1897], p. 42.
9 Hamilton, *Remembering My Good Friends*, p. 37.
10 V. Glendinning, *A Suppressed Cry: Life and Death of a Quaker Daughter*, p. 17 (London: Routledge & Kegan Paul, 1969).
11 Jebb Family Papers (JFP), Dorothy Jebb Diary, June 1891.
12 Purvis, *A History of Women's Education*, p. 112.
13 Mitchell, *The New Girl*, p. 61.
14 Ussher, Jebb Family History, p. 4.
15 JFP, Arthur Trevor Jebb to Eglantyne Louisa Jebb, 4 October 1891.
16 Family papers show that Tye supported the higher education of women. JFP, Arthur Trevor Jebb to Eglantyne Louisa Jebb, 4 October 1891.
17 H. M. Swanwick, *I Have Been Young*, p. 116 (London: V. Gollancz, 1935).
18 Wilson, *Rebel Daughter*, pp. 55–56.
19 Ibid., p. 57.

20 V. Brittain, *The Women at Oxford*, pp. 87–110; (London: Harrap, 1960) W. Peck, *A Little Learning: A Victorian Childhood*, pp. 153–184 (London: Faber and Faber, 1952).

21 Dyhouse, *No Distinction of Sex*, p. 58.

22 JFP, G. Jebb, Recollections of Eglantyne Senior (Unpublished), p. 1.

23 SCF, GP, D. Kempe, 'First Term at Lady Margaret Hall, 1895–1896', p. 1.

24 Ibid., Introduction to Section 1 of Letters, 1895–6, p. 2.

25 Gardiner assembled these letters at the request of Dorothy Jebb Buxton after Eglantyne's death. The original letters were rarely dated and Gardiner numbered them. I have included Gardiner's number and Eglantyne's dates. Gardiner was the author of many books including, *English Girlhood at School* (London: Oxford University Press, 1929). June Purvis regards this as the first 'classic' in the field of women's education. See: J. Purvis, (ed.) *Women's History in Britain, 1850–1945*, p. 129 (London: University London College Press, 1995).

26 SCF, GP, EJ to DK, Introduction to Section 1 of Letters, 1895–6, p. 2.

27 V. Glendinning, *A Suppressed Cry: Life and Death of a Quaker Daughter*, p. 17 (London: Routledge & Kegan Paul, 1969).

28 Wilson, *Rebel Daughter*, pp. 57–58.

29 Purvis, *A History of Women's Education*, p. 118.

30 Swanwick, *I Have Been Young*, p. 118.

31 Mitchell, *The New Girl*, p. 55.

32 SCF, GP, EJ to DK, Letter 19, 1896, p. 20.

33 Purvis, *A History of Women's Education*, p. 118.

34 Lodge, 'Growth', p. 74.

35 SCF, GP, EJ to DK, Letter 5, 1895, p. 7.

36 Ibid., Letter 2, 1895, p. 6.

37 Ibid., Kempe, 'First Term at Lady Margaret Hall, 1895–1896', p. 2. Ibid., Letter 4, 21 March 1896, p. 7.

38 R. McWilliams Tullberg, *Study of Women at Cambridge*, p. 104 (Cambridge: Cambridge University Press, 1998); V. Brittain, *The Women at Oxford*.

39 SCF, GP, EJ to DK, Letter 7, pp. 9–10.

40 Ibid., Letter 8, 26 June 1896, p. 11.

41 Ibid., Letter 11, pp. 13–14.

42 Ibid., Letter 16, p. 17.

43 Ibid., Letter 19, pp. 20–21.

44 Ibid., Letter 12, p. 15.

45 Ibid., Letter 45, p. 42.

46 Ibid., Letter 61 [Autumn 1897], p. 51. Mitchell stressed that universities were 'not as straight laced as we perhaps imagine'. It was professors who demanded chaperons and professors who married their students. Mitchell, *The New Girl*, p. 67.

47 Ibid., Letter 62 [Autumn 1897], p. 52.

48 It was not until 1921 that Oxford awarded women degrees on the same terms as men. Cambridge did not capitulate until 1947. Purvis, *Women and Education*, p. 119.

49 British Library, John Maynard Keynes Papers, John Maynard Keynes to Duncan Grant, 16 February 1909.

50   Skidelsky, R. *John Maynard Keynes, vol. 1: Hopes Betrayed 1883–1920*, p. 212 (London: Macmillan, 1983).
51   Ibid., Letter 22, 21 October 1896, pp. 24b–25.
52   Ibid., Letter 32 [November 1896], p. 30.
53   Ibid., Letter 33 [November 1896], p. 30.
54   F. Lannon, 'Wordsworth, Dame Elizabeth (1840–1932)', in Oxford Dictionary of National Biography, http://www.oxforddnb.com/view/article/37024 (accessed 25 August 2008).
55   M. Lochhead, *Young Victorians*, p. 176 (London: John Murray, 1959).
56   Lodge 'Growth', p. 74.
57   R. McWilliams Tullberg, *Study of Women at Cambridge*, p. 81.
58   SCF, GP, EJ to DK, Letter 23 [1896], p. 25.
59   Mitchell, *The New Girl*, p. 50.
60   Ibid., p. 68.
61   SCF, GP, EJ to DK, Letter 26, 11 November 1896, p. 28.
62   Ibid., Letter 21, 22 November 1896, p. 24.
63   Ibid., Letter 32, 33, p. 30.
64   Ibid., Letter 26, 11 November 1896, p. 35.
65   Ibid., Letter 38, p. 34
66   Ibid., Letter 22, 21 October 1896, p. 24b.
67   Ibid., Letter 26, 11 November 1896, pp. 28–29.
68   Ibid., Letter 57, p. 47. Mitchell, *The New Girl*, p. 52
69   Lannon, 'Wordsworth, Dame Elizabeth (1840–1932)'.
70   Purvis, *A History of Women's Education*, p. 119.
71   Brittain, *The Women at Oxford*, p. 74.
72   SCF, GP, EJ to DK, Letter 22, 21 October 1896, p. 24b.
73   Ibid., Letter 25, 3 November 1896, p. 27.
74   For Kathleen Courtney and Maude Royden see: B. Haslam, *From Suffrage to Internationalism: The Political Evolution of Three British Feminists* (New York: Peter Lang, 1999).
75   Purvis, *A History of Women's Education*, p. 112.
76   Ibid., Letter 45 [Spring 1897], pp. 41–42.
77   Ibid., Letter 1, 29 December 1895, p. 5.
78   Mitchell, The *New Girl*, p. 63.
79   Dyhouse, *Girls Growing Up*, p. 72.
80   Ibid., p. 75.
81   SCF, GP, EJ to DK, Letter 6, p. 8.
82   Brittain, *The Women at Oxford*, p. 47.
83   SCF, GP, EJ to DK, Letter 10, 1895, p. 12.
84   G. Finlayson, *Citizen, State, and Social Welfare in Britain 1830–1990* pp. 131–132 (Oxford: Clarendon Press, 1994).
85   S. Meacham, *Toynbee Hall and Social Reform, 1880–1914* (New Haven: Yale University Press, 1987); K. B. Beauman, *Women and the Settlement Movement* (New York: Radcliffe, 1996); S. Koven, 'From Rough Lads to Hooligans: Boy Life, National Culture and Social Reform', in A. Parker et al. (eds) *National isms and Sexualities*, pp. 365–395 (New York: Routledge, 1992); Dyhouse, *No Distinction of Sex*, pp. 221–223.
86   R. Humphreys, *Sin, Organized Charity and the Poor Law in Victorian England* p. 115 (New York: St. Martin's Press, 1995).

87 Dyhouse, *Girls Growing Up*, p. 76

88 SCF, GP, Kempe, 'Section II, 1896–1897, p. 1.

89 Wilson, *Rebel Daughter*, p. 67.

90 K. Beauman argues that board schools were the centre and origin of many projects. 'The schoolchildren provided, as always, the best introduction to friendship and families'. Beauman, *Women and the Settlement Movement*, p. 22; D. Copelman links settlement work and professionalisation of teacher. D. Copelman, *London's Women Teachers: Gender, Class and Feminism, 1870–1930*, pp. 162–175 (London: Routledge, 1996).

91 Purvis, *Women and Education*, p. 120.

92 SCF, GP, EJ to DK, Letter 52 [Spring 1897], p. 45.

93 '...Indeed and indeed I feel rather heartbroken'. Ibid., Letter 76, 18 June [1897], pp. 66–67.

94 Brittain, *The Women at Oxford*, p. 97.

Chapter 4

1 Save the Children Fund (SCF) Archive, Gardiner Papers (GP), Eglantyne Jebb (EJ) to Dorothy Kempe (DK), Letter 55, 1898, p. 67.

2 S. Pedersen, *Eleanor Rathbone and the Politics of Conscience*, p. 54 (New Haven: Yale University Press, 2004).

3 SCF, GP, EJ to DK, Letter 83a, 18 September 1898, p. 74.

4 'To the Editor', *Times*, 3 September 1873, p. 9.

5 M. Jeanne Peterson, 'The Victorian Governess: Status Incongruence in Family and Society,' *Victorian Studies*, Vol. 14:1, pp. 7–26 (September, 1970); K. Hughes, *The Victorian Governess*, p. 47 (London: Hambeldon Press, 1983).

6 F. Widdowson, '"Educating Teachers": Women and Elementary Teaching in London, 1900–1914', in L. Davidoff and B. Westover (eds) *Our Work, Our Lives, Our Words: Women's History and Women's Work*, p. 99 (Basingstoke: Macmillan, 1986); A. Oram, *Women Teachers and Feminists: Politics, 1900–1939*, p. 23 (Manchester: Manchester University Press, 1996).

7 'Elementary Schoolmistresses', *Times*, 3 September 1873, p. 9.

8 Widdowson, 'Educating Teachers', p. 107.

9 A. Anderson, 'Victorian High Society and Social Duty: The Promotion of "Recreative Learning and Voluntary Teaching"', *History of Education*, 31:4 (2002), pp. 311, 315.

10 L. McDonald, *Roses Over No Man's Land*, p. 27 (New York: Penguin, 1980); D. Copelman, *London's Women Teachers: Gender, Class and Feminism, 1870–1930*, p. 12 (London: Routledge, 1996); Oram, *Women Teachers*, p. 14. 'It could be said "a lady, to be such, must be a mere lady and nothing else. She must not work for profit, or engage on any occupation that money can command, lest she invade the rights of the working classes"'. The Diary of Margaret Greg, quoted in F. Prochaska, *Women and Philanthropy in Nineteenth-Century England*, p. 5 (Oxford: Clarendon Press, 1980).

11 Hubbard, 'Elementary Schoolmistresses', *Times*, 5 September 1873, p. 4; A. Tropp, *The School Teacher*, p. 23 (London: Heinemann, 1957).

12 Oram, *Women Teachers*, p. 14.

13 Hubbard, *Times*, 5 September 1873, p. 4.

14 C. Dyhouse, *Girls Growing Up in Late Victorian and Edwardian England*, p. 76 (Boston: Routledge and Kegan Paul Ltd., 1981).

15 Copelman links settlement work and professionalization of teacher. Copelman, *London's Women Teachers*, p. 162. Beauman argues 'schoolchildren provided, as always, the best introduction to friendship and families'. K. B. Beauman, *Women and the Settlement Movement*, p. 22 (New York: Radcliffe, 1996); F. Wilson, *Rebel Daughter of a Country House: The Life of Eglantyne Jebb, Founder of the Save the Children Fund*, p. 81 (London: Allen & Unwin, 1967).

16 Copelman, *London's Women Teachers*, pp. 10–11.

17 Seth Koven, *Slumming, Sexual and Social Politics in Victorian London*, p. 183 (Princeton: Princeton University Press, 2004).

18 Wilson, *Rebel Daughter*, p. 80.

19 Copelman, *London's Women Teachers*, p. 10.

20 Buxton Family Papers (BFP), G. Jebb, Recollections of Eglantyne Senior, n.d., p. 1.

21 Wilson, *Rebel Daughter*, p. 80.

22 Jebb Family Papers, E. L. Jebb, *The Rights of Women*, 1882, p. 2.

23 Oram, *Women Teachers*, pp. 17–19.

24 SCF, GP, EJ to DG, Letter 162, October 1900, p. 37.

25 Ibid., Letter 80, pp. 67–68. Ibid., Letter 81, p. 69.

26 Ibid., Letter 82, 25 August 1898, p. 70.

27 Years later, she confided to her cousin Geraldine Jebb, that her decision to enrol in teachers' college was 'based on the belief that she was too stupid to do anything else'. BFP, G. Jebb, Recollections of Eglantyne Senior, n.d., p. 10.

28 SCF, GP, EJ to DK, Letter 82, 25 August 1898, p. 70. Teachers in grammar schools possessed a degree and were not required to take a teacher-training course. 'Teachers divided along the lines of the type of school, nursery (working-class children up to age 5), elementary (working-class children aged 5 to 14) or grammar school (predominantly middle-class children aged 11 to 16 or 18), in which they worked. There was a clear pecking order between schools, which reflected the schools' resources, the age and social class of pupils, and the level of the teachers' education and qualification.' H. Jones, *Women in British Public Life, 1914–50: Gender, Power, and Social Policy*, p. 56 (London: Longman, 2000).

29 Tropp, *The School Teacher*, pp. 18–23, 169.

30 SCF, GP, EJ to DK, Letter 82, 25 August 1898, p. 70.

31 British Session Papers (BSP), *Report on Training Colleges*, Cd. 226 xx, 1898–1899, p. 3.

32 Dyhouse, *Girls Growing Up*, p. 69; Copelman, *London's Women Teachers*, pp. 10–11.

33 Oram, *Women Teachers*, p. 33. For student numbers see: BSP, Cd. 597 xxi.1, *Report on Training Colleges*, 1900–1, p. 6. Ibid., Cd. 226 xx, 1899–1900, p. 2.

34 Developed by James Kay-Shuttleworth in 1838. 'In the training of teachers, [he] was insistent on the need for guarding the teacher's mind from "the evils to which it is especially prone: intellectual pride, assumption of superiority, selfish ambition"'. Tropp, *The School Teacher*, pp. 14–15.

35 W. Robinson, 'Sarah Jane Bannister and Teacher Training in Transition 1870–1918' in Hilton, M. and P. Hirsch (eds) *Practical Visionaries: Women,*

Education and Social Progress, 1790–1930, p. 19 (London: Longman, 2000); E. Edwards, 'Mary Miller Allan: The Complexity of Gender Negotiation for a Woman Principal of a Teachers Training College', in Hilton, M. and P. Hirsch (eds) *Practical Visionaries: Women, Education and Social Progress, 1790–1930*, p. 151 (London: Longman, 2000).

36 BSP, *Report on Training Colleges*, Cd. 226 xx, 1899–1900, p. 5.
37 SCF, GP, EJ to DG, Letter 83, 12 September 1898, p. 73.
38 'The Late Lydia Manley', *The Times Higher Education Supplement*, 1 August 1911; S. Harrop, 'Committee Women: Women on the Consultative Committee of the Board of Education, 1900–1944', in Goodman, J. and S. Harrop, *Women, Educational Policy-Making and Administration in England*, p. 158 (London: Routledge, 2000).
39 BSP, *Report on Training Colleges*, Cd. 226 xx, 1898–1899, p. 54.
40 SCF, GP, EJ to DK, Letter 83a, 18 September 1898, p. 74.
41 'In 1899, 18 took advantage of the permission; this year (1900) about 60 have been admitted'. BSP, *Report on Training Colleges*, Cd. 597 xxi.1, 1900–1901, p. 19. Eglantyne wrote that 'one great pleasure to me is the way in which mother entered into my plans. When she came up and saw the college and we talked together, she was most enthusiastic and encouraging, alas—I never told her how I contemplated failure'. SCF, GP, EJ to DK, Letter 83a, 12 September 1898, pp. 74–75.
42 BSP, *Report on Training Colleges*, Cd. 226 xx, 1898–1899, p. 54.
43 SCF, GP, EJ to DG, Letter 99, p. 87.
44 Ibid., Letter 87, p. 79.
45 Ibid., Letter 83, 12 September 1898, pp. 73–74.
46 Ibid., D. Kempe, Introduction to Section 4, 1928, pp. 71–72.
47 Widdowson, 'Educating Teachers', pp. 100, 108.
48 Oram, *Women Teachers*, p. 8.
49 'The Late Lydia Manley', 1 August 1911.
50 Tropp, *The School Teacher*, p. 19; GP, EJ to DK, Letter 83a, 18 September 1898, pp. 74–75; H. Corke, *In Our Infancy: An Autobiography, 1882–1912*, p. 103 (Cambridge: Cambridge University Press, 1975).
51 Widdowson, 'Educating Teachers', p. 104.
52 BSP, *Report on Training Colleges*, Cd. 226 xx, 1889–1900, p. 54.
53 SCF, GP, EJ to DG, Letter 88, 1899, p. 80.
54 Robinson, 'Sarah Jane Bannister and Teacher Training in Transition 1870–1918', p. 134.
55 Letter from 'A Certificated Mistress', *Times*, 5 September 1873, p. 7.
56 Ibid., 16 September 1873, p. 9.
57 Koven, *Slumming*, p. 191.
58 Wilson, *Rebel Daughter*, pp. 81–82.
59 Widdowson, 'Educating Teachers', p. 119.
60 Oram, *Women Teachers*, p. 15.
61 SCF, GP, EJ to DG, Letter 100, p. 88.
62 Ibid., Letter 83a, 12 September 1898, pp. 74–75.
63 Tropp, *The School Teachers*, p. 126.
64 'Middle class girls were often notoriously deficient in the 3R's, although well educated in other matters'. Widdowson, 'Educating Teachers', p. 100.
65 SCF, GP, EJ to DG, Letter 85, p. 76.

66 A. Turnbull, 'Learning Her Womanly Work: The Elementary School Curriculum, 1870–1914', in Hunt, F. (ed.) *Lessons for Life*, pp. 85–86 (Oxford: Basil Blackwell, 1987).

67 Turnbull explains that the maxim 'love of needles encouraged love of domesticity' reinforced thrift, neatness, cleanliness and self-respect. In the 1900s concerns were raised about the effect of this on young scholars' eyesight'. Ibid., pp. 88, 91.

68 SCF, GP, EJ to DG, Letter 87, p. 78. Ibid., Letter 92, 11 December 1899, p. 86. Turnbull points out that while patching and mending are the realities of working-class life, throughout the 1890s Singer sewing machines were widely available and the poor were buying ready-made clothing and cheap paper patterns. Turnbull, 'Learning Her Womanly Work', pp. 87–88.

69 Koven, *Slumming*, p. 187.

70 SCF, GP, EJ to DG, Letter 119, September, p. 9.

71 Ibid., Letter 90, 20 November, p. 84.

72 Ibid., Letter 88, n.d., p. 79. Ibid., Letter 85, p. 77. Ibid., Letter 90, 20 November 1898, p. 83.

73 Ibid., Letter 87, n.d., pp. 77–79.

74 Ibid., Letter 90, 20 November, pp. 83–84.

75 Ibid.

76 'Gentleman Schoolmistresses', *Times*, 5 September 1873, p. 4.

77 Ibid., 6 September 1873, p. 7.

78 BSP, *Report on Training Colleges*, Cd. 226 xx, 1898–1899, p. 16.

79 Ibid., Cd. 597 xxi.1, 1900–1901, p. 10.

80 SCF, GP, EJ to DG, Letter 83b, 19 September 1898, p. 76.

81 Tropp, *The School Teacher*, p. 119.

82 G. Sutherland, *Policy-making in Elementary Education, 1870–1895*, p. 56 (Oxford: Oxford University Press, 1973).

83 JFP, Arthur Jebb to Eglantyne Louisa Jebb, 7 June 1873.

84 Ibid., 24 May 1873.

85 Sutherland, *Policy-making*, pp. 65, 75.

86 Tropp, *The School Teacher*, p. 119.

87 P. Gordon, 'Katharine Bathurst: A Controversial Women Inspector', *History of Education*, 17: 3 (1988), p. 193. By the 1890s women [like Bathurst] meeting the criteria for the Inspectorate had university education, 'teaching experience and...an enormous amount of zeal for, and the desire to promote the interests of education'. Quoted in J. Goodman and S. Harrop, *Women, Educational Policy-Making and Administration in England*, pp. 139–140 (London: Routledge, 2000).

88 Oram, *Women Teachers*, p. 8.

89 From a certificated board teacher's point of view, promotion to the Inspectorate should follow naturally upon a minimum of seven years' teaching experience. Sutherland, *Policy-making*, pp. 62–63; Tropp, *The School Teacher*, p. 119.

90 Copelman, *London's Women Teachers*, p. 50; A. O'Hanlon-Dunn, 'Women as Witness: Elementary Schoolmistresses and the Cross Commission, 1885–1888', in J. Goodman and S. Harrop, *Women, Educational Policy-Making and Administration in England*, pp. 120–121 (London: Routledge, 2000); Sutherland, *Policy-making*, p. 195; P. Gordon, 'Edith Mary Deverell: An Early Woman Inspector', *History of Education Society Bulletin*, 22 (1978), p. 8.

91 SCF, GP, EJ to DG, Letter 83b, 19 September 1898, p. 77.

92 Ibid., Letter 88, 1898, pp. 79–81.
93 Ibid., Letter 83b, 19 September 1898, pp. 75–77.
94 Ibid., Letter 88, 1898, pp. 79–81.
95 Ibid., Letter 83a ,18 September 1898, pp. 74–75.
96 Wilson, *Rebel Daughter*, pp. 82–83.
97 SCF, Letter 83b, 19 September 1898, pp. 75–77.
98 Ibid., GP, EJ to DG, Letter 105, p. 92.

Chapter 5

1   Save the Children Fund (SCF) Archive, Gardiner Papers (GP), Eglantyne Jebb (EJ) to Dorothy Kempe Gardiner (DK), Letter 102, 3 April, 1899.
2   Ibid., Letter 101, p. 89.
3   F. Wilson, *Rebel Daughter of a Country House: The Life of Eglantyne Jebb, Founder of the Save the Children Fund*, p. 84 (London: Allen & Unwin, 1967).
4   SCF, GP, EJ to DK, Letter 111, 29 May 1899, p. 96.
5   H. Jones, *Women in British Public Life, 1914–50: Gender, Power, and Social Policy*, p. 9 (London: Longman, 2000).
6   SCF, GP, EJ to DK, Letter 109, p. 95.
7   Ibid., Letter 101, p. 88.
8   Ibid., Letter 109, p. 95.
9   Ibid.
10 Ibid., Letter 101, p. 89; Letter 102, 3 April 1899, p. 90.
11 Ibid., Letter 111, 26 May 1899, p. 96.
12 Ibid., Letter 102, 3 April 1899, p. 90.
13 Jebb Family Papers (JFP), E. L. Jebb, *The Right of Women* (Leaflet), 1882, p. 1.
14 JFP, Arthur Trevor Jebb to Eglantyne Louisa Jebb, 4 October 1891.
15 S. Koven, *Slumming: Sexual and Social Politics in Victorian London*, p. 19 (Princeton: Princeton University Press, 2004).
16 Ibid., p. 191.
17 SCF, GP, EJ to DK, Letter 158, 20 July 1900. Eglantyne would use masquerading again in the SCF years by adopting a form of aesthetic dress. See Chapter 10.
18 Ibid., Letter 167, November 1900, p. 43.
19 'The truest economy is to buy as good a material as you can afford'. Ibid.
20 Ibid., Letter 119, September 1899, p. 10.
21 E. Ross (ed.) *Slum Travelers: Ladies and London Poverty, 1860–1920*, p. 81 (Berkeley: University of California Press, 2007).
22 SCF, GP, EJ to DK, Letter 122, September 1899, p. 11; Letter 123, September 1899, p. 12.
23 Ibid., 199 September 1899, p. 9. '[S]isterhood was at best a fragile enterprise in a world in which one group of women was destined to clean the dirt created by another'. Koven, *Slumming*, p. 191.
24 SCF, GP, EJ to DK, Letter 169, November 1900, p. 44.
25 Eglantyne said, 'this little school is under the charge of Miss Arch...who manages it entirely by herself. It did one good to see her, so youthful and genuine and capable, as to be able to take an honest pride in her work'. JFP, Marlborough Diary, 10 May 1900.
26 SCF, GP, EJ to DK, Letter 88, 1898, p. 81.

27   Ibid., Letter 89, 13 November 1898, p. 82. Although Eglantyne declined a position as school inspector, she toured many schools and described them to Kempe. JFP, Marlborough Diary, 10 May 1900.

28   Ibid., 31 August 1899.

29   Ibid., April 1900.

30   Ibid., 20 November 1899.

31   'Ladies as Elementary Governesses', *London Times*, 16 September 1873, p. 9.

32   S. Cave, 'Ladies as Elementary School Mistresses', *London Times*, 6 September 1873, p. 7.

33   SCF, GP, EJ to DK, Letter 122, September 1899, Letter 127, October 1899, p. 18.

34   C. Steedman, 'Prisonhouses', *Feminist Review*, 20 (1985), p. 16.

35   SCF, GP, EJ to DK, Letter 169, November 1900, p. 43, Letter 138, 22 January 1900, p. 27.

36   JFP, Marlborough Diary, 23 November 1900; SCF, GP, EJ to DK Letter 169, November 1900, p. 43.

37   L. Mahood, *Policing Gender, Class and Family: Britain, 1850–1940*, p. 147 (London: University College London, 1995).

38   JFP Marlborough Diary, 31 August 1899.

39   Ibid., 31 August 1899.

40   Ibid., 30 April 1899.

41   Ibid., 17 July 1899.

42   Steedman, *Tidy House*, p. 76 (London: Virago, 1982).

43   E. Jebb, *Cambridge: A Social Study in Social Questions*, p. 171 (Cambridge: McMillan & Bowes, 1906).

44   Ibid., p. 172.

45   JFP, Marlborough Diary, 1 May 1900.

46   Ibid., 8 May 1900.

47   Ibid., 31 August 1899.

48   E. Ross, *Slum Travelers*, p. 82.

49   SCF, GP, EJ to DK, Letter 123, September 1899, p. 12.

50   Ibid., Letter 124, October 1899, p. 13.

51   Ibid., Letter 126, October 1899, p. 16.

52   Ibid., Letter 166, October 1900, p. 40.

53   Ibid., Letter 165, October 1900, p. 40.

54   JFP, Marlborough Diary, April 1900.

55   Ibid., 30 July 1900.

56   Ibid.

57   Wilson, *Rebel Daughter*, p. 83.

58   Steedman, 'Prisonhouses', p. 16.

59   Koven, *Slumming*, p. 193.

60   JFP, Marlborough Diary, 21 November 1899.

61   Ibid.

62   Ibid., 31 August 1900. In *The Right of the Child*, Edward Fuller recounted a story that Dorothy told about Eglantyne: 'One day Eglantyne Jebb called at Mattie's house to see why she had not been to school. She knocked; there was no answer. She knocked again; still no answer. She pushed the door open and looked in. A scene of indescribable filth and disorder met her gaze—the bare floor littered with rags and broken crockery; no furniture but

makeshift junk; even the baby's pram full of dirty plates and dishes. And where was Mattie? Overcome with shame, she had fled down the street from the back door as soon as she saw her teacher approaching the house. It was only afterwards that Eglantyne Jebb discovered the immediate effect of her call. Its long-term effect on her own life was comparable to that of the experience of the seventh Earl of Shaftesbury when, as a school boy at Harrow, he saw a pauper's funeral, and there upon decided to devote his life to the welfare of the poor. The ideal began to form itself in her mind that the world had a duty to many a "Mattie"—and not in this land alone'. E. Fuller, *The Right of the Child*, pp. 20–21 (London: Gollancz, 1951). There is no mention of this episode anywhere else in Jebb's papers or letters.

63 JFP, Marlborough Diary, 31 August 1900.
64 Ibid. [Autumn] 1899.
65 Ibid., 21 November 1899.
66 SCF, GP, EJ to DK, Letter 171, December 1900, p. 46.
67 Ruth Wordsworth writes to Mrs Jebb, 'I am sure the work is too great a strain on her and that her delicate organism suffers for the disagreeables of elementary school life…I think she is a most lovable girl and with the sort of longing for self-abnegation that would make a martyr but who in ordinary life is apt to make one tremble for her health'. JFP, Ruth Wordsworth to Eglantyne Louisa Jebb, 30 May 1898.
68 JFP, R. Wordsworth, Recollections of EJ, Holy Innocents Day 1928.
69 '… I am, and was, as well as I usually am at the end of term, i.e. very well, tho' not extravagantly plump or vigorous, really and truly I can't understand what made my mother think otherwise—or for that matter that doctor—or the many people who at once declared that they had long thought me ill!' SCF, GP, EJ to DK, Letter 170, December 1900, pp. 45–46; Ibid.
70 Oram, *Women Teachers*, p. 8.
71 'Of course it will be very nice to be able to sleep well on Sunday nights…I console myself by the thought that I may yet get another chance, and may go back <u>soon</u>'. SCF, GP, EJ to DK, Letter 172, 29 December, 1900, p. 46.

Chapter 6

1 Save the Children Fund (SCF) Archive, Gardiner Papers (GP), Eglantyne Jebb (EJ) to Dorothy Kempe (DK), Letter 233, 24 November 1902, p. 27.
2 L. H. Lees, *The Solidarities of Strangers: The English Poor Laws and the People, 1700–1948*, pp. 269–271 (Cambridge and New York: Cambridge University Press, 1998); F. Prochaska, *Christianity and Social Service in Modern Britain: The Disinherited Spirit*, p. 76 (Oxford and New York: Oxford University Press, 2006); R. Humphreys, *Sin, Organized Charity and the Poor Law in Victorian England*, p. 54 (New York: St. Martin's Press, 1995); G. Finlayson, *Citizen, State, and Social Welfare in Britain 1830–1990*, pp. 71, 171–173 (Oxford: Clarendon Press, 1994).
3 SCF, GP, EJ to DK, Letter 233, 24 November 1902, p. 27.
4 S. Koven, *Slumming: Sexual and Social Politics in Victorian London*, pp. 187–188 (Princeton and Oxford: Princeton University Press, 2004).

5   SCF, GP, EJ to DK, Letter 233, 24 November 1902, p. 27.
6   Seth Koven uses this term to describe where historical primary sources including fictional writing can show how elite women's past experiences and personal or intimate desires structured the initiatives they undertook in slum philanthropy. Koven, *Slumming*, p. 204.
7   Sophia Smith Collection (SSC), Box 1, File 1–18, Caroline Jebb to Mary, 15 January 1895.
8   Lady Jebb said, my sister-in-law 'finding the Lyth too dreary now that Dick is married…I shall be interested to see what happens'. Ibid., Caroline Jebb to Emma, 23 October 1900.
9   Richard Claverhouse Jebb (1841–1905) was first offered a peerage in 1897, declined for his own reasons and accepted in 1900. 'Cara no doubt got a great pleasure out of being Lady Jebb.' M. Bobbitt, *With Dearest Love To All: The Life and Letters of Lady Jebb*, p. 246 (Chicago: Regency, 1960). She will be referred to as Lady Jebb in this chapter and the remainder of the book.
10 Ibid., p. 15.
11 G. M. Raverat, *Period Piece: A Cambridge Childhood*, p. 89 (London: Faber and Faber Limited, 1885).
12 Bobbitt, *With Dearest Love*, p. 76.
13 SSC, Box 1, File 1–18, Caroline Jebb to my dear sister, 15 December 1874.
14 Bobbitt, *With Dearest Love*, pp. 105–106.
15 Raverat, *Period Piece*, p. 78.
16 Jebb Family Papers (JFP), Arthur Trevor Jebb to Eglantyne Louisa Jebb, 23 November 1874.
17 Ibid., 5 December 1879.
18 JFP, Eglantyne Louisa Jebb Diary, 8 August 1882.
19 L. Davidoff, *The Best Circles: Society, Etiquette and the Season*, p. 38 (London: Croom Helm, 1973).
20 SCF, GP, EJ to DK, Letter 196, 22 November 1901, p. 13.
21 Buxton Family Papers (BFP), Dorothy Francis Buxton's Questions to Mrs Keynes, May 1929.
22 JFP, R. Wordsworth, Recollections of EJ, Holy Innocents Day 1928.
23 D. F. Buxton and E. Fuller *The White Flame*, p. 3 (Toronto: The Weardale Press, Ltd., 1931).
24 SCF, GP, EJ to DK, Letter 180, May 1901, p. 4.
25 Ibid., Letter 192, p. 10.
26 Ibid.
27 SCF, Oral History Interview with David Buxton by Douglas Keay, 22 June 1993.
28 Lees, *The Solidarities of Strangers*, p. 273.
29 Ibid., 269. Cambridge County Record Office (CCRO); D. Stephenson, *Cambridge Central Aid Society*, p. 245.
30 CCRO, Charity Organization Society, *Twenty-sixth Annual Report 1905*, p. 5 (Cambridge: Jonathon Palmer, 1906).
31 Lees, *The Solidarities of Strangers*, p. 269; Eglantyne described an investigation. She wrote, 'Enquiries are made, references are asked for, and visits are paid to the applicant's home with a view to obtaining the knowledge of the history and conditions which are necessary in order to ascertain the causes of distress and the best means of remedying it'. E. Jebb, *Cambridge:*

A Social Study in Social Questions, pp. 200–201 (Cambridge: McMillan & Bowes, 1906).

32 Lees, *The Solidarities of Strangers*, pp. 268–269.

33 E. Ross, (ed.) *Slum Travelers: Ladies and London Poverty, 1860–1920*, p. 1 (Berkeley: University of California Press, 2007).

34 SSC, Box 1, File 1–18, Caroline Jebb to Carrie, 3 January 1901.

35 SCF, GP, EJ to DK, Letter 196, 22 November 1901, p. 13.

36 The Ladies Discussion Society amalgamated with the National Union of Women Workers in 1913. CCRO, Cambridge Ladies Discussion Society, *Scrapbook, 1886–1928*.

37 CCRO, 'Cambridge Central Aid Society' in Cambridge Ladies Discussion Society, *Minutes with Membership Lists, 1886–1928*.

38 Settlement work represented the softer-sided of scientific Charity Organization Society. R. Humphreys, *Sin, Organized Charity and the Poor Law in Victorian England*, p. 155 (New York: St. Martin's Press, 1995).

39 CCRO, Cambridge Ladies Discussion Society, *Annual Meeting Volume*, 1922.

40 CCRO, Cambridge Ladies Discussion Society, *Minute Book*, 1897.

41 CCRO, Cambridge Ladies Discussion Society, *Scrapbook, 1886–1928*.

42 F. Spalding, F. *Gwen Raverat*, p. 402 (London: Harvill, 2001). Wilson read *Period Piece* and drew heavily on the Cambridge material when writing *Rebel Daughter*. Wilson, F. *Rebel Daughter of a Country House: The Life of Eglantyne Jebb, Founder of the Save the Children Fund*, p. 98 (London: Allen & Unwin, 1967).

43 Spalding, *Gwen Raverat*, p. 112.

44 SCF, GP, EJ to DK, Letter 204, 19 March 1902, p. 11.

45 Ibid.

46 Margaret Keynes Hill was worried that G. M. Trevelyan was mentioned by name in *Rebel Daughter*. 'He was happily married'. Wilson asserted that she had made no suggestion that he was one of Eglantyne's suitors. BFP, F. Wilson, Visit With Margaret Hill, 5 October 1966; Wilson, *Rebel Daughter*, p. 102.

47 Lady Jebb supposedly received 37 marriage proposals in her lifetime, the first when she was 14. Bobbitt, *With Dearest Love*, p. 76.

48 Wilson, *Rebel Daughter*, p. 103.

49 BFP, E. Buxton, Eglantyne's Notes on Eglantyne Jebb: Mostly Prompted by the Inadequacies of Francesca Wilson's *Rebel Daughter*, n.d., p. 11. Margaret Keynes said that Eglantyne 'only spoke to her once of how she had been in love as a young girl, saying that it was a horsy fellow and that it would never have done'. Eglantyne never told Margaret his name. She did tell her he was 'melancholy'. Today he would be diagnosed with a bipolar disorder. Eglantyne told Margaret that 'he committed suicide after his marriage. He had three children'. BFP, F. Wilson, Talk with Margaret Hill, 28 September 1966. In 'The Ring Fence', Hugh and Freda fall passionately in love while riding horses.

50 S. Jeffreys, *The Spinster and Her Enemies: Feminism and Sexuality, 1880–1930*, p. 87 (London: Pandora Press, 1985).

51 BFP, E. Buxton, Notes by Dorothy Frances Buxton for Eglantyne Jebb Biography, p. 11.

52 JFP, E. Jebb, 'The Ring Fence,' pp. 697–698.

53 BFP, E. Buxton, Notes by Dorothy Frances Buxton for Eglantyne Jebb Biography, p. 1.
54 Ibid., SCF, GP, EJ to DK, Letter 240, 5 February 1903, p. 2.
55 JFP, Jebb, 'The Ring Fence', p. 482.
56 Koven, *Slumming*, p. 199.
57 Ibid., p. 199.
58 SCF, GP, EJ to DK, Letter 233, 24 November 1902, p. 27.
59 Lewis, *Women and Social Action*, p. 11.
60 SCF, GP, EJ to DK, Letter 240, 5 February 1903, p. 2; R. McWilliams Tullberg, 'Marshal, Mary (1850–1944)', *Dictionary of National Biography* (Oxford University Press, September 2004) http://www.oxforddnb.com/view/article/ 39167, accessed 10 Sept 2008.
61 Victorian Glendenning argued that she 'embod[ied] all that was most romantic and idealist about the first girl undergraduates'. V. Glendinning, *A Suppressed Cry: Life and Death of a Quaker Daughter*, p. 62 (London: Routledge & Kegan Paul, 1969).
62 SCF, GP, EJ to DK, Letter 240, 5 February 1903, p. 2; BFP, E. Buxton, Notes by Dorothy Frances Buxton for Eglantyne Jebb Biography, p. 2.
63 R. McWilliams Tullberg, 'Keynes, Florence Ada (1861–1958)', *Dictionary of National Biography* (Oxford University Press, September 2004). http://www. oxforddnb.com/view/article/39171, assessed 10 Sept 2008.
64 Florence Keynes would enter the world of politics through this COS work. F. A. B. Keynes, *Gathering Up the Threads: A Study in Family Biography* (Cambridge: W. Heffer & Sons Ltd., 1950).
65 SCF, GP, EJ to DK, Letter 254, 4 June 1903, p. 6.
66 Ibid., Letter 245, 18 March 1903, p. 3.
67 Ibid., Letter 272, 15 November 1903, p. 20.
68 Letter from Gwen Darwin to Margaret Darwin, August 1905 in Spalding *Gwen Raverat*, p. 113. Edward Fuller compares the survey to Booth's 'classic London Life and Labor' in *The Right of the Child*; E. Fuller, *The Right of the Child*, p. 21 (London: Gollancz, 1951).
69 Finlayson, *Citizen, State*, p. 120.
70 Jebb, *Cambridge*, pp. 19–21.
71 Ibid., p. 21.
72 Ross, *Slum Travelers*, p. 14.
73 Jebb, *Cambridge*, p. 172.
74 L. Mahood, *Policing Gender, Class and Family: Britain, 1850–1940*, pp. 39–63 (London: University College London, 1995).
75 Jebb, *Cambridge*, p. 156.
76 Ibid., p. 129.
77 Ibid., pp. 162–163.
78 Ibid., p. 173.
79 Ibid., p. 176.
80 Ibid., p. 181.
81 Ibid., p. 176.
82 Ibid., p. 177.
83 Wilson, *Rebel Daughter*, p. 58; C. Dyhouse, *Girls Growing Up in Late Victorian and Edwardian England*, p. 73 (Boston: Routledge and Kegan Paul Ltd., 1981).

84 Jebb, *Cambridge*, p. 179.
85 Ibid., pp. 181–182.
86 Ibid., p. 180.
87 Eglantyne would later work this principle into her SCF work although she no more believed it in 1919 than she did in 1906. F. Prochaska, *Christianity and Social Service in Modern Britain: The Disinherited Spirit*, p. 76 (Oxford and New York: Oxford University Press, 2006).
88 SCF, Eglantyne Jebb Papers, EJ to Mrs. Florence Keynes, 18 April 1906.
89 Ibid., 2 October 1906.
90 Jebb, *Cambridge*, p. 182.
91 CCRO, Charity Organization Society, *Twenty-fifth Annual Report 1904*, p. 3; Charity Organization Society, Twenty-*sixth Annual Report 1905*, p. 3; Charity Organization Society, *Twenty-seventh Annual Report 1906*, pp. 1, 4.
92 Ibid., Charity Organization Society, *Twenty-sixth Annual Report 1905*, p. 5.
93 BFP, G. Jebb, Memories of Eglantyne Senior, n.d., p. 2.
94 Bedford College Archive, Geraldine Emma May Papers, 1942–1952; E. M. Jebb, *A Personal Memoir of Her Sister*, n.d.
95 In their memoirs they wrote that Eglantyne Jebb's influence on them was enormous, for both attended university, became lecturers and had distinguished careers as British educationalists. 'Miss E. M. Jebb', *Times*, 11 May 1978; F. Wilson, *Gem Jebb: A Portrait by Francesca Wilson*, Bedford College, [n.d.]; Royal Holloway, University of London Archives (BC RF141/1/1); E. J. Jebb, *A Personal Memoir of her Sister* [n.d.]; Royal Holloway, University of London Archives (BC RF141/1/1).
96 BFP, Jebb, Memories of Eglantyne Senior, p. 2.
97 B. Haslam, *From Suffrage to Internationalism: The Political Evolution of Three British Feminists, 1908–1939*, p. 17 (New York: Peter Lang, 1999).
98 W. Peck, *A Little Learning: A Victorian Childhood*, p. 164 (London: Faber and Faber, 1952).
99 Spalding, *Gwen Raverat*, p. 112.
100 SCF, Eglantyne Jebb Papers, EJ to DK, 18 May 1906.
101 BFP, Wilson, Talk with Margaret Hill, 25 September 1966.
102 Koven, *Slumming*, p. 188.
103 Spalding, *Gwen Raverat*, p. 112.
104 JFP, D. F. Buxton, *Boots Scribbler*, Margaret Keynes to EJ, 5 May 1911.
105 Margaret told Eglantyne, 'Of course he will reduce my allowance, but he thinks it nicer for me to think that at any rate part of my income is really mine'. Ibid., 9 December 1911.
106 Ibid., 5 May 1911. Prochaska says that COS work seemed 'cold, impersonal and unbending' to many young women who were frustrated by the 'normal' channels of 'do-goodery'. F. Prochaska, *Women and Philanthropy in Nineteenth-Century England*, p. 106 (Oxford: Clarendon Press, 1980).
107 JPF, Buxton, *Boots Scribbler*, Margaret Keynes to EJ, December 1911.
108 SCF, GP, EJ to DK, Letter 233, 24 November 1902, p. 27.
109 JFP, Jebb, 'The Ring Fence', p. 642.
110 Ibid., p. 291.
111 Ibid., p. 298.
112 Spalding, *Gwen Raverat*, p. 113.

Chapter 7

1 *Times* reader describing modern girls who 'are a law unto themselves' 'Unmarried Daughters' (Letter to the Editor), *London Times*, 15 December 1909, p. 12.

2 Jebb Family Papers (JFP), D. F. Buxton, transcribed these letters into a *Boots Scribbling Diary* (Boots), Margaret Keynes (MK) to Eglantyne Jebb (EJ), 9 November 1911. Some letters are irregularly dated.

3 JFP, Boots MK to EJ, September 1910.

4 JFP, Boots MK to EJ, 9 November 1911.

5 JFP, Boots MK to EJ, 10 April 1908.

6 The terms 'daughter-at-home' and earlier 'daughter-of-the-house' were still in use in 1909. Deborah Gorham argues that according to Victorian prescriptive literature it was maintained that 'a mother should have a special relationship with her daughter. More than any other individual, the good mother could teach a daughter how to be truly feminine. A girl who had such a mother was thought to owe her several kinds of filial duties. The role of daughter-at-home referred to an unmarried daughter or daughters remaining financially dependent with their aging parents'. D. Gorham *The Victorian Girl and the Feminine Ideal*, p. 47 (Bloomington: Indiana University Press, 1982).

7 M. Vicinus, *Independent Women: Work and Community for Single Women 1850–1920*, p. 158 (London: Virago Press, 1985). See also: M. Vicinus *Intimate Friends: Women Who Loved Women, 1778–1928* (Chicago: The University of Chicago Press, 2004).

8 C. Dyhouse, *Feminism and the Family in England, 1880–1939*, pp. 25, 26 (Oxford: Basil Blackwell Ltd., 1989).

9 *Times* debate in letter to the editor pages, see 'Unmarried Daughters', *London Times*, 25 November 1909 to 28 December 1909. Contributors agreed that the age of 30 was the turning point. 'Unmarried Daughters', *London Times* 26 November 1909. Ibid., 9 December 1909. Ibid., 10 December 1909. Ibid. 15 December 1909.

10 Ibid., 10 December 1909, p. 12.

11 Ibid., 15 December 1909, p. 12.

12 E. Gordon and G. Nair *Public Lives: Women, Family and Society in Victorian Britain*, p. 175 (New Haven and London: Yale University Press, 2003). The Victorians attributed the surplus of unmarried daughters, called 'spinsters' to middle-class marriage customs, but they saw the real problem in terms of Malthusian fears concerning the natural balance between the sexes and the potential economic and political disruption that an excessive number of redundant and dependent women would cause. Spinsters were believed to have 'failed to perform their life's work of servicing men' and many Victorians recommended emigration, to restore the balance. S. Jeffreys, *Th Spinster and Her Enemies: Feminism and Sexuality, 1880–1930*, p. 87 (London Pandora Press, 1985).

13 'Unmarried Daughters', *London Times,* 11 December 1909.

14 Ibid., 15 December 1909.

15 Ibid., 26 November 1909. Ibid., 13 December 1909.

16 Ibid., 26 November 1909.

17 Ibid., 7 December 1909.
18 Ibid., 10 December 1909.
19 JFP, Eglantyne Jebb, Cambridge Diary, September 1906. The Cambridge diary covers 19 May–5 December 1906.
20 Ibid., 31 May 1906.
21 Ibid., 1–13 June 1906.
22 Ibid., 13–14 June 1906.
23 Buxton Family Papers (BFP), F. Wilson, Talk Margaret Hill, 28 September 1966.
24 Sophia Smith Collection (SSC), Box 1, File 1–18, Caroline Jebb to Polly, letter 8 January 1887, Bobbitt, *With Dearest Love To All: The Life and Letters of Lady Jebb*, p. 129 (Chicago: Regency, 1960).
25 JFP, EJ Cambridge Diary, 9 July 1906.
26 Ibid., 14 June 1906.
27 In his study of Dora Marsden, Les Gardner raises the question of Marsden's poor health and its influence on her physical strength and psyche. Eglantyne's thyroid disease did affect her psychological functioning, possibly causing depression; however, it may perhaps also have been a source of creative energy. See: L. Garner, *A Brave and Beautiful Spirit: Dora Marsden, 1882–1960* (Brookfield: Avebury, 1990).
28 BFP, Dorothy Frances Buxton, Talk With Margaret Hill, 10 October 1929, p. 6.
29 Pedersen, S. *Eleanor Rathbone and the Politics of Conscience*, p. 163 (New Haven: Yale University Press, 2004).
30 Vicinus, *Independent Women*, p. 158. Also see, Vicinus, *Intimate Friends* and S. Pedersen, *Eleanor Rathbone and the Politics of Conscience*, p. 96 (New Haven: Yale University Press, 2004).
31 Jeffreys argues that in the Victorian period women's intimate friendships 'were seen by men as useful because they trained women in the ways of love in preparation for marriage'. Jeffreys, *The Spinster,* p. 102.
32 Vicinus, *Intimate Friends*. Also see: J. Murray, *Journal of Women's History*, forthcoming 2008; L. Faderman, *Odd Girls and Twilight Lovers: A History of Lesbian Life in Twentieth-Century America*, p. 48 (New York: Penguin Books, 1992).
33 I am grateful to Professor Jacqueline Murray, University of Guelph, for clarification on the naming of women's sexual practices. J. Bennett, 'Lesbian-Like and the Social History of Lesbians', *Journal of the History of Sexuality*, 9:1, pp. 16, 21 (January/April 2000).
34 M. Foucault, *The History of Sexuality*, p. 17, trans. R. Hurley (New York: Random House, 1980).
35 O. Banks, *Faces of Feminism: A Study of Feminism as a Social Movement*, p. 97 (New York: St. Martin's Press, 1981).
36 Jeffreys, *The Spinster,* p. 100.
37 C. Bolt, *Feminist Ferment: "The Woman Question" in the USA and England, 1870–1940*, pp. 20–21 (London: UCL Press, 1995).
38 BFP, Wilson, Visit to Margaret Hill, 5 October 1966.
39 F. A. B. Keynes, *Gathering Up the Threads: A Study in Family Biography*, pp. 69, 75 (Cambridge: W. Heffer & Sons Ltd., 1950).
40 R. Skidelsky, *John Maynard Keynes, vol. 1: Hopes Betrayed 1883–1920*, p. 122 (London: Macmillan, 1983).

41 Keynes, *Gathering Up the Threads,* p. 76.
42 Seth Koven observes that we know a great deal more about men's same-sex relationships among social reformers and settlement workers because more diaries, letters and court transcripts have survived. As with men, social work created a 'space' where women could explore their own erotic sexual feelings. S. Koven, *Slumming: Sexual and Social Politics in Victorian London,* pp. 203–204 (Princeton and Oxford: Princeton University Press, 2004).
43 'Unmarried Daughters', *London Times,* 11 December 1909. Ibid., 21 December 1909.
44 Skidelsky, *John Maynard Keynes,* p. 268.
45 This is how Margaret describes herself. BFP, Wilson, Talk with Margaret Hill, 28 September 1966.
46 Cambridge County Records Office (CCRO), Charity Organization Society, *Twenty-seventh Annual Report 1906,* p. 14.
47 Ibid., p. 15.
48 Save the Children Archive, Eglantyne Jebb Papers, EJ to Dorothy Kempe, 18 May 1906.
49 BFP, F. Wilson to David Buxton, 7 August 1967.
50 Clay argues that 'letters create, as well as reflect, the relationship, and through the process of projection and construction allow the possibility for expressing, in textual form, multiple selves that are uniquely fashioned in relation to the addressee and recipient'. C. Clay, *British Women Writers, 1914–1945: Professional Work and Friendship,* pp. 30–31 (Hampshire: Ashgate Publishing Limited, 2006).
51 JFP, Boots, MK to EJ, 19 October 1911.
52 Ibid., 23 December 1912.
53 Ibid., 17 October 1911.
54 Ibid., 29 October 1911.
55 Ibid., September 1910.
56 Ibid., 3 May 1911.
57 Skidelsky, *John Maynard Keynes,* p. 269.
58 JFP, Boots, MK to EJ, 6 March 1911.
59 Ibid., 10 March 1911.
60 Ibid., 1 February 1913. Middle-class girls who did unpaid or poorly paid social work and did not require an income were called 'pocket money girls'. 'Unmarried Daughters', *London Times,* 9 December 1909.
61 Ibid., 27 November 1911.
62 Ibid., 29 October 1911.
63 Ibid., 10 March 1911.
64 Ibid., 22 October 1911.
65 Ibid., 12 March 1911.
66 Ibid., 20 September 1911.
67 Ibid., 17 October 1911.
68 Ibid., 22 October 1911.
69 JFP, EJ to MK, 4 March 1911.
70 JFP, Boots, MK to EJ, 12 December 1912.
71 Ibid., 3 November 1911.
72 Ibid., 22 October 1911. Ibid., 23 October 1911.
73 Ibid., 3 February 1911.

74 Ibid., 2 February 1912.

75 Ibid., 10 April 1908.

76 Ibid., 21 February 1911. F. Wilson, *Rebel Daughter of a Country House: The Life of Eglantyne Jebb, Founder of the Save the Children Fund*, p. 29 (London: Allen & Unwin, 1967).

77 JFP, EJ, Little Diary Journal at Octz, 10 November 1911.

78 Koven, *Slumming*, p. 204.

79 E. Ross (ed.) *Slum Travelers: Ladies and London Poverty, 1860–1920*, p. 25 (Berkeley: University of California Press, 2007).

80 E. Jebb, 'The Ring Fence', p. 203 (Unpublished novel, written between 1911 and 1912).

81 Ibid., pp. 802, 827.

82 Koven, *Slumming*, pp. 204–205.

83 Jebb, 'The Ring Fence', p. 811.

84 Ibid., p. 891.

85 Ibid., pp. 556, 558.

86 Ibid., p. 557.

87 Ibid., p. 1034.

88 Ibid., p. 802.

89 Ibid., p. 827.

90 Ibid., p. 663.

91 JFP, Boots, MK to EJ, 13 October 1911.

92 Ibid., 11 October 1911.

93 BFP, D. F. Buxton, A Talk with Margaret Hill, 19 October 1929, p. 4.

94 JFP, Boots, MK to EJ, 18 September 1911.

95 Ethel Sidgwick said 'such books ought to be printed and kept locally, as records, infinitely valuable, of the distinct they describe…The squatter's family, and the dreadful cottages…She had enough material for a dozen modern books'. BFP, Ethel Sidgwick to DFB, 1 January 1929.

96 S. Pedersen and P. Mandler, *After the Victorians: Private Conscience and Public Duty in Modern Britain*, p. 13 (London: Routledge, 1994).

97 Pedersen, S. *Eleanor Rathbone and the Politics of Conscience*, p. 163 (New Haven: Yale University Press, 2004).

98 'A Mother in Mayfair', *London Times*, 11 December 1909.

99 Ibid.

100 Letter to the Editor, *London Times*, 11 December 1909.

101 Pedersen and Mandler, *After the Victorians,* p. 13.

102 JFP, Boots, MK to EJ, 17 April 1911.

103 Ibid., 6 December 1911.

104 Skidelsky, *John Maynard Keynes,* p. 122.

105 British Library John Maynard Keynes Papers (JMKP), John Maynard Keynes to Duncan Grant, 27 July 1908. Skidelsky says, 'Both Maynard's brother and sister had bisexual inclinations'. Skidelsky, *John Maynard Keynes*, p. 128.

106 Maynard said, 'We had the Darwins to tea. Mgt. Darwin:…was Oscar Wilde imprisoned for stealing? Mgt Keynes…Oh, I don't know. For that and other things. So perhaps she may have known what she was saying in the morning'. JMKP, John Maynard Keynes to Duncan Grant, 26 December 1908.

107   Ibid., 11 October 1909.
108   JFP, Boots, MK to EJ, 6 December 1911.
109   'Mother thinks she might come to Killarney'. Ibid., 4 August 1912.
110   Ibid., 27 December 1912. Mrs Jebb 'likes the idea of the little house in Kensington...I believe she knows how much we want to be together and will help us'.
111   Ibid., 1 February 1912.
112   Ibid., 20 February 1921.
113   JFP, Boots, MK to EJ, 6 January 1913.
114   JFP, EJ to Emily Ussher, 10 January 1913.
115   Ibid.
116   Faderman, *Odd Girls*, p. 12.
117   Skidelsky, *John Maynard Keynes*, p. 268.
118   JFP, Boots, MK to EJ, 29 December 1912.
119   Ibid., 22 January 1913.
120   Ibid., 31 January 1913.
121   Ibid., 1 February 1913.
122   Ibid., 24 January 1913.
123   JMKP, John Maynard Keynes to Duncan Grant, 23 January 1913.
124   Ibid., 8 August 1908.
125   Skidelsky, *John Maynard Keynes*, p. 129.
126   JMKP, John Maynard Keynes to Duncan Grant, 28 July 1908.
127   Ibid., 8 August 1908.
128   Ibid., 23 January 1913.
129   Faderman, *Odd Girls*, p. 12.
130   JMKP, John Maynard Keynes to Duncan Grant, 12 February 1913.
131   JFP, Boots, MK to EJ, 24 January 1913.
132   JMKP, John Maynard Keynes to Duncan Grant, 12 February 1913.
133   JFP, EJ to MK, 14 February 1913.
134   The letter continues, '...If you don't reform I will never let you have soul charge for Polly for more than a week at a time' [Dorothy inserted: 'E would never have wished to take over charge of a baby!]' JFP, Boots, MK to EJ, 5 June 1914.
135   See: L. Stanley, 'Romantic Friendship? Some Issues in Researching Lesbian History and Biography', *Women's History Review*, 1:2 (1992), p. 197.
136   R. Hall, *The Well of Loneliness*, pp. 436–437 (New York: Random House, 1990).
137   See: L. Doan, *Fashioning Sapphism: The Origins of a Modern English Lesbian Culture* (New York: Columbia University Press, 2001).
138   Pedersen, *Eleanor Rathbone*, p. 171.
139   M. Jolly, *In Love and Struggle*, p. 207 (New York: Columbia University Press, 2008). For Jolly the 'burned letter' is the 'archetypal motif of revenge, cleansing and commemoration' p. 19.
140   BFP, D. F. Buxton, A Talk with Margaret Hill, 10 October 1929, pp. 1–3.
141   Buxton, D. F. and E. Fuller *The White Flame*, p. 3 (Toronto: The Weardale Press, Ltd., 1931).
142   E. Buxton, Talk with Margaret Hill, 28 September 1966.
143   The first full biography of J. M. Keynes came out in 1944 when this correspondence and Keynes' own sexuality was concealed. His first biographer,

Roy Harrod complained that he had to show the book to 'old Mrs. Keynes, Geoffrey and Mrs. Hill'. Skidelsky, *John Maynard Keynes*, pp. xx–xxi.
144 Pedersen, *Eleanor Rathbone*, pp. 172–173.
145 BFP, D. Buxton, Notes on Eglantyne Jebb, p. 11.
146 Ibid.
147 BFP, Francesca Wilson to David Buxton, 7 August 1967.
148 Letter to the Editor, *London Times*, 26 November 1909. The letter was signed, 'A MOTHER OF DAUGHTERS'.

Chapter 8

1 Jebb Family Papers (JFP), 'Raise the Blockade Leaflet, *Times*, 16 May 1919, p. 9; 'What Does Britain Stand for? *Daily Herald*, 16 May 1919, pp. 1, 8.
2 Ibid., p. 8.
3 L. Rupp, *Worlds of Women: The Making of an International Women's Movement*, p. 297 (Princeton: Princeton University Press, 1997).
4 F. Prochaska, *Women and Philanthropy in Nineteenth-Century England*, pp. 228–230 (Oxford: Clarendon Press, 1980).
5 J. Alberti, *Beyond Suffrage: Feminists in War and Peace, 1914–1928*, p. 22 (Hampshire: Macmillan, 1989).
6 H. Jones, *Women in British Public Life, 1914–50: Gender, Power, and Social Policy*, p. 13 (London: Longman, 2000).
7 J. Parker, *Women and Welfare*, p. 188 (New York: St. Martin's Press, 1989).
8 S. Koven, *Slumming: Sexual and Social Politics in Victorian London*, p. 203 (Princeton: Princeton University Press, 2004).
9 Mary Agnes Hamilton was Labour MP for Blackburn (1929–1931), editor of British socialist newspapers, the Leader in 1920, broadcaster and Governor of the BBC (1933–1937). M. A. Hamilton, *Remembering My Good Friends*, pp. 47–48 (London: Jonathon Cape Ltd., 1944).
10 R. Skidelsky, *John Maynard Keynes, vol. 1: Hopes Betrayed 1883–1920*, p. 212 (London: Macmillan, 1983).
11 Buxton Family Papers (BFP), D. Keay, Interview with David Buxton, 22 June 1993, pp. 2–3.
12 V. de Bunsen, *Charles Roden Buxton*, p. 49 (London: George Allen & Unwin, 1948).
13 Hamilton, *Remembering My Good Friends*, p. 46.
14 C. V. J. Griffiths, 'Buxton, Charles Roden (1875–1942)', in *Oxford Dictionary of National Biography*, http://www.oxforddnb.com/view/article/74568 (accessed 17 July 2008).
15 V. de Bunsen, *Charles Roden Buxton*, p. 26.
16 Ibid., p. 27.
17 Ibid., p. 34.
18 M. J. Peterson, 'No Angel in the House: The Victorian Myth and the Paget Women', *The American Historical Review*, 89: 3 (1984), p. 678.
19 S. Pedersen and Mandler, P., *After the Victorians: Private Conscience and Public Duty in Modern Britain*, p. 15 (London: Routledge, 1994).
20 J. Lewis, *Women and Social Action in Victorian and Edwardian England* (California: Stanford University Press, 1991).

21 B. Buxton, 'Dorothy Buxton's Long Crusade for Social Justice', *Cambridge: The Magazine of the Cambridge Society*, 50 (2002), p. 74.
22 Hamilton, *Remembering My Good Friends*, p. 45.
23 C. Dyhouse, *Feminism and the Family in England, 1880–1939*, pp. 174–184 (Oxford: Basil Blackwell Ltd., 1989); C. Dyhouse, *Girls Growing Up in Late Victorian and Edwardian England*, pp. 31–33 (Boston: Routledge and Kegan Paul Ltd., 1981).
24 Newnham lecturer, Jane Harrison approved of the match. She predicted a 'dream marriage' along progressive ideals. She told Victoria that she was 'only a little sad that it will be all politics and philanthropy now—and no literature, poor old literature'. V. de Bunsen, *Charles Roden Buxton*, p. 42.
25 Hamilton, *Remembering My Good Friends*, p. 45.
26 Pedersen and Mandler, *After the Victorians*, p. 15.
27 V. de Bunsen, *Charles Roden Buxton*, p. 42.
28 S. Koven, *Slumming*, pp. 25–87.
29 M. Anderson, *Noel Buxton, a Life*, p. 27 (London: George Allen, 1952).
30 F. Wilson, *Rebel Daughter of a Country House: The Life of Eglantyne Jebb, Founder of the Save the Children Fund*, p. 111 (London: Allen & Unwin, 1967).
31 Ibid.
32 JFP, *Cambridge Independent Press*, July 8 circa 1910. BFP, G. Jebb, *Recollections of Eglantyne Senior* [n.d.], p. 4.
33 E. Fuller, *The Right of the Child*, p. 22 (London: Gollancz, 1951).
34 JFP, D. F. Buxton (ed.), *Boots Scribbling Diary* (Boots), Margaret Keynes (MK) to Eglantyne Jebb (EJ), 9 January 1913. Margaret wrote, 'It is extraordinary to think that three months ago…nothing was further from our thoughts than the present situation, though of course you had wanted to go to Bulgaria.'
35 Mosa Anderson explains that Noel Buxton's reason for starting the Balkan Committee in 1903 was that, in 1899 Noel found Greeks and Serbs had been 'crushed' under Turkish rule. 'With its incitement of race against race…People have been brutalized'. Anderson, *Noel Buxton*, p. 33, V. de Bunsen, *Charles Roden Buxton,* p. 54.
36 JFP, Letter from EJ to MK, 9 January 1913.
37 JFP, Letter from EJ to MK, Friday January 1913.
38 K. Freeman, *If Any Man Build, Let Him Build on a Sure Foundation*, p. 13 (London: Save the Children Fund, 1965).
39 JFP, E. Jebb, 'Where War Has Been: Lady's Work in Macedonia', *The High Street, Ayr,* 30 May 1913.
40 JFP, Letter EJ to MK, 6 March 1913.
41 Save the Children Fund (SCF) Archives, Gardiner Papers (GP), EJ to Dorothy Kempe (DK), Letter 10, 1895, p. 2.
42 JFP, 'Where War Has Been'.
43 Ibid. Also see: K. Freeman, *If Any Man Build*, p. 13 (London: Save the Children Fund, 1965).
44 JFP, 'Where War Has Been'.
45 Ibid.
46 JFP, Letter, EJ to MK, 30 April 1913.
47 Ibid., 4 May 1913.
48 J. Thirsk, *Alternative Agriculture: A History From the Black Death to Present Day*, p. 214 (Oxford: Oxford University Press, 1997).

49 Ibid., p. 204.
50 'Mrs. Roland Wilkins', *London Times*, 29 January 1929.
51 Lil set up the first Women's National Land Services Corps, which was taken over by the British government in 1917. J. Martin, 'Wilkins, Louisa (1873–1929)', in *Oxford Dictionary of National Biography*, http://www.oxforddnb.com/view/article/50178 (accessed 18 July 2008).
52 H. Pluckett, Ellice Pilkington and George Russell, *The United Irishwomen: Their Place. Work and Ideals*, p. 13 (Dublin: Maunsel, 1911).
53 L. Jebb, *The Small Holdings of England: A Survey of Various Existing Systems*, p. 202 (London: John Murray, 1907).
54 Ibid., pp. 32–33.
55 Ibid., p. 191.
56 Eglantyne mentions having a membership in co-op stores in London. JFP, Letter EJ to MK, March 1914. During the war, Emily Ussher planned to set up a local co-operative store to 'stimulate production' and 'sell their own oatmeal to it'. JFP, Letter EJ to MK, 15 March 1918.
57 SCF, GP, D. Kempe, Description of Eglantyne's Work in 1913–1914, n.d.
58 Ibid. Many Co-operators were arguing that 'cooperation is the only possible foundation for a new rural society'. See: Pluckett, *The United Irishwomen*, p. 13.
59 'Mrs. Roland Wilkins', 25 January 1929.
60 SCF, GP, Kempe, Description of Eglantyne's Work, EJ to DK, 25 September 1913.
61 JFP, Letter EJ to MK, 12 March 1914.
62 Ibid., 2 March 1914.
63 Colonel H. L. Pilkington Obituary, *London Times*, 6 March 1914.
64 Ellice Pilkington wrote influential pamphlet, Horace Pluckett, *The United Irishwomen*, pp. v, 2; Coulter, *The Hidden Tradition: Feminism, Women and Nationalism in Ireland*, pp. 31–32 (Cork: Cork University Press, 1993).
65 JFP, Maud Holgate to Dorothy Buxton, 7 December 1933.
66 SCF, GP, Kempe, Description of Eglantyne's Work, EJ to DK, 17 March 1914.
67 JFP, Letter EJ to MK, 11 March 1914, SCF, GP, Kempe, Description of Eglantyne's Work, EJ to DK, 17 March 1914.
68 JFP, Boots, MK to EJ, 15 March 1914. 'I am very glad that Miss Holgate is able to be with you. You never write to me now but I know you are probably busy. The only thing is you always will be busy in future'. Ibid., 5 June 1914.
69 JFP, Maud Holgate to Dorothy Buxton, 20 April 1934.
70 Ibid., 7 December 1933, 20 April 1934.
71 JFP, E. Jebb, Conversations With a Departed Friend, 15–19 March 1913.
72 JFP, E. Ussher, Jebb Family History (Unpublished Manuscript), c.1930, p. 28.
73 In 1875 she wrote to her sister that it amused her to watch the 'great geniuses' look for meaning in the center of a millstone. M. Bobbitt, *With Dearest Love To All: The Life and Letters of Lady Jebb*, p. 110 (Chicago: Regency, 1960).
74 JFP, EJ, Marlborough Diary, 3 June 1900.
75 JFP, Maude Holgate to Dorothy Buxton, 20 April 1934.

76 Ibid., 7 December 1933.
77 BFP, D. F. Buxton, Interview with Mrs Florence Keynes, p. 2.
78 SCF, GP, Kempe, Description of Eglantyne's Work. Eglantyne Mary Jebb and Eglantyne Roden Buxton heard the same story from Jebb.
79 Ibid.
80 JFP, Boots, MK to EJ, 25 February 1914.
81 BFP, D. Buxton 'A Talk With Margaret Hill', 10 October 1929, pp. 1–2.
82 BFP, F. Wilson, 'Visit to Margaret Hill', 5 October 1966.
83 JFP, Boots, MK to EJ, 19 February 1914. Margaret wrote, 'Now remember you are only going for three months and it is your bound duty to come back after that and you must make it an understood thing from the beginning. I am convinced it is not your duty to stay longer...so don't be weak about it'. Ibid., 25 February 1914.
84 Eglantyne was very disappointed with the attitude of the MRF Committee. She had worked out a detailed proposal to establish co-operative colonies for refugees, however the Committee 'would have none of it...not because it is impossible...[they] prefer meeting once in ten months to allocate 100 pounds here and there to envisaging the fact that we've been throwing money into the sea and are continuing to dispose of it thus through sheer slackness'. JFP, Letter from EJ to MK, 25 February 1914.
85 BFP, D. F. Buxton 'A talk with Margaret Hill', 10 October 1929, p. 2
86 JFP, Maude Holgate to Dorothy Buxton, 7 December 1933, SCF, GP, Kempe, Description of Eglantyne's Work, EJ to DK, 17 March 1914.
87 T. Heinrich and G. Grahm, 'Hypothyroidism Presenting as Psychosis: Myxedema Madness Revisited', *Journal Clinical Psychiatry*, 2003, 5, pp. 260–266, p. 261.
88 E. Kubler Ross, *On Death and Dying* (London, Routledge, 1973).
89 In a letter to Margaret, Eglantyne said, 'my fits of depression for instance must have been very trying to those around me...you tried so hard to cheer me up'. JFP, EJ to MK, 25 April 1914.
90 JFP, Boots, MK to EJ, 7 March 1913, 13 March 1913, 23 March 1913, 24 March 1913, 23 December 1913.
91 Dorothy Buxton wrote in the margins to Holgate: 'Do you think one mind or two were having these conversations?' E. Jebb, Conversations, 8 March 1913, p. 12.
92 JFP, Letter from EJ to MK, 12 March 1914.
93 James Hournan argues that experiences traditionally known as 'haunting or poltergeist episodes are commonly reported in many cultures throughout the world...and involve measured or inferred physical changes such as object movements, electrical failures, or strange sounds...reports of psychological experiences include "odd feelings", intelligible phrases and sometimes the perception of human forms.' Spirit infestation is also associated with some kinds of illness and psychological distress. See: J. Hournan, V. K. Kumar, M. Thalbourne and N. Lavertue, 'Haunted by Somatic Tendencies: Spirit Infestation as Psychogenic Illness', *Mental Health, Religion and Culture*, 5:2, 2002, p. 120.
94 JFP, Maud Holgate to Dorothy Buxton, 7 December 1933.
95 JFP, EJ to MK, 9 September 1917.
96 Ibid.

97 Pedersen and Mandler, *After the Victorians*, pp. 9, 15. Frank Prochaska argues that 'the Labour Party grew out of a voluntary culture'. F. Prochaska, *Schools of Citizenship: Charity and Civic Virtue*, p. 31 (London: Civitas: Institute for the Study of Civil Society, 2002).

98 B. Buxton, 'A Real National Movement', *The Friend*, 21 May 1999, p. 4; B. Buxton, 'Dorothy Buxton's Long Crusade', pp. 74–75.

99 Bernard de Bunsen *Adventures in Education*, p. 15 (Kendal: Titus Wilson, 1995).

100 BFP, Keay, Interview with David Buxton, pp. 1–11. Another account of family life by Buxton children can be gleaned from her daughter. BFP, E. R. Buxton, Miscellaneous Notes on Eglantyne Jebb and Dorothy Buxton, 1965, pp. 1–11. Also See: V. de Bunsen, *Charles Roden Buxton,* pp. 46–47.

101 The Buxton's did not reclaim the house until 1921. McMaster University (MAC) Archives, Charles Kay Ogden Papers, D. F. Buxton to C. K. Ogden, 17 May 1921.

102 B. Buxton, 'Dorothy Buxton's Long Crusade', p. 75.

103 MAC, C. K. Ogden Papers, D. F. Buxton to C. K. Ogden, 12 August 1915.

104 W. T. Gordon, *C.K. Ogden: A Bio-Bibliographic Study*, p. 13 (London: The Scarecrow Press, Inc., 1990).

105 Ibid., p. 17. B. Buxton, 'A Real National Movement', pp. 4–5.

106 Wilson, *Rebel Daughter*, p. 170.

107 BFP, Keay, Interview with David Buxton, pp. 3–4.

108 Fuller, *The Right of The Child*, pp. 22–23.

109 Ibid., p. 23.

110 JFP, EJ to 'Italian Woman', 6 October 1918.

111 BFP, Keay, Interview with David Buxton, p. 3.

112 Ibid., pp. 2–3.

113 Gordon, *C. K. Ogden*, p. 17.

114 MAC, Box 104, File 3, Dr Foakes-Jackson to C. K. Ogden, n.d.

115 MAC, Box 106, File 1, Mrs. Crofsland to C. K. Ogden, 12 January 1917.

116 Gordon, *C. K. Ogden*, p. 17.

117 *London Times*, 11 January 1916.

118 MAC, Box 105, File 1, William Cadbury to C. K. Ogden, n.d.

119 Ibid., C. Franklin Angus to D. Buxton, n.d.

120 Ibid., A. B. Cleworth to C. K. Ogden, 27 March 1917.

121 BFP, Keay, Interview with David Buxton, p. 9.

122 MAC, Box 104, File 11, D. F. Buxton to C. K. Ogden, n.d.

123 Ibid. [1916, n.d.].

124 Ibid., 24 April 1916.

125 B. de Bunsen, *Adventures in Education*, p. 16.

126 MAC, D. F. Buxton to C. K. Ogden, 28 December 1918.

127 Fuller, *The Right of the Child*, pp. 35–36.

128 Buxton, 'A Real National Movement', p. 5; V. de Bunsen, *Charles Roden Buxton,* p. 76.

129 Ibid., p. 71.

130 Wilson, *Rebel Daughter*, p. 174.

131 B. Buxton, 'Dorothy Buxton's Long Crusade', p. 75.

132 G. Bussey and M. Tims, *Some Notes on the Founding*, pp. 1, 17; Alberti, *Beyond Suffrage*, p. 85.

133 B. Haslam, *From Suffrage to Internationalism: The Political Evolution of Three British Feminists, 1908–1939* (New York: Peter Lang, 1999), p. 145, London School of Economics Archive (LSEA), Women's International League, Executive Minutes, 6 March 1918. G. Bussey and M. Tims, *Some Notes on the Founding of Women's International League for Peace and Freedom*, p. 17.

134 Dorothy Buxton was present at the first meeting and donated 45 pounds. Victoria de Bunsen donated 100 pounds. LSEA, Women's International League, First Report, October 1915–1916. Records motion 'in support of aims embodied in resolution of Miss Ellis's report "Fight Famine Council." Ayrton Gould representative of FFC committee'. LSEA, Women's International League, Executive Minutes, 23 January 1918. '[C]ouncil...demands that allied government should openly and immediately endorse the policy put forward in the 5 points of President Woodrow Wilson'. Ibid., 22 October 1918; E. Pethick-Lawrence, *My Part in a Changing World* (London: V. Gollancz, 1938).

135 SCF, D. F. Buxton, Memorandum to Delegates of the Women's International Committee in Zurich, 8 May 1919.

136 SCF, D. F. Buxton, Fight the Famine Council Appeal Letter, 11 May 1919, LSEA, Women's International League, 'Zurich Conference, 12–17 May 1919', Women's International League *Fourth Yearly Report*, 1919.

137 LSEA, Women's International League, *Third Yearly Report*, 14 July 1918; Ibid., Executive Minutes, 3 April 1919. Minutes state, 'handed out 20,000 handbills'. Ibid., Executive Minutes, 17 October 1918. Minutes state, 'DORA required the submission of all leaflets and pamphlets dealing with war or the making of peace to be submitted to the press bureau before publication'. Ibid., Executive Minutes, 3 April 1919.

138 The National Labour Press was fined 80 pounds with 10 guineas costs; Mr Moss was fined 15 pounds with 5 guineas cost; Messers Proteaus were fined 4 pounds with 2 guineas costs. British Library (BL), *The Daily Herald*, 16 May 1919, p. 8.

139 Ibid.

140 Serena Kelly, 'Gould, Barbara Bodichon Ayrton (1886–1950)', Oxford Dictionary of National Biography, Oxford University Press, 2004 [http://www.oxforddnb.com.subzero.lib.uoguelph.ca/view/article/50046, [accessed June 2007].

141 LSEA, Women's International League, *Third Report,* 17 October 1918, p. 6.

142 BL, *The Daily Herald*, 16 May 1919.

143 Ibid.

144 Swanwick advised her that the WIL, '(through you) should plead not guilty...It is most important work for the moment to keep pegging at the abomination of starving little children...I think you should keep out of prison if you can, so as to go on with the work. I think the WIL ought to raise the money for a fine. I feel very little doubt that we can'. LSEA, WIL correspondence, Swanwick to Aytron Gould, 12 May 1919.

145 BL, *The Daily Herald*, 16 May 1919.

146 The National Labour Press was fined 80 pounds with 10 guineas costs; Mr Moss was fined 15 pounds with 5 guineas cost; Messers Proteaus were fined 4 pounds with 2 guineas costs. Ibid., p. 8, Women's International League records minutes show that, Lady Parmoor (Marion Ellis) also contributed 60 pounds. LSEA, Women's International League, Executive Minutes, 5 June 1919.

147 JFP, EJ to Eglantyne Louisa Jebb, 14 May 1919; LSEA, Women's International League, Executive Minutes, 5 June 1919.
148 BFP, Keay, Interview with David Buxton, p. 3; BFP, E. R. Buxton, 'Miscellaneous Notes on Eglantyne Jebb and Dorothy Francis Buxton', 1965, pp. 5, 7.
149 Fuller, *The Right of the Child*, p. 27.
150 K. Pickels, *Transnational Outrage: The Death and Commemoration of Edith Cavell*, pp. 39–42 (London: Palgrave, 2007).
151 On 21 May 1919 a press release signed by Eglantyne Jebb was submitted to newspapers. *The Daily News* supported Jebb's line that 'famine is a medical and religious question and should never be made a question of party interest'. *The Daily Herald* published the leaflets and photos on 16 May 1919. 'The Case For The Children', *The Daily News*, 17 May 1919, BL, *The Daily Herald*, 16 May 1919.
152 Ibid.
153 Ibid.
154 BFP, Keay, Interview with David Buxton, p. 3
155 E. Jebb, 'The Ring Fence' (Unpublished Novel, 1912), pp. 552–555.
156 Pickels, *Transnational Outrage*, p. 88
157 JFP, 'Where War Has Been'.
158 BFP, Notes made by ERB in 1928 (Dictated by EJ), E. R. Buxton, 'Miscellaneous Notes on Eglantyne Jebb and Dorothy Francis Buxton', p. 4.

Chapter 9

1 Jebb Family Papers, (JFP), Eglantyne Jebb (EJ) to Victoria de Bunsen, 10 March 1922.
2 D. Buxton and Fuller, The *White Flame*, p. 5 (London: Longmans, 1931).
3 Save the Children Fund (SCF) Archive, Eglantyne Jebb Papers, EJ to Mrs A. V. Hill [Margaret Keynes], 25 April 1921.
4 British Library (BL), *The World's Children: A Quarterly Journal of Child Care and Protection Considered from an International Point of View,* 1 January 1921, p. 119.
5 H. Cunningham, *Children and Childhood in Western Society Since 1500*, p. 136 (London and New York: Longman, 1995).
6 M. May, 'Innocence and Experience: The Evolution of the Concept of Juvenile Delinquency in the Mid-nineteenth Century', *Victorian Studies*, 17, 1973–1974, pp. 7–29.
7 Cunningham, *Children and Childhood*, p. 137. Also see: E. Ross, *Love and Toil: Motherhood in Outcast London, 1870–1918* (New York: Oxford University Press, 1993); L. Mahood, *Policing Gender, Class and Family: Britain, 1850–1940* (London: University College London, 1995).
8 December 1921 the SCF was incorporated under the Companies Act as a nonprofit association. SCF, Save the Children Fund, *Annual Report,* 1922, p. 1. The first aid was sent on 28 May 1919 to Vienna, 12 June to Armenia, 14 June to Germany. BL, E. Jebb, 'A History', *The Record of the Save the Children Fund*, 3:1 (1922), p. 2; E. Fuller, *The Right of the Child*, p. 25 (London: Gollancz, 1951). The FFC's next big project was a conference. On 1 November 1920 delegates from Belgium, Norway, the United States, France, Holland and Germany attended an economic conference in London. *Times,*

1 November 1920, p. 12. Ibid., 3 November, p. 13; SCF, *Annual Report,* 1920, p. 3.

9 BL, Jebb, 'A History', p. 10.

10 Buxton Family Papers (BFP), E. R. Buxton, Miscellaneous Notes on Eglantyne Jebb and Dorothy Francis Buxton, 1965; Fuller, *Right of the Child,* p. 25; JFP, E. Fuller to Dorothy Buxton, 23 February 1953.

11 D. Marshall, 'Humanitarian Sympathy for Children in Times of War and the History of Children's Rights, 1919–1959', in J. Martin (ed.), *Children and War,* p. 187 (New York: New York University Press, 2002).

12 Eglantyne told Suzanne Ferrière, 'I was trained in social work by the Charity Organization Society and since [sic] I trained social workers myself at Cambridge'. *Archives d'Etat,* Geneva (G), Save the Children International Union Papers (1919–1946), EJ to Suzanne Ferrière, 24 June 1926.

13 SCF, E. Lawrence, Random Memories of the Save the Children Fund from 1921, 1 April 1957, p. 1.

14 Ibid., pp. 1–2.

15 Ibid., p. 1.

16 SCF, EJ to Grace Vulliamy, 27 November 1919.

17 Fuller, *Right of the Child,* p. 43.

18 Ibid., p. 66.

19 The position of the Labour Party was 'charity is only a palliative'. G, EJ to Suzanne Ferrière (SF), 20 April 1920.

20 H. M. Swanwick, *I Have Been Young,* p. 315 (London: V. Gollancz, 1935); JFP, Florence Haughton to DFB, 25 October 1919. Ibid., 20 October 1919. B. Haslam, *From Suffrage to Internationalism: The Political Evolution of Three British Feminists, 1908–1939,* p. 135 (New York: Peter Lang, 1999).

21 JFP, M. P. Willcocks to DFB, 5 December 1919.

22 SCF, Report on Staffing (Office Memorandum), December 1919.

23 Eglantyne liked him because he supported the League of Nations, M. Macmillan, *Paris 1919: Six Months that Changed the World,* p. 90 (New York: Random House, 2002).

24 JFP, J. F. Parsons, Friends Emergency Committee to SCF General Council, 25 September 1919. Ibid., 6 October 1919; JFP, E. Hobhouse to Dorothy Buxton, 7 February 1920. JFP, D. Buxton, Mr Pease and D. Sanger, *Report on Staffing Committee,* December 1919.

25 JFP, F. Houghton to Dorothy Buxton, 25 October 1919.

26 G, EJ to Suzanne Ferrière, 29 January 1920.

27 G. Orwell, *The Road to Wigan Pier,* pp. 173–174 (London: Victor Gollancz, 1937).

28 JFP, D. Buxton, Reminiscing About the Early Days of the Save the Children Fund, n.d.

29 E. Jebb, 'Ring Fence' (unpublished novel, 1912), pp. 144, 166.

30 G. Finlayson, *Citizen, State, and Social Welfare in Britain 1830–1990,* p. 218 (Oxford: Clarendon, 1994).

31 JFP, EJ to Eglantyne Louisa Jebb, 15 November 1919.

32 'I beg your eminence's kind help for the accomplishment of a mission to which we attach the deepest importance...I am accompanied by Dr. Munro—a doctor who earned many distinctions in the course of the war and is now generously giving his services to the cause of children...[W]e have

ventured to ask if we might be accorded the great privilege of an audience with his holiness…' JFP, EJ to The Pope (undated draft circa, November 1919).

33 S. Raitt, and T. Tate (eds) *Women's Fiction and the Great War*, pp. 72–73 (Oxford: Oxford University Press, 1997). Munro was a Scottish doctor who specialized in auto-suggestion and nature cure methods in medicine. F. Wilson, *Rebel Daughter of a Country House: The Life of Eglantyne Jebb, Founder of the Save the Children Fund*, p. 178 (London: Allen & Unwin, 1967).

34 JFP, Dorothy Buxton to Eglantyne Louisa Jebb, 25 November 1919.

35 Eglantyne wrote, 'our first idea was to utilize an existing committee'; by 1924 they had abandoned this plan. SCF, Jebb, 'Nonproductive Stunts', p. 2. Ibid., EJ to Margaret Keynes, 25 April 1921.

36 BL, Jebb, 'A History', p. 3. '[I]n the event of [the Comité] refusing the invitation contained in resolution 3 "co-operation" the SCF shall proceed Forthwith to open an office in Geneva'. SCF, *Protocoles du Comité d' Initiative*, meeting at Hotel des Familles, Geneva, 19 November 1919.

37 JFP, Dorothy Buxton to Eglantyne Louisa Jebb, 25 November 1919.

38 JFP, EJ to Eglantyne Louisa Jebb, 15 November 1919.

39 Wilson, *Rebel Daughter*, pp. 177–178.

40 R. Morton, 'Benedict XV and the Save the Children Fund', *The Month* (July, 1995, pp. 281–283), p. 281

41 SCF, *Annual Report*, 1920, p. 3. 'This was the first time in history when the churches of Christendom took united action in offering prayers and almsgiving on the same day and it is a most remarkable fact that is was the thought of the suffering child which called for this combined effort'. BL, Jebb, 'A History', p. 3.

42 Lady Sara Blomfield came on the executive in 1922. SCF, EJ to Lady Blomfield, 24 October 1920; JFP, Blomfield to Abdul Baha, 25 November 1920. The letter was sent on behalf of Eglantyne Jebb.

43 R. Humphreys, *Sin, Organized Charity and the Poor Law in Victorian England*, p. 144 (New York: St. Martin's Press, 1995).

44 '[S]ituation here is not very satisfying as all-Russian Famine Relief Fund is being set up apparently by representatives of the International War Relief Fund, the British Red Cross and League of Red Cross Societies and Quakers and Archbishop and various Labour people who they have detached from us. They appear to be at dissension amongst themselves, being only at one in their anxiety to promote a rival appeal to ours, and they are carefully ignoring us. It is lamentable that these petty rivalries should distract attention from the main issues when 30 million people are in danger of starvation'. SCF, E. Jebb, Private Correspondence, 2 August 1921. See J. F. Hutchinson, *Champions of Charity: War and the Rise of the Red Cross* (Oxford: Westview, 1996).

45 International Committee of the Red Cross, *International Review of the Red Cross*, November 1976, p. 550.

46 Eglantyne wanted the SCF to have 'an international centre in a neutral country'. G, L. B. Golden to W. Mackenzie, 19 July 1921.

47 Another important relationship that helped Eglantyne move the SCF from a British-based charity to the international stage was with Suzanne Ferrière

(1886–1970) who was very active in the Social Sector Committee of the International Committee of the Red Cross. Eglantyne called her 'international sister' and 'understudy' in Geneva.

48 G, EJ to Suzanne Ferrière, 30 October 1920.

49 JFP, Dorothy Buxton to Eglantyne Louisa Jebb, 25 November 1919.

50 She invited Herbert Hoover of the American Relief Administration to become General Secretary. After he declined, Eglantyne approached Etienne Clouzot of the Red Cross who accepted. SCF, Memorandum from Eglantyne Jebb, 1919. For history of Red Cross see: J. Hutchinson, *Champions of Charity*, pp. 256, 280.

51 JFP, Dorothy Buxton to Eglantyne Louisa Jebb, 25 November 1919.

52 G, EJ to SCF Executive Council, Memorandum, 27 November 1919.

53 JFP, Dorothy Buxton to Eglantyne Louisa Jebb, 25 November 1919.

54 JFP, EJ to Eglantyne Louisa Jebb, 29 November 1919.

55 L. Rupp, *Worlds of Women: The Making of an International Women's Movement*, p. 297 (Princeton: Princeton University Press, 1977).

56 M. MacMillan, *1919*, p. 94.

57 M. Anderson, *Noel Buxton: A Life*, pp. 125–126 (London: George Allen 1952).

58 C. Miller, '"Geneva—the Key to Equality": Inter-war Feminists and the League of Nations', *Women's History Review*, 3:2, 1994, p. 220.

59 Rupp, *Worlds of Women*, p. 120; SCF, E. Jebb, 'Nonproductive Stunts' 9 September 1924, p. 2.

60 L. Mahood and V. Satzewich, 'The Save the Children Fund and the Russian Famine, 1921–1923 Claims and Counterclaims about Feeding "Bolshevik" Children', *Journal of Historical Sociology*, 22:1 (March 2009).

61 JPF, Lady Norah Bentnick to Victoria de Bunsen, 26 September 1919.

62 BFP, D. Keay, interview with David Buxton, 1993; E. Jebb, *The Real Enemy* (London: Weardale Press, 1928).

63 Buxton's resignation letter. SCF, Dorothy Buxton to EJ, 4 September 1919 'I myself abandoned politics altogether when I took up the SCF and now that I think it is time to take up politics again I am withdrawing from the SCF work'. JFP, Dorothy Buxton to Fru Schreiden [n.d.].

64 Finlayson, *Citizen, State*, p. 202.

65 J. Best, 'Rhetoric in Claims-Making: Constructing the Missing Children Problem', *Social Problems*, 34:2 (April 1987), p. 106.

66 Best, 'Rhetoric in Claims Making', p. 106.

67 *Daily Express*, 19 November 1921.

68 SCF, Executive Council Minutes, 24 January 1924.

69 SCF, L. B. Golden, Memorandum to Save the Children Fund Executive Council, 28 May 1929, pp. 2–4.

70 SCF, EJ to Mackenzie, 25 April 1920. Fuller, *The Right of a Child*, pp. 91–92.

71 Hamilton shot footage in Austria (1922), Hungary (1922), Greece and Turkey (1923). SCF Archive, Annual Report 1923, p. 9.

72 JFP, EJ to William Mackenzie, 3 February 1920.

73 R. Symonds, *Far Above Rubies* (Leominster: Gracewing, 1993), p. 81.

74 JFP, E. Hobhouse to Dorothy Buxton, 7 February 1920.

75 SCF, EJ to Mackenzie, 25 April 1920.

76 BL, *The World's Children*, 1 January 1921, p. 119.

77 A letter published in the *Westminster Gazette* objected to sensational advertising. 'The statement by the SCF authorities that there were starving children in London and the industrial centre is being objected to by many philanthropic workers. Mr Woolcombe, Secretary of the COS informed...The SCF's appeal ought not to be as sensational as it was...It cannot really justify the facts'. SCF, Executive Minutes, 27 January 1921, BL, *World's Children,* January 1924, p. 48.

78 BL, Jebb, 'A History', p. 5.

79 G, Translation of Circular, Kinderhilfe, Nurmberge, Easter 1921.

80 Cunningham, *Children and Childhood,* pp. 134–135.

81 BL, *The Record*, October 1921, p. 21.

82 Ibid., 15 January 1922, p. 135.

83 Ibid.

84 F. Prochaska, *Schools of Citizenship: Charity and Civic Virtue*, p. 45 (London: Civitas: Institute for the Study of Civil Society, 2002).

85 Their first response was to get to know him better. SCF, Save the Children Fund Office to Miss Houghton, 19 May 1922.

86 JFP, Violet Hanbury to Charles Buxton, 10 October 1919.

87 P. Panayi (ed.) 'Anti-immigrant Riots in Nineteenth and Twentieth Century Britain', in *Racial Violence Britain, 1840–1950*, pp. 1–23 (London: Leicester University Press, 1993).

88 G, EJ to Suzanne Ferrière, 11 May 1921.

89 SCF, E. Lawrence, 'Random Memories', p. 2.

90 JPF, Lady Norah Bentnick to Victoria de Bunsen, 26 September 1919. Bentnick joined the general council in 1930 but was adamant that 'she wished the council to understand clearly that she was interested in the British side of the work and was only prepared to help on that side'. SCF, Executive Council Minutes, 6 November 1930.

91 Ibid.

92 JFP, Violet Hanbury to C. R. Buxton, 10 October 1919.

93 JFP, Norah Bentnick to Victoria de Bunsen to EJ, 26 September 1919.

94 BL, E. Jebb, 'A History', p. 9.

95 R. Huntford, *Nansen* (London: Duckworth, 1998), p. 505. BL, *The Record of the Save the Children Fund,* 1 September 1921, p. 315.

96 Ibid., BL, 1 September 1921, p. 316.

97 D. Arnold, *Famine: Social Crisis and Historical Change* (Oxford: Oxford University Press, 1988).

98 BL, *The Record*, 1 July 1922, p. 308.

99 Ibid., 21 October 1921, p. 20.

100 A. Chrisholm, A. *Lord Beaverbrook : A Life* (New York: Alfred A. Knopf, 1993).

101 A. J. P. Taylor, *Beaverbrook* (London: Hamish Hamilton, 1972), p. 177.

102 *Daily Express*, 18 November, 1921. Ibid., 23 November 1921.

103 Ibid., 5 January 1922.

104 *Daily Express*, 5 January 1922; Chisholm, *Lord Beaverbrook*, p. 209.

105 SCF, EJ to R. D. Blumenfeld, 21 November 1921.

106 *Daily Express,* 6 December 1921.

107 Ibid., 30 November 1921.

108 In Ireland 'violence had never been far from the surface' since the suppression of the Easter Rising in 1916. It erupted again in 1920, which is

why Eglantyne had to set up the Irish SCF through Suzanne Ferrière's office in Geneva. The Sinn Fein wanted an independent united Ireland, and when it rejected the government's proposal to divide the predominantly Protestant northern counties from the Catholic south and to allow both home rule, violence erupted. B. Haslam, *From Suffrage to Internationalism*, p. 160. In response, the British government imposed martial law and assembled the Royal Irish Constabulary, which was nicknamed the 'Black and Tans'. This militia force soon became a by-word for brutality. *The Daily Express*, 19 November 1921.

109 JFP, EJ to Mackenzie, 3 February 1920.
110 SCF, Executive Council Minutes, January 1921, W. Plender, 'Letter to the Editor', *The Daily Express*, 7 December 1921; L. B. Golden to *The Daily Express* 24 November 1921.
111 SCF, Lord Weardale, 'Letter to the Editor', *The Daily Express*, February 10, 1922.
112 'Editorial', *The Daily Express*, 26 April 1923.
113 Ibid.
114 BL, *The World's Children*, July 1924, p. 179.
115 Fuller, *The Right of the Child*, p. 94.
116 SCF, Executive Council Minutes, 21 March 1927. The description of the colonists and co-operative agricultural village life is reminiscent of those recommended in Louisa Jebb's small holding study of 1907. See: Buxton and Fuller, *White Flame*, pp. 55–60.
117 JFP, Victoria de Bunsen to EJ, 20 April circa 1926.
118 G. Finlayson, *Citizen, State*, pp. 217–218, 221–222.
119 G, EJ to Suzanne Ferrière, 11 May 1921.
120 ...Private charity...does not touch the fringe of the problem...The League of Nations should also be induced to take in hand the question of the position of children of subject races. In some countries in Europe there are a large number of children of subjects of a different nationality from the dominant race, and there is always a temptation...to deny them hospital treatment and schooling. To obtain these reforms, a great deal of initial and preparatory work is required from the Voluntary Societies...I believe that in future the SCF may be able to do most valuable work in such directions. For this work we should not require a large amount of money, but we should require a very large number of people behind us backing our work by small contributions and by helping to form 'public opinion' SCF Jebb, 'Nonproductive Stunts', 9 September 1924, p. 1.
121 G, EJ to Suzanne Ferrière, 11 May 1921.
122 BFP, E. Buxton, Eglantyne's Notes on Eglantyne Jebb, Mostly Prompted by the Inadequacies of Francesca Wilson's *Rebel Daughter* [n.d.], p. 13.

Chapter 10

1 Buxton Family Papers (BFP), E. Buxton, Eglantyne's Notes on Eglantyne Jebb Mostly Prompted by the Inadequacies of Francesca Wilson's *Rebel Daughter* [n.d.], p. 14.
2 *London Times*, 2 January 1946, p. 8.

3 British Library (BL), 'Eglantyne Jebb, 'The World Pays Tribute', *The World's Children: A Quarterly Journal of Child Care and Protection Considered from an International Point of View,* February 1929, p. 76. A Hungarian volunteer, Rozsi Vajkai, said, 'There will come a day when the world will realize that Eglantyne Jebb's name should be placed next to those pioneers of humanitarian thought and feeling, such as Jane Adams and Florence Nightingale'. Ibid., 26 June 1935, p. 2.

4 BFP, Buxton, Eglantyne's Notes on Eglantyne Jebb (Dictated by EJ), p. 1.

5 D. F. Buxton and E. Fuller *The White Flame*, p. 8 (Toronto: The Weardale Press, Ltd., 1931).

6 C. Heilburn, *Writing a Woman's Life*, pp. 24, 130 (New York: Norton, 1988).

7 Buxton and Fuller, *The White Flame*, p. 15.

8 Ibid.

9 Eglantyne contrasted the old-fashioned order of social workers—the dowdies with the 'modern woman—that sort of woman who sits on public bodies and talks socialism'. Jebb Family Papers (JFP), E. Jebb, 'The Ring Fence' (unpublished novel, 1912), pp. 636, 857.

10 Ibid.

11 Save the Children Fund (SCF) Archive, M. Vajkai, *From 1928–1950: Some Decisive Moments of the Save Children International Union* [n.d.].

12 Premature grey hair was a genetic Jebb family trait. BFP, D. Keay, Interview with David Buxton, 22 June 1993, p. 2.

13 Vajkai, 'frail, almost ethereal figure'. BL, *The World's Children*, February 1929, p. 73.

14 She did not make the link between clothing and child labour in garment manufacture. E. Jebb, *The Real Enemy*, p. 10 (London: Weardale Press, 1928).

15 JFP, EJ to Eglantyne Louisa Jebb, 25 September 1921.

16 JFP, Copy of Medical Report, June 1924, R. Symonds, *Far Above Rubies: The Women Uncommemorated by the Church of England*, p. 85 (Leominster: Gracewing, 1993).

17 JFP, EJ to Eglantyne Louisa Jebb, 30 November 1919. Dorothy Buxton revealed personal information about Eglantyne's health in *White Flame*, making her out to be a martyr. She wrote that Eglantyne said, 'I often said to myself that if only we had money I should be well'. D. Buxton and Fuller, *The White Flame*, p. 14.

18 City Archive, *Archives d'Etat*, Geneva (G), Save the Children International Union Papers (1919–1946), L. B. Golden to Suzanne Ferrière, 19 May 1921.

19 G, EJ to William Mackenzie, 25 April 1920. In summer 1922 her doctor urged her to take a three-week long 'holiday in the Savoy after the conference on Moral Education is over'. G, EJ to Suzanne Ferrière, [circa summer 1922]. 'I am not sure yet how long I should stay…no one seems willing to count my being in Geneva as part of my holiday.' Ibid., 15 August 1922.

20 JFP, Letter EJ to Margaret Keynes, 2 March 1924.

21 JFP Papers, Copy of Medical Report, June 1924.

22 J. Whorton, *Nature Cures: The History of Alternative Medicine in America*, p. 123 (Oxford, Oxford University Press, 2002).

23 SCF, E. Lawrence, Random Memories of the Save the Children Fund From 1921, 1 April 1957, pp. 1–2.

24 JFP, EJ to Victoria de Bunsen, 10 March 1922.
25 In 1918 Eglantyne began a sleep experiment and kept a diary of her dream JFP, E. Jebb, Book of Dreams, 24 April 1918. Ibid., 8 November 1918.
26 F. Wilson, *Rebel Daughter of a Country House: The Life of Eglantyne Jebb, Found* *of the Save the Children Fund*, p. 211 (London: Allen & Unwin, 1967).
27 JFP, EJ to Victoria de Bunsen, 10 May 1922; BL, *The World's Children*, Februar 1929, p. 75.
28 Wilson, *Rebel Daughter*, p. 182.
29 Ibid., p. 165.
30 BFP, 'Dorothy Francis Buxton's Questions to Mrs. Keynes', May 1929.
31 JFP, Letter Emily Ussher to Dorothy Buxton [n.d.].
32 JFP, Dorothy Buxton to Eglantyne Louisa Jebb, 16 July 1919.
33 Ibid., 17 August 1924.
34 JFP, Copy of Medical Report, June 1924.
35 BFP, E. R. Buxton, 'Miscellaneous Notes on Eglantyne Jebb and Doroth Francis Buxton', 1965, p. 10.
36 Eglantyne believed that 'selfishness and indifference' were the enemies c society. See her book of prose and verse written during her final illnes dedicated to Dorothy. Jebb, *The Real Enemy* (London, Weardale, 1928).
37 JFP, Copy of Medical Report, June 1924.
38 JFP, Letter EJ to Margaret Keynes, 18 June 1927.
39 JFP, EJ to Eglantyne Louisa Jebb, 25 September 1921.
40 G, EJ to Suzanne Ferrière, 20 April 1920. These concerns are the subject c her essays in *The Real Enemy*. SCF, Save the Children Fund, *Annual Repor* 1921, p. 4.
41 F. Prochaska, *Schools of Citizenship: Charity and Civic Virtue*, p. 29 (Londor Civitas: Institute for the Study of Civil Society, 2002).
42 JFP, Florence Haughton to Dorothy Buxton, 25 October 1919. Ibid 20 October 1919.
43 G, EJ to Suzanne Ferrière, 20 April 1920.
44 JFP, E. L. Jebb, *The Rights of Women* (Leaflet), 1882, p. 1.
45 H. M. Swanwick, *I Have Been Young*, p. 316 (London: V. Gollancz, 1935) C. Law, *Suffrage and Power: The Women's Movement 1918–1928*, p. 239 (Londor I. B. Tauris, 2000).
46 BL, *The World's Children*, 1 September 1921, p. 318. Ibid., *The World'* *Children*, November 1924, p. 25. Very few of these women started ou as experts in child welfare. Most were like the SCIU volunteer, Julia Ev Vajkai, a Hungarian novelist who later became a vice-president of th SCF. In 1919 while working in a prisoner of war camp she came up wit the idea for a 'little appeal' for infants, which she launched throug the Red Cross. She asked that 'everyone should send 3 napkins for th use of infants', which at the time were being 'wrapped in old newspaper for lack of garments'. Thousands of people from Europe and Nort America responded, and amidst the mountainous stacks of cotton Vajka said she found herself 'suddenly classed as an expert in matters pertain ing to the protection of children'. By 1923 she was in charge of nin SCF funded children's workrooms in Budapest, which targeted homeles children. G, J. Vajkai, 'For the 25th Anniversary of the SCIU', October 1944 p. 2.

47 B. Haslam, *From Suffrage to Internationalism: The Political Evolution of Three British Feminists, 1908–1939*, p. 135 (New York: Peter Lang, 1999).

48 G. Finlayson, *Citizen, State, and Social Welfare in Britain 1830–1990*, p. 221 (Oxford: Clarendon Press, 1994).

49 Ibid., pp. 221–222.

50 Ibid., p. 222.

51 SCF, Save the Children Fund, *Annual Report*, 1921. Ibid., 1922; BL, E. Jebb, 'A History of the Save the Children Fund', *The Record of the Save the Children Fund*, September 1922, p. 9.

52 SCF, Save the Children Fund, *Annual Report*, 1923, pp. 3–5. Ibid., 1924, p. 5. Ibid., 1926, pp. 6–7.

53 Ibid. 1924, p. 5. Ibid., 1926, p. 7.

54 Many SCF nursery schools were given government grants in the 1930s and 1940s. This was interpreted as the successful contribution of voluntary service to the public service. In the late 1930s the SCF appointed joint committees with the Council for German Jewry, the German-Jewish Aid Society, the Society of Friends and the Church of England to aid Jewish and non-Jewish refugees. The SCF placed a number of refugee children in English boarding schools and with English families.

55 SCF, Save the Children Fund, *Annual Report*, 1926, pp. 6–7. Ibid., 1929, p. 6.

56 L. Rupp, *Worlds of Women: The Making of an International Women's Movement*, p. 297 (Princeton: Princeton University Press, 1997); H. Jones, *Women in British Public Life, 1914–50: Gender, Power, and Social Policy*, pp. 107–108 (London: Longman, 2000).

57 E. Picton-Turbervill, *Life is Good: An Autobiography*, vol. 3, p. 154 (London: F. Muller, 1939).

58 BFP, E. Buxton, Notes on Eglantyne Jebb, p. 20.

59 BL, Jebb, 'A History of the Save the Children Fund', p. 7.

60 Buxton and Fuller, *The White Flame*, p. 23.

61 London School of Economics Archive, Women's International League, *Fifth Yearly Report*, October 1920.

62 BL, *The World's Children*, 15 May 1921, p. 106.

63 JFP, E. M. Pye to EJ, circa 1919; Jones, *Women in British Public Life*, pp. 40, 117.

64 L. Leneman L. *In the Service of Life: The Story of Elsie Inglis and the Scottish Women's Hospitals*, p. 199 (Edinburgh: Mercat Press, 1994).

65 BL, *The World's Children*, December 1920, pp. 46–47.

66 'When the political situation worsened she accompanied refugee women and children to Constantinople. She married Major T. H. Hutton and wrote *The Hygiene of Marriage*, a sex manual…She became involved in the women's movement in India and director of Indian Red Cross Welfare during WWII'. Leneman, *In the Service of Life*, p. 209.

67 The hospital was founded in 1919 with a small English nursing staff. Leneman, *In the Service of Life*, pp. 90, 207–211; Buxton and Fuller, *The White Flame*, p. 68.

68 L. B. Golden told Suzanne Ferrière that the only way to save the SCIU was to divide it into a theoretical side and a practical side. G, L. B. Golden to Suzanne Ferrière, 8 September 1927.

69 G, EJ to Suzanne Ferrière, 15 October 1925.

70 JFP, Miss Hobhouse to Dorothy Buxton, 7 February 1920.
71 In 1946 the SCIU merged with her Belgian International Association for Child Welfare and became the International Union of Child Welfare E. Fuller, *The Right of the Child*, p. 50 (London: Gollancz, 1951).
72 D. Marshall, 'The Construction of Children as an Object of International Relations: The Declaration of Children's Right and Child Welfare Committee of League of Nations, 1900–1924', *The International Journal of Children's Rights* 7 (1999), p. 130.
73 BFP, E. Buxton, Eglantyne's Notes on Eglantyne Jebb, p. 25.
74 Ibid., p. 20.
75 EJ to Suzanne Ferrière, 24 January 1923.
76 Buxton and Fuller, *The White Flame*, p. 6.
77 SCF Archive; R. Breen, The Origins of the Declaration of the Right of the Child, 1994; Fuller, *The Right of the Child*, p. 72; BL, *The World's Children* June 1925, p. 142.
78 'Though it was essentially an inspirational document, by introducing basic principles on the international plan it did prepare the ground for the pro gressive development of international norms'. These principles were later to form the structure of the UN Declaration on the Rights of the Child. The Declaration, 'speaks, for the first time in terms of rights and entitlement. As a resolution of the General Assembly it was nonbinding'. H. Heintze, 'The UN Convention and the Network of the International Human Rights Pro tection by the Union', in M. Freeman and P. Veerman (eds) *The Ideologies of Children's Rights*, pp. 73–74 (London: Martinus Nijhoff, 1992).
79 Milne, B. 'From Chattels to Citizens? Eighty Years of Eglantyne Jebb's Legacy to Children and Beyond', in A. Invernizzi and J. Williams, *Children and Citizenship*, pp. 44–54 (London: Sage, 2008).
80 G, EJ to Suzanne Ferrière, 2 February 1923.
81 EJ's memorandum for proposed children's charter noted. SCF, SCF Executive Minutes, 28 July 1922. Jebb reports that the SCIU are interested in the charter idea and recommends that the Union would do 'propa ganda' and a 'practical work...itself in order to emphasize the international character of the undertaking'. Ibid., 1 September 1922, de Bunsen updates committee on her work. 'The charter was not a fresh departure but a continuation of work already undertaken by SCF [no mention of ICW's charter]...various societies had also been consulted in order to have the opinion of people of divergent views'. Ibid., 26 January 1923; SCF R. Breen, The Origins of the Declaration of the Rights of the Child, 1994.
82 JFP, Lady Aberdeen to Victoria de Buxton, 8 April 1924.
83 Rupp, *Worlds of Women*, p. 14.
84 Ibid., p. 15.
85 International Council of Women, *Women in a Changing World: The Dynamic Story of the International Council of Women Since 1888*, p. 125 (London Routledge and Kegan Paul, 1966).
86 Ibid., p. 45.
87 Rupp, *Worlds of Women*, p. 297. See: Miller, C. '"Geneva—the Key to Equal ity": Inter-War Feminists and the League of Nations', *Women's History Review* 3:2 (1994), p. 220.
88 D. French, *Ishbel and the Empire: A Biography of Lady Aberdeen*, p. 305 (Toronto: Dundurn Press, 1988).

89 International Council of Women, *Women and Change*, p. 45; French, *Ishbel and the Empire*, p. 306.

90 SCF Archive; Breen, The Origins of the Declaration.

91 London Metropolitan Archives (LMA), National Council of Women of Great Britain, Executive Minutes, 20 April 1924. Ibid., 11 May 1923, '...joint Children's Charter had been drafted', Save the Children Fund, *Annual General Meeting*, 18 September 1925.

92 JFP, R. Wordsworth, Recollections of EJ, Holy Innocents Day 1928.

93 W. Blunt, *Lady Muriel: Lady Muriel Paget, Her Husband, and Her Philanthropic Work in Central and Eastern Europe*, p. 45 (London: Methuen, 1962).

94 SCF, Save the Children Fund, Executive Minutes, 26 April 1921, 15 March 1921, 19 May 1922. In 1925, the Hungarian government began to pay half the cost of the workrooms and local factory owners offered jobs to the children. SCF, Save the Children Fund, *Annual Report,* 1925, p. 6.

95 Blomfield was on the SCF executive for 19 years. Many Bahai publications and writing of faith founder Abdul Baha (1844–1921) are reviewed at length in the *World's Children* book review section. Eglantyne and Dorothy struck up a correspondence with Abdul Baha in 1920. See: BL, L. Blomfield, 'The Child and the Future: Some Bahai Thought', *The World's Children*, September 1925, p. 170.

96 JFP, Lord Aberdeen, Haddo House to DFB, 24 January 1920.

97 G, EJ to Etienne Clouzot, 16 December 1920.

98 LMA, National Council of Women of Great Britain, Executive Minutes, 15 April 1921.

99 'Victoria de Bunsen has been working very hard on it and collecting opinions and information from no end of people and as we are anxious that the charter should be at the same time sound and comprehensive on the one hand and noncontroversial on the other hand—two extremely difficult things to combine!...As V. is doing all the work it is not necessary for me to attend Charter meetings'. JFP, EJ to Dorothy Buxton, 21 January 1923.

00 Letter from Lady Aberdeen to Victoria de Bunsen copied into minutes. SCF, Save the Children Fund, Executive Minutes, 8 April 1924.

01 SCF, Save the Children Fund, Executive Minutes, 18 July 1924. LMA, National Council of Women of Great Britain, Executive Minutes, 19 September 1924.

02 SCF, Save the Children Fund, Executive Minutes, 8 April 1924.

03 Cunningham, *Children and Childhood*, pp. 157, 161.

04 G, EJ to Suzanne Ferrière, 2 February 1923.

05 Prochaska, *Schools of Citizenship*, p. 11.

06 G, Eglantyne told Ferrière, 'the result is ludicrous.' EJ to Suzanne Ferrière, 31 January 1923. Ibid., 2 February 1923.

07 Ibid.

08 Ibid.

09 SCF, Emergency Meeting for Council, Consider Draft of Children's Charter, April, 11, 1924, pp. 46–47. Four months earlier Eglantyne wrote: 'I am sorry to say the charter I drafted originally has been completely spoilt. Some members of our Committee who do not seem to have been at all in sympathy... have insisted on some parts being omitted and others added and others changed...If I had wanted a charter of a different type, I should have written it from the beginning...Another difficulty which had arisen about the charter

is that Lady Aberdeen seems indignant that we take up instead that [
the International Council of Women, which she considered much better.
G, EJ to Suzanne Ferrière, 31 January 1923; Breen, The Origins of th
Declaration.

110   G, EJ to Suzanne Ferrière, 2 February 1923.

111   Eglantyne's letters indicate that she fully expected Ferrière to support he
point of view regarding the charter. G, EJ to Suzanne Ferrière, 2 Janua
1923, 24 January 1923; 31 January 1923, 2 February 1923.

112   Fuller, *The Right of the Child*, p. 71.

113   SCF Archive, Breen, The Origins of the Declaration; Miller, *Geneva—the K*
to Equality, p. 220.

114   G, EJ to Professor Atkinson, 15 January 1925.

115   D. Marshall, 'The Construction of Children as an Object of Internation
Relations: The Declaration of Children's Rights and the Child Welfa
Committee of League of Nations, 1900–1924', *The International Journal*
Children's Rights, 7, 1999, p. 129.

116   P. Veerman, *The Right of the Child and the Changing Image of Childhoo*
p. 156 (Netherlands: Martinus Nijhoff, 1992).

117   D. Marshall, 'The Construction of Children', p. 128.

118   S. Pedersen, 'Back to the League of Nations', *American Historical Review*, 11
(October, 2007), p. 1091.

119   SCF, Save the Children Fund, Executive Minutes, 27 June 1924, p. 996.

120   Ibid., 14 December 1924. BL, *The World's Children*, 11 April 1924, p. 139.

121   SCF Archive, Annual Report, 1931, p. 5.

122   Lady Aberdeen indicated a degree of anger with Eglantyne. She wrote to d
Bunsen: 'The ICW would be glad to repeat its endorsement of your Genev
declaration and the principles therein contained being after all very simil
to those contained in the preamble of our Charter', SCF, Save the Childre
Fund, Executive Minutes, 8 April 1892; BL, *The World's Children*, 11 Apr
1924, p. 49. Ibid., July 1925, p. 166.

123   Ibid., May 1925, p. 108.

124   G, EJ to Suzanne Ferrière, 24 January 1923. In 1925 she told 200 delegate
at the International Summer School in Geneva that child welfare was ju
the jumping-off point for a much larger social movement: 'Our object is t
rally the people of goodwill of every race and clime into a common effo
to carry out the *Declaration of Geneva* and to make it the charter of a ne
civilization.' Ibid.

125   The minutes contain a memorandum by EJ called 'The Future of the Save th
Children Fund' where she states, 'My personal conclusion is therefore that
would be better to sacrifice any other branch of our work rather than ou
international relief, if it is impossible to maintain this it might be better t
liquidate our work. It may also be pointed out that were the opinion of thos
who hold the national point of view to prevail, the quickest and best way t
carry them into effect would no doubt be to liquidate and let a new societ
be started upon quite different lines'. SCF, Save the Children Fund, Executiv
Minutes, 6 December 1929, p. 7; BL, *The World's Children*, October 1925
p. 3.

126   SCF, Save the Children Fund, *Annual Report*, 1926, p. 9; BL, *The World'*
Children, 25 July, 1925, p. 166.

27 BL, E. Jebb, 'What the League of Nations Can Do For Children', *The World's Children*, June 1927, p. 130; BL, E. Jebb, 'The League and the Child', *The World's Children*, June 1925, pp. 153–155.

28 G, *The Church of England Newspaper*, 15 August 1925 [press clipping]; BL, *The World's Children*, January 1929, p. 144.

29 Ibid., May 1929, pp. 141–143.

30 JFP, Emily Ussher to Louisa Jebb, 25 March 1925. In a letter to Tye, Eglantyne thanks her for the 'magnificent contribution to our work—which I cannot see how you can possibly afford. I should not give more the 50 pounds for the time and see how you are later'. JFP, EJ to Eglantyne Louisa Jebb [n.d.].

31 Wilson states the death of the elder Jebb women was a terrible loss to the biographer, for after this there are fewer personal letters. Wilson, *Rebel Daughter*, p. 210.

32 G, EJ to Suzanne Ferrière, 30 November 1925.

33 Ibid., 9 March 1926. Ibid., 18 June 1927. Eglantyne apologized for missing the Crystal Palace event. 'It was obvious that I should faint on the way if I attempted it'. JFP, EJ to Margaret Keynes, 18 June 1927.

34 G, EJ to Suzanne Ferrière, 10 April 1926.

35 BL, World's Children, April 1929, p. 190.

36 R. Wordsworth, 'The Brown Book', *Lady Margaret Chronicle*, n.d., p. 34.

37 BL, *The World's Children*, July 1927, p. 53. Ibid., E. Jebb, 'International Social Service', *The World's Children*, July 1928, pp. 151–153.

38 BFP, Buxton, Miscellaneous Notes on Eglantyne Jebb and Dorothy Frances Buxton, 1965, p. 5; BFP, Buxton, Eglantyne's Notes on Eglantyne Jebb, p. 25.

39 G. Finlayson, *Citizen, State*, p. 201.

40 Fuller, *Right of the Child*, p. 50; Y. Beigbeder, *The Role and Status of International Humanitarian Volunteers and Organizations*, pp. 192–193 (Dordrecht: Martinus Nijhoff, 1911).

41 BL, E. Jebb, 'International Responsibilities for Child Welfare', *The World's Children*, October 1927, pp. 4–6.

42 Ibid., E. Jebb, 'The New Education', *The World's Children*, April–May 1927, pp. 103–104.

43 Ibid., 'The War on Poverty', *The World's Children*, August–September 1927, pp. 155–157.

44 JFP, EJ to Margaret Keynes, 26 September 1928.

45 BFP, E. Buxton, Notes Made by ERB in 1928, p. 1.

46 BL, E. Jebb, 'The Dawn of a New Era, *The World's Children*, January 1928, pp. 50–51.

47 JFP, EJ to Mrs Radcliffe, 12 December 1928; BL, *The World's Children*, February 1925, p. 14.

48 Her sister Emily recorded last days of Eglantyne's life. She told the family that Eglantyne's 'whole left side, face and arm were ridged, but she could still smile from one side of her mouth and her speech was still understandable'. Eglantyne's throat was partially paralysed and she had trouble swallowing, but Emily thought that the stroke had 'knotted up the guts' and told Mabel Few that she would 'never forget the moans, broken with snatches of psalms and hymns'. JFP, Emily Ussher to Mabel Few, 21 December 1928.

149   BL, *The World's Children*, March 1929, p. 94.
150   *Times*, 19 December 1928, p. 14.
151   Including a tribute from the Red Cross of the Soviet Union, with th‹ inscription, 'the Children of Russia'. Fuller, *The Right of the Child*, p. 15‹ BL, *The World's Children*, January 1929, p. 47.
152   BFP, Buxton, Eglantyne's Notes on Eglantyne Jebb (Dictated by EJ), p. 1.

Epilogue

1   Buxton Family Papers (BFP), E. Buxton, Notes for a Possible Biography ‹ Miss Eglantyne Jebb, pp. 1–2.
2   BFP, E. Buxton to David Buxton, 29 June 1967.
3   Buxton told her brother David, 'I wrote several times to Cousin Eglantyn‹ about my dissatisfaction, and once at my club I told her verbally mo‹ strongly how I felt'. Ibid. After the book appeared, Eglantyne Buxton wrot‹ a 25-page response to Wilson's *Rebel Daughter*, which is referred to a‹ Eglantyne's Notes on Eglantyne Jebb, Mostly Prompted by the Inadequacie‹ of Francesca Wilson's *Rebel Daughter* [n.d.].
4   BFP, E. Buxton to David Buxton, 11 June 1967.
5   R. Symonds, *Far Above Rubies: The Women Uncommemorated by the Church ‹ England*, p. 274 (Leominster: Gracewing, 1993).
6   Save the Children Fund (SCF) Archive, General Council Minutes, 3 Januar‹ 1930. Ibid., 6 February 1930; B. Buxton, 'Dorothy Buxton's Long Crusad‹ for Social Justice', *Cambridge: The Magazine of the Cambridge Society*, 5‹ (2002), p. 76.
7   SCF council minutes state that Buxton planned to approach Basil Matthew‹ (1879–1951), a well-known writer on interfaith and missionary organization‹ to write Jebb's biography. SCF, Save the Children Fund, Executive Minute‹ 1 January 1931; D. Buxton and E. Fuller, *The White Flame* (Toronto: Th‹ Weardale Press, Ltd., 1931), p. 1. Katie Pickles' analysis of the propagand‹ images of Edith Cavell can be applied to Eglantyne Jebb who was onl‹ five years older when she died. Buxton and Fuller's *The White Flame* tries t‹ show that Eglantyne was not a disappointed spinster but motivated by dee‹ religiosity and a mission to 'save' children, reminiscent of the social mother‹ hood doctrines of the previous century. To construct her as a 'child-lover‹ Buxton and Fuller down played Jebb's involvement in other social causes‹ Eglantyne regarded 'the world's children' as a metaphor for a new inter‹ national world order. She had no commitment to social motherhood and n‹ particular interest in children. K. Pickles, *Transitional Outrage: The Death an‹ Commemoration of Edith Cavell*, p. 90 (London: Palgrave, 2007).
8   E. Buxton, Notes on Eglantyne Jebb, p. 21.
9   C. Steedman, *Childhood, Culture and Class in Britain: Margaret McMillan‹ pp. 5–6 (New Jersey: Rutgers University Press, 1990).
10   R. Pesman, 'Autobiography, Biography and Ford Madox Ford's Women‹ *Women's History Review*, 8:4 (1999), p. 655.
11   L. Stanley, 'Romantic Friendship? Some Issues in Researching Lesbian Histor‹ and Biography', *Women's History Review*, 1:2 (1992), p. 194.
12   C. Heilbrun, *Writing a Woman's Life*, p. 130 (New York: Norton, 1988).

3 City Archive, Geneva (G) EJ to Suzanne Ferrière, 15 October 1925.

4 H. Jones, *Women in British Public Life, 1914–50: Gender, Power, and Social Policy* (London: Longman, 2000), p. 13.

5 Ibid., p. 74. J. Alberti, *Beyond Suffrage: Feminists in War and Peace, 1914–1928*, p. 22 (Hampshire: Macmillan, 1989).

6 B. Haslam, *From Suffrage to Internationalism: The Political Evolution of Three British Feminists, 1908–1939*, p. 135 (New York: Peter Lang, 1999); H. M. Swanwick, *I Have Been Young*, p. 315 (London: V. Gollancz, 1935).

7 The British Library (BL), *The Record of the Save the Children Fund*, 1 November 1920, p. 27; L. Leneman, *In the Service of Life: The Story of Elsie Inglis and the Scottish Women's Hospitals*, p. 209 (Edinburgh: Mercat Press, 1994).

8 S. Raitt and T. Tate (eds) *Women's Fiction and the Great War*, pp. 72–73 (Oxford: Oxford University Press, 1997).

9 Leneman, *In the Service of Life*, p. 2.

0 BL, *The World's Children: A Quarterly Journal of Child Care and Protection Considered from an International Point of View*, 1 May 1921, p. 191.

1 Leneman, *In the Service of Life*, pp. 207–211.

2 Lil Jebb wrote about her adventures with de Bunsen. See: Mrs Roland Wilkins, *By Desert Ways to Baghdad* (London: Charles Scribner, 1909); see: V. de Bunsen, *The Soul of a Turk* (New York: J. Lane, 1910); BL, 'Child Life in Turkey', *The World's Children*, January 1925, p. 57. Ibid., 'Cures in Turkey', July 1924, p. 163.

3 Ibid., *The World's Children*, January 1924, p. 49.

4 SCF, Save the Children Fund, Annual *Report*, 1925, p. 5.

5 Ibid., 1922, p. 7.

6 Ibid., 1925, p. 9.

7 V. Brittain, *Pethick-Lawrence: A Portrait*, p. 84 (London: G. Allen & Unwin, 1963).

8 SCF, Lawrence, Random Memories, p. 1.

9 Ibid., p. 2.

0 E. Ross (ed.) *Slum Travelers: Ladies and London Poverty, 1860–1920*, p. 12 (Berkeley: University of California Press, 2007).

1 The *World's Children* can be regarded as a literary and historical account of how women saw the world in the 1920s. See: Ross, *Slum Travelers*, p. 10.

2 SCF, D. Buxton, Appeal Letter, 11 May 1919.

3 JFP, Dorothy Buxton from Miss Hobhouse, 7 February 1920; L. Mahood, 'Feminists, Politics and Children's Charity: The Formation of the Save the Children Fund', *Voluntary Action*, 5 (2002), p. 79.

4 M. Mulvihill, *Charlotte Despard: A Biography*, pp. 129–130 (London: Pandora, 1989); C. Law, *Suffrage and Power: the Women's Movement 1918–1928*, p. 369 (London: I. B. Tauris, 2000).

5 J. Alberti, *Beyond Suffrage: Feminists in War and Peace, 1914–1928*, p. 86 (Hampshire: Macmillan, 1989).

6 She reported on her trip to Vienna and Budapest in *The World's Children*. BL, *The World's Children*, 1 February 1921, p. 92. Ibid., December 1920.

7 Ibid., 15 April 1921, p. 173.

8 JFP, E. Jebb, private papers [circa, 1928]. In *The White Flame*, Dorothy published a great deal of Eglantyne's personal writing including, 'Heart trouble set in, due (from a medical point of view) to other causes...I took

long journeys, travelling as simply as possible in order to economize, an generally by myself. Sometimes I wondered whether I should still be aliv when I reached by journey's end...it was strange I knew I was killing my se for nothing...'. Dorothy editorialized: 'It was true she was killing herself Within eighteen months of writing these words she died. D. Buxton an Fuller, *The White Flame*, pp. 14–15.

39   K. Jayawardena, *The White Women's Other Burden: Western Women and Sout Asia During British Rule* (London: Routledge, 1995), p. 2.
40   Ibid., pp. 21, 65–66. H. Jones, *Women in British Public Life, 1914–195(Gender, Power and Social Policy*, pp. 112–113 (London: Longmans, 2000).
41   E. Jebb, 'What the League of Nations can do for Children, June, 192; *The World's Children*, p. 130; E. Jebb, *Save the Child!: A Posthumous Essa* pp. 49–50 (London: Weardale Press, 1929). Eglantyne quoting Andre Gid and Nina Boyle, writes, 'Wherever the education of girls is neglected, an especially where marriage is allowed too early...there is the danger of th condition of marriage degenerating into a system of [sexual] slavery; at an rate in many individual cases...'. E. Jebb, *The Real Enemy*, p. 27 (Londor Weardale Press, 1928); Jones, *Women in British Public Life*, p. 112.
42   Jebb, *The Real Enemy*, pp. 6, 42.
43   D. Buxton and Fuller, *The White Flame*, p. 7. Hawes argues that since the lat nineteenth century 'cruelty societies' had been raising the question of chi dren's rights and publicized child abuse but they failed to understand th realities of life among the poor. J. Hawes, *The Children's Rights Movemen A History of Advocacy and Protection*, p. 24 (Boston: Twayne Publisher: 1991).
44   K. Jayawardena, *The White Woman's Other Burden: Western Women an South Asia*, p. 96 (London: Routledge, 1995).
45   Jebb, *The Real Enemy*, p. 16.
46   This technique began with the SCF's photograph of a dead Russia boy, which they published repeatedly in major British papers in 192] Koven argues that *Save the Child* did better than *Barnardos* regarding exploi ative images of children. In response to criticism, in the 1980s th *Save the Children Fund* developed strict guidelines concerning the image of children and the preservation of human dignity; Koven, *Slummin;* pp. 134–138.
47   JFP, Nora Bentwich to Victoria de Bunsen, 26 September 1919.
48   D. Marshall, 'Humanitarian Sympathy for Children in Times of War an the History of Children's Rights, 1919–1959', in J. Marten (ed.) *Children an War* (New York: New York University Press, 2002), p. 196. There used to b a moneybox circa 1920s in the SCF archive, with the slogan: '*Sambo* say Save the Children!'
49   Symonds, *Far Above Rubies*, p. 88.
50   Jebb, *The Real Enemy*, p. 9.
51   BFP, E. Buxton, Notes made by ERB in 1928 (dictated by EJ).
52   SCF, Gardiner Papers, EJ to Dorothy Kempe, Letter 83b, 19 September 189; pp. 75–77.
53   SCF, Save the Children Fund, Executive Minutes, 23 January 1932.
54   Eglantyne first used this term in a letter to Suzanne Ferrière. G, EJ to Suzann Ferrière, 19 March 1921, 'a line to ask you to stay with me when you come t

London…I have so many things to discuss with you and it would give me great pleasure if you could'. G, EJ to Suzanne Ferrière, 11 July 1926.

5 SCF, Geneva Papers, Eglantyne Jebb Obituary (Newspaper Clipping), n.d.
6 BL, *The World's Children*, February 1929, p. 76.
7 B. Milne, 'Chattels to Citizens? Eighty Years of Eglantyne Jebb's Legacy to Children and Beyond', in A. Invernizzi and J. William, *Children and Citizenship*, p. 46 (London: Sage, 2008).
8 E. Clift, Women, *Philanthropy and Social Change: Visions for a Just Society*, (Medford: Tufts University Press, 2005).

Bibliography

Secondary Sources

Abbott, M. *Family Ties: English Families, 1540–1920* (London: Routledge, 1993)

Alberti, J. *Beyond Suffrage: Feminists in War and Peace, 1914–1928* (Hampshire Macmillan, 1989).

Anderson, A. 'Victorian High Society and Social Duty: The Promotion of "Recreat ive Learning and Voluntary Teaching"', *History of Education*, 31:4 (2002).

Anderson, M. *Noel Buxton: A Life* (London: George Allen & Unwin Ltd., 1952).

Andrew, D. T. *Philanthropy and Police: London Charity in the Eighteenth Centur* (Princeton: Princeton University Press, 1989).

Arnold, D. *Famine: Social Crisis and Historical Change* (Oxford: Oxford Universit Press, 1988).

Banks, O. *Faces of Feminism: A Study of Feminism as a Social Movement* (New Yorl St. Martin's Press, 1981).

Banks, J. A. and Banks, O. *Feminism and Family Planning in Victorian Englan* (Liverpool: Liverpool University Press, 1965).

Beauman, K. B. *Women and the Settlement Movement* (New York: Radcliffe, 1996

Beigbeder, Y. *The Role and Status of International Humanitarian Volunteers an Organizations* (Dordrecht: Martinus Nijhoff, 1911).

Bennett, J. 'Lesbian-Like and the Social History of Lesbians', *Journal of the Histor of Sexuality*, 9:1 (January/April 2000).

Best, J. 'Rhetoric in Claims-Making: Constructing the Missing Children Problem *Social Problems*, 34:2 (April 1987).

——. *Threatened Children: Rhetoric and Concern about Child-victims* (Chicago Chicago University Press, 1990).

Birkett, D. and J. Wheelwright '"How Could She?" Unpalatable Facts an Feminists' Heroines', *Gender & History*, 2:1 (Spring 1990).

Blunt, W. *Lady Muriel: Lady Muriel Paget, Her Husband, and Her Philanthropi Work in Central and Eastern Europe* (London: Methuen, 1962).

Bobbitt, M. *With Dearest Love To All: The Life and Letters of Lady Jebb* (Chicago Regency, 1960).

Bolt, C. *Feminist Ferment: "The Woman Question" in the USA and England, 1870–194* (London: UCL Press, 1995).

Brandon, R. *The New Women and the Old Men: Love, Sex and the Woman Questio* (London: Secker & Warburg, 1990).

Brittain, V. *Pethick-Lawrence: A Portrait* (London: G. Allen & Unwin, 1963).

——. *The Women at Oxford* (London: Harrap, 1960).

Broughton, T. L. and H. Rogers (eds) *Gender and Fatherhood in the Nineteent Century* (New York: Palgrave Macmillan, 2007).

Burstyn, J. N. *Victorian Education and the Ideal of Womanhood* (London: Croon Helm, 1980).

Buxton, B. 'A Real National Movement', *The Friend* (May 1999).

——. 'Dorothy Buxton's Long Crusade for Social Justice', *Cambridge: Th Magazine of the Cambridge Society*, 50 (2002).

Buxton, D. F. and E. Fuller *The White Flame* (Toronto: The Weardale Press, Ltd., 1931).

——. *English Feminism, 1780–1980* (Oxford: Oxford University Press, 1997).

Chisholm, A. *Lord Beaverbrook: A Life* (New York: Alfred A. Knopf, 1993).

Clay, C. *British Women Writers, 1914–1945: Professional Work and Friendship* (Hampshire: Ashgate Publishing Limited, 2006).

Clift, E. *Women, Philanthropy and Social Change: Visions for a Just Society* (Medford: Tufts University Press, 2005).

Copelman, D. *London's Women Teachers: Gender, Class and Feminism, 1870–1930* (London: Routledge, 1996).

Corke, H. *In Our Infancy: An Autobiography, 1882–1912* (Cambridge: Cambridge University Press, 1975).

Cunningham, H. *Children and Childhood in Western Society Since 1500* (London: Longman, 1995).

Davidoff, L. *The Best Circles: Society, Etiquette and the Season* (London: Croom Helm, 1973).

Davidoff, L., M. Doolittle, J. Fink and K. Holden *The Family Story: Blood, Contract and Intimacy, 1830–1960* (London: Longman, 1999).

Davidoff, L. and C. Hall *Family Fortunes: Men and Women of the English Middle Class, 1780–1850* (London: The University of Chicago Press, 1987).

de Bunsen, B. *Adventures in Education* (Kendal: Titus Wilson, 1995).

de Bunsen, V. *Charles Roden Buxton* (London: George Allen & Unwin, 1948).

——. *The Soul of a Turk* (New York: J. Lane, 1910).

Doan, L. *Fashioning Sapphism: The Origins of a Modern English Lesbian Culture* (New York: Columbia University Press, 2001).

Donzelot, J. *The Policing of Families,* trans. R. Hurley (New York: Random House, 1979).

Dyhouse, C. *Feminism and the Family in England, 1880–1939* (Oxford: Basil Blackwell Ltd., 1989).

——. *Girls Growing Up in Late Victorian and Edwardian England* (Boston: Routledge and Kegan Paul Ltd., 1981).

——. *No Distinction of Sex? Women in British Universities, 1870–1939* (London: University College Press, 1995).

Edwards, E. 'Mary Miller Allan: The Complexity of Gender Negotiation for a Woman Principal of a Teacher's Training College' in M. Hilton and P. Hirsch (eds) *Practical Visionaries: Women, Education and Social Progress* (London: Longman, 2000).

Faderman, L. *Odd Girls and Twilight Lovers: A History of Lesbian Life in Twentieth-Century America* (New York: Penguin Books, 1992).

Fletcher, A. *Growing Up in England: The Experience of Childhood, 1600–1914* (New Haven: Yale University Press, 2008).

Finlayson, G. *Citizen, State, and Social Welfare in Britain 1830–1990* (Oxford: Clarendon Press, 1994).

Freeman, K. *If Any Man Build, Let Him Build on a Sure Foundation* (London: Save the Children Fund, 1965).

Fieldson, K. 'Samuel Smiles and Self-Help', *Victorian Studies*, xii (December 1968).

French, D. *Ishbel and the Empire: A Biography of Lady Aberdeen* (Toronto: Dundurn Press, 1988).

Foucault, M. *The History of Sexuality: An Introduction*, Volume 1, trans, R. Hurley (New York: Random House, 1980).

Fuller, E. *The Right of the Child* (London: Gollancz, 1951).

Garner, L. *A Brave and Beautiful Spirit: Dora Marsden, 1882–1960* (Brookfield: Avebury, 1990).

Glendinning, V. *A Suppressed Cry: Life and Death of a Quaker Daughter* (London: Routledge & Kegan Paul, 1969).

Goodman, J. and S. Harrop *Women, Educational Policy-Making and Administration in England* (London: Routledge, 2000).

Gordon, E. and G. Nair *Public Lives: Women, Family and Society in Victorian Britain* (London: Yale University Press, 2003).

Gordon, P. 'Edith Mary Deverell: An Early Woman Inspector', *History of Education Society Bulletin*, 22 (1978).

——. 'Katharine Bathurst: A Controversial Women Inspector', *History of Education*, 17:3 (1988).

Gordon, W. T. *C. K. Ogden: A Bio-Bibliographic Study* (London: The Scarecrow Press, Inc., 1990).

Gorham, D. *The Victorian Girl and the Feminine Ideal* (Bloomington: Indiana University Press, 1982).

Gorham, D. *Vera Brittain: A Feminist Life* (Oxford: Blackwell, 1996).

Hall. R. *Well of Loneliness* (New York: Random House, 1990).

Hamilton, M. A. *Remembering My Good Friends* (London: Jonathon Cape Ltd., 1944).

Heinrich, T. and G. Grahm 'Hypothyroidism Presenting as Psychosis: Myxedema Madness Revisited', *Journal of Clinical Psychiatry*, 5, 2003.

Heintze, H-J. 'The UN Convention and the Network of International Human Rights Protection by the UN', in M. D. A. Freeman and P. E. Veerman (eds) *The Ideologies of Children's Rights* (London: Martinus Nijhoff, 1992).

Harrison, B. 'Philanthropy and the Victorians', *Victorian Studies,* June, 1966.

Harrison, J. E. C. *Late Victorian Britain, 1875–1901* (London: Fontana Press, 1990).

Harrop, S. 'Committee Women: Women on the Consultative Committee of the Board of Education, 1900–1944', in J. Goodman and S. Harrop *Women, Educational Policy-Making and Administration in England* (London: Routledge, 2000).

Haslam, B. *From Suffrage to Internationalism: The Political Evolution of Three British Feminists, 1908–1939* (New York: Peter Lang, 1999).

Hawes, J. *The Children's Rights Movement: A History of Advocacy and Protection* (Boston: Twayne Publishers, 1991).

Heilburn, C. *Writing a Woman's Life* (New York: Norton, 1988).

Hellerstein, E. O., L. P. Hume and K. M. Offen (eds) *Victorian Women: A Documentary Account of Women's Lives in Nineteenth-century England, France, and the United States* (Stanford: Stanford University Press, 1981).

Hewa, S. and D. H. Stapleton (eds) *Globalization, Philanthropy, and Civil Society: Toward a New Political Culture in the Twenty-First Century* (New York: Springer, 2005).

Hilton, M. and P. Hirsch (eds) *Practical Visionaries: Women, Education and Social Progress, 1790–1930* (London: Longman, 2000).

Horn, P. *Ladies of the Manor: Wives and Daughters in Country-House Society 1830–1918* (Gloucestershire: Alan Sutton Publishing Ltd., 1991).

Huntford, R. *Nansen* (London: Duckworth, 1998).

Hollis, P. *Women in Public: The Women's Movement* (London: George Unwin, 1979).

Hournan, J., V. Kumar, M. Thalbourne and N. Lavertue 'Haunted by Somatic Tendencies: Spirit Infestation as Psychogenic Illness', *Mental Health, Religion and Culture*, 5:2, 2002, p. 120.

Howard, P. *Beaverbrook: A Study of Max the Unknown* (New Brunswick: Brunswick Press, 1964).

Hughes, K. *The Victorian Governess* (London: Hambeldon Press, 1983).

Humphreys, R. *Sin, Organized Charity and the Poor Law in Victorian England* (New York: St. Martin's Press, 1995).

Hunt, F. (ed.) *Lessons for Life* (Oxford: Basil Blackwell, 1987).

Hutchinson, J. *Champions of Charity: War and the Rise of the Red Cross* (Oxford: Westview, 1996).

International Council of Women, *Women in a Changing World: The Dynamic Story of the International Council of Women Since 1888* (London: Routledge and Keagan Paul, 1966).

Jalland, P. *Death in the Victorian Family* (New York: Oxford University Press, 1996).

Jayawardena, K. *The White Woman's Other Burden: Western Women and South Asia* (London: Routledge, 1995).

Jebb, E. *Cambridge: A Social Study in Social Questions* (Cambridge: McMillan & Bowes, 1906).

——. *Save the Child!: A Posthumous Essay* (London: Weardale Press, 1929).

——. *The Real Enemy* (London: Weardale Press, 1928).

Jebb, L. *The Small Holdings of England: A Survey of Various Existing Systems* (London: John Murray, 1907).

Jeffreys, S. *The Spinster and Her Enemies: Feminism and Sexuality, 1880–1930* (London: Pandora Press, 1985).

Jolly, M. *In Love and Struggle* (New York: Columbia University Press, 2008).

Jones, H. *Women in British Public Life, 1914–50: Gender, Power, and Social Policy* (London: Longman, 2000).

Kean, H. 'Some Problems of Constructing and Reconstructing a Suffragette's Life: Mary Richardson, Suffragette, Socialist and Fascist', *Women's History Review*, 7:4 (1998).

Keynes, F. A. B. *Gathering Up the Threads: A Study in Family Biography* (Cambridge: W. Heffer & Sons Ltd., 1950).

Koven, S. and S. Michel (eds) *Mothers of a New World: Maternalist Politics and the Origins of Welfare States* (New York: Routledge, 1993).

——. 'From Rough Lads to Hooligans: Boy Life, National Culture and Social Reform', in A. Parker et al. (eds) *Nationalisms and Sexualities* (New York: Routledge, 1992).

——. *Slumming: Sexual and Social Politics in Victorian London* (Princeton: Princeton University Press, 2004).

Kubler Ross, E. *On Death and Dying* (London: Routledge, 1973).

Law, C. *Suffrage and Power: The Women's Movement 1918–1928* (London: I. B. Tauris, 2000).

Lees, L. H. *The Solidarities of Strangers: The English Poor Laws and the People,* *1700–1948* (Cambridge: Cambridge University Press, 1998).
Leland, C. G. *The Minor Arts: Porcelain Painting, Wood-carving, Stenciling,* *Modeling, Mosaic Work, Etc.* (London: Macmillan, 1880).
Leneman, L. *In the Service of Life: The Story of Elsie Inglis and the Scottish Women's* *Hospitals* (Edinburgh: Mercat Press, 1994).
Lepore, J. 'Historian Who Love too Much: Reflections on Microhistory and Biography', *Journal of American History*, 88:1, 2001.
Lewis, J. *Women and Social Action in Victorian and Edwardian England* (California: Stanford University Press, 1991).
Lochhead, M. *Young Victorians* (London: John Murray, 1959).
Lodge, E. 'Growth', in G. Bailey (ed.) *Lady Margaret Hall* (London: Oxford University Press, 1923).
Loseke, D. R. '"The Whole Spirit of Modern Philanthropy": The Construction of the Idea of Charity, 1912–1992', *Social Problems*, 44:4 (November 1997).
Luddy, M. *Women and Philanthropy in Nineteenth-Century Ireland* (Cambridge: Cambridge University Press, 1995).
MacMillan, M. *Paris 1919: Six Months that Changed the World* (New York: Random House, 2002).
Mahood, L. and V. Satzewich 'The Save the Children Fund and the Russian Famine, 1921–1923 Claims and Counterclaims about feeding "Bolshevik" Children', *Journal of Historical Sociology*, 22:1 (March 2009).
Mahood, L. 'Eglantyne Jebb: Remembering, Representing and Writing a Rebel Daughter', *Women's History Review*, 17:1 (February 2008).
———. 'Feminists, Politics and Children's Charity: The Formation of the Save the Children Fund', *Voluntary Action*, 5 (2002).
———. *Policing Gender, Class and Family: Britain, 1850–1940* (Edmonton: University of Alberta Press, 1995).
Margaretson, S. *Victorian High Society* (New York: Homes and Myers, 1980), p. 94.
Mason, P. *The English Gentleman: The Rise and Fall of an Ideal* (London: André Deutsch Limited, 1982).
Marshall, D. 'Humanitarian Sympathy for Children in Times of War and the History of Children's Rights, 1919–1959', in J. Marten (ed.) *Children and War* (New York: New York University Press, 2002).
———. 'The Construction of Children as an Object of International Relations: The Declaration of Children's Right and Child Welfare Committee of League of Nations, 1900–1924', *The International Journal of Children's Rights*, 7 (1999).
May, M. 'Innocence and Experience: The Evolution of the Concept of Juvenile Delinquency in the Mid-nineteenth Century', *Victorian Studies*, 17, 1973–1974.
McBriar, A. M. *An Edwardian Mixed Doubles: The Bosanquets versus The Webbs* (Oxford: Clarendon Press, 1987).
McDonald, L. *Roses Over No Man's Land* (New York: Penguin, 1980).
McCarthy K. (ed.) *Lady Bountiful Revisited: Women Philanthropy and Power* (New Jersey: Rutgers University Press, 1990).
McWilliams Tullberg, R. *Study of Women at Cambridge* (Cambridge: Cambridge University Press, 1998).
McWilliams Tullberg, R. 'Marshall, Mary (1850–1944)', *Dictionary of National Biography* (Oxford University Press, September 2004) http://www.oxforddnb.com/view/article/39167.

McWilliams Tullberg, R. 'Keynes, Florence Ada (1861–1958)', *Dictionary of National Biography* (Oxford University Press, September 2004).

Meacham, S. *Toynbee Hall and Social Reform, 1880–1914* (New Haven: Yale University Press, 1987).

Miller, C. '"Geneva—the Key to Equality": Inter-War Feminists and the League of Nations', *Women's History Review*, 3:2 (1994).

Mills, C. W. 'The Promise', in C. W. Mills, *The Sociological Imagination* (Oxford: Oxford University Press, 2000).

Milne, B. 'From Chattels to Citizens? Eighty Years of Eglantyne Jebb's Legacy to Children and Beyond', in A. Invernizzi and J. Williams *Children and Citizenship* (London: Sage, 2008).

Mitchell, S. *The New Girl* (New York: Columbia University Press, 1995).

——. *Frances Power Cobbe* (Charlottesville: University of Virginia Press, 2004).

Mulvihill, M. *Charlotte Despard: A Biography* (London: Pandora, 1989).

Murray, J. *Strong Minded Women & Other Lost Voices from 19th Century England* (New York: Pantheon Books, 1982).

Myall, M. '"Only be ye strong and very courageous": The Militant Suffragism of Lady Constance Lytton', *Women's History Review*, 7:1 (1998).

O'Day, A. *Irish Home Rule, 1867–1921* (Manchester: Manchester University Press, 1998).

O'Hanlon-Dunn, A. 'Women as Witness: Elementary Schoolmistresses and the Cross Commission, 1885–1888', in J. Goodman and S. Harrop *Women, Educational Policy-Making and Administration in England* (London: Routledge, 2000).

Oram, A. *Women Teachers and Feminist Politics, 1900–1939* (Manchester: Manchester University Press, 1996).

Orwell, G. *The Road to Wigan Pier* (London: Victor Gollancz, 1937).

Panayi, P. (ed.) 'Anti-immigrant Riots in Nineteenth and Twentieth Century Britain', in *Racial Violence Britain, 1840–1950* (London: Leicester University Press, 1993).

Parker, J. *Women and Welfare* (New York: St. Martin's Press, 1989).

Peck, W. A *Little Learning: A Victorian Childhood* (London: Faber and Faber, 1952).

Pedersen, S. and P. Mandler *After the Victorians: Private Conscience and Public Duty in Modern Britain* (London: Routledge, 1994).

Pedersen, S. *Eleanor Rathbone and the Politics of Conscience* (New Haven: Yale University Press, 2004).

——. 'Back to the League of Nations', *American Historical Review*, 112 (October, 2007).

Pesman, R. 'Autobiography, Biography and Ford Madox Ford's Women', *Women's History Review*, 8:4 (1999).

Peterson, M. J. 'The Victorian Governess: Status Incongruence in Family and Society', *Victorian Studies*, Vol. 14:1 (September, 1970).

——. *Family, Love, and Work in the Lives of Victorian Gentlewomen* (Indianapolis: Indiana University Press, 1989).

——. 'No Angel in the House: The Victorian Myth and the Paget Women', *The American Historical Review*, 89: 3 (1984).

Pethick-Lawrence, E. *My Part in a Changing World* (London: V. Gollancz, 1938).

Pickels, K. *Transnational Outrage: The Death and Commemoration of Edith Cavell* (London: Palgrave, 2007).

Picton-Turbervill, E. *Life is Good: An Autobiography*, vol. 3 (London: F. Muller, 1939).

Platt, A. *The Child-Savers: The Invention of Delinquency* (Chicago: Chicago University Press, 1969).

Pluckett, H., E. Pilkington and G. Russell *The United Irishwomen: Their Place, Work and Ideals*, (Dublin: Maunsel, 1911).

Prochaska, F. *Christianity and Social Service in Modern Britain: The Disinherited Spirit* (Oxford: Oxford University Press, 2006).

——. *Schools of Citizenship: Charity and Civic Virtue* (London: Civitas: Institute for the Study of Civil Society, 2002).

——. *Women and Philanthropy in Nineteenth-Century England* (Oxford: Clarendon Press, 1980).

Purvis, J. *A History of Women's Education in England* (Milton Keynes: Open University Press, 1991).

——. *Emmeline Pankhurst: A Biography* (New York: Routledge, 2002).

——. (ed.) *Women's History in Britain, 1850–1945* (London: University London College Press, 1995).

Raitt, S. and T. Tate (eds) *Women's Fiction and the Great War* (Oxford: Oxford University Press, 1997).

Raverat, G. M. *Period Piece: A Cambridge Childhood* (London: Faber and Faber Limited, 1885).

Robinson, W. 'Sarah Jane Bannister and Teacher Training in Transition 1870–1918', in M. Hilton and P. Hirsch (eds) *Practical Visionaries: Women, Education and Social Progress, 1790–1930* (London: Longman, 2000).

Ross, E. *Love and Toil: Motherhood in Outcast London, 1870–1918* (New York: Oxford University Press, 1993).

——. (ed.) *Slum Travelers: Ladies and London Poverty, 1860–1920* (Berkeley: University of California Press, 2007).

Rothstein, E. *George Farquhar* (Berkeley: University of California, 1967).

Rupp, L. *Worlds of Women: The Making of an International Women's Movement* (Princeton: Princeton University Press, 1997).

Skidelsky, R. *John Maynard Keynes, vol. 1: Hopes Betrayed 1883–1920* (London: Macmillan, 1983).

Smiles, S. *Self-help* (London: John Murray, 1905).

Spalding, F. *Gwen Raverat* (London: Harvill, 2001).

Spender, D. *Man Made Language*, 2nd edition (New York: Routledge, 1985).

Spongberg, M., B. Caine and A. Curthoys (eds) *Companion to Women's Historical Writing* (London: Palgave, 2005).

Stanley, L. 'Biography as Microscope or Kaleidoscope? The Case of "Power" in Hanna Cullwick's Relationship with Arthur Munby', *Women's Studies International Forum*, 10:1 (1987).

——. 'Mimesis, Metaphor and Representation: Holding Out an Olive Branch to Emergent Schreiner Canon', *Women's History Review*, 10:1 (2001).

——. 'Romantic Friendship? Some Issues in Researching Lesbian History and Biography', *Women's History Review*, 1:2 (1992).

——. *The Auto/Biographical I: Theory and Practice of Feminist Auto/Biography* (Manchester: Manchester University Press, 1992).

Steedman, C. 'Prisonhouses', *Feminist Review*, 20 (1985).

——. *The Tidy House* (London: Virago Press Limited, 1982).

——. *Childhood, Culture and Class in Britain* (New Jersey: Rutgers University Press, 1990).

Sutherland, G. *Policy-making in Elementary Education, 1870–1895* (Oxford: Oxford University Press, 1973).

Swanwick, H. M. *I Have Been Young* (London: V. Gollancz, 1935).

Symonds, R. *Far Above Rubies: The Women Uncommemorated by the Church of England* (Leominster: Gracewing, 1993).

Taylor, A. J. P. *Beaverbrook* (London: Hamish Hamilton, 1972).

Tanner, L. B. (ed.) *Voices From Women's Liberation* (New York: New American Library, 1970).

Thirsk, J. *Alternative Agriculture: A History From the Black Death to Present Day* (Oxford: Oxford University Press, 1997).

Tosh, J. *A Man's Place: Masculinity and the Middle-Class Home in Victorian England* (New Haven: Yale University Press, 1999).

Tropp, A. *The School Teacher* (London: Heinemann, 1957).

Turnbull, P. 'Learning Her Womanly Work: The Elementary School Curriculum, 1870–1914', in Hunt, F. (ed.) *Lessons for Life* (Oxford: Basil Blackwell, 1987).

Vammen, T. 'Forum: Modern English Auto/biography and Gender', *Gender and History*, 2:1 (1990).

Vicinus, M. *Independent Women: Work and Community for Single Women, 1850–1920* (London: Virago Press, 1985).

——. *Intimate Friends: Women Who Loved Women, 1778–1928* (Chicago: The University of Chicago Press, 2004).

Widdowson, F. '"Educating Teachers": Women and Elementary Teaching in London, 1900–1914', in L. Davidoff and B. Westover (eds) *Our Work, Our Lives, Our Words: Women's History and Women's Work* (Basingstoke: Macmillan, 1986).

Wilson, F. *Aftermath: France, Germany, Austria, Yugoslavia, 1945 and 1946* (Harmondsworth: Penguin Books, 1947).

——. *They Came as Strangers: The Story of Refugees in Britain* (London: Hamilton, 1959).

——. *Rebel Daughter of a Country House: The Life of Eglantyne Jebb, Founder of the Save the Children Fund* (London: Allen & Unwin, 1967).

——. *In the Margins of Chaos: Recollections of Relief Work in and Between Three Wars* (London: John Murray, 1944).

Yeo, E. 'Social Motherhood and the Sexual Communion of Labour in British Social Science, 1850–1950', *Women's History Review*, 1:1 (1992).

Index